SOCIOLOGICAL
METHODOLOGY
2005

SOCIOLOGICAL METHODOLOGY 2005

VOLUME 35

EDITOR: Ross M. Stolzenberg

MANAGING EDITOR: Ray Weathers

An official publication by Blackwell Publishing for

THE AMERICAN SOCIOLOGICAL ASSOCIATION

SALLY T. HILLSMAN, *Executive Officer*

Library of Congress Catalog Card Information
Sociological Methodology, 1969–85
   San Francisco, Jossey-Bass. 15 v. illus. 24 cm. annual. (Jossey-Bass behavioral
   science series)
      Editor: 1969, 1970: E. F. Borgatta; 1971, 1972, 1973–74: H. L. Costner;
      1975, 1976, 1977: D. R. Heise; 1978, 1979, 1980: K. F. Schuessler;
      1981, 1982, 1983–84: S. Leinhardt; 1985: N. B. Tuma

Sociological Methodology, 1986–88
   Washington, DC, American Sociological Association. 3 v. illus. 24 cm. annual.
      Editor: 1986: N. B. Tuma; 1987, 1988: C. C. Clogg

Sociological Methodology, 1989–1992
   Oxford, Basil Blackwell. 4 v. illus. 24 cm. annual.
      Editor: 1989, 1990: C. C. Clogg; 1991, 1992: P. V. Marsden
      "An official publication of the American Sociological Association."
      1. Sociology—Methodology—Year books. I. American Sociological
      Association. II. Borgatta, Edgar F., 1924-ed.

HM24.S55   301'.01'8   68-54940
                           rev.
Library of Congress   [r71h2]

British Cataloguing in Publication Data
Sociological Methodology. Vol. 30
1. Sociology. Methodology
301'.01'8

ISBN 1-4051-5068-8
ISSN 0081-1750

Library of Congress Cataloging-in-Publication Data is available at the Library of
Congress

REVIEWERS

Paul D. Allison
Hans-Peter Blossfeld
Eugene P. Ericksen
George Farkas
Katherine Faust
John D. Fox
Roberto Franzosi
Leonid Gavrilov
Andrew Gelman
Rick Grannis
David Grusky
Patrick Heuveline
Paul T. von Hippel

Jon A. Krosnick
Kai Larsen
Edward J. Lawler
Tim F. Liao
Rod Little
Michael Lovaglia
Robert D. Mare
Barry Markovsky
Linda Molm
Daniel A. Powers
Lincoln Quillan
Ken Rasinski
Stephen W. Raudenbush

Sean Reardon
Carl W. Roberts
Barbara Schneider
Robert Schoen
Michael Sobel
Stephen M. Stigler
Jeffrey M. Timberlake
Roger Tourangeau
David L. Weakliem
Bruce Western
Michael J. White
Andres Villareal

CONTENTS

CONTRIBUTORS

Avinash Singh Bhati

Avinash Singh Bhati is a Research Associate at the Justice Policy Center of the Urban Institute. He is interested in developing and applying information and entropy-based econometric methods for the analysis of complex social, economic, and behavioral phenomena.

J. Scott Brown

J. Scott Brown is an Assistant Professor of Sociology and Gerontology at Miami University (Oxford, OH). His research interests focus on wealth and health inequalities across the life course with particular emphasis on gender and race differences in physical and mental health; the use of Bayesian statistical methods to provide new insights into current social and demographic research; and the investigation of the initiation of and changes in social security policies.

Jacob E. Cheadle

Jacob E. Cheadle is a Robert Wood Johnson Postdoctoral Scholar in Health Policy Research at the University of Michigan. His research interests include multilevel structural equation modeling and the consequences of family environments and parenting practices on children's academic competencies.

Mark S. Handcock

Mark S. Handcock is Professor of Statistics and Sociology in the Department of Statistics at the University of Washington. His recent work focuses on combining population-level and individual-level information, statistical models for the analysis of social network data, spatial processes, and labor economics. He is a core faculty member of the Center for Statistics and the Social Sciences and the Center for Studies in Demography and Ecology.

James J. Heckman

James J. Heckman is the Henry Schultz Distinguished Service Professor of Economics at the University of Chicago, where he also serves as director of the Economics Research Center and the Center for Social Program Evaluation. He is a Senior Research Fellow at the American Bar Foundation and is affiliated with University College London and Peking University. Heckman's work has been devoted to the development of a scientific basis for economic policy evaluation, with special emphasis on models of individuals and disaggregated groups, and on the problems and possibilities created by heterogeneity, diversity, and unobserved counterfactual states. He also does research on human development and life-cycle skill formation.

Scott M. Lynch

Scott M. Lynch is Assistant Professor of Sociology and a Faculty Associate in the Office of Population Research at Princeton University. His substantive research interests include studying life course and cohort patterns in the relationship between education and health, the relationship between socioeconomic status and active life expectancy, and the interrelationships between stress, disability, social support, and depression in later life. His methodological interests include the use of Bayesian estimation methods in social science research.

Lisa Slattery Rashotte

Lisa Slattery Rashotte is Associate Professor of Sociology at the University of North Carolina at Charlotte. Her research focuses on small group interaction, nonverbal behaviors, gender, and expectations. Currently, she is conducting projects on altering the status meaning of gender and, with Murray Webster, on the effect of behaviors on inequality structures in small groups.

Michael S. Rendall

Michael S. Rendall is Senior Social Scientist at the RAND Corporation and Adjunct Associate Professor of Sociology and Demography at Pennsylvania State University. His recent studies include (with Jonsson) the fertility impact of international migration (*Demography* 41, 2004).

Michael E. Sobel

Michael E. Sobel is a Professor at Columbia University. His statistical research has focused on causal inference, models for categorical data, and structural equation models. His substantive research has been primarily in the area of social stratification. Current interests include neighborhood effects and applications of finance.

Murray Webster Jr.

Murray Webster Jr. is Professor of Sociology at the University of North Carolina at Charlotte. With Whitmeyer and Rashotte, he has recently completed a series of experiments on status claims (*Social Science Research* 33, 4, and *Social Psychology Quarterly* 68, 2). With Rashotte, he is currently studying effects of behavior patterns on group structure, and with Jane Sell he is editing a book on experimental methods in the social sciences (*Elsevier*).

Joseph M. Whitmeyer

Joseph M. Whitmeyer is Professor of Sociology at the University of North Carolina at Charlotte. Two of his current projects are development and tests of a theory of attachment inequalities in network structures, with Rafael Wittek, and determination of presidential power over the Supreme Court through appointment.

ACKNOWLEDGMENTS

Many people contributed to the publication of this volume. First, I thank those who submitted papers for consideration. Scholars benefit from having their work published, but they are scholars with or without their publications. Journals, however, cannot exist without articles to publish. So I am very grateful to all who submitted papers to *Sociological Methodology*, whether or not those papers were accepted for publication.

Second, I thank Ray Weathers for his essential contributions as managing editor of *Sociological Methodology*. The last twelve months have been an unusually demanding period for me, and I simply could not have edited this volume without the extraordinary skill, overflowing good will, and abundantly practical optimism that Ray Weathers brought to the enterprise each and every day. His expertise, efficiency, great care, marvelous good humor, and his distinctive and enjoyable personality have made it a true pleasure to work with him.

Third, I thank the reviewers who spent so much time evaluating the papers that were submitted for publication in this volume. Methodological papers are time-consuming and difficult to review. We rely upon reviewers to vet the accuracy of mathematical derivations as well as the more general features of submitted papers. Without these careful, painstaking, and insightful reviews, *Sociological Methodology* would vanish in an instant. I also thank the editorial board members and deputy editors of *Sociological Methodology* for their contributions.

I express my gratitude to Jennifer Scarano and other staff at Blackwell Publishing who produced *Sociological Methodology*. These people brought technical expertise, good business judgment, constructive attitudes, flexibility, and hard work to the production of *Sociological Methodology*. They make this journal possible in ways that I greatly appreciate but do not understand. I am also grateful to Stephanie Magean for quickly, efficiently, and cheerfully copyediting all of the articles in this volume. Karen Edwards of the American Sociological Association has helped in numerous ways, and has smilingly conspired with Ray Weathers to work around my abundant bureaucratic failings.

For unusual reasons, editing *Sociological Methodology* has consumed much more time than I could have anticipated. I am enormously grateful to Craig Coelen, the president of NORC, for making available the resources that have permitted me to find that time among my other responsibilities.

Finally, I thank the American Sociological Association for its support of *Sociological Methodology*. A discipline's journals reflect the interests of its practitioners as well as the intellectual content of the field itself. Thus, the publication of *Sociological Methodology* by the American Sociological Association confirms that sociology, sociologists, and the association itself all share a deep and abiding interest in the methods by which sociological research is done. Without that interest, our claims to scientific inquiry would be hollow, and we would be little more than a loosely coupled collection of artisans bringing idiosyncratic methods of unknown quality to the production of disconnected projects.

Ross M. Stolzenberg
Editor

SUBMISSION INFORMATION FOR AUTHORS

Sociological Methodology is an annual compendium of advances in the methodology of social research. These articles promise to advance the quality and efficiency of sociological research, or to make accessible to sociologists recent methodological advances in related disciplines. *Sociological Methodology* is an official publication of the American Sociological Association.

Sociological Methodology seeks contributions that address the full range of problems confronted by empirical work in the contemporary social sciences, including conceptualization and modeling, research design, data collection, measurement, and data analysis. Work on the methodological problems involved in any approach to empirical social science is appropriate for *Sociological Methodology*. Chapters present original methodological contributions, expository statements on and illustrations of recently developed techniques, and critical discussions of research practice.

The content of each annual volume of *Sociological Methodology* is driven by submissions initiated by authors; the volumes do not have specific themes. Editorial decisions about manuscripts submitted are based on the advice of expert referees. Criteria include originality, breadth of interest and applicability, and expository clarity. Discussions of implications for research practice are vital, and authors are urged to include empirical illustrations of the methods they discuss.

Authors should submit five copies of manuscripts to

Ross M. Stolzenberg
Sociological Methodology
The University of Chicago
Department of Sociology
307 Social Science Building
1126 East 59th Street
Chicago, Illinois 60637

Manuscripts should include an informative abstract of not more than one double-spaced page, and should not identify the author within the text. Submission of a manuscript for review by *Sociological Methodology* implies that it has not been published previously and that it is not under review elsewhere.

Inquiries concerning the appropriateness of material and/or other aspects of editorial policies and procedures are welcome; prospective authors should correspond with the editor by E-mail at r-stolzenberg@ uchicago.edu.

EDITOR'S INTRODUCTION

One of the attractions of methodology is the infinitely variable scale of its topics. For example, when we want big thoughts about big questions, we can turn to the topic of causal effects. Causation can be irresistibly attractive because it is the fundamental topic of all scientific inquiry. We build theories to organize and codify ideas about causation. We meticulously record data on circumstances and events so that we might one day have the raw materials to make a theory of how those circumstances and events cause each other, or to test theories that are already proposed to do the explaining. We go to great lengths to measure the impact of causes on their effects. Ideas about causation tell us what to find interesting (i.e., effects and their proposed causes) and what we should do to investigate those objects of interest (experiments, for example, if we can do them). Causation is a necessary topic because it is woven through the entire enterprise of research and theory-construction. We can never escape from questions about causation and the measurement of causal effects.

To the vexation of many and the delight of a few, causation is a construct that cannot be observed. The unobservable nature of causation guarantees uncertainty about its nature and ensures that debates about it will never end. Thus, causation is a generous and dependable source of new activity for those whose vocation is scholarly debate; it is an indefatigable generator of new work for those who study it; and is a philosopher's stone for those who seek their gold in the methods of research.

This volume of *Sociological Methodology* includes a major essay on causation by James J. Heckman, and a lively critique of that chapter by Michael E. Sobel. Both of these papers are insightful and instructive considerations of the biggest of big questions in social science methodology: What is a cause and how do we measure it?

Big questions are important, but answers to smaller questions often make the difference between outstanding research and questionable findings. Four chapters in this volume address questions that are smaller than the subject of causality itself, but still seem likely to spell the difference between ambiguous findings and successful, useful research: Rashotte, Webster, and Whitmeyer remind readers that small differences in instruction wording can produce substantial differences in findings. Lynch and Brown give readers new methods for calculating the life table quantities that are the mainstay not only of formal demography but many applied social science topics and policy research subjects that rely on the life table. Bhati proposes new methods for examining the spatial distribution of rare events — a subject that has frustrated those who study not only crime but epidemiology and related topics. Handcock, Rendall, and Cheadle conclude this volume with a paper that demonstrates useful methods for incorporating into a multivariate analysis extraneously learned information about a bivariate relationship. Once again, we are shown that all information contributes to the quality of statistical analyses, if only one can find a way to incorporate that information into the calculations.

❧ 1 ❧

THE SCIENTIFIC MODEL OF CAUSALITY

*James J. Heckman**

Causality is a very intuitive notion that is difficult to make precise without lapsing into tautology. Two ingredients are central to any definition: (1) a set of possible outcomes (counterfactuals) generated by a function of a set of "factors" or "determinants" and (2) a manipulation where one (or more) of the "factors" or "determinants" is changed. An effect is realized as a change in the argument of a stable function that produces the same change in the outcome for a class of interventions that change the "factors" by the same amount. The outcomes are compared at different levels of the factors or generating variables. Holding all factors save one at a constant level, the change in the outcome associated with manipulation of the varied factor is called a causal effect of the manipulated factor. This definition, or some version of it, goes back to Mill (1848) and Marshall (1890). Haavelmo's (1943) made it more precise within the context of linear equations models. The phrase '*ceteris paribus*' (everything else held constant) is a mainstay of economic analysis

This research was supported by NSF 97-09-873, 00-99195, NSF SES-0241858, NIH R01-HD043411, and the American Bar Foundation. An earlier version of this paper was presented at the ISI meeting in Seoul, Korea, in August 2001. I am grateful to Jaap Abbring and Edward Vytlacil for very helpful discussions about the topics of this paper over the past five years. Yu Xie and especially T. N. Srinivasan made helpful comments on this version. Some of the material in this paper also appears in Heckman and Vytlacil (2006a,b).

*University of Chicago, University College London, and the American Bar Foundation

1

and captures the essential idea underlying causal models. This paper develops the scientific model of causality developed in economics and compares it to methods advocated in epidemiology, statistics, and in many of the social sciences outside of economics that have been influenced by statistics and epidemiology.

I make two main points that are firmly anchored in the econometric tradition. The first is that causality is a property of a model of hypotheticals. A fully articulated model of the phenomena being studied precisely defines hypothetical or counterfactual states.[1] A definition of causality drops out of a fully articulated model as an automatic by-product. A model is a set of possible counterfactual worlds constructed under some rules. The rules may be the laws of physics, the consequences of utility maximization, or the rules governing social interactions, to take only three of many possible examples. A model is in the mind. As a consequence, causality is in the mind.

In order to be precise, counterfactual statements must be made within a precisely stated model. Ambiguity in model specification implies ambiguity in the definition of counterfactuals and hence of the notion of causality. The more complete the model of counterfactuals, the more precise the definition of causality. The ambiguity and controversy surrounding discussions of causal models are consequences of analysts wanting something for nothing: a definition of causality without a clearly articulated model of the phenomenon being described (i.e., a model of counterfactuals). They want to describe a phenomenon as being modeled "causally" without producing a clear model of how the phenomenon being described is generated or what mechanisms select the counterfactuals that are observed in hypothetical or real samples. In the words of Holland (1986), they want to model the effects of causes without modeling the causes of effects. Science is all about constructing models of the causes of effects. This paper develops the scientific model of causality and shows its value in analyzing policy problems.

My second main point is that the existing literature on "causal inference" in statistics confuses three distinct tasks that need to be carefully distinguished:

---

[1] I will use the term *counterfactual* as defined in philosophy. A counterfactual need not be contrary to certain facts. It is just a hypothetical. The term *hypothetical* would be better and I will use the two concepts interchangeably.

- Definitions of counterfactuals.
- Identification of causal models from population distributions (infinite samples without any sampling variation). The hypothetical populations producing these distributions may be subject to selection bias, attrition, and the like. However, issues of sampling variability of empirical distributions are irrelevant for the analysis of this problem.
- Identification of causal models from actual data, where sampling variability is an issue. This analysis recognizes the difference between empirical distributions based on sampled data and population distributions generating the data.

Table 1 represents these three tasks.

The first task is a matter of science, logic, and imagination. It is also partly a matter of convention. A model of counterfactuals is more widely accepted the more widely accepted are its ingredients, which are

- the rules of the derivation of a model including whether or not the rules of logic and mathematics are followed;
- its agreement with other theories; and
- its agreement with the accepted interpretations of facts.

Models are not empirical statements or descriptions of actual worlds. They are descriptions of hypothetical worlds obtained by varying—hypothetically—the factors determining outcomes.

TABLE 1
Three Distinct Tasks Arising from Analysis of Causal Models

Task	Description	Requirements
1	Defining the Set of Hypotheticals or Counterfactuals	A Scientific Theory
2	Identifying Parameters (Causal or Otherwise) from Hypothetical Population Data	Mathematical Analysis of Point or Set Identification
3	Identifying Parameters from Real Data	Estimation and Testing Theory

The second task is one of inference in very large samples. Can we recover counterfactuals (or means or distributions of counterfactuals) from data that are free of sampling variation? This is the identification problem. It abstracts from any variability in estimates due to sampling variation. It is strictly an issue of finding unique mappings from population distributions, population moments or other population measures to causal parameters.

The third task is one of inference in practice. Can one recover a given model or the desired causal parameters from a given set of data? This entails issues of inference and testing in real world samples. This is the task most familiar to statisticians and empirical social scientists. This essay focuses on the first two tasks. Identification is discussed, but issues of sampling distributions of estimators, such as efficiency, are not.

Some of the controversy surrounding counterfactuals and causal models is partly a consequence of analysts being unclear about these three distinct tasks and often confusing solutions to each of them. Some analysts associate particular methods of estimation (e.g., matching or instrumental variable estimation) with causal inference and the definition of causal parameters. Such associations confuse the three distinct tasks of definition, identification, and estimation. Each method for estimating causal parameters makes some assumptions and forces certain constraints on the counterfactuals.

Many statisticians are uncomfortable with counterfactuals. Their discomfort arises in part from the need to specify models to interpret and identify counterfactuals. Most statisticians are not trained in science or social science and adopt as their credo that they "should stick to the facts." An extreme recent example of this discomfort is expressed by Dawid (2000), who denies the need for, or validity of, counterfactual analysis. Tukey (1986) rejects the provisional nature of causal knowledge—i.e., its dependence on *a priori* models to define the universe of counterfactuals and the mechanisms of selection and the dependence of estimators of causal parameters on *a priori*, untestable assumptions.[2] Cox (1992) appears to accept the provisional nature of causal knowledge (see also Cox and Wermuth 1996). Science is based on counterfactuals and theoretical models.

---

[2]The exchange between Heckman and Tukey in Wainer (1986) anticipates many of the issues raised in this paper.

Human knowledge is produced by constructing counterfactuals and theories. Blind empiricism unguided by a theoretical framework for interpreting facts leads nowhere.

Causal models which are widely used in epidemiology and statistics are incompletely specified because they do not delineate selection mechanisms for how hypothetical counterfactuals are realized or how hypothetical interventions are implemented even in hypothetical populations. They focus only on outcomes of treatment, leaving the model-selecting outcomes only implicitly specified. In addition, in this literature the construction of counterfactual outcomes is based on intuition and not on explicit formal models. Instead of modeling outcome selection mechanisms, a metaphor of "random selection" is adopted. This emphasis on randomization or its surrogates (like matching) rules out a variety of alternative channels of identification of counterfactuals from population or sample data. It has practical consequences because of the conflation of step one with steps two and three in Table 1. Since randomization is used to define the parameters of interest, this practice sometimes leads to the confusion that randomization is the only way— or at least the best way—to identify causal parameters from real data. In truth, this is not always so, as I show in this paper.

Another reason why epidemiological and statistical models are incomplete is that they do not specify the sources of randomness generating the unobservables in the models—i.e., they do not explain why observationally identical people make different choices and have different outcomes given the same choice. Modeling these unobservables greatly facilitates the choice of estimators to identify causal parameters. Statistical and epidemiological models are incomplete because they are recursive. They do not allow for simultaneous choices of outcomes of treatment that are at the heart of game theory and models of social interactions (e.g., see Tamer 2003; Brock and Durlauf 2001). They rule out the possibility that one outcome can cause another if all outcomes are chosen simultaneously. They are also incomplete because the ingredients of the "treatments" are not considered at a finer level. "Treatment" is usually a black box of many aggregate factors that are not isolated or related to underlying theory in a precise way. This makes it difficult to understand what factor or set of factors produces the "effect" of the intervention being analyzed. The treatment effects identified in the statistical literature cannot be used to forecast out-of-sample to new populations. They are incomplete because they do not distinguish uncertainty from the point of view of the agent being analyzed from variability as analyzed by the observing social scientist.

Economists since the time of Haavelmo (1943, 1944) have recognized the need for precise models to construct counterfactuals and to answer "causal" questions and more general policy evaluation questions, including making out-of-sample forecasts. The econometric framework is explicit about how counterfactuals are generated and how interventions are assigned (the rules of assigning "treatment"). The sources of unobservables, in both treatment assignment equations and outcome equations, and the relationship between the unobservables are studied. Rather than leaving the rule governing selection of treatment implicit, the econometric approach explicitly models the relationship between the unobservables in outcome equations and selection equations to identify causal models from data and to clarify the nature of identifying assumptions. The theory of structural modeling in econometrics is based on these principles.

The goal of the econometric literature, like the goal of all science, is to model phenomena at a deeper level, to understand the causes producing the effects so that we can use empirical versions of the models to forecast the effects of interventions never previously experienced, to calculate a variety of policy counterfactuals, and to use scientific theory to guide the choices of estimators and the interpretation of the evidence. These activities require development of a more elaborate theory than is envisioned in the current literature on causal inference in epidemiology and statistics.

This essay is in five parts. Section 1 discusses policy evaluation questions as a backdrop against which to compare alternative approaches to causal inference. A notation is developed and both individual-level and population-level causal effects are defined. Population-level effects are defined both in terms of means and distributions. Uncertainty at the individual level is introduced to account for one source of randomness across persons in terms of outcomes and choices.

Section 2 is the heart of the paper. It defines causality using structural econometric models and analyzes both objective outcomes and subjective evaluations. It defines structural models and policy-invariant structural parameters. A definition of causality in models with simultaneously determined outcomes is presented. A distinction between conditioning and fixing variables is developed. The Neyman (1923)–Rubin (1978) model advocated in statistics is compared to the scientific model. Marschak's maxim is defined. This maxim links the statistical treatment effect literature to the literature on structural models by showing that statistical treatment effects focus on answering one narrow question while the structural approach attempts to answer many questions. It is usually easier to answer one question well than to answer many questions at the same time but the narrowness of the question answered in the treatment effect literature limits the applicability of the answer obtained to address other questions.

Section 3 briefly discusses the identification problem at a general level (task 2 in Table 1). Section 4 applies the framework of the paper to the identification of four widely used estimators for causal inference and the implicit identifying assumptions that justify their application. This section is only intended as a comprehensive survey. Section 5 concludes.

1. POLICY EVALUATION QUESTIONS AND CRITERIA OF INTEREST

This paper discusses questions of causal inference in terms of policy evaluation and policy forecasting problems. Such a focus appears to limit the scope of the inquiry. In fact, it makes the discussion more precise by placing it in a concrete context. By focusing on policy questions, the discussion gains tangibility, something often lacking in the literature on causality. In social science, a major use of causal analysis is in determining "effects" of various policies. Causal analysis is almost always directed toward answering policy questions.

This section first presents three central policy evaluation questions. It then defines the notation used in this paper and the definition of individual-level causal effects or treatment effects. The policy evaluation problem is discussed in general terms. Population-level mean treatment parameters are then defined and distributional criteria are also presented. We discuss, in general terms, the type of data needed to construct the policy evaluation criteria.

1.1. *Three Policy Evaluation Problems*

Three broad classes of policy evaluation questions are of general interest. Policy evaluation question one is:

P1: *Evaluating the impact of historical interventions on outcomes including their impact in terms of welfare.*

By historical, I refer to interventions actually experienced. A variety of outcomes and welfare criteria might be used to form these evaluations. By impact, I mean constructing either individual-level or population-level counterfactuals and their valuations. By welfare, I mean the valuations of the outcomes obtained from the intervention by the agents being analyzed or some other party (e.g., the parents of the agent).

P1 is the problem of *internal validity*. It is the problem of identifying a given treatment parameter or a set of treatment parameters in a given environment (see Campbell and Stanley 1963). This is the policy question addressed in the epidemiological and statistical literature on causality. A drug trial for a particular patient population is the prototypical problem in that literature.

Most policy evaluation is designed with an eye toward the future and toward decisions about new policies and application of old policies to new environments. I distinguish a second task of policy analysis:

P2: *Forecasting the impacts (constructing counterfactual states) of interventions implemented in one environment in other environments, including their impacts in terms of welfare.*

Included in these interventions are policies described by generic characteristics (e.g., tax or benefit rates, etc.) that are applied to different groups of people or in different time periods from those studied in previous implementations of these policies. This is the problem of *external validity*: taking a treatment parameter or a set of parameters estimated in one environment to another environment. The "environment" includes the characteristics of individuals and of their social and economic setting.

Finally, the most ambitious problem is forecasting the effect of a new policy, never previously experienced:

P3: *Forecasting the impacts of interventions (constructing counterfactual states associated with interventions) never historically experienced to other environments, including their impacts in terms of welfare.*

This problem requires that one use past history to forecast the consequences of new policies. It is a fundamental problem in knowledge.[3] I now present a framework within which one can address these problems in a systematic fashion. It is also a framework that can be used for causal inference.

1.2. *Notation and Definition of Individual-Level Treatment or Causal Effects*

To evaluate is to value and to compare values among possible outcomes. These are two distinct tasks that I distinguish in this essay. Define outcomes corresponding to state (policy, treatment) s for person ω as $Y(s, \omega)$, $\omega \in \Omega$. One can think of Ω as a universe of individuals each characterized by their own element ω. The ω encompass all features of individuals that affect Y outcomes. $Y(s, \omega)$ may be generated from a scientific or social science theory. $Y(s, \omega)$ may be vector valued. The components of $Y(s, \omega)$ may also be interdependent, as in the Cowles Commission simultaneous equations model developed by Haavelmo (1943, 1944) and discussed in Section 2. The components of $Y(s, \omega)$ may be discrete, continuous, or mixed discrete-continuous random variables.

I use "ω" as a shorthand descriptor of the state of a person. We (the analyst) may observe variables $X(\omega)$ that characterize the person as well. In addition, there may be model unobservables. I develop this distinction further in Section 2.

The $Y(s, \omega)$ are outcomes after treatment is chosen. In advance of treatment, agents may not know the $Y(s, \omega)$ but may make forecasts about them. These forecasts may influence their decisions to participate in a treatment or may influence the agents who make decisions about whether or not an individual participates in the treatment. Selection into the program based on actual or anticipated components of outcomes gives rise to the selection problem in the evaluation literature.

Let S be the set of possible treatments denoted by s. For simplicity of exposition, I assume that this set is the same for all ω.[4] For each choice of $s \in S$ and for each person ω, we obtain a collection of possible outcomes given by $\{Y(s, \omega)\}_{s \in S}$. The set S may be finite

---

[3]Knight (1921:313) succinctly summarizes the problem: "The existence of a problem in knowledge depends on the future being different from the past, while the possibility of a solution of the problem depends on the future being like the past."

[4]At the cost of a more cumbersome notation, this assumption can be modified so that S sets are ω-specific.

(e.g., J states with $\mathcal{S} = \{1, \ldots J\}$), countable, or may be defined on the continuum (e.g., $\mathcal{S} = [0, 1]$) so there are an uncountable number of states. For example, if $\mathcal{S} = \{0, 1\}$, there are two policies (or treatments), one of which may be a no-treatment state—for example, $Y(0, \omega)$ is the outcome for a person ω not getting a treatment like a drug, schooling, or access to a new technology, while $Y(1, \omega)$ corresponds to person ω getting the drug, schooling or access.

Each "state" (treatment, policy) may consist of a compound of subcomponent states. In this case, we can define s as a vector (e.g., $s = (s_1, s_2, \ldots, s_k)$) corresponding to the different components that comprise treatment. Thus a job training program typically consists of a package of treatments. We might be interested in the package or one (or more) of its components. Thus s_1 may be months of vocational education, s_2 quality of training and so forth. The outcomes may be time subscripted as well, with $Y_t(s, \omega)$ corresponding to outcomes of treatment measured at different times. The index set for t may be the integers, corresponding to discrete time, or an interval, corresponding to continuous time.[5] The $Y_t(s, \omega)$ are realized or *ex post* (after treatment) outcomes. When choosing treatment, these values may not be known. Gill and Robins (2001), Abbring and Van Den Berg (2003), Lechner (2004), Heckman and Vytlacil (2006a,b), and Heckman and Navarro (2006) develop models for dynamic counterfactuals.

Each policy regime $p \in \mathcal{P}$ consists of a collection of possible treatments $\mathcal{S}_p \subseteq \mathcal{S}$. Different policy regimes may include some of the same subsets of $\mathcal{S}$. Associated with each policy regime is an assignment mechanism $\tau \in \mathcal{T}_p$, where $\mathcal{T}_p$ is the set of possible mechanisms under policy p. (Some policy regimes may rule out some assignment mechanisms.) The assignment mechanism determines the allocation of persons $\omega \in \Omega$ to treatment. It implicitly sets the scale of the program. The mechanism could include randomization so that the assignment mechanism would assign probabilities $\pi_s^\tau \in [0, 1]$ to each treatment $s \in \mathcal{S}_p$. Let Π_p denote the set of families $(\pi_s)_{s \in \mathcal{S}_p}$, $\pi_s \in [0, 1]$, such that $\Sigma_{s \in \mathcal{S}_p} \pi_s = 1$. Then,

$$\Phi^p : \Omega \times \mathcal{T}_p \to \Pi_p,$$

---

[5]In principle, in addition to indexing $\mathcal{S}$ by ω ($\mathcal{S}_\omega$) so there are person-specific treatment possibility sets, we could index by t ($\mathcal{S}_{\omega,t}$), but we assume, for simplicity, a common $\mathcal{S}$ for all ω and t.

where $\Phi^p(\omega, \tau) \in \Pi_p$ is a family of probabilities which we note alternatively $\left(\pi_s^\tau(\omega)\right)_{s \in \mathcal{S}_p}$. This signifies that, under policy p with assignment mechanism τ, person ω receives treatment s_p with probability $\pi_{s_p}^\tau(\omega)$. For each person ω, the special case of deterministic assignment sets $\pi_{s_0}^\tau(\omega) = 1$ for exactly one treatment $s_0 \in \mathcal{S}_p$ and sets $\pi_{s_0}^\tau(\omega) = 0$ for all $s \in \mathcal{S}_p \backslash \{s_0\}$.

For deterministic policy assignment rules, a universal policy may consist of a single treatment ($\mathcal{S}_p$ may consist of a single element). Treatment can include direct receipt of some intervention (e.g., a drug, education) as well as the tax payment for financing the treatment. For some persons, the assigned treatment may only be the tax payment. In the special case where some get no treatment ($\omega \in \Omega_0$) and others get treatment ($\omega \in \Omega_1$), and there are two elements in $\mathcal{S}_p$ (e.g., $\mathcal{S}_p = \{0, 1\}$), we produce the classical binary treatment-control comparison.

Two assumptions are often invoked in the literature.[6] In our notation, they are:

$$Y(s, \omega, p, \tau) = Y(s, \omega, p', \tau) = Y(s, \omega, \tau) \text{ for } s \in \mathcal{S}_p \cap \mathcal{S}_{p'},$$
$$\tau \in \mathcal{T}_p \cap \mathcal{T}_{p'}, \text{ for all } p, p' \in \mathcal{P} \text{ and } \omega \in \Omega \tag{A-1}$$

This assumption says that outcomes for person ω under treatment s with assignment mechanism τ are the same in two different policy regimes which both include s as a possible treatment. It rules out social interactions and general equilibrium effects. A second assumption rules out any effect of the assignment mechanism on potential outcomes.

Irrespective of assignment mechanism τ, for all policies
$p \in \mathcal{P}, Y(s, \omega, \tau) = Y(s, \omega)$ for all $s \in \mathcal{S}_p$ and
$\omega \in \Omega$, so the outcome is not affected by the assignment. (A-2)

This assumption maintains that the outcome is the same no matter what the choice of assignment mechanism. (A-2) rules out, among other things, the phenomenon of randomization bias discussed in Heckman, LaLonde, and Smith (1999) where agent behavior is

---

[6]See, e.g., Holland (1986) or Rubin (1986).

affected by the act of participating in an experiment. Such effects are also called "Hawthorne" effects.

Heckman, LaLonde, and Smith (1999) discuss the evidence against both assumptions. In much of this essay, I maintain these strong assumptions mostly to simplify the discussion. But the reader should be aware of the strong limitations imposed by these assumptions. Recent work in economics tests and relaxes these assumptions (see Heckman and Vytlacil 2006a).

Under these assumptions, the *individual-level treatment effect* for person ω comparing outcomes from treatment s with outcomes from treatment s' is

$$Y(s,\omega) - Y(s',\omega), \quad s \neq s', \tag{1}$$

where two elements are selected $s, s' \in \mathcal{S}$.[7] This is also called an *individual-level causal effect*. This may be a random variable or a constant. Our framework accommodates both interpretations. Thus the same individual with the same choice set and characteristics may have the same outcome in a sequence of trials or it may be random across trials. We discuss intrinsic variability at the individual level in Section 2.[8]

Other comparisons might be made. Comparisons can be made in terms of utilities (personal, $V(Y(s, \omega), \omega)$, or in terms of planner preferences, V_G). Thus one can ask if $V(Y(s, \omega), \omega) > V(Y(s', \omega), \omega)$ or not (is the person better off as a result of treatment s compared to treatment s'?) Treatments s and s' may be bundles of components

[7]One could define the treatment effect more generally as

$$Y(s,\omega,p,\tau) - Y(s',\omega,p,\tau).$$

This makes clear that the policy treatment effect is defined under a particular policy regime and for a particular mechanism of selection within a policy regime. One could define treatment effects for policy regimes or regime selection mechanisms by varying the arguments p or τ respectively, holding the other arguments fixed.

[8]There is a disagreement in the literature on whether or not the individual-level treatment effects are constants or random at the individual level. I develop both cases in this paper.

as previously discussed. One could define the treatment effect as $1[V(Y(s, \omega), \omega) > V(Y(s', \omega), \omega)]$ where $1[\cdot] = 1$ if the argument in brackets is true and is zero otherwise. These definitions of treatment effects embody Marshall's notion of *ceteris paribus*. Holding ω fixed holds all features about the person fixed except the treatment assigned s.[9]

Social welfare theory constructs aggregates over Ω or subsets of Ω (Sen 1999). A comparison of two policies $\{s_p(\omega)\}_{\omega \in \Omega}$ and $\{s_{p'}(\omega)\}_{\omega \in \Omega}$, using the social welfare function $V_G(\{Y(s(\omega), \omega)\}_{\omega \in \Omega})$, can be expressed as

$$V_G(\{Y(s_p, \omega), \omega\}_{\omega \in \Omega}) - V_G(\{Y(s_{p'}, \omega), \omega\}_{\omega \in \Omega}).$$

We can use an indicator function to denote when this term is positive: $1[V_G(\{Y(s_p(\omega), \omega)\}_{\omega \in \Omega}) > V_G(\{Y(s_{p'}(\omega), \omega)\}_{\omega \in \Omega})]$. A special case of this analysis is cost-benefit analysis in economics where willingness to pay measures $W(s(\omega), \omega)$ are associated with each person. The cost-benefit comparison of two policies is

$$\textbf{Cost Benefit}: \textbf{CB}_{p,p'} = \int_\Omega W(Y(s_p(\omega), \omega)) d\mu(\omega) - \int_\Omega W(Y(s_{p'}(\omega), \omega)) d\mu(\omega),$$

[9]One might compare outcomes in different sets that are ordered. Thus, for a particular policy regime and assignment mechanism, if $Y(s, \omega)$ is scalar income and we compare outcomes for $s \in S_A$ with outcomes for $s' \in S_B$, where $S_A \cap S_B = \varnothing$, then one might compare $Y_{s_A} - Y_{s_B}$, where

$$s_A = \arg\max_{s \in S_A}(Y(s, \omega)) \quad \text{and} \quad s_B = \arg\max_{s \in S_B}(Y(s, \omega)).$$

This compares the best in one choice set with the best in the other. A particular case is the comparison of the best choice with the next best choice. To do so, define $s' = \arg\max_{s \in S}(Y(s, \omega))$, $S_B = S \setminus \{s'\}$ and define the treatment effect as $Y_{s'} - Y_{s_B}$. This is the comparison of the highest outcome over S with the next best outcome. In principle, many different individual level comparisons might be constructed, and they may be computed using personal preferences, V_ω, using the preferences of the planner, V_G, or using the preferences of the planner over preferences of agents.

where p, p' are two different policies, p' may correspond to a benchmark of no policy, and $\mu\,(\omega)$ is the distribution of ω.[10] The distribution $\mu\,(\omega)$ is constructed over the individual characteristics ω (e.g., age, sex, race, income) The Benthamite criterion replaces $W(Y(s(\omega),\,\omega))$ with $V(Y(s(\omega),\,\omega))$ in the preceding expressions and integrates utilities across persons:

$$\textbf{Benthamite}: \mathbf{B}_{p,p'} = \int_\Omega V(Y(s_p(\omega),\omega))d\mu(\omega) - \int_\Omega V(Y(s_{p'}(\omega),\omega))d\mu(\omega).$$

I now discuss a fundamental problem that arises in constructing these and other criteria from data. This takes me to the problem of causal inference, the second task delineated in Table 1. Recall that I am talking about inference in a population, not in a sample, so no issues of sampling variability arise.

1.3. *The Evaluation Problem*

Operating purely in the domain of theory, I have assumed a world with a well-defined set of individuals $\omega \in \Omega$ and a universe of counterfactuals or hypotheticals defined for each person $Y\,(s,\,\omega)$, $s \in \mathcal{S}$. Different policies $p \in \mathcal{P}$ select treatment for persons. Each policy can in principle assign treatment to persons by different mechanisms $\tau \in \mathcal{T}$. In the absence of a theory, there are no well-defined rules for constructing counterfactual or hypothetical states or constructing the assignment to treatment rules Φ_τ^p.[11] Scientific theories provide algorithms for generating the universe of internally consistent, theory-consistent counterfactual states.

These hypothetical states are possible worlds. They are products of a purely mental activity. No empirical problem arises in constructing these theoretically possible worlds. Indeed, in forecasting new policies, or projecting the effects of old policies to new

---

[10]These willingness-to-pay measures are standard in the economics literature (e.g., see Boadway and Bruce 1984).

[11]Efforts like those of Lewis (1974) to define admissible counterfactual states without an articulated theory as "closest possible worlds" founder on the lack of any meaningful metric or topology to measure "closeness" among possible worlds. Statisticians often appeal to this theory, but it is not operational (e.g., see Gill and Robins 2001 for one such appeal).

environments, some of the $Y(s, \omega)$ may have never been observed for anyone. Different theories produce different outcomes $Y(s, \omega)$ and different $\Phi^p_\tau(\omega)$.

The evaluation problem, in contrast to the model construction problem, is an identification problem that arises in constructing the counterfactual states and treatment assignment rules produced by abstract models from population data. This is the second task presented in Table 1.

This problem is not precisely stated until the data available to the analyst are precisely defined. Different subfields in science and social science assume access to different types of data. They also make different assumptions about the underlying models generating the counterfactuals and mechanisms for selecting which counterfactuals are actually observed.

At any point in time, we can observe person ω in one state but not in any of the other states. The states are mutually exclusive. Thus we do not observe $Y(s', \omega)$ for person ω if we observe $Y(s, \omega)$, $s \neq s'$. Let $D(s, \omega) = 1$ if we observe person ω in state s. Then $D(s', \omega) = 0$ for $s \neq s'$. $D(s, \omega)$ is generated by $\Phi^p_\tau(\omega) : D(s, \omega) = 1$ if $\Phi^p(\omega) = s$.

We observe $Y(s, \omega)$, if $D(s, \omega) = 1$ but we do not observe $Y(s', \omega)$, $s \neq s'$. We can define observed $Y(\omega)$ as

$$Y(\omega) = \sum_{s \in \mathcal{S}} D(s, \omega) Y(s, \omega).^{12} \tag{2}$$

Without further assumptions, constructing an empirical counterpart to equation (1) is impossible from the data on $(Y(\omega), D(\omega))$, $\omega \in \Omega$. This formulation of the evaluation problem is known as Quandt's switching regression model (Quandt 1958, 1974) and is attributed in statistics to Neyman (1923), Cox (1958), and Rubin (1978). A revision of it is formulated in a linear equations context for a continuum of treatments by Haavelmo (1943). The Roy model (Roy 1951) in economics is another version of it with two possible treatment outcomes ($\mathcal{S} = \{0,1\}$) and a scalar outcome measure and a particular selection mechanism $\tau \in \mathcal{T}$ which is that $D(1, \omega) = \mathbf{1}\,(Y(1, \omega) > Y(0, \omega))$ where "$\mathbf{1}[\cdot]$" is an indicator function which equals 1 when the event inside the

---

[12]In the general case, $Y(\omega) = \int_{\mathcal{S}} D(s, \omega) Y(s, \omega) ds$ where $D(s, \omega)$ is a Dirac function.

parentheses is true and is zero otherwise.[13] The mechanism of selection depends on the potential outcomes. Agents choose the sector with the highest outcome, so the actual selection mechanism is not a randomization.

Social experiments attempt to create assignment rules so that $D(s, \omega)$ is random with respect to $\{Y(s, \omega)\}_{s \in \mathcal{S}}$ for each ω (i.e., so that receipt of treatment is independent of the outcome of treatment). When agents self-select into treatment, rather than being randomly assigned, in general the $D(s, \omega)$ are not independent of $\{Y(s, \omega)\}_{s \in \mathcal{S}}$. This arises in the Roy model example. This selection rule creates the potential for *self-selection bias in inference*. We discuss this problem at length in Section 4.

The problem of self-selection is an essential aspect of the evaluation problem when data are generated by choices of agents. The agents making choices may be different from the agents receiving treatment (e.g., parents making choices for children). Such choices can include compliance with the protocols of a social experiment as well as ordinary choices about outcomes that people make in everyday life. Observe that in the Roy model, the choice of treatment (including the decision not to attrite from a program) is informative on the relative valuation of the $Y(s, \omega)$. This point is more general and receives considerable emphasis in the econometric literature but none in the statistical or epidemiological literature. Choices of treatment provide information on subjective relative evaluations of treatment by the decision maker and provides analysts with information on agent valuations of outcomes that are of independent interest.

A central problem considered in the literature on causal inference is the absence of information on outcomes for person ω other than the outcome that is observed. Even a perfectly implemented social experiment does not solve this problem (Heckman 1992) and, even under ideal conditions, randomization identifies only one component of $\{Y(s, \omega)\}_{s \in \mathcal{S}}$. In addition, even with ideal data and infinite samples some of the $s \in \mathcal{S}$ may not be observed if one is seeking to evaluate policies that produce new outcome states.

There are two main avenues of escape from this problem. The first, featured in explicitly formulated econometric models, often called "structural econometric analysis," is to model $Y(s, \omega)$ explicitly in terms of its determinants as specified by theory. This entails

---

[13]In terms of the assignment mechanism, $\Phi^p(\omega, \tau) = 1$ for ω such that $Y(1, \omega) > Y(0, \omega)$.

describing ω and carefully distinguishing what agents know and what the analyst knows. This approach also models $D(s, \omega)$—or $\Phi^p(\omega)$—and the dependence between $Y(s, \omega)$ and $D(s, \omega)$ produced from variables common to $Y(s, \omega)$ and $D(s, \omega)$. The Roy model, previously discussed, explicitly models this dependence.[14] Like all scientific models, this approach seeks to understand the factors underlying outcome, choice of outcome equations, and their relationship. Empirical models explicitly based on economic or social theory pursue this avenue of investigation. Some statisticians call this the "scientific approach" and are surprisingly hostile to it (Holland 1986).[15]

A second avenue of escape, and the one pursued in the recent epidemiological and statistical treatment effect literature, defines the problem away from estimating $Y(s, \omega)$ to be one of estimating some population version of equation (1), most often a mean, without modeling those factors giving rise to the outcome or the relationship between the outcomes and the mechanism selecting outcomes. Agent valuations of outcomes are ignored. The treatment effect literature focuses almost exclusively on policy problem P1 for the subset of outcomes that is observed. It ignores the problems of forecasting a policy in a new environment (problem P2) or a policy never previously experienced (problem P3). Forecasting the effects of new policies is a central task of science and public policy analysis that the treatment effect literature ignores.[16]

1.4. *Population-Level Treatment Parameters*

Constructing equation (1) or any of the other individual-level parameters defined in Section 1.2 for a given person is a difficult task because we rarely observe the same person ω in distinct s states. In addition, some of the states in S may not be experienced by anyone. The conventional approach in the treatment effect literature is to reformulate the parameter of interest to be some summary measure of the population distribution of treatment

[14]See Heckman and Honoré (1990) for a discussion of this model.

[15]I include in this approach methods based on panel data or more generally the method of paired comparisons, as applications of the scientific approaches. Under special conditions discussed in Heckman and Smith (1998), we can observe the same person in states s and s' in different time periods and can construct (1) for all ω.

[16]See Heckman and Vytlacil (2005) for one synthesis of the treatment effect and the structural literatures.

effects, most often a mean, or sometimes the distribution itself, rather than attempting to identify individual treatment effects. This approach focuses on presenting some summary measure of outcomes, not analyzing determinants of outcomes.[17] This approach also confines attention to the subsets of S that are observed states. Thus the objects of interest are redefined to be the distributions of $(Y(j, \omega) - Y(k, \omega))$ over ω, conditional on known components of ω, or certain means (or quantiles) of the distribution of $(Y(j, \omega) - Y(k, \omega))$ over ω, conditional on known components of ω (Heckman, Smith, and Clements 1997) or of $Y(j, \omega)$ and $Y(k, \omega)$ separately (Abadie, Angrist, and Imbens 2002). The standard assumptions in the treatment effect literature are that all states in S are observed, and that assumptions (A-1) and (A-2) hold (see Holland 1986; Rubin 1986).

The conventional parameter of interest, and the focus of many investigations in economics and statistics, is the average treatment effect (ATE). For program (treatment) j compared to program (treatment) k, this parameter is

$$ATE(j,k) = E_\omega(Y(j,\omega) - Y(k,\omega)), \tag{3a}$$

where "E_ω" means that we take expectations with respect to distribution of the factors generating outcomes and choices that characterize ω. Conditioning on covariates X, which are observed components associated with ω (and hence working with conditional distributions), this parameter is

$$ATE(j,k \mid x) = E_\omega(Y(j,\omega) - Y(k,\omega) \mid X = x). \tag{3b}$$

This is the effect of assigning a person to a treatment—taking someone from the overall population (3a) or a subpopulation conditional on X (3b) and determining the mean gain of the move from base state k, averaging over the factors that determine Y but are not captured by X. This parameter is also the effect of moving the society from a universal policy (characterized by policy k) and moving to a universal policy of j (e.g., from no social security to full population coverage). Such a policy would likely induce social interaction and general equilibrium effects that are

---

[17]The effects of causes and not the causes of effects, in the language of Holland (1986).

assumed away by (A-1) in the treatment effect literature and which, if present, fundamentally alter the interpretation placed on this parameter.

A second conventional parameter in this literature is the average effect of treatment on the treated. Letting $D(j, \omega) = 1$ denote receipt of treatment j, the conventional parameter is

$$TT(j,k) = E_\omega(Y(j,\omega) - Y(k,\omega) \mid D(j,\omega) = 1). \tag{4a}$$

For a population conditional on $X = x$, it is

$$TT(j,k \mid x) = E_\omega(Y(j,\omega) - Y(k,\omega) \mid D(j,\omega) = 1, X = x). \tag{4b}$$

These are, respectively, the mean impact of moving persons from k to j for those people who get treatment, unconditional and conditional on $X = x$.

A parallel pair of parameters for nonparticipants is treatment on the untreated, where $D(j, \omega) = 0$ denotes no treatment at level j:

$$TUT(j,k) = E_\omega(Y(j,\omega) - Y(k,\omega) \mid D(j,\omega) = 0) \tag{5a}$$

$$TUT(j,k \mid x) = E_\omega(Y(j,\omega) - Y(k,\omega) \mid D(j,\omega) = 0, X = x). \tag{5b}$$

These parameters answer (conditionally and unconditionally) the question of how extension of a program to nonparticipants as a group would affect their outcomes.[18]

The population treatment parameters just discussed are average effects: how the average in one treatment group compares with the average for another. The distinction between the marginal and average return has wide applicability in many areas of social science. The average student going to college may have higher earnings than the marginal student who is indifferent between going to school or not. It is often of interest to evaluate the impact of marginal extensions (or contractions) of a program. Incremental cost-benefit analysis is conducted in terms of marginal gains and benefits. The *effect of treatment for people at the margin of indifference* (*EOTM*) between

[18]Analogous to the pairwise comparisons, we can define setwise comparisons as is done in footnote 9.

j and k, given that these are the best two choices available is, with respect to personal preferences, and with respect to choice-specific costs P (j, ω),

$$EOTM_\omega^V(Y(j,\omega) - Y(k,\omega))$$

$$= E_\omega \left(Y(j,\omega) - Y(k,\omega) \left| \begin{array}{c} V(Y(j,\omega), P(j,\omega), \omega) = V(Y(k,\omega), P(k,\omega), \omega); \\[2mm] \left. \begin{array}{c} V(Y(j,\omega), P(j,\omega), \omega) \\[2mm] V(Y(k,\omega), P(k,\omega), \omega) \end{array} \right\} \geq V(Y(l,\omega), P(l,\omega), \omega), \\[2mm] l \neq j, k \end{array} \right. \right).$$

$$(6)$$

This is the mean gain to people indifferent between j and k, given that these are the best two options available. In a parallel fashion, we can define $EOTM_\omega^{V_G}(Y(j) - Y(k))$ using the preferences of another person (e.g., the parent of a child or a paternalistic bureaucrat).[19]

A generalization of this parameter called the *marginal treatment effect*—developed in Heckman and Vytlacil (1999, 2000, 2005, 2006b), Heckman (2001), and estimated in Carneiro, Heckman, and Vytlacil (2005)—plays a central role in organizing and interpreting a wide variety of evaluation estimators. Many other mean treatment parameters can be defined depending on the choice of the conditioning set. Analogous definitions can be given for median and other quantile versions of these parameters (see Heckman, Smith, and Clements 1997; Abadie, Angrist, and Imbens 2002). Although means are conventional, distributions of treatment parameters are also of considerable interest, and we consider them in the next section.

Mean treatment effects play a special role in the statistical approach to causality. They are the centerpiece of the Rubin (1986)–Holland (1986) model and in many other studies in statistics and epidemiology. Social experiments with full compliance and no disruption can identify these means because of a special mathematical property of means. If we can identify the mean of $Y(j, \omega)$ and the mean of $Y(k, \omega)$ from an experiment where j is the treatment and k is the baseline, we can form the average treatment effect for j compared

---

[19]An analogous parameter can be defined for mean setwise comparisons as in footnote 9.

with k (3a). These can be formed over two different groups of people classified by their X values. By a similar argument, we can form the treatment on the treated parameter (TT) (4a) or (TUT) (5a) by randomizing over particular subsets of the population ($D = 1$ or $D = 0$, respectively) assuming full compliance and no randomization (disruption) bias. Disruption bias arises when the experiment itself affects outcomes $(Y(s, \omega))_{\omega \in \Omega}$ and (A-2) is violated.[20]

The case for randomization is weaker if the analyst is interested in other summary measures of the distribution, or the distribution itself. Experiments do not solve the problem that we cannot form $Y(s, \omega) - Y(s', \omega)$ for any person. Randomization is not an effective procedure for identifying median gains, or the distribution of gains, under general conditions. The elevation of population means to be the central population-level "causal" parameters promotes randomization as an ideal estimation method. By focusing exclusively on mean outcomes, the statistical literature converts a metaphor for outcome selection—randomization—into an ideal.

1.5. Criteria of Interest Besides the Mean: Distributions of Counterfactuals

Although means are traditional, the answer to many interesting policy evaluation questions requires knowledge of features of the distribution of program gains other than some mean. It is also of interest to know the following for scalar outcomes

a. The proportion of people taking the program j who benefit from it relative to some alternative k, $\Pr_\omega(Y(j, \omega) > Y(k, \omega)|D(j, \omega) = 1)$;
b. The proportion of the total population that benefits from the program k compared with program j, $\Pr_\omega(Y(j, \omega) > Y(k, \omega))$, sometimes called the *voting criterion*;
c. Selected quantiles of the impact distribution;[21]
d. The distribution of gains at selected base state values, (the distribution of $Y(j, \omega) - Y(k, \omega)$ given $Y(k, \omega) = y(k)$).

---

[20]Such disruptions leading to changed outcomes are also called Hawthorne effects; see Heckman (1992) and Heckman, LaLonde, and Smith (1999).
[21]$\inf \{\delta : F_\Delta (\delta) \geq q\}$ where q is a quantile of the distribution and F_Δ is the distribution function of $\Delta = Y(j, \omega) - Y(k, \omega)$.

Each of these measures can be defined conditional on observed characteristics X. Measure (a) is of interest in determining how widely program gains are distributed among participants. Voters in an electorate in a democratic society are unlikely to assign the same weight to two programs with the same mean outcome, one of which produced large favorable outcomes for only a few persons while the other distributed smaller gains more broadly. This issue is especially relevant if program benefits are not transferrable or if restrictions on feasible social redistributions prevent distributional objectives from being attained.

Measure (b) is the proportion of the entire population that benefits from a program. In a study of the political economy of interest groups, it is useful to know which groups benefit from a program and how widely distributed the program benefits are. Measure (c) reveals the gains at different percentiles of the impact distribution. Criterion (d) focuses on the distribution of impacts for subgroups of participants with particular outcomes in the nonparticipation state. Concerns about the impact of policies on the disadvantaged emphasize such criteria (Rawls 1971). All of these measures require knowledge of features of the joint distribution of outcomes for participants for their construction, not just the mean. Identifying distributions is a more demanding task than identifying means.

Distributions of counterfactuals are also required in computing the option values conferred by social programs.[22] Heckman and Smith (1998), Aakvik, Heckman, and Vytlacil (1999, 2005), Carneiro, Hansen, and Heckman (2001, 2003), and Cunha, Heckman, and Navarro (2005a) develop methods for identifying distributions of counterfactuals.

1.6. *Accounting for Private and Social Uncertainty*

Persons do not know the outcomes associated with possible states not yet experienced. If some potential outcomes are not known at the time treatment decisions are made, the best that agents can do is to forecast them with some rule. Even if, *ex post*, agents know their outcome in a benchmark state, they may not know it *ex ante*, and they may always

---

[22]Heckman, Smith, and Clements (1997) present estimates of the option values of social programs.

be uncertain about what they would have experienced in alternative states. This creates a further distinction between *ex ante* and *ex post* evaluations of both subjective and objective outcomes. This distinction is missing from the statistical treatment effect literature.

In the literature on social choice, one form of decision-making under uncertainty plays a central role. The *Veil of Ignorance* of Vickrey (1945, 1960) and Harsanyi (1955, 1975) postulates that individuals are completely uncertain about their position in the distribution of outcomes under each policy considered, or should act as if they are completely uncertain, and they should use expected utility criteria (Vickrey-Harsanyi) or a maximin strategy (Rawls 1971) to evaluate their welfare under alternative policies. Central to this viewpoint is the anonymity postulate that claims the irrelevance of any particular person's outcome to the overall evaluation of social welfare. This form of ignorance is sometimes justified as an ethically correct position that captures how an objectively detached observer should evaluate alternative policies even if actual participants in the political process use other criteria. An approach based on the Veil of Ignorance is widely used in applied work in evaluating different income distributions (see Foster and Sen 1998). It only requires information about the marginal distributions of outcomes produced under different policies. If the outcome is income, policy j is preferred to policy k if the income distribution under j stochastically dominates the income under k.[23]

An alternative criterion is required if it is desired to model social choices where persons act in their own self-interest, or in the interest of certain other groups (e.g., the poor, the less able) and have at least partial knowledge about how they (or the groups they are interested in) will fare under different policies. The outcomes in different regimes may be dependent so that persons who benefit under one policy may also benefit under another (see Carneiro, Hansen, and Heckman 2001, 2003).

Because agents typically do not possess perfect information, the simple voting criterion assuming perfect foresight discussed in Section 1.5 may not accurately predict choices and requires

---

[23]See Foster and Sen (1998) for a definition of stochastic dominance. It compares one distribution with another and determines which, if either, has more mass at favorable outcomes.

modification. Let $\mathcal{I}_\omega$ denote the information set available to agent ω. The agent evaluates policy j against k using that information. Under an expected utility criterion, person ω prefers policy j over k if

$$E_\omega(V(Y(j,\omega),\omega) \mid \mathcal{I}_\omega) > E_\omega(V(Y(k,\omega),\omega) \mid \mathcal{I}_\omega).$$

The proportion of people who prefer j is

$$PB(j \mid j,k) = \int \mathbf{1}\begin{bmatrix} E_\omega(V(Y(j,\omega),\omega)|\mathcal{I}_\omega) > \\ E_\omega(V(Y(k,\omega),\omega) \mid \mathcal{I}_\omega) \end{bmatrix} d\mu(\omega), \qquad (7)$$

where $\mu(\omega)$ is the distribution of ω in the population.[24] The voting criterion previously discussed in Section 1.5 is the special case where $I_\omega = (Y(j, \omega), Y(k, \omega))$, so there is no uncertainty about $Y(j, \omega)$ and $Y(k, \omega)$. In the more general case, the expectation is computed against the distribution of $(E_\omega(V(Y(j, \omega), \omega|\mathcal{I}_\omega)), E_\omega(V(Y(k, \omega), \omega)|\mathcal{I}_\omega))$.[25]

Accounting for uncertainty in the analysis makes it essential to distinguish between *ex ante* and *ex post* evaluations. *Ex post*, part of the uncertainty about policy outcomes is resolved although individuals do not, in general, have full information about what their potential outcomes would have been in policy regimes they have not experienced and may have only incomplete information about the policy they have experienced (e.g., the policy may have long run consequences extending after the point of evaluation). It is useful to index the information set $\mathcal{I}_\omega$ by t, $\mathcal{I}_{\omega,t}$, to recognize that information about the outcomes of policies may accrue over time. *Ex ante* and *ex post* assessments of a voluntary program need not agree. *Ex post* assessments of a program through surveys administered to persons who have completed it (see Katz, Gutek, Kahn, and Barton 1975) may disagree with *ex ante* assessments of the program. Both may reflect honest valuations of the program but they are reported when agents have different information about it or have their preferences

---

[24]Persons would not necessarily vote "honestly," although in a binary choice setting they do and there is no scope for strategic manipulation of votes (see Moulin 1983). *PB* is simply a measure of relative satisfaction and need not describe a voting outcome when other factors come into play.
    [25]See Cunha, Heckman, and Navarro (2005b) for computations regarding both types of joint distributions.

altered by participating in the program. Before participating in a program, persons may be uncertain about the consequences of participation. A person who has completed program j may know $Y(j, \omega)$ but can only guess at the alternative outcome $Y(k, \omega)$ which they have not experienced. In this case, *ex post* "satisfaction" with j relative to k for agent ω is synonymous with the inequality

$$V(Y(j,\omega),\omega) > E_\omega(V(Y(k,\omega),\omega) \mid \mathcal{I}_\omega), \qquad (8)$$

where the information is post-treatment. Survey questionnaires about "client" satisfaction with a program may capture subjective elements of program experience not captured by "objective" measures of outcomes that usually exclude psychic costs and benefits. (Heckman, Smith, and Clements 1997 and Heckman and Smith 1998 present evidence on this question.) Carneiro, Hansen, and Heckman (2001, 2003), Cunha, Heckman, and Navarro (2005a,b), and Heckman and Navarro (2004, 2006) develop econometric methods for distinguishing *ex ante* from *ex post* evaluations of programs.

1.7. *Information Needed to Construct Various Criteria*

Four ingredients are required to implement the criteria discussed in this section: (1) private preferences, including preferences over outcomes by the decision maker; (2) social preferences, as exemplified by social welfare function $V_G(\{Y(s_p(\omega), \omega)\}_{\omega \in \Omega})$; (3) distributions of outcomes in alternative states, and for some criteria, such as the voting criterion, *joint* distributions of outcomes *across* policy states; and (4) *ex ante* and *ex post* information about outcomes. Cost-benefit analysis requires only information about means of measured outcomes and for that reason is easier to implement. The treatment effect literature in epidemiology and statistics largely focuses on means. Recent work in econometrics analyzes distributions of treatment effects (see Heckman, Smith, and Clements 1997; Carneiro, Hansen, and Heckman 2001, 2003; Cunha, Heckman, and Navarro 2005a). The rich set of questions addressed in this section contrasts sharply with the focus on mean outcome parameters in the epidemiology and statistics literatures, which ignore private and social preferences and ignore distributions of outcomes. Carneiro, Hansen, and Heckman (2001, 2003), Cunha, Heckman, and Navarro (2005a,b), and

Heckman and Navarro (2006) present methods for extracting private information on evaluations and their evolution over time. I now exposit more formally the econometric approach to formulating causal models.

2. COUNTERFACTUALS, CAUSALITY, AND STRUCTURAL ECONOMETRIC MODELS

This section formally defines structural models as devices for generating counterfactuals. I consider both outcome and treatment choice equations. The scientific model of econometrics is compared with the Neyman (1923)–Rubin (1978) model of causality that dominates discussions in epidemiology, in statistics, and in certain social sciences outside of economics. The structural equations approach and treatment effects approach are compared and evaluated.

2.1. *Generating Counterfactuals*

The treatment effect and structural approaches differ in the detail with which they specify counterfactual outcomes, $Y(s, \omega)$. The scientific approach embodied in the structural economics literature models the counterfactuals more explicitly than is common in the statistical treatment effect literature. This facilitates the application of theory to provide interpretation of counterfactuals and comparison of counterfactuals across empirical studies using basic parameters of social theory. These models also suggest strategies for identifying parameters (task 2 in Table 1). Models for counterfactuals are the basis for extending historically experienced policies to new environments and for forecasting the effects of new policies never previously experienced. These are policy questions P2 and P3 stated in Section 1.

Models for counterfactuals are in the mind. They are internally consistent frameworks derived from theory. Verification and identification of these models from data are separate tasks from the purely theoretical act of constructing internally consistent models. No issue of sampling, inference, or selection bias is entailed in constructing theoretical models for counterfactuals.

The traditional model of econometrics is the "all causes" model.[26] It writes outcomes as a deterministic function of inputs:

$$y(s) = g_s(x, u_s), \tag{9}$$

where x and u_s are fixed variables specified by the relevant economic theory for person ω.[27] All outcomes are explained in a functional sense by the arguments of g_s in equation (9). If we model the *ex post* realizations of outcomes, it is entirely reasonable to invoke an all causes model because *ex post* all uncertainty has been resolved. Equation (9) is a "production function" relating inputs (factors) to outputs (outcomes). The notation x and u_s anticipates the econometric problem that some arguments of functional relationship (9) are observed while other arguments may be unobserved by the analyst. In the analysis of this section, their roles are symmetric.

My notation allows for different unobservables from a common list u to appear in different outcomes.[28] g_s maps (x, u_s) into y. The domain of definition $\mathcal{D}$ of g_s may differ from the empirical support. Thus we can think of (9) as mapping logically possible inputs into logically possible *ex post* outcomes, but in a real sample we may observe only a subset of the domain of definition.

A "deep structural" version of (9) models the variation across the g_s in terms of s as a function of generating characteristics c_s that capture what "s" is:[29]

$$y(s) = g(c_s, x, u_s). \tag{10}$$

The components c_s provide the basis for generating the counterfactuals across treatments from a base set of characteristics. This approach models different treatments as consisting of different bundles of characteristics. g maps c, s, u_s into $y(s)$, where the domain of definition $\mathcal{D}$ of g may differ from its empirical support. Different treatments s are characterized by different bundles of the same characteristics that generate all outcomes. This framework provides the

[26]This term is discussed in Dawid (2000).
[27]Denote $\mathcal{D}$ as the domain of $g_s : \mathcal{D} \to \mathcal{R}^y$ where $\mathcal{R}^y$ is the range of y.
[28]An alternative notation would use a common u and let g_s select out s-specific components.
[29]Now the domain of g, $\mathcal{D}$, is defined for c_s, x, u_s and $g : \mathcal{D} \to \mathcal{R}^y$.

basis for solving policy problem P3 since new policies (treatments) are generated as different packages of common characteristics, and all policies are put on a common basis. If a new policy is characterized by known transformations of (c, x, u_s) that lie in the known empirical support of g, policy forecasting problem P3 can be solved.[30] This point is discussed further in the Appendix.

Part of the *a priori* specification of a causal model is the choice of the arguments of the functions g_s and g. Analysts may disagree about appropriate arguments to include based on alternative theoretical frameworks. One benefit of the statistical approach that focuses on problem P1 is that it works solely with the outcomes rather than the inputs. However, it is silent on how to solve problems P2 and P3 and provides no basis for interpreting the population-level treatment effects.

Consider alternative models of schooling outcomes of pupils where s indexes the schooling type (e.g., regular public, charter public, private secular, and private parochial). The c_s are the observed characteristics of schools of type s. The x are the observed characteristics of the pupil. The u_s are the unobserved characteristics of both the schools and the pupil. If we can characterize a proposed new type of school as a new package of different levels of the same ingredients x, c_s, and u_s and we can identify (10) over the domain defined by the new package, we can solve problem P3. If the same schooling input (same c_s) is applied to different students (those with different x) and we can identify (9) or (10) over the new domain of definition, we solve problem P2. By digging deeper into the "causes of the effects" we can do more than just compare the effects of treatments in place with each other. In addition, as we shall see, modeling the u_s and its relationship with the corresponding unobservables in the treatment choice equation is informative on appropriate identification strategies.

Equations (9) and (10) describing *ex post* outcomes are sometimes called Marshallian causal functions (see Heckman 2000). Assuming that the components of (x, u_s) or (c_s, x, u_s) can be independently varied or are variation-free,[31] a feature that may or may not be

---

[30]See Heckman and Vytlacil (2005, 2006a).
[31]The requirement is that if $(\mathcal{X}, \mathcal{U})$ or $(\mathcal{C}, \mathcal{X}, \mathcal{U})$ are the domains of (9) and (10), $(\mathcal{X}, \mathcal{U}) = (\mathcal{X}_1 \times \cdots \times \mathcal{X}_N \times \mathcal{U}_1 \times \cdots \times \mathcal{U}_M)$ or $(\mathcal{C}, \mathcal{X}, \mathcal{U}) = (\mathcal{C}_1 \times \cdots \times \mathcal{C}_K \times \mathcal{X}_1 \times \cdots \times \mathcal{X}_N \times \mathcal{U}_1 \times \cdots \times \mathcal{U}_M)$, where we assume K components in $\mathcal{C}$, N components in $\mathcal{X}$, and M components in $\mathcal{U}$. This means that we can vary one variable without necessarily varying another.

produced by the relevant theory, we may vary each argument of these functions to obtain a causal effect of that argument on the outcome. These thought experiments are for hypotheticals.

Changing one coordinate while fixing the others produces a Marshallian *ceteris paribus* causal effect of a change in that coordinate on the variable. Varying c_s sets different treatment levels. Variations in x, u_s among persons explains why people facing the same characteristics c_s respond differently to the same treatment s. Variations in u_s not observed by the analyst explain why people with the same x values respond differently.

The *ceteris paribus* variation used to define causal effects need not be for a single variable of the function. A treatment generally consists of a package of characteristics and if we vary the package from c_s to $c_{s'}$, we get different treatment effects.

I use lowercase notation produced from the theory to denote fixed values. I use uppercase notation to denote random variables. In defining equations (9) and (10), I have explicitly worked with fixed variables that are manipulated in a hypothetical way as in algebra or elementary physics. In a purely deterministic world, agents would act on these nonstochastic variables. Even if the world is uncertain, *ex post*, after the realization of uncertainty, the outcomes of uncertain inputs are deterministic. Some components of u_s may be random shocks realized after decisions about treatment are made.

Thus if uncertainty is a feature of the environment, equations (9) and (10) can be interpreted as *ex post* realizations of the counterfactual as uncertainty is resolved. *Ex ante* versions of these relationships may be different. From the point of view of agent ω with information set $\mathcal{I}_\omega$, the *ex ante* expected value of $Y(s, \omega)$ is,[32]

$$E(Y(s, \omega) \mid \mathcal{I}_\omega) = E(g(C_s(\omega), X(\omega), U(s, \omega)) \mid \mathcal{I}_\omega), \qquad (11)$$

where C_s, X, U_s are random variables generated from a distribution that depends on the agent's information set, indexed by $\mathcal{I}_\omega$. This distribution may differ from the distribution produced by "reality"

---

[32]The expectation might be computed using the information sets of the relevant decision maker (e.g., the parents in the case of the outcomes of the child) who might not be the agent whose outcomes are measured. These random variables are drawn from agent ω's subjective distribution.

or nature if agent expectations are different from objective reality.[33] In the presence of intrinsic uncertainty, the relevant decision maker acts on equation (11), but the *ex post* counterfactual is

$$Y(s,\omega) = E(Y(s,\omega) \mid \mathcal{I}_\omega) + \nu(s,\omega), \qquad (12)$$

where $\nu(s, \omega)$ satisfies $E(\nu(s, \omega)|\mathcal{I}_\omega) = 0$. In this interpretation, the information set of agent ω before realizations occur, $\mathcal{I}_\omega$, is part of the model specification. This discussion clarifies the distinction between deterministic (*ex post*) outcomes and intrinsically random (*ex ante*) outcomes discussed in Section 1.

This statement of the basic deterministic model reconciles the all causes model (9) and (10) with a model of intrinsic uncertainty favored by some statisticians (see Dawid 2000 and the following discussion). *Ex ante*, there is uncertainty at the agent (ω) level but *ex post* there is not. Realization $\nu(s, \omega)$ is an ingredient of the *ex post* all causes model but not the subjective *ex ante* all causes model. The probability law used by the agent to compute the expectation of $C_s(\omega)$, $X(\omega)$, $U_s(\omega)$ may differ from the objective distribution, i.e., the distribution that generates the observed data. In the *ex ante* all causes model, manipulations of $\mathcal{I}_\omega$ define the *ex ante* Marshallian causal parameters.

Thus from the point of view of the agent we can vary elements in $\mathcal{I}_\omega$ to produce Marshallian *ex ante* causal response functions. The *ex ante* treatment effect from the point of view of the agent for treatment s and s' is

$$E(Y(s,\omega)|\mathcal{I}_\omega) - E(Y(s',\omega) \mid \mathcal{I}_\omega). \qquad (13)$$

However, agents may not act on these *ex ante* effects if they have decision criteria (utility functions) that are not linear in $Y(s, \omega)$, $s = 1, \ldots, \bar{S}$. I discuss *ex ante* valuations of outcomes in the next section.

The value of the scientific (or explicitly structural) approach to the construction of counterfactuals is that it explicitly models the unobservables and the sources of variability among observationally

---

[33]Thus agents do not necessarily use rational expectations, so the distribution used by the agent to make decisions need not equal the distribution generating the data.

identical people. Since it is the unobservables that give rise to selection bias and problems of inference that are central to empirically rigorous causal analysis, analysts using the scientific approach can draw on scientific theory and in particular choice theory to design and justify methods to control for selection bias. This avenue is not available to adherents of the statistical approach. Statistical approaches that are not explicit about the sources of the unobservables make strong implicit assumptions which, when carefully exposited, are often unattractive. We exposit some of these assumptions in Section 5.

The models for counterfactuals—equations (9)–(13)—are derived from theory. The arguments of these functions are varied by hypothetical manipulations to produce outcomes. These are thought experiments. When analysts attempt to construct counterfactuals empirically, they must carefully distinguish between these theoretical relationships and the empirical relationships determined by the available evidence.

The data used to determine these functions may be limited in their support. (The support is the region of the domain of definition where we have data on the function.)[34] In this case we cannot fully identify the theoretical relationships. In addition, in the support, the components of X, U_s and $\mathcal{I}_\omega$ may not be variation-free even if they are in the hypothetical domain of definition of the function. A good example is the problem of multicollinearity. If the X in a sample are linearly dependent, it is not possible to identify the Marshallian causal function with respect to variations in x over the available support even if we can imagine hypothetically varying the components of x over the domains of definition of the functions (9) or (10).

Thus in the available data (i.e., over the empirical support), one of the X (gender) may be perfectly predictable by the other X. With limited empirical supports that do not match the domain of definition of the outcome equations, one may not be able to identify the Marshallian causal effect of gender even though one can define it in some hypothetical model. In empirical samples, gender may be predictable in a statistical sense by other empirical factors. Holland's 1986 claim that the causal effects of race or gender are meaningless conflates an empirical problem (task 2 in Table 1) with a problem of theory (task 1 in Table 1). The scientific

---

[34]Thus if $\mathcal{D}_x$ is the domain of x, the support of x is the region *Supp* $(x) \subset \mathcal{D}_x$ such that the data density $f(x)$ satisfies the condition $f(x) > 0$ for $x \in$ *Supp* (x).

approach sharply distinguishes these two issues. One can in theory define the effect even if one cannot identify it from population or sample data.

I next turn to an important distinction between fixing and conditioning on factors that gets to the heart of the distinction between causal models and correlational relationships. This point is independent of any problem with the supports of the samples compared to the domains of definition of the functions.

2.2. Fixing Versus Conditioning

The distinction between *fixing* and *conditioning* on inputs is central to distinguishing true causal effects from spurious causal effects. In an important paper, Haavelmo (1943) made this distinction in linear equations models. It is the basis for Pearl's (2000) book on causality that generalizes Haavelmo's analysis to nonlinear settings. Pearl defines an operator "do" to represent the mental act of fixing a variable to distinguish it from the action of conditioning which is a statistical operation. If the conditioning set is sufficiently rich, fixing and conditioning are the same in an *ex post* all causes model.[35] Pearl suggests a particular physical mechanism for fixing variables and operationalizing causality, but it is not central to his or any other definition of causality. Pearl's analysis conflates the three tasks of Table 1.

An example of fixing versus conditioning is most easily illustrated in a linear regression model of the type analyzed by Haavelmo (1943). Let $y = x\beta + u$. Although both y and u are scalars, x may be a vector. The linear equation maps (x, u) into y: $(x, u) \mapsto y$. Suppose that the support of random variable (X, U) in the data is the same as the domain of (x, u) that are fixed in the hypothetical thought experiment and that the (x, u) are variation-free (i.e., they can be independently varied coordinate by coordinate). Thus we abstract from the problem of limited support that is discussed in the preceding section. We may write (dropping the "ω" notation for random variables)

$$Y = X\beta + U.$$

[35]Florens and Heckman (2003) carefully distinguish conditioning from fixing, and generalize Pearl's analysis to both static and dynamic settings.

Here "nature" or the "real world" picks (X, U) to determine Y. X is observed by the analyst and U is not observed, and (X, U) are random variables. This is an all causes model in which $(X, U) \mapsto Y$. The variation generated by the hypothetical model varies one coordinate of (X, U), fixing all other coordinates to produce the effect of the variation on the outcome Y. Nature (as opposed to the model) may not permit such variation.

Formally, we can write this model formulated at the population level as a conditional expectation,

$$E(Y|X, U) = X\beta + U.$$

Since we condition on both X and U, there is no further source of variation in Y. This is a deterministic model that coincides with the all causes model. Thus on the support, which is also assumed to be the domain of definition of the function, this model is the same model as the deterministic, hypothetical model, $y = x\beta + u$. Fixing X at different values corresponds to doing different thought experiments with the X. Fixing and conditioning are the same in this case.

If, however, we only condition on X in the sample, we obtain

$$E(Y|X) = X\beta + E(U|X).^{36} \tag{14}$$

This relationship does not generate U-constant (Y, X) relationships. It generates only an X-constant relationship. Unless we condition on all of the "causes" (the right hand side variables), the empirical relationship (14) does not identify causal effects of X on Y. The variation in X also moves the conditional mean of U unless U is independent of X.

This analysis readily generalizes to a general nonlinear model $y = g(c, x, u)$. A model specified in terms of random variables C, X, U with the same support as c, x, u has as its conditional expectation $g(C, X, U)$ under general conditions. Conditioning only on C, X does not in principle identify $g(c, x, u)$ or any of its derivatives (if they exist) or differences of outcomes defined in terms of c and x.

---

[36]I assume that the mean of U is finite.

Conditioning and fixing on the arguments of g or g_s are the same in an "all causes" model if all causes are accounted for. Otherwise, they are not the same. This analysis can be generalized to account for the temporal resolution of uncertainty if we include ν (s, ω) as an argument in the *ex post* causal model. The outcomes can include both objective outcomes $Y(s, \omega)$ and subjective outcomes $V(Y(s, \omega), \omega)$.

Statisticians and epidemiologists have great difficulty with the distinction between fixing and conditioning because they typically define the models they analyze in terms of some type of conditioning. However, thought experiments in models of hypotheticals that vary factors are distinct from variations in conditioning variables that conflate the effects of variation in X, holding U fixed, with the effects of X in predicting the unobserved factors (the U) in the outcome equations.

2.3. *Modeling the Choice of Treatment*

Parallel to the models for outcomes are models for the choice of treatment. Consider *ex ante* personal valuations of outcomes based on expectations of gains from receiving treatment s:

$$E[V(Y(s,\omega), P(s,\omega), C_s(\omega), \omega)|\mathcal{I}_\omega], s \in S,$$

where $P(s, \omega)$ is the price or cost the agent must pay for participation in treatment s. We write $P(s, \omega) = K(Z(s, \omega), \eta(s, \omega))$. I allow utility V to be defined over the characteristics that generate the treatment outcome (e.g., quality of teachers in a schooling choice model) as well as other attributes of the consumer. In parallel with the g_s function generating the $Y(s, \omega)$, we write

$$V(Y(s,\omega), P(s,\omega), C_s(\omega), \omega) = f(Y(s,\omega), Z(s,\omega), C_s(\omega), \eta(s,\omega), \omega).$$

Parallel to the analysis of outcomes, we may keep $C_s(\omega)$ implicit and use f_s functions instead of f.

My analysis includes both measured and unmeasured attributes. The agent computes expectations against his/her subjective distribution of information. I allow for imperfect information by postulating an ω-specific information set. If agents know all components of future outcomes, the uppercase letters become lower-case variables that are known constants. The $\mathcal{I}_\omega$ are the causal factors for ω. In a utility-maximizing framework, choice $\hat{s}$ is made if $\hat{s}$ is maximal in the set of valuations of potential outcomes:

$$\{E[V(Y(s,\omega), P(s,\omega), C_s(\omega), \omega)|\mathcal{I}_\omega] : s \in S\}.$$

In this interpretation, the information set plays a key role in specifying agent preferences. Actual realizations may not be known at the time decisions are made. Accounting for uncertainty and subjective valuations of outcomes (e.g., pain and suffering for a medical treatment) is a major contribution of the scientific approach. The factors that lead an agent to participate in treatment s may be dependent on the factors affecting outcomes. Modeling this dependence is a major source of information used in the scientific approach to constructing counterfactuals from real data, as I demonstrate in Section 4. A parallel analysis can be made if the decision maker is not the same as the agent whose objective outcomes are being evaluated.

2.4. The Scientific Model Versus the Neyman–Rubin Model

Many statisticians and social scientists invoke a model of counterfactuals and causality attributed to Donald Rubin by Paul Holland (1986) but which actually dates back to Neyman (1923).[37] Neyman and Rubin postulate counterfactuals $\{Y(s, \omega)\}_{s \in \mathcal{S}}$ without modeling the factors determining the $Y(s, \omega)$ as I have done in equations (9)–(12), using the scientific, structural approach. Rubin and Neyman offer no model of the choice of which outcome is selected. Thus there no "lowercase," all causes models explicitly specified in this approach, nor is there any discussion of the science or theory producing the outcomes studied.

In my notation, Rubin assumes (A-1) and (A-2) as presented in Section 1.[38] Recall that (A-1) assumes no general equilibrium effects or social interactions among agents. Thus the outcome for the person is the

---

[37]The framework attributed to Rubin was developed in statistics by Neyman (1923), Cox (1958), and others. Parallel frameworks were independently developed in psychometrics (Thurstone 1930) and economics (Haavelmo 1943; Roy 1951; Quandt 1958, 1972).

[38]Rubin (1986) calls these two assumptions "SUTVA" for Stable Unit Treatment Value Assumption.

same whether one person receives treatment or many receive treatment. (A-2) says that however ω receives s, the same outcome arises. (A-2) also rules out randomization bias where the act of randomization affects the potential outcomes.[39]

More formally, the Rubin model assumes the following:

> **R-1** $\{Y(s, \omega)\}_{s \in \mathcal{S}}$, a set of counterfactuals defined for *ex post* outcomes (no valuations of outcomes or specification of treatment selection rules).
>
> **R-2** (A-1) (No social interactions).
>
> **R-3** (A-2) (Invariance of counterfactual to assignment mechanism of treatment).
>
> **R-4** P1 is the only problem of interest.
>
> **R-5** Mean causal effects are the only objects of interest.
>
> **R-6** There is no simultaneity in causal effects, i.e., outcomes cannot cause each other reciprocally (see Holland 1988).

The scientific model (1) decomposes the $Y(s, \omega)$, $s \in \mathcal{S}$ into its determinants; (2) considers valuation of outcomes as an essential ingredient of any study of causal inference; (3) models the choice of treatment and uses choice data to infer subjective valuations of treatment; (4) uses the relationship between outcomes and treatment choice equations to motivate, justify, and interpret alternative identifying strategies; (5) explicitly accounts for the arrival of information through *ex ante* and *ex post* analyses; (6) considers distributional causal parameters as well as mean effects; (7) addresses problems P1–P3; (8) allows for nonrecursive (simultaneous) causal models. I develop nonrecursive models in the next section.

In the Neyman–Rubin model, the sources of variability generating $Y(s, \omega)$ as a random variable are not specified. The "causal effect" of s compared to s' is defined as the treatment effect in equation (1). Holland (1986, 1988) argues that it is an advantage of the Rubin model that it is not explicit about the sources of variability among observationally identical people, or about the factors that

---

[39]See Heckman (1992) or Heckman, LaLonde, and Smith (1999) for discussions and evidence on this question.

generate $Y(s, \omega)$. Holland and Rubin focus on mean treatment effects as the interesting causal parameters.

The scientific (econometric) approach to causal inference supplements the model of counterfactuals with models of the choice of counterfactuals $\{D(s, \omega)\}_{s \in \mathcal{S}}$ generated by the maps $\Phi_\tau^p(\omega)$ and the relationship between choice equations and the counterfactuals. The $D(s, \omega)$ are assumed to be generated by the collection of random variables $(C_s(\omega), Z(s, \omega), \eta(s, \omega), Y(s, \omega) | \mathcal{I}_\omega)$, $s \in \mathcal{S}$, where $C_s(\omega)$ is the characteristic of the treatment s for person ω, $Z(s, \omega)$ are observed determinants of costs, the $\eta(s, \omega)$ are unobserved (by the analyst) cost (or preference) factors and $Y(s, \omega)$ are the outcomes, and the "|" denotes that these variables are defined conditional on $\mathcal{I}_\omega$ (the agent's information set).[40] Along with the *ex ante* valuations that generate $D(s, \omega)$ are the *ex post* valuations discussed in Section 1.6.

Random utility models generating $D(s, \omega)$ go back to Thurstone (1930) and McFadden (1974, 1981).[41] The full set of counterfactual outcomes for each agent is assumed to be unobserved by the analyst. It is the dependence of unmeasured determinants of treatment choices with unmeasured determinants of potential outcomes that gives rise to selection bias in empirically constructing counterfactuals and treatment effects, even after conditioning on the observables. Knowledge of the relationship between choices and counterfactuals suggests appropriate methods for solving selection problems. By analyzing the relationship of the unobservables in the outcome equation, and the unobservables in the treatment choice equation, the analyst can use *a priori* theory to devise appropriate estimators to identify causal effects.

The scientific approach is more general than the Neyman–Rubin model because it emphasizes the welfare of the agents being studied (through V_G or $V(Y(s, \omega), \omega)$)—the "subjective evaluations"— as well as the objective evaluations. The econometric approach also

---

[40]If other agents make the treatment assignment decisions, then the determinants of $D(s, \omega)$ are modified according to what is in their information set.

[41]Corresponding to these random variables are the deterministic all causes counterparts $d(s)$, c_s, $z(s)$, $\eta(s)$, $\{y(s)\}$, i, where the $(\{z(s)\}_{s \in \mathcal{S}}, \{c_s\}_{s \in \mathcal{S}}, \{\eta(s)\}_{s \in \mathcal{S}}, \{y(s)\}_{s \in \mathcal{S}}, i)$ generate the $d(s) = 1$ if $(\{z(s)\}_{s \in \mathcal{S}}, \{c_s\}_{s \in \mathcal{S}}, \{\eta(s)\}_{s \in \mathcal{S}}, \{y(s)\}_{s \in \mathcal{S}}) \in \Psi$, a subset of the domain of the generators of $d(s)$. Again the domain of definition of $d(s)$ is not necessarily the support of $z(s, \omega), c_s(\omega), \eta(s, \omega), \{Y(s, \omega)\}_{s \in \mathcal{S}}$ and $\mathcal{I}_\omega$.

distinguishes *ex ante* from *ex post* subjective evaluations, so it can measure both agent satisfaction and regret.[42]

In addition, modelling $Y(s, \omega)$ in terms of characteristics of treatment, and of the treated, facilitates comparisons of counterfactuals and derived causal effects across studies where the composition of programs and treatment group members may vary. It also facilitates the construction of counterfactuals on new populations and the construction of counterfactuals for new policies. The Neyman–Rubin framework focuses exclusively on population-level mean "causal effects" or treatment effects for policies actually experienced and provides no framework for extrapolation of findings to new environments or for forecasting new policies (problems P2 and P3). Its focus on population mean treatment effects elevates randomization and matching to the status of preferred estimators. Such methods cannot identify distributions of treatment effects or general quantiles of treatment effects.

Another feature of the Neyman–Rubin model is that it is recursive. It cannot model causal effects of outcomes that occur simultaneously. I now present a model of simultaneous causality.

2.5. *Nonrecursive (Simultaneous) Models of Causality*

A system of linear simultaneous equations captures interdependence among outcomes Y. For simplicity, I focus on *ex post* outcomes so I ignore the revelation of information over time. To focus on the main ideas of this section, I assume that the domain of definition of the model is the same as the support of the population data. Thus the model for values of uppercase variables has the same support as the domain of definition for the model in terms of lowercase variables.[43] The model developed in this section is rich enough to model interactions among agents.[44] I write this model in terms of parameters (Γ, B), observables (Y, X), and unobservables U as

$$\Gamma Y + BX = U, \qquad E(U) = 0, \tag{15}$$

[42]See Cunha, Heckman, and Navarro (2005a,b) for estimates of subjective evaluations and regret in schooling choices.

[43]This approach merges tasks 1 and 2 in Table 1. I do this here because the familiarity of the simultaneous equations model as a statistical model makes the all causes *ex post* version confusing to many readers familiar with this model.

[44]For simplicity, I work with the linear model in the text, developing the nonlinear case in footnotes.

where Y is now a vector of endogenous and interdependent variables, X is exogenous ($E(U|X) = 0$), and Γ is a full rank matrix. A better nomenclature, suggested by Leamer (1985), is that the Y are internal variables determined by the model and the X are external variables specified outside the model.[45] This definition distinguishes two issues: (1) defining variables (Y) that are determined from inputs outside the model (the X) and (2) determining the relationship between observables and unobservables.[46] When the model is of full rank (Γ^{-1} exists), it is said to be "complete." A complete model produces a unique Y from a given (X, U). A complete model is said to be in reduced form when equation (15) is multiplied by Γ^{-1}. The reduced form is $Y = \Pi X + R$ where $\Pi = -\Gamma^{-1}B$ and $R = \Gamma^{-1}U$.[47] This is a linear-in-parameters "all causes" model for vector Y, where the causes are X and R. The "structure" is (Γ, B), Σ_U, where Σ_U is the variance-covariance matrix of U. The reduced form slope coefficients are Π, and Σ_R is the variance-covariance matrix of R.[48] In the population generating (15), least squares recovers Π provided Σ_X, the variance of X, is nonsingular (no multicollinearity). In this linear-in-parameters equation setting, the full rank condition for Σ_X is a variation-free condition on the external variables. The reduced form solves out for the dependence among the Y. The linear-in-parameters model is traditional. Nonlinear versions are available (Fisher 1966; Matzkin 2004).[49] For simplicity, I stick to the linear version, developing the nonlinear version in footnotes.

The structural form (15) is an all causes model that relates in a deterministic way outcomes (internal variables) to other outcomes (internal variables) and external variables (the X and U). Without some restrictions, certain *ceteris paribus* manipulations associated

---

[45]This formulation is static. In a dynamic framework, Y_t would be the internal variables and the lagged Y, Y_{t-k}, $k > 0$, would be external to period t and be included in the X_t. Thus we could work with lagged dependent variables. The system would be $\Gamma Y_t + BX_t = U_t$, $E(U_t) = 0$.

[46]In a time-series model, the internal variables are Y_t determined in period t.

[47]In this section only, Π refers to the reduced form coefficient matrix and not the set of policies Π_p, as in earlier sections.

[48]The original formulations of this model assumed normality so that only means and variances were needed to describe the joint distributions of (Y, X).

[49]The underlying all causes model writes $\Gamma y + Bx = u$, $y = \Pi x + r$ and $\Pi = -\Gamma^{-1} B$, $r = \Gamma^{-1}u$. Recall that I assume that the domain of the all causes model is the same as the support of (x, u). Thus there is a close correspondence between these two models.

with the effect of some components of Y on other components of Y are not possible within the model. I now demonstrate this point.

For specificity, consider a two-person model of social interactions. Y_1 is the outcome for person 1; Y_2 is the outcome for person 2. This could be a model of interdependent consumption where the consumption of person 1 depends on the consumption of person 2 and other person-1-specific variables (and possibly other person-2-specific variables). It could also be a model of test scores. We can imagine populations of data generated from sampling the same two-person interaction over time or sampling different two-person couplings at a point in time.

Assuming that the preferences are interdependent, we may write

$$Y_1 = \alpha_1 + \gamma_{12} Y_2 + \beta_{11} X_1 + \beta_{12} X_2 + U_1 \qquad (16a)$$

$$Y_2 = \alpha_2 + \gamma_{21} Y_1 + \beta_{21} X_1 + \beta_{22} X_2 + U_2. \qquad (16b)$$

This model is sufficiently flexible to capture the notion that the consumption of person 1 (Y_1) depends on the consumption of person 2 (if $\gamma_{12} \neq 0$), as well as person 1's value of X (if $\beta_{11} \neq 0$), X_1 (assumed to be observed), person 2's value of X, X_2 (if $\beta_{12} = 0$), and unobservable factors that affect person 1 (U_1). The determinants of person 2's consumption are defined symmetrically. I allow U_1 and U_2 to be freely correlated. I assume that U_1 and U_2 are mean independent of (X_1, X_2) so

$$E(U_1|X_1, X_2) = 0 \qquad (17a)$$

and

$$E(U_2|X_1, X_2) = 0. \qquad (17b)$$

Completeness guarantees that (16a) and (16b) have a determinate solution for (Y_1, Y_2).

Applying Haavelmo's argument to (16a) and (16b), the causal effect of Y_2 on Y_1 is γ_{12}. This is the effect on Y_1 of fixing Y_2 at different values, holding constant the other variables in the equation. Symmetrically, the causal effect of Y_1 on Y_2 is γ_{21}. Conditioning,—that is, using least squares—which is the method of matching, in general fails to identify these causal effects because U_1 and U_2 are correlated with Y_1 and Y_2. This is a traditional argument. It is based on the correlation between Y_2 and U_1. But even if $U_1 = 0$ and $U_2 = 0$, so that there are no unobservables, matching or least squares breaks down because Y_2 is perfectly predictable by X_1 and X_2. We cannot simultaneously vary Y_2, X_1, and X_2. This is the essence of the problem of defining a causal effect. To see why, we derive the reduced form of this model.

Assuming completeness, the reduced form outcomes of the model after social interactions are solved out can be written as

$$Y_1 = \pi_{10} + \pi_{11}X_1 + \pi_{12}X_2 + R_1 \tag{18a}$$

$$Y_2 = \pi_{20} + \pi_{21}X_1 + \pi_{22}X_2 + R_2. \tag{18b}$$

Least squares (matching) can identify the *ceteris paribus* effects of X_1 and X_2 on Y_1 and Y_2 because $E(R_1|X_1, X_2) = 0$ and $E(R_2|X_1, X_2) = 0$. Simple algebra informs us that

$$\pi_{11} = \frac{\beta_{11} + \gamma_{21}\beta_{21}}{1 - \gamma_{12}\gamma_{21}} \quad \pi_{12} = \frac{\beta_{12} + \beta_{22}\gamma_{12}}{1 - \gamma_{12}\gamma_{21}}$$
$$\pi_{21} = \frac{\gamma_{21}\beta_{11} + \beta_{21}}{1 - \gamma_{12}\gamma_{21}} \quad \pi_{22} = \frac{\gamma_{12}\beta_{12} + \beta_{22}}{1 - \gamma_{12}\gamma_{21}} \tag{19}$$

and

$$R_1 = \frac{U_1 + \gamma_{21}U_2}{1 - \gamma_{12}\gamma_{21}}$$
$$R_2 = \frac{\gamma_{12}U_1 + U_2}{1 - \gamma_{12}\gamma_{21}}.$$

Observe that because R_2 depends on both U_1 and U_2 in the general case, Y_2 is correlated with U_1 (through the direct channel of U_1 and through the correlation between U_1 and U_2). Without any further information on the variances of (U_1, U_2) and their relationship to the causal parameters, we cannot isolate the causal effects γ_{12} and γ_{21} from the reduced form regression coefficients. This is so because holding X_1, X_2, U_1, and U_2 fixed in (16a) or (16b), it is not *in principle* possible to vary Y_2 or Y_1, respectively, because they are exact functions of X_1, X_2, U_1, and U_2.

This exact dependence holds true even if $U_1 = 0$ and $U_2 = 0$ so that there are no unobservables.[50] In this case, which is thought to be the most favorable to the application of least squares or matching to (16a) and (16b), it is evident from (18a) and (18b) that when $R_1 = 0$ and

---

[50]See Fisher (1966).

$R_2 = 0$, Y_1 and Y_2 are exact functions of X_1 and X_2. There is no mechanism yet specified within the model to independently vary the right-hand sides of equations (16a) and (16b).[51] The X effects on Y_1 and Y_2, identified through the reduced forms, combine the direct effects (through β_{ij}) and the indirect effects (as they operate through Y_1 and Y_2, respectively).

If we assume exclusions ($\beta_{12} = 0$) or ($\beta_{21} = 0$) or both, we can identify the *ceteris paribus* causal effects of Y_2 on Y_1 and of Y_1 on Y_2 respectively. Thus if $\beta_{12} = 0$ from the reduced form,

$$\frac{\pi_{12}}{\pi_{22}} = \gamma_{12}.$$

If $\beta_{21} = 0$, we obtain

$$\frac{\pi_{21}}{\pi_{11}} = \gamma_{21}.$$

These exclusions say that the social interactions only operate through the Y's. Person 1's consumption depends only on person 2's consumption and not on his or her X_2 or directly through his or her U_2. Person 2 is modeled symmetrically versus person 1. Observe that I have *not* ruled out correlation between U_1 and U_2. When the procedure for identifying causal effects is applied to samples, it is called indirect least squares. The method traces back to Haavelmo (1943, 1944).[52]

The intuition for these results is that if $\beta_{12} = 0$, we can vary Y_2 in equation (16a) by varying the X_2. Since X_2 does not appear in the

---

[51]Some readers of an earlier draft of this paper suggested that the mere fact that we can write (16a) and (16b) means that we "can imagine" independent variation. By the same token, we can imagine a model

$$Y = \varphi_0 + \varphi_1 X_1 + \varphi_2 X_2,$$

but if part of the model is (∗) $X_1 = X_2$, the rules of the model constrain $X_1 = X_2$. No causal effect of X_1 holding X_2 constant is possible. If we break restriction (∗) and permit independent variation in X_1 and X_2, we can define the causal effect of X_1 holding X_2 constant.

[52]The analysis for social interactions in this section is of independent interest. It can be generalized to the analysis of N person interactions if the outcomes are continuous variables. For binary outcomes variables, the same analysis goes through for the special case analyzed by Heckman and MaCurdy (1985). However, in the general case, for discrete outcomes generated by latent variables it is necessary to modify the system to obtain a coherent probability model; see Heckman (1978).

equation, under exclusion, we can keep U_1, X, fixed and vary Y_2 using X_2 in (18b) if $\beta_{22} \neq 0$.[53] Symmetrically, by excluding X_1 from (16b), we can vary Y_1, holding X_2 and U_2 constant. These results are more clearly seen when $U_1 = 0$ and $U_2 = 0$.

Observe that in the model under consideration, where the domain of definition and the supports of the variables coincide, the causal effects of simultaneous interactions are defined if the parameters are identified in the traditional Cowles definition of identification (e.g., see Ruud 2000 for a modern discussion of these conditions). A hypothetical thought experiment justifies these exclusions. If agents do not know or act on the other agents X, these exclusions are plausible.

An implicit assumption in using (16a) and (16b) for causal analysis is invariance of the parameters (Γ, β, Σ_U) to manipulations of the external variables. This invariance embodies the key idea in assumption (A-2). Invariance of the coefficients of equations to classes of manipulation of the variables is an essential part of the definition of structural models that I develop more formally in the next section.

This definition of causal effects in an interdependent system generalizes the recursive definitions of causality featured in the statistical treatment effect literature (Holland 1988; Pearl 2000). The key to this definition is manipulation of external inputs and exclusion, not randomization or matching. Indeed matching or, equivalently, *OLS*, using the right-hand side variables of (16a) and (16b), does not identify causal effects as Haavelmo (1943) established long ago. We can use the population simultaneous equations model to define the class of admissible variations and address problems of definitions (task 1 in Table 1). If for a given model, the parameters of (16a) or (16b) shift when external variables are manipulated, or if external variables cannot be independently manipulated, causal effects of one internal variable on another cannot be defined *within that model*. If people were randomly assigned to pair with their neighbors, and the parameters of (16a) were not affected by the randomization, then Y_2 would be exogenous in equation (16b) and we could identify causal

---

[53]Notice that we could also use U_2 as a source of variation in (18b) to shift Y_2. The roles of U_2 and X_2 are symmetric. However, if U_1 and U_2 are correlated, shifting U_2 shifts U_1 unless we control for it. The component of U_2 uncorrelated with U_1 plays the role of X_2.

effects by least squares. At issue is whether such a randomization would recover γ_{12}. It might fundamentally alter agent 1's response to Y_2 if that person is randomly assigned as opposed to being selected by the agent. Judging the suitability of an invariance assumption entails a thought experiment—a purely mental act.

Controlled variation in external forcing variables is the key to defining causal effects in nonrecursive models. It is of some interest to readers of Pearl (2000) to compare my use of the standard simultaneous equations model of econometrics in defining causal parameters to his. In the context of equations (16a) and (16b), Pearl defines a causal effect by "shutting one equation down" or performing "surgery" in his colorful language.

He implicitly assumes that "surgery," or shutting down an equation in a system of simultaneous equations, uniquely fixes one outcome or internal variable (the consumption of the other person in my example). In general, it does not. Putting a constraint on one equation places a restriction on the entire set of internal variables. In general, no single equation in a system of simultaneous equations uniquely determines any single outcome variable. Shutting down one equation might also affect the parameters of the other equations in the system and violate the requirements of parameter stability.

A clearer manipulation is to assume that it is possible to fix Y_2 by setting $\gamma_{12} = 0$. Assume that U_1 and U_2 are uncorrelated.[54] This makes the model recursive. It assumes that person 1 is unaffected by the consumption of person 2. Under these assumptions, we can regress Y_1 on Y_2, X_1, and X_2 in the population and recover all of the causal parameters of (16a). Variation in U_2 breaks the perfect collinearity among Y_2, X_1, and X_2. It is far from obvious, however, that one can freely set parameters without affecting the rest of the parameters of the model.

Shutting down an equation or fiddling with the parameters in Γ is not required to *define* causality in an interdependent, nonrecursive system or to identify causal parameters. The more basic idea is *exclusion* of different external variables from different equations which, when manipulated, allow the analyst to construct the desired causal quantities.

---

[54]Alternatively, we can assume that it is possible to measure U_1 and control for it.

One can move from the problem of definition (task 1 in Table 1) to identification (task 2) by using population analog estimation methods—in this case the method of indirect least squares.[55] There are many ways other than through exclusions of variables to identify this and more general systems. Fisher (1966) presents a general analysis of identification in both linear and nonlinear simultaneous equations systems. Matzkin (2004) is a recent substantial extension of this literature.

In the context of the basic nonrecursive model, there are many possible causal variations, richer than what can be obtained from the reduced form. Using the reduced form ($Y = X\Pi + R$), we can define causal effects as *ceteris paribus* effects of variables in X or R on Y. This definition solves out for all of the intermediate effects of the internal variables on each other. Using the structure in equation (15), we can define the effect of one internal variable on another holding constant the remaining internal variables and (X, U). It has just been established that such causal effects may not be defined within the rules specified for a particular structural model. Exclusions and other restrictions discussed in Fisher (1966) make definitions of causal effects possible under certain conditions.

One can, in general, solve out from the general system of equations for subsets of the Y (e.g., Y^* where $Y = (Y^*, Y^{**})$) using the reduced form of the model and use *quasi-structural* models to define a variety of causal effects that solve out for some but not all of the possible causal effects of Y on each other. These quasi-structural models may be written as

$$\Gamma^{**} Y^{**} = \Pi^{**} X + U^{**}.$$

This expression is obtained by using the reduced form for component Y^*: $Y^* = \Pi^* X + R^*$ and substituting for Y^* in (15). U^{**} is the error term associated with this representation. There are many possible quasi-structural models. Causal effects of internal variables may or may not be defined within them, depending on the assumed *a priori* information.

The causal effect of one component of Y^{**} on another does not fix Y^* but allows the Y^* components to adjust as the components of Y^{**} and the X are varied. Thus the Y^* are not being held fixed when

---

[55]Two-stage least squares would work as well.

X and/or components of the Y^{**} are varied. Viewed in this way, the reduced form and the whole class of quasi-structural models do not define any *ceteris paribus* causal effect relative to all of the variables (internal and external) in the system since they do not fix the levels of the other Y or Y^* in the case of the quasi-structural models. Nonetheless, the reduced form may provide a good guide to forecasting the effects of certain interventions that affect the external variables. The quasi-structural models may also provide a useful guide for predicting certain interventions, where Y^{**} are fixed by policy. The reduced form defines a net causal effect of variations in X as they affect the internal variables. There are many quasi-structural models and corresponding thought experiments.

This discussion demonstrates another reason why causal knowledge is provisional. Different analysts may choose different subsystems of equations derived from equation (15) to work with and define different causal effects within the different possible subsystems. Some of these causal effects may not be identified, while others may be. Systems smaller or larger than (15) can be imagined. The role of *a priori* theory is to limit the class of models and the resulting class of counterfactuals and to define which ones are interesting.

I now present a basic definition of structure in terms of invariance of equations to classes of interventions. Invariance is a central idea in causal analysis and in policy analysis.

2.6. *Structure as Invariance*

A basic definition of a system of structural relationships is that it is a system of equations invariant to a class of modifications or interventions. In the context of policy analysis, this means a class of policy modifications. This is the definition that was proposed by Hurwicz (1962). It is implicit in Marschak (1953) and it is explicitly utilized by Sims (1977), Lucas and Sargent (1981), and Leamer (1985), among others. This definition requires a precise definition of a policy, a class of policy modifications, and specification of a mechanism through which policy operates.

The mechanisms generating counterfactuals and the choices of counterfactuals have already been characterized in Sections 2.1 and 2.3. Policies can act on preferences and the arguments of preferences (and hence choices), on outcomes $Y(s, \omega)$ and the determinants affecting outcomes or on the information facing agents. Recall that g_s, $s \in \mathcal{S}$, generates outcomes while f_s, $s \in \mathcal{S}$, generates evaluations. Specifically,

1. Policies can shift the distributions of the determinants of outcomes and choices (C, Z, X, U, η), where $C = \{C_s(\omega)\}_{s \in \mathcal{S}}$, $Z = \{Z(s, \omega)\}_{s \in \mathcal{S}}$, $\eta = \{\eta(s, \omega)\}_{s \in \mathcal{S}}$ and $U = \{U_s(\omega)\}_{s \in \mathcal{S}}$ in the population. This may entail defining the g_s and f_s over new domains. Let $Q = (C, Z, X, U, \eta)$. Policies shifting the distributions of these variables are characterized by maps $T_Q : Q \longmapsto Q'$.
2. Policies may select new f, g or $\{f_s, g_s\}_{s \in \mathcal{S}}$ functions.[56] In particular, new arguments (e.g., amenities or characteristics of programs) may be introduced as a result of policy actions creating new attributes. Policies shifting functions map f, g or $\{f_s, g_s\}_{s \in \mathcal{S}}$ into new functions $T_f : f_s \longmapsto f'_s$; $T_g : g_s \longmapsto g'_s$. This may entail changes in functional forms with a stable set of arguments as well as changes in arguments of functions.
3. Policies may affect individual information sets $(\mathcal{I}_\omega)_{\omega \in \Omega}$. $T_{\mathcal{I}\omega} : \mathcal{I}_\omega \longmapsto \mathcal{I}'_\omega$.

Clearly, any particular policy may incorporate elements of all three types of policy shifts.

Parameters of a model or parameters derived from a model are said to be policy invariant if they are not changed (are invariant) when policies are implemented. This notion is partially embodied in assumption (A-2), which is defined solely in terms of *ex post* outcomes. More generally, policy invariance for f, g or $\{f_s, g_s\}_{s \in S}$ requires the following:

> **(A-3)** The functions f, g or $\{f_s, g_s\}_{s \in S}$ are the same for all values of the arguments in their domain of definition no matter how their arguments are determined.

This definition can be made separately for f, g, f_s, g_s or any function derived from them. It requires that when we change an argument of a function it does not matter how we change it.

---

[56]By f_s, we mean s-specific valuation functions.

In the simultaneous equations model analyzed in the last section, invariance requires stability of Γ, B, and Σ_U to interventions. Such models can be used to accurately forecast the effects of policies that can be cast as variations in the inputs to the model. Policy-invariant parameters are not necessarily causal parameters, as we noted in our analysis of reduced forms in the preceding section. Thus, in the simultaneous equations model, depending on the *a priori* information available, no causal effect of one internal variable on another may be defined but if Π is invariant to modifications in X, the reduced form is policy invariant for those modifications. The class of policy-invariant parameters is thus distinct from the class of causal parameters, but invariance is an essential attribute of a causal model. For counterfactuals $Y(s, \omega)$, if assumption (A-3) is not postulated, all of the treatment effects defined in Section 1 would be affected by policy shifts. Rubin's assumption (A-2) makes $Y(s, \omega)$ invariant to policies that change f but not policies that change g or the support of Q. Within the treatment effects framework, a policy that adds a new treatment to S is not policy invariant for treatment parameters comparing the new treatment to any other treatment unless the analyst can model all policies in terms of a generating set of common characteristics specified at different levels. The lack of policy invariance makes it difficult to forecast the effects of new policies using treatment effect models within the framework of the Appendix.

"Deep structural" parameters generating the f and g are invariant to policy modifications that affect technology, constraints, and information sets except when the policies extend the historical supports. Invariance can only be defined relative to a class of modifications and a postulated set of preferences, technology, constraints, and information sets. Thus causal parameters can be precisely identified only within a class of modifications.

2.7. *Marschak's Maxim and the Relationship Between Structural Literature and Statistical Treatment Effect Literature*

The absence of explicit models is a prominent feature of the statistical treatment effect literature. Scientifically well-posed models make explicit the assumptions used by analysts regarding preferences, technology, the information available to agents, the constraints under which they operate, and the rules of interaction among agents in market and social settings and the sources of variability among persons. These explicit features make these models, like all scientific models, useful vehicles: (1) for interpreting empirical evidence using theory; (2) for collating and synthesizing evidence using theory; (3) for measuring the welfare effects of policies; and (4) for forecasting the welfare and direct effects of previously implemented policies in new environments and the effects of new policies.

These features are absent from the modern treatment effect literature. At the same time, this literature makes fewer statistical assumptions in terms of exogeneity, functional form, exclusion, and distributional assumptions than the standard structural estimation literature in econometrics. These are the attractive features of this approach.

In reconciling these two literatures, I reach back to a neglected but important paper by Jacob Marschak. Marschak (1953) noted that for many specific questions of policy analysis, it is unnecessary to identify full structural models, where by structural I mean parameters invariant to classes of policy modifications as defined in the last section. All that is required are combinations of subsets of the structural parameters, corresponding to the parameters required to forecast particular policy modifications, which are much easier to identify (i.e., require fewer and weaker assumptions). Thus in the simultaneous equations system examples, policies that only affect X may be forecast using reduced forms, not knowing the full structure, provided that the reduced forms are invariant to the modifications.[57] Forecasting other policies may require only partial knowledge of the system. I call this principle *Marschak's maxim* in honor of this insight. I interpret the modern statistical treatment effect literature as implicitly implementing Marschak's maxim where the policies analyzed are the treatments and the goal of policy analysis is restricted to evaluating policies in place (task 1; P1) and not in forecasting the effects of new policies or the effects of old policies on new environments.

Population mean treatment parameters are often identified under weaker conditions than are traditionally assumed in econometric structural analysis. Thus to identify the average

---

[57]Thus we require that the reduced form Π does not change when we change the X.

treatment effect for s and s' we require only $E(Y(s, \omega) \mid X = x) - E(Y(s', \omega) \mid X = s)$. We do not have to know the full functional form of the generating g_s functions nor does X have to be exogenous. The treatment effects may, or may not, be causal parameters depending on what else is assumed about the model.

Considerable progress has been made in relaxing the parametric structure assumed in the early structural models in econometrics (see Matzkin 2006). As the treatment effect literature is extended to address the more general set of policy forecasting problems entertained in the structural literature, the distinction between the two literatures will vanish although it is currently very sharp. Heckman and Vytlacil (2005, 2006a,b) and Heckman (2006) are attempts to bridge this gulf.

Up to this point in the essay, everything that has been discussed precisely is purely conceptual, although I have alluded to empirical problems and problems of identification going from data of various forms to conceptual models. Models are conceptual and so are the treatment effects derived from them. The act of defining a model is distinct from identifying it or estimating it although statisticians often conflate these distinct issues. I now discuss the identification problem, which must be solved if causal models are to be empirically operational.

3. IDENTIFICATION PROBLEMS: DETERMINING MODELS FROM DATA

Unobserved counterfactuals are the source of the problems considered in this paper. For a person in state s, we observe $Y(s, \omega)$ but not $Y(s', \omega)$, $s' \neq s$. A central problem in the literature on causal inference is how to identify counterfactuals and the derived treatment parameters. Unobservables, including missing data, are at the heart of the identification problem considered here.

Estimators differ in the amount of knowledge they assume that the analyst has relative to what the agents being studied have when making their program enrollment decisions (or their decisions are made for them as a parent for a child). This is strictly a matter of the quality of the available data. Unless the analyst has access to all of the relevant information that produces the dependence between outcomes and treatment rules (i.e., that produces selection bias), he or she must devise methods to control for the unobserved components of relevant information. Heckman and Vytlacil (2006b) and Heckman and Navarro (2004) define relevant information precisely. Relevant information is the information which, if available to the analyst and conditioned on, would eliminate selection bias. Intuitively, there may be a lot of information known to the agent but not known to the observing analyst that is irrelevant in creating the dependence between outcomes and choices. It is the information that gives rise to the dependence between outcomes and treatment choices that matters for eliminating selection bias.

A priori one might think that the analyst knows a lot less than the agent whose behavior is being analyzed. At issue is whether the analyst knows less *relevant* information, which is not so obvious, if only because the analyst can observe the outcomes of decisions in a way that agents making decisions cannot. This access to *ex post* information can sometimes give the analyst a leg up on the information available to the agent.

The policy forecasting problems P2 and P3 raise the additional issue that the support over which treatment parameters and counterfactuals are identified may not correspond to the support to which the analyst seeks to apply them. Common to all scientific models, there is the additional issue of how to select (X, Z), the conditioning variables, and how to deal with them if they are endogenous. Finally, there is the problem of lack of knowledge of functional forms of the models. Different econometric methods solve these problems in different ways. I now present a precise discussion of identification.

3.1. *The Identification Problem*

The identification problem asks whether theoretical constructs have any empirical content in a hypothetical population or in real samples. This formulation considers tasks 2 and 3 in Table 1 together, although some analysts like to separate these issues, focusing solely on task 2. The identification problem considers what particular models within a broader class of models are consistent with a given set of data or facts. Specifically, we can consider a model space M. This is the set of admissible models that are produced by some theory for generating counterfactuals. Elements $m \in M$ are admissible theoretical models.

We may be interested in only some features of a model. For example, we may have a rich model of counterfactuals $\{Y(s, \omega)\}_{s \in \mathcal{S}}$, but we may be interested in only the average treatment effect $E_\omega[Y(s, \omega) - Y(s', \omega)]$. Let the objects of interest be $t \in T$, where "t" stands for the target—the goal of the analysis. The target space T may be the whole model space M or something derived from it.

Define map $g: M \rightarrow T$. This maps an element $m \in M$ into an element $t \in T$. In the example in the preceding paragraph, T is the space of all average treatment effects produced by the models of counterfactuals. I assume that g is into.[58] Associated with each model is an element t derived from the model, which could be the entire model itself. Many models may map into the same t so the inverse map (g^{-1}), mapping T to M, may not be well-defined. Thus many different models may produce the same average treatment effect.

Let the class of possible information or data be I. Define a map $h: M \rightarrow I$. For an element $i \in I$, which is a given set of data, there may be one or more models m consistent with i. If i can be mapped only into a single m, the model is exactly identified.[59] If there are multiple m's, consistent with i, these models are not identified. Thus, in Figure 1, many models (elements of M) may be consistent with the same data (single element of I).

Let $M_h(i)$ be the set of models consistent with i. $M_h(i) = h^{-1}(\{i\}) = \{m \in M : h(m) = i\}$. The data i reject the other models $M \backslash M_h(i)$, but are consistent with all models in $M_h(i)$. If $M_h(i)$ contains more than one element, the data produce set-valued instead of point-valued identification. If $M_h(i) = \emptyset$, the empty set, no

---

[58]By this, we mean that for every $t \in T$, there is an element $m \in M$ such that g sends m to t, i.e., the image of g is the entire set T. Of course, g may send many elements of M to a single element of T.

[59]Associated with each data set i is a collection of random variables $Q(i)$, which may be a vector. Let $F_Q(q|m)$ be the distribution of q under model m. To establish identification on nonnegligible sets, one needs that, for some true model m^*,

$$\Pr(|F_Q(q|m^*) - F_Q(q|m)| > \varepsilon) > 0$$

for some $\varepsilon > 0$ for all $m \neq m^*$. This guarantees that there are observable differences between the data generating process for Q given m and for Q given m^*. We can also define this for $F_Q(q|t^*)$ and $F_Q(q|t)$.

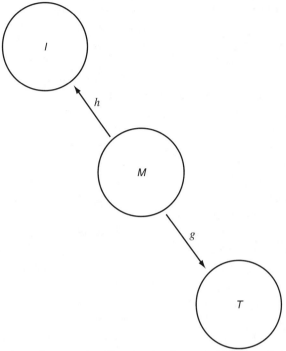

FIGURE 1. Are elements in T uniquely determined from elements in I? Sometimes $T = M$. Usually T consists of elements derived from M.

model is consistent with the data. By placing restrictions on models, we can sometimes reduce the number of elements in $M_h(i)$ if it has multiple members. Let $R \subset M$ be a set of restricted models. It is sometimes possible by imposing restrictions to reduce the number of models consistent with the data. Recall that in the two-person model of social interactions, if $\beta_{12} = 0$ and $\beta_{21} = 0$ we could uniquely identify the remaining parameters under the other conditions maintained in Section 2.5. Thus $R \cap M_h(i)$ may contain only a single element. Another way to solve this identification problem is to pick another data source $i' \in I$, which may produce more restrictions on the class of admissible models. More information provides more hoops for the model to jump through.

Going after a more limited class of objects such as features of a model ($t \in T$) rather than the full model ($m \in M$) is another way to secure unique identification. Let $M_g(t) = g^{-1}(\{t\}) = \{m \in M : g(m) = t\}$.

Necessary and sufficient conditions for the existence of a unique map $f: I \to T$ with the property $f \circ h = g$ are (a) h must map M *onto* I and (b) for all $i \in I$, there exists $t \in T$ such that $M_h(i) \subseteq M_g(t)$. Condition (b) means that even though one element $i \in I$ may be consistent with many elements in M, so that $M_h(i)$ consists of more than one element, it may be that all elements in $M_h(i)$ are mapped by g into a single element of T. The map f is onto since $g = f \circ h$ and g is onto by assumption. In order for the map f to be one-to-one, it is necessary and sufficient to have equality of $M_h(i)$ and $M_g(t)$ instead of simply inclusion.

If we follow Marschak's maxim and focus on a smaller target space T, it is possible that g maps the admissible models into a smaller space. Thus the map f described above may produce a single element even if there are multiple models m consistent with the data source i. This would arise, for example, if for a given set of data i, we could only estimate the mean μ_1 of Y_1 up to a constant c and the mean μ_2 of Y_2 up to the same constant c. But we could uniquely identify the element $\mu_1 - \mu_2 \in T$.[60] In general, identifying elements of T is easier than identifying elements of M. Thus, in Figure 1, even though many models (elements of M) may be consistent with the same $i \in I$, only one element of T may be consistent with that i. I now turn to empirical causal inference and illustrate the provisional nature of causal inference.

4. THE PROVISIONAL NATURE OF CAUSAL INFERENCE[61]

This section develops the implicit assumptions underlying four widely used methods of causal inference applied to data: (1) matching, (2) control functions, (3) instrumental variable methods, and (4) the method of directed acyclic graphs promoted by Pearl (2000) (or the g-computation method of Robins 1989). It is not intented as an

---

[60]Most modern analyses of identification assume that sample sizes are infinite, so that enlarging the sample size is not informative. However, in any applied problem this distinction is not helpful. Having a small sample (e.g. fewer observations than regressors) can produce an identification problem. This definition combines task 3 and task 2 if we allow for samples to be finite.

[61]Portions of this section are based on Heckman and Navarro (2004).

exhaustive survey of the literature. I demonstrate the value of the scientific approach to causality by showing how explicit analysis of the choice of treatment (or the specification of the selection equations) and the outcomes, including the relationship between the unobservables in the outcome and selection equations clarifies the implicit assumptions being made in each method. This enables the analyst to use behavioral theory aided by statistics to choose estimators and interpret their output. This discussion also clarifies that each method of inference makes implicit identifying assumptions in going from samples to make inferences about models. There is no assumption-free method of causal inference.[62]

I do not discuss randomization systematically except to note that randomization does not in general identify distributions of treatment effects (Heckman 1992; Heckman and Smith 1998; Heckman, Smith, and Clements 1997; Heckman and Vytlacil 2006b). Matching implicitly assumes a randomization by nature in the unobservables producing the choice treatment equation relative to the outcome equation, so my analysis of matching implicitly deals with randomization.

I focus primarily on identification of mean treatment effects in this paper. Discussions of identification of distributions of treatment effects are presented in Aakvik, Heckman, and Vytlacil (1999, 2005), Carneiro, Hansen, and Heckman (2001, 2003), and Heckman and Navarro (2006). I start by presenting a prototypical econometric selection model.

4.1. *A Prototypical Model of Treatment Choice and Outcomes*

To focus the discussion, and to interpret the implicit assumptions underlying the different estimators presented in this paper, I present a benchmark model of treatment choice and treatment outcomes. For simplicity I consider two potential outcomes (Y_0, Y_1). I drop the individual (ω) subscripts to avoid notational clutter. $D = 1$ if Y_1 is selected; $D = 0$ if Y_0 is selected. Agents pick the realized outcome based on their evaluation of the outcomes, given their information. The agent picking the treatment might be different from the person experiencing the outcome

---

[62]This is true for experiments as well. See Heckman (1992).

(e.g., the agent could be a parent choosing outcomes for the child). Let V be the agent's valuation of treatment. I write

$$V = \mu_V(W, U_V) \quad D = \mathbf{1}(V > 0), \tag{20}$$

where the W are factors (observed by the analyst) determining choices, U_V are the unobserved (by the analyst) factors determining choice. Valuation function (20) is a centerpiece of the scientific model of causality but is not specified in the statistical approach.

Potential outcomes are written in terms of observed variables (X) and unobserved (by the analyst) outcome-specific variables

$$Y_1 = \mu_1(X, U_1) \tag{21a}$$

$$Y_0 = \mu_0(X, U_0). \tag{21b}$$

I assume throughout that U_0, U_1, and U_V are continuous random variables and that all means are finite.[63] The individual level treatment effect is thus

$$\Delta = Y_1 - Y_0.$$

More familiar forms of (20), (21a), and (21b) are additively separable expressions,

$$V = \mu_V(W) + U_V \quad E(U_V) = 0, \tag{22a}$$

$$Y_1 = \mu_1(X) + U_1 \quad E(U_1) = 0, \tag{22b}$$

$$Y_0 = \mu_0(X) + U_0 \quad E(U_0) = 0. \tag{22c}$$

Additive separability is not strictly required in modern econometric models (e.g., see Matzkin 2003). However, I use the additively separable representation throughout most of this section because of its familiarity, noting when it is a convenience and when it is an essential part of a method.

The distinction between X and Z is crucial to the validity of many econometric procedures. In matching as conventionally

---

[63]Strictly speaking, absolutely continuous with respect to the Lebesgue measure.

formulated there is no distinction between X and Z. The roles of X and Z in alternative estimators are explored in this section.

A simple example will serve to fix ideas. It will enable me to synthesize the main results of the first three sections of this paper and lay the ground for this section.

Suppose that we use linear-in-parameters expressions. We write the potential outcomes for the population as

$$Y_1 = X\beta_1(C_1) + U_1 \tag{23a}$$

$$Y_0 = X\beta_0(C_0) + U_0, \tag{23b}$$

where we let X be the characteristics of persons and we let the β depend on C_1 and C_0, the characteristics of the programs. These are linear-in-parameters versions of equation (10) for $s = 0,1$. The U_1 and U_0 are the unobservables arising from omitted X, C_1, and C_0 components. Included among the X is "1" so that the characteristics of the programs are allowed to enter directly and in interaction with the X. By modeling how β_1 and β_0 depend on C_1 and C_0, we can answer policy question P3 for new programs that offer new packages of C, assuming we can account for the effects C_i on generating U_1 and U_0.

A version of the model most favorable to solving problems P2 and P3 writes

$$\beta_1(C_1) = \Lambda C_1'$$
$$\beta_0(C_0) = \Lambda C_0',$$

where C_1 and C_0 are $1 \times J$ vectors of characteristics of programs, and C_1' and C_0' are their transposes. Assuming that X is a $1 \times K$ vector of person-specific characteristics, Λ is a $K \times J$ matrix. This specification enables us to represent all of the coefficients of the outcome equations in terms of a base set of generator characteristics.

For each fixed set of characteristics of a program, we can model how outcomes are expected to differ when we change the characteristics of the people participating in them (the X). This is an ingredient for solving problem P3.

Equations (23a) and (23b) are in *ex post* all causes form. For information set $\mathcal{I}$, we can write the *ex ante* version as $E(Y_1|\mathcal{I})$ and $E(Y_0|\mathcal{I})$ (see equation 11). The decision-making agent may be uncertain about the X, the β_i, the C_i, and the U_i. The *ex ante* version reflects this uncertainty. Cunha, Heckman, and Navarro (2005a,b) provide examples of *ex ante* outcome models. *Ex ante* Marshallian causal functions are defined in terms of variations in $\mathcal{I}$. *Ex post* and *ex ante* outcomes are connected by shock ν (s, ω), as in equation (12).

The choice equation may depend on expected rewards and costs, as in Section 2.3. Let

$$V = E(Y_1 - Y_0 - (P_1 - P_0)|\mathcal{I}), \qquad (24)$$

where P_i is the price of participating in i and $P_i = Z\varphi_i + \eta_i$. In the special case of perfect foresight, $\mathcal{I} = (U_1, U_0, C_1, C_0, X, Z, \Lambda, \varphi_1, \varphi_2)$.

To focus on some main ideas, suppose that we work with β_1 and β_0, leaving the C_i implicit. Substituting for the P_i in equation (24) and for the outcomes (23a) and (23b), we obtain after some algebra

$$V = E[X(\beta_1 - \beta_0) - Z(\varphi_1 - \varphi_0) + (U_1 + U_0) - (\eta_1 - \eta_0) \mid \mathcal{I}],$$

where $\mathcal{I}$ is the information set at the time the agent is making the participation decision. Let $W = (X, Z)$, $U_W = (U_1 - U_0) - (\eta_1 - \eta_0)$, and $\gamma = (\beta_1 - \beta_0, -(\varphi_1 - \varphi_0))$. We can then represent the choice equation as

$$V = E[W\gamma + U_W|\mathcal{I}],$$

where

$$D = \mathbf{1}(V > 0).$$

Let U_V be the random variable of U_W conditional on $\mathcal{I}$. For simplicity, we assume that agents know $W = (X, Z)$ but not all of the components of U_W when they make their treatment selection decisions. We also assume that the analyst knows $W = (X, Z)$.

The selection problem arises when D is correlated with (Y_0, Y_1). This can happen if the observables or the unobservables in (Y_0, Y_1) are correlated with or dependent on D. Thus there may be common observed or unobserved factors connecting V and (Y_0, Y_1).

If D is not independent of (Y_0, Y_1), the observed (Y_0, Y_1) are not randomly selected from the population distribution of (Y_0, Y_1). In the Roy model, discussed in Section 1, $\varphi_1 = \varphi_0 = 0$, $\eta_1 = \eta_0 = 0$, and selection is based on Y_1 and Y_0 ($D = \mathbf{1}(Y_1 > Y_0)$). Thus we observe Y_1 if $Y_1 > Y_0$ and we observe Y_0 if $Y_0 \geq Y_1$.

If conditioning on W makes (Y_0, Y_1) independent of D, selection on observables is said to characterize the selection process.[64] This is the motivation for the method of matching. If conditional on W, (Y_0, Y_1) are not independent of D, then we have selection on unobservables and alternative methods must be used.

For the Roy model, Heckman and Honoré (1990) show that it is possible to identify the distribution of treatment outcomes $(Y_1 - Y_0)$ under the conditions they specify. Randomization can identify only the marginal distributions of Y_0 and of Y_1, not the joint distribution of $(Y_1 - Y_0)$ or the quantiles of $(Y_1 - Y_0)$. Thus, under its assumptions, the Roy model is more powerful than randomization in producing the distributional counterfactuals.[65]

The role of the choice equation is to motivate and justify the choice of an evaluation estimator. This is a central feature of the econometric approach that is missing from the statistical and epidemiological literature on treatment effects. Heckman and Smith (1998), Aakvik, Heckman, and Vytlacil (2005), Carneiro, Hansen, and Heckman (2003), and Cunha, Heckman, and Navarro (2005a,b) extend these results to estimate distributions of treatment effects.

4.2. Parameters of Interest

There are many different treatment parameters that can be derived from this model if $U_1 \neq U_0$ and agents know or partially anticipate U_0, U_1 in making their decisions (Heckman and Robb 1985; Heckman 1992; Heckman, Smith, and Clements 1997: Heckman 2001; Heckman and Vytlacil 2000; Cunha, Heckman, and Navarro 2005a,b). For specificity, I focus on certain means because they are traditional. As noted in Section 2 and in Heckman and Vytlacil (2000, 2005) and Heckman (2001), the traditional means often do not answer interesting social and economic questions.

[64]See Heckman and Robb (1985).
[65]The same analysis applies to matching, which cannot identify the distributions of $(Y_1 - Y_0)$ or derived quantiles.

The traditional means conditional on covariates are as follows:

Average Treatment Effect $(ATE) : E(Y_1 - Y_0|X)$
Treatment on the Treated $(TT) : E(Y_1 - Y_0|X, D = 1)$
Marginal Treatment Effect $(MTE) : E(Y_1 - Y_0|X, Z, V = 0)$.

The MTE is the marginal treatment effect introduced into the evaluation literature by Björklund and Moffitt (1987). It is the average gain to persons who are indifferent to participating in sector 1 or sector 0 given X, Z. These are persons at the margin, defined by (W) so Z plays a role in the definition of the parameter by fixing $\mu_V(W)$ in equation (20) or equation (22a) and hence fixing U_V. It is a version of $EOTM$ as defined in Section 1. An alternative definition in this setup is $MTE = E(Y_1 - Y_0|X, U_V)$. Heckman and Vytlacil (1999, 2005, 2006b) show how the MTE can be used to construct all mean treatment parameters, including the policy relevant treatment parameters, under the conditions specified in their papers. These parameters can be defined for the population as a whole not conditioning on X or Z.[66]

4.3. The Selection Problem Stated in Terms of Means

Let $Y = DY_1 + (1 - D)Y_0$. Samples generated by choices have the following means which are assumed to be known:

$$E(Y|X, Z, D = 1) = E(Y_1|X, Z, D = 1)$$

and

$$E(Y|X, Z, D = 0) = E(Y_0|X, Z, D = 0)$$

for outcomes Y_1 for participants and the outcomes Y_0 for nonparticipants, respectively. In addition, choices are observed so that in large samples $\Pr(D = 1|X, Z)$ is known—that is, the probability of choosing treatment is known. From the sample data, we can also construct

$$E(Y_1|X, D = 1) \quad \text{and} \quad E(Y_0|X, D = 0).$$

[66]The average marginal treatment effect is
$$E(Y_1 - Y_0|V = 0) = \int E(Y_1 - Y_0|X, Z, V = 0)f(X, Z|V = 0)dXdZ.$$

The conditional biases from using the difference of these means to construct the three parameters studied in this paper are

$$\text{Bias } TT = [E(Y|X, D = 1) - E(Y|X, D = 0)] - E(Y_1 - Y_0|X, D = 1)$$
$$= [E(Y_0|X, D = 1) - E(Y_0|X, D = 0)].$$

In the case of additive separability

$$\text{Bias } TT = E(U_1|X, D = 1) - E(U_0|X, D = 0).$$

For ATE,

$$\text{Bias } ATE = E(Y|X, D = 1) - E(Y|X, D = 0) - [E(Y_1 - Y_0|X)].$$

In the case of additive separability

$$\text{Bias } ATE = [E(U_1|X, D = 1) - E(U_1|X)] - [E(U_0|X, D = 0) - E(U_0|X)].$$

For MTE,

$$\begin{aligned}
\text{Bias } MTE &= E(Y|X, Z, D = 1) - E(Y|X, Z, D = 0) \\
&\quad - E(Y_1 - Y_0|X, Z, V = 0) \\
&= [E(U_1|X, Z, D = 1) - E(U_1|X, Z, V = 0)] \\
&\quad - [E(U_0|X, Z, D = 0) - E(U_0|X, Z, V = 0)],
\end{aligned}$$

for the case of additive separability in outcomes. The MTE is defined for a subset of persons indifferent between the two sectors and so is defined for X and Z. The bias is the difference between average U_1 for participants and marginal U_1 minus the difference between average U_0 for nonparticipants and marginal U_0. Each of these terms is a bias that can be called a selection bias. These biases can be defined conditional on X (or X and Z or X, Z, and V in case of the MTE) or unconditionally.

4.4. How Different Methods Eliminate the Bias

In this section I consider the identification conditions that underlie matching, control functions, and instrumental variable methods to identify the three parameters using the data on mean outcomes. I also briefly discuss the method of directed acyclic graphs or the g-computation method for one causal parameter. I discuss sources of unobservables, implicit assumptions about how unobservables are eliminated as sources of selection problems, and the assumed relationship between outcomes and choice equations. I start with the method of matching.

4.4.1. *Matching*

The method of matching as conventionally formulated makes no distinction between X and Z. Define the conditioning set as $W = (X, Z)$. The strong form of matching advocated by Rosenbaum and Rubin (1983) and in numerous predecessor papers, assumes that

$$(Y_1, Y_0) \perp\!\!\!\perp D \mid W \qquad\qquad \text{(M-1)}$$

and

$$0 < \Pr(D = 1 \mid W) = P(W) < 1, \qquad\qquad \text{(M-2)}$$

where "$\perp\!\!\!\perp$" denotes independence given the conditioning variables after "$\mid$". $P(W)$ is the probability of selection into treatment and is sometimes called the propensity score. Condition (M-2) implies that the mean treatment parameters can be defined for all values of W (i.e., for each W, in very large samples, there are observations for which we observe a Y_0 and other observations for which we observe a Y_1). Rosenbaum and Rubin (1983) show that under (M-1) and (M-2)

$$(Y_1, Y_0) \perp\!\!\!\perp D \mid P(W). \qquad\qquad \text{(M-3)}$$

This reduces the dimensionality of the matching problem. They assume that P is known. When it is not known, it is necessary to estimate it. Nonparametric estimation of $P(W)$ restores the dimensionality problem but shifts it to the estimation of $P(W)$.[67] Under these

---

[67]Rosenbaum (1987) or Rubin and Thomas (1992) consider the distribution of the matching estimator when P is estimated under special assumptions about the distribution of the matching variables. Papers that account for estimated P under general conditions include Heckman, Ichimura, and Todd (1997, 1998) and Hahn (1998).

assumptions, conditioning on P eliminates all three biases defined in Section 4.3 for parameters defined conditional on P because

$$E(Y_1|D = 0, P(W)) = E(Y_1|D = 1, P(W)) = E(Y_1|P(W))$$
$$E(Y_0|D = 1, P(W)) = E(Y_0|D = 0, P(W)) = E(Y_0|P(W)).$$

Thus for TT one can identify counterfactual mean $E(Y_0|D = 1, P(W))$ from $E(Y_0|D = 0, P(W))$. In fact, one only needs the weaker condition $Y_0 \perp\!\!\!\perp D|P(W)$ to remove the bias[68] because $E(Y_1|D = 1, P(W))$ is known, and only $E(Y_0|D = 1, P(W))$ is unknown. From the observed conditional means one can form ATE. Since the conditioning is on $P(W)$, the parameter is defined conditional on it and not X or (X, Z). Integrating out $P(W)$ produces unconditional ATE. Integrating out $P(W)$ given $D = 1$ produces unconditional TT.[69]

Observe that since $ATE = TT$ for all X, Z under (M-1) and (M-2), the effect for the average person participating in a program is the same as the effect for the marginal person, conditional on W, and there is no bias in estimating MTE.[70] The strong implicit assumption that the marginal participant in a program gets the same return as the average participant in the program, conditional on W, is an unattractive implication of these assumptions (see Heckman 2001 and Heckman and Vytlacil 2005, 2006a,b). The method assumes that all of the dependence between U_V and (U_1, U_0) is eliminated by conditioning on W,

$$U_V \perp\!\!\!\perp (U_1, U_0)|W.$$

This motivates the term "selection on observables" introduced in Heckman and Robb (1985, 1986).

Assumption (M-2) has the unattractive feature that if the analyst has too much information about the decision of who takes treatment so that $P(W) = 1$ or 0, the method breaks down because people cannot be compared at a common W. The method of matching

---

[68]See Heckman, Ichimura, and Todd (1997) and Abadie (2003).
[69]To estimate the parameters conditional on W, one cannot use $P(W)$ but must use the full W vector.
[70]As demonstrated in Carneiro (2002), one can still distinguish marginal and average effects in terms of observables.

assumes that, given W, some unspecified randomization device allocates people to treatment. The fact that the cases $P(W) = 1$ and $P(W) = 0$ must be eliminated suggests that methods for choosing which variables enter W based on the fit of the model to data on choices (D) are potentially problematic; see Heckman and Navarro (2004) and Heckman and Vytlacil (2005) for further discussion of this point.

What justifies (M-1) or (M-3)? Absent an explicit theoretical model of treatment assignment and an explicit model of the sources of randomness, analysts are unable to justify the assumption except by appeal to convenience. Because there are no exclusion restrictions in the observables, the only possible source of variation in D given W are the unobservable elements generating D. These elements are assumed to act like an ideal randomization that assigns person to treatment but is independent of (U_1, U_2), the unobservables generating (Y_0, Y_1), given W.

If agents partially anticipate the benefits of treatment and make enrollment decisions based on these anticipations, (M-1) or (M-3) is false. In the extreme case of the Roy model, where $D = \mathbf{1}(Y_1 > Y_0)$, (M-1) or (M-3) is certainly false. Even if agents are only imperfectly prescient but can partially forecast (Y_1, Y_0) and use that information in deciding whether or not to participate, (M-1) or (M-3) is false.

Without a model of interventions justifying these assumptions, and without a model of the sources of unobservables, (M-1) or (M-3) cannot be justified. The model cannot be tested without richer sources of data.[71] Judgments about whether agents are as ignorant about potential outcomes given W, as is assumed in (M-1) or (M-3), can only be settled by the theory unless it is possible to randomize persons into treatment, and randomization does not change the outcome— that is, under assumption (A-2). The matching model makes strong implicit assumptions about the unobservables.

In the recent literature, the claim is sometimes made that matching is "for free" (e.g., see Gill and Robins 2001). The idea underlying this claim is that since $E(Y_0|D = 1, W)$ is not observed, we might as well set it to $E(Y_0|D = 0, W)$, an implication of (M-1). This argument

---

[71]See Heckman, Ichimura, Smith, and Todd (1998) for a test of matching assumptions using data from randomized trials.

is correct so far as data description goes. Matching imposes just-identifying restrictions and in this sense—at a purely empirical level—is as good as any other just-identifying assumption in describing the data.

However, the implied behavioral restrictions are not "for free." Imposing that—conditional on X and Z or conditional on $P(W)$ the marginal person entering a program is the same as the average person— is a strong and restrictive implication of the conditional independence assumptions and is not a "for free" assumption in terms of its behavioral content.[72] In the context of estimating the economic returns to schooling, it implies that, conditional on W, the economic return to schooling for persons who are just at the margin of going to school are the same as the return for persons with strong preferences for schooling.

Introducing a distinction between X and Z allows the analyst to overcome the problem arising from perfect prediction of treatment assignment for some values of (X, Z) if there are some variables Z not in X. If P is a nontrivial function of Z (so $P(X, Z)$ varies with Z for all X) and Z can be varied independently of X for all points of support of X,[73] and if outcomes are defined solely in terms of X, the problem of perfect classification can be solved. Treatment parameters can be defined for all support values of X since for any value (X, Z) that perfectly classifies D, there is another value (X, Z'), $Z' \neq Z$, that does not (see Heckman, Ichimura, and Todd 1997).

Offsetting the disadvantages of matching, the method of matching with a known conditioning set that satisfies (M-1) does not require separability of outcome or choice equations into observable and unobservable components, exogeneity of conditioning variables, exclusion restrictions, or adoption of specific functional forms of outcome equations. Such assumptions are commonly used in conventional selection (control function) methods and conventional applications of IV although recent work in semiparametric estimation

---

[72]As noted by Heckman, Ichimura, Smith, and Todd (1998), if one seeks to identify $E(Y_1 - Y_0|D = 1, W)$ one only needs to impose a weaker condition $[E(Y_0|D = 1, W) = E(Y_0|D = 0, W)]$ or $Y_0 \perp\!\!\!\perp D|W$ rather than (M-1). This imposes the assumption of no selection on levels of Y_0 (given W) and not the assumption of no selection on levels of Y_1 or on $Y_1 - Y_0$, as (M-1) does. Marginal can be different from average in this case.

[73]A precise sufficient condition is that $Supp(Z|X) = Supp(Z)$. We can get by with a weaker condition that in any neighborhood of X, there is a Z^* such that $0 < \Pr(D = 1|X, Z^*) < 1$, and that Z^* is in the support of $Z|X$.

relaxes many of these assumptions, as I note below (see also Heckman and Vytlacil 2005, 2006b). Moreover, the method of matching does not strictly require (M-1). One can get by with weaker mean independence assumptions,

$$
\begin{aligned}
E(Y_1|W, D = 1) &= E(Y_1|W), \\
E(Y_0|W, D = 0) &= E(Y_0|W),
\end{aligned}
\tag{M-1$'$}
$$

in the place of the stronger (M-1) conditions. However, if (M-1$'$) is invoked, the assumption that one can replace W by P (W) does not follow from the analysis of Rosenbaum and Rubin, and is an additional new assumption.

4.4.2. Control Functions
The principle motivating the conventional method of control functions is different. (See Heckman 1976, 1978, 1980 and Heckman and Robb 1985, 1986, where this principle was first developed.) Like matching, it works with conditional expectations of (Y_1, Y_0) given (X, Z and D). Conventional applications of the control function method assume additive separability that is not required in matching. Strictly speaking, additive separability in the outcome equation is not required in the application of control functions either.[74] What is required is a model relating the outcome unobservables to the observables, including the choice of treatment. The method of matching assumes that, conditional on the observables (X, Z), the unobservables are independent of D.[75] For the additively separable case, control functions based on the principle of modeling the conditional expectations of Y_1 and Y_0 given X, Z, and D can be written as

$$
\begin{aligned}
E(Y_1|X, Z, D = 1) &= \mu_1(X) + E(U_1|X, Z, D = 1) \\
E(Y_0|X, Z, D = 0) &= \mu_0(X) + E(U_0|X, Z, D = 0).
\end{aligned}
$$

---

[74]Examples of nonseparable selection models are found in Cameron and Heckman (1998).

[75]Or mean independent in the case of mean parameters.

In the method of control functions if one can model $E(U_1|X, Z, D = 1)$ and $E(U_0|X, Z, D = 0)$ and these functions can be independently varied against μ_1 (X) and μ_0 (X) respectively, one can identify μ_1 (X) and μ_0 (X) up to constant terms.[76] Nothing in the method intrinsically requires that X or Z be stochastically independent of U_1 or U_0, although conventional methods often assume this.

If one assumes that $(U_1, U_V)\perp\!\!\!\perp(X, Z)$ and adopts equation (22a) as the treatment choice model augmented so X and Z are determinants of treatment choice, one obtains

$$E(U_1|X, Z, D = 1) = E(U_1|U_V \geq -\mu_V(X, Z)) = K_1(P(X, Z)),$$

so the control function depends only on $P(X, Z)$. By similar reasoning, if $(U_0, U_V) \perp\!\!\!\perp (X, Z)$,

$$E(U_0|X, Z, D = 0) = E(U_0|U_V < -\mu_V(X, Z)) = K_0(P(X, Z))$$

and the control function depends only on the probability of selection ("the propensity score"). The key assumption needed to represent the control function solely as a function of $P(X, Z)$ is

$$(U_1, U_0, U_V) \perp\!\!\!\perp (X, Z). \tag{C-1}$$

Under this condition

$$E(Y_1|X, Z, D = 1) = \mu_1(X) + K_1(P(X, Z))$$
$$E(Y_0|X, Z, D = 0) = \mu_0(X) + K_0(P(X, Z))$$

---

[76]Heckman and Robb (1985, 1986) introduce this general formulation of control functions. The identifiability requires that the members of the pairs $(\mu_1(X), E(U_1|X, Z, D = 1))$ and $(\mu_0(X), E(U_0|X, Z, D = 0))$ be "variation free" so that they can be independently varied against each other; see Heckman and Vytlacil (2006a, b) for a precise statement of these conditions.

with $\lim_{P \to 1} K_1(P) = 0$ and $\lim_{P \to 0} K_0(P) = 0$ where it is assumed that Z can be independently varied for all X, and the limits are obtained by changing Z while holding X fixed.[77] These limit results simply state that when the values of X, Z are such that the probability of being in a sample is 1, there is no selection bias. One can approximate the $K_1(P)$ and $K_0(P)$ terms by polynomials in P (Heckman 1980; Heckman and Robb 1985, 1986; Heckman and Hotz 1989).

If $K_1(P(X, Z))$ can be independently varied from $\mu_1(X)$ and $K_0(P(X, Z))$ can be independently varied from $\mu_0(X)$, one can identify $\mu_1(X)$ and $\mu_0(X)$ up to constants. If there are limit sets $\mathbb{Z}_0$ and $\mathbb{Z}_1$ such that for each X $\lim_{Z \to \mathbb{Z}_0} P(X, Z) = 0$ and $\lim_{Z \to \mathbb{Z}_1} P(X, Z) = 1$, then one can identify these constants, since in those limit sets we identify $\mu_1(X)$ and $\mu_0(X)$.[78] Under these conditions, it is possible to nonparametrically identify all three conditional treatment parameters:

$$ATE(X) = \mu_1(X) - \mu_0(X)$$
$$TT(X, D = 1) = \mu_1(X) - \mu_0(X) + E(U_1 - U_0 | X, D = 1)$$
$$= \mu_1(X) - \mu_0(X) + E_{Z|X, D=1}$$
$$\left[K_1(P(X, Z)) + \left(\frac{1 - P}{P} \right) K_0(P(X, Z)) \right],^{79}$$

---

[77]More precisely, assume that *Supp* $(Z|X) = $ *Supp* (Z) and that limit sets of Z, $\mathbb{Z}_0$, and $\mathbb{Z}_1$ exist such that as $Z \to \mathbb{Z}_0$, $P(Z, X) \to 0$ and as $Z \to \mathbb{Z}_1$, $P(Z, X) \to 1$. This is also the support condition used in the generalization of matching by Heckman, Ichimura, and Todd (1997).

[78]This condition is sometimes called "identification at infinity"; see Heckman (1990) or Andrews and Schafgans (1998).

[79]Since

$$E(U_0) = 0$$
$$= E(U_0 | D = 1, X, Z) P(X, Z) + E(U_0 | D = 0, X, Z)(1 - P(X, Z))$$
$$E(U_0 | D = 1, X, Z) = -\frac{(1 - P(X, Z))}{P(X, Z)} E(U_0 | D = 0, X, Z) = -\frac{(1 - P(X, Z))}{P(X, Z)} K_0(P(X, Z))$$

See Heckman and Robb (1986). The expression $E_{Z|X, D=1}$ integrates out Z for a given $X, D = 1$.

$$
\begin{aligned}
MTE(X, Z, V = 0) &= \mu_1(X) - \mu_1(X) + E(U_1 - U_0 \mid \mu_V(Z, X) \\
&= -U_V) \\
&= \mu_1(X) - \mu_0(X) \\
&\quad + \frac{\partial[E(U_1 - U_0 \mid X, Z, D = 1)P(X, Z)]}{\partial(P(X, Z))}.
\end{aligned}
$$[80]

Unlike the method of matching, the method of control functions allows the marginal treatment effect to be different from the average treatment effect or from the effect of treatment on the treated (i.e., the second term on the right-hand side of the first equation for $MTE(X, Z, U = 0)$ is, in general, nonzero). Although conventional practice is to derive the functional forms of $K_0(P)$ and $K_1(P)$ by making distributional assumptions (e.g., normality or other conventional distributional assumptions about (U_0, U_1, U_V); see Heckman, Tobias, and Vytlacil 2001, 2003), this is not an intrinsic feature of the method and there are many non-normal and semiparametric versions of this method (see Powell 1994 or Heckman and Vytlacil 2006a,b for surveys).

Without invoking parametric assumptions, the method of control functions requires an exclusion restriction (a Z not in X) to achieve nonparametric identification.[81] Without any functional form assumptions, one cannot rule out a worst-case analysis where—for example, if $X = Z$, $K_1(P(X)) = \alpha\mu(X)$ where α is a scalar. Then, there

---

[80]As established in Heckman and Vytlacil (2000, 2005) and Heckman (2001), under assumption (C-1) and additional regularity conditions

$$
E(U_1 - U_0 \mid X, Z, D=1)P(X,Z) = \int_{-P(X,Z)}^{1} \int_{-\infty}^{\infty} (U_1 - U_0) f(U_1 - U_0 \mid U_V^*) d(U_1 - U_0) dU_V^*,
$$

where $U_V^* = F_V(U_V)$, so

$$
\frac{\partial[E(U_1 - U_0 \mid X, Z, D=1)P(X,Z)]}{\partial P(X,Z)} = E(U_1 - U_0 \mid U_V^* = -P(X,Z)).
$$

The third expression follows from algebraic manipulation. Expressions conditional on X and $V = 0$ are obtained by integrating out Z conditional on X and $V = 0$.

[81]For many common functional forms for the distributions of unobservables, no exclusion is required.

is perfect collinearity between the control function and the conditional mean of the outcome equation, and it is impossible to control for selection with this method. Even though this case is not generic, it is possible. The method of matching does not require an exclusion restriction because it makes a stronger assumption, which we clarify below. Without additional assumptions, the method of control functions requires that, for some Z values for each X, $P(X, Z) = 1$ and $P(X, Z) = 0$ to achieve full nonparametric identification.[82] The conventional method of matching excludes this case.

Both methods require that treatment parameters be defined on a common support that is the intersection of the supports of X given $D = 1$ and X given $D = 0$:

$$Supp\ (X|D = 1) \cap Supp\ (X|D = 0).$$

A similar requirement is imposed on the generalization of matching with exclusion restrictions introduced in Heckman, Ichimura, Smith, and Todd (1998). Recall that exclusion (adding a Z in the probability of treatment equation that is not in the outcome equation where $\Pr(D = 1|X, Z)$ is the choice probability), both in matching and selection models, enlarges the set of X values that satisfy this condition. If $P(X, Z)$ depends on Z, then even if $P(X, Z) = 1$ for some $Z = z$ it can be that $P(X, Z) < 1$ for $Z = z'$ if $z \neq z'$. A similar argument applies to $P(X, Z) = 0$ for $Z = z''$ but $P(X, Z) > 0$ for $Z = z'''$ if $z'' \neq z'''$. This requires the existence of such Z values in the neighborhood of all values of X, Z such that $P(X, Z) = 0$ or 1.

In the method of control functions, $P(X, Z)$ is a conditioning variable used to predict U_1 conditional on D, X, and Z and U_0 conditional on D, X, and Z. In the method of matching, it is used to characterize the stochastic independence between (U_0, U_1) and D. In the method of control functions, as conventionally applied, $(U_0, U_1) \perp\!\!\!\perp (X, Z)$, but this assumption is not intrinsic to the method.[83]

---

[82]Symmetry of the errors can be used in place of the appeal to limit sets that put $P(X, Z) = 0$ or $P(X, Z) = 1$; see Chen (1999).

[83]Relaxing it, however, requires that the analyst model the dependence of the unobservables on the observables and that certain variation-free conditions are satisfied; see Heckman and Robb (1985).

This assumption plays no role in matching if the correct conditioning set is known (i.e., one that satisfies (M-1) and (M-2)). However, as noted in Heckman and Navarro (2004), exogeneity plays a key role in devising rules to select appropriate conditioning variables. The method of control functions does not require that $(U_0, U_1) \perp\!\!\!\perp D|(X, Z)$, which is a central requirement of matching. Equivalently, the method of control functions does not require

$$(U_0, U_1) \perp\!\!\!\perp U_V|(X, Z)$$

whereas matching does. Thus matching assumes access to a richer set of conditioning variables than is assumed in the method of control functions.

The method of control functions is more robust than the method of matching, in the sense that it allows for outcome unobservables to be dependent on D even after conditioning on (X, Z), and it models this dependence, whereas the method of matching assumes no such dependence. Matching under the assumed conditions is a special case of the method of control functions[84] in which under assumptions (M-1) and (M-2),

$$E(U_1|X, Z, D = 1) = E(U_1|X, Z)$$
$$E(U_0|X, Z, D = 0) = E(U_0|X, Z).$$

In the method of control functions in the case when $(X, Z) \perp\!\!\!\perp (U_0, U_1, U_V)$

$$
\begin{aligned}
E(Y|X, Z, D) &= E(Y_1|X, Z, D = 1)D + E(Y_0|X, Z, D = 0)(1 - D) \\
&= \mu_0(X) + (\mu_1(X) - \mu_0(X))D \\
&\quad + E(U_1|X, Z, D = 1)D + E(U_0|P(X, Z), D = 0)(1 - D) \\
&= \mu_0(X) + (\mu_1(X) - \mu_0(X))D \\
&\quad + E(U_1|P(X, Z), D = 1)D + E(U_0|P(X, Z), D = 0)(1 - D) \\
&= \mu_0(X) + [\mu_1(X) - \mu_0(X) + K_1(P(X, Z)) - K_0(P(X, Z))]D \\
&\quad + K_0(P(X, Z)).
\end{aligned}
$$

---

[84]See Aakvik et al. (2005); Carneiro et al. (2003); and Cunha et al. (2005a, 2005b) for a generalization of matching that allows for selection on unobservables by imposing a factor structure on the errors and estimating the distribution of the unobserved factors.

To identify $\mu_1(X) - \mu_0(X)$, the average treatment effect, one must isolate it from $K_1(P(X, Z))$ and $K_0(P(X, Z))$. The coefficient on D in this regression does not correspond to any one of the treatment effects presented above.

Under assumptions (M-1) and (M-2) of the method of matching, one may write expressions conditional on $P(W)$:

$$E(Y|P(W), D) = \mu_0(P(W)) +$$
$$[(\mu_1(P(W)) - \mu_0(P(W))) + E(U_1|P(W)) - E(U_0|P(W))]$$
$$D + \{E(U_0|P(W))\}.$$

Notice that if the analyst further invokes (C-1)

$$E(Y|P(W), D) = \mu_0(P(W)) + [\mu_1(P(W)) - \mu_0(P(W))]D,$$

since $E(U_1|P(W)) = E(U_0|P(W)) = 0$. A parallel argument can be made conditioning on X and Z instead of $P(W)$.

Under the assumptions that justify matching, treatment effects ATE or TT (conditional on $P(W)$) are identified from the coefficient on D in either of the two preceding equations. It is not necessary to invoke (C-1) in the application of matching although it simplifies expressions. One can define the parameters conditional on X, allowing the X to be endogenous. Condition (M-2) guarantees that D is not perfectly predictable by W so the variation in D identifies the treatment parameter. Thus the coefficient on D in the regression associated with the more general control function model does not correspond to any treatment parameter whereas the coefficient on D in the regression associated with matching corresponds to a treatment parameter under the assumptions of the matching model. Under (C-1), $\mu_1(P(W)) - \mu_0(P(W)) = ATE$ and $ATE = TT = MTE$, so the method of matching identifies all of the (conditional on $P(W)$) mean treatment parameters.[85] Under the assumptions justifying matching, when means of Y_1 and Y_0 are the

---

[85]This result also holds if (C-1) is not satisfied, but then the treatment effects include

$$E(U_1|P(W)) - E(U_0|P(W))$$

.

parameters of interest, and W satisfies (M-1) and (M-2), the bias terms defined in Section 4.3 vanish. They do not in the more general case considered in the method of control functions. The vanishing of the bias terms in matching is the mathematical counterpart of the randomization implicit in matching: conditional on W or $P(W)$, (U_1, U_0) are random with respect to D. The method of control functions allows them to be nonrandom with respect to D. In the absence of functional form assumptions, an exclusion restriction is required in the analysis of control functions to separate out $K_0(P(X, Z))$ from the coefficient on D. Matching produces identification without exclusion restrictions whereas identification with exclusion restrictions is a central feature of the control function method in the absence of functional form assumptions. The implicit randomization in matching plays the role of an exclusion restriction in the method of instrumental variables.

The work of Rosenbaum (1995) and Robins (1997) implicitly recognizes that the control function approach is more general than the matching approach. Their sensitivity analyses for matching when there are unobserved conditioning variables are, in their essence, sensitivity analyses using control functions.[86] Aakvik, Heckman, and Vytlacil (2005), Carneiro, Hansen, and Heckman (2003), and Cunha, Heckman, and Navarro (2005a) explicitly model the relationship between matching and selection models using factor structure models, treating the omitted conditioning variables as unobserved factors and estimating their distribution.

Tables 2 and 3 perform sensitivity analyses under different assumptions about the parameters of the underlying selection model. In particular, I assume that the data are generated by the model of equations (22a)–(22c), with (22c) having the explicit representation

$$V = Z\gamma + U_V,$$
$$(U_1, U_0, U_V)' \sim N(0, \Sigma)$$
$$corr\ (U_j, U_V) = \rho_{jV}$$
$$var\ (U_j) = \sigma_j^2; \quad j = \{0, 1\}.$$

---

[86]See also Vijverberg (1993), who performs a sensitivity analysis in a parametric selection model with an unidentified parameter.

TABLE 2
Mean Bias for Treatment on the Treated

ρ_{0V}	Average Bias ($\sigma_0 = 1$)	Average Bias ($\sigma_0 = 2$)
−1.00	−1.7920	−3.5839
−0.75	−1.3440	−2.6879
−0.50	−0.8960	−1.7920
−0.25	−0.4480	−0.8960
0.00	0.0000	0.0000
0.25	0.4480	0.8960
0.50	0.8960	1.7920
0.75	1.3440	2.6879
1.00	1.7920	3.5839

$$\text{BIAS}_{TT} = \rho_{0V} * \sigma_0 * M(p)$$

$$M(p) = \frac{\varphi(\Phi^{-1}(p))}{[p^*(1-p)]}$$

I assume no X and that $Z \perp\!\!\!\perp (U_1, U_0, U_V)$. Using the formulas presented in the appendix of Heckman and Navarro (2004), one can write the biases conditional on $Z = z$ as

$$\text{Bias } TT(Z = z) = \text{Bias } TT(P(Z) = p(z)) = \sigma_0 \rho_{0V} M(p(z))$$
$$\text{Bias } ATE(Z = z) = \text{Bias } ATE(P)Z) = p(z))$$
$$= M(p(z))[\sigma_1 \rho_{1V}(1 - p(z)) + \sigma_0 \rho_{0V} p(z)]$$
$$\text{Bias } MTE(Z = z) = \text{Bias } MTE(P(Z) = p(z))$$
$$= M(p(z))[\sigma_1 \rho_{1V}(1 - p(z)) + \sigma_0 \rho_{0V} p(z)]$$
$$- \Phi^{-1}(1 - p(z))[\sigma_1 \rho_{1V} - \sigma_0 \rho_{0V}]$$

where $M(p(z)) = \frac{\phi(\Phi^{-1}(1-p(z)))}{p(z)(1-p(z))}$, $\phi(\cdot)$ and $\Phi(\cdot)$ are the probability density function (pdf) and cumulative distribution function (cdf) of a standard normal random variable and $p(z)$ is the propensity score evaluated at $Z = z$. I assume that $\mu_1 = \mu_0$ so that the true average treatment effect is zero.

I simulate the mean bias for TT (Table 2) and ATE (Table 3) for different values of the ρ_{jV} and σ_j. The results in the tables show that, as one lets the variances of the outcome equations grow, the value of the mean bias that one obtains can become substantial. With larger correlations come larger biases. These

TABLE 3
Mean Bias for Average Treatment Effect

$(\sigma_0 = 1)$

ρ_{0V}	-1.00	-0.75	-0.50	-0.25	0	0.25	0.50	0.75	1.00
					$\rho_{1V}\,(\sigma_1 = 1)$				
-1.00	-1.7920	-1.5680	-1.3440	-1.1200	-0.8960	-0.6720	-0.4480	-0.2240	0
-0.75	-1.5680	-1.3440	-1.1200	-0.8960	-0.6720	-0.4480	-0.2240	0	0.2240
-0.50	-1.3440	-1.1200	-0.8960	-0.6720	-0.4480	-0.2240	0	0.2240	0.4480
-0.25	-1.1200	-0.8960	-0.6720	-0.4480	-0.2240	0	0.2240	0.4480	0.6720
0	-0.8960	-0.6720	-0.4480	-0.2240	0	0.2240	0.4480	0.6720	0.8960
0.25	-0.6720	-0.4480	-0.2240	0	0.2240	0.4480	0.6720	0.8960	1.1200
0.50	-0.4480	-0.2240	0	0.2240	0.4480	0.6720	0.8960	1.1200	1.3440
0.75	-0.2240	0	0.2240	0.4480	0.6720	0.8960	1.1200	1.3440	1.5680
1.00	0	0.2240	0.4480	0.6720	0.8960	1.1200	1.3440	1.5680	1.7920
					$\rho_{1V}\,(\sigma_1 = 2)$				
-1.00	-2.6879	-2.2399	-1.7920	-1.3440	-0.8960	-0.4480	0	0.4480	0.8960
-0.75	-2.4639	-2.0159	-1.5680	-1.1200	-0.6720	-0.2240	0.2240	0.6720	1.1200
-0.50	-2.2399	-1.7920	-1.3440	-0.8960	-0.4480	0	0.4480	0.8960	1.3440
-0.25	-2.0159	-1.5680	-1.1200	-0.6720	-0.2240	0.2240	0.6720	1.1200	1.5680
0	-1.7920	-1.3440	-0.8960	-0.4480	0	0.4480	0.8960	1.3440	1.7920
0.25	-1.5680	-1.1200	-0.6720	-0.2240	0.2240	0.6720	1.1200	1.5680	2.0159
0.50	-1.3440	-0.8960	-0.4480	0	0.4480	0.8960	1.3440	1.7920	2.2399
0.75	-1.1200	-0.6720	-0.2240	0.2240	0.6720	1.1200	1.5680	2.0159	2.4639
1.00	-0.8960	-0.4480	0	0.4480	0.8960	1.3440	1.7920	2.2399	2.6879

$\text{BIASATE} = \rho_{1V} * \sigma_1 * M_1(p) - \rho_{0V} * \sigma_0 * M_0(p)$
$\text{BIASMTE} = \text{BIASATE} - \Phi^{-1}(1 - p) * (\rho_{1V} * \sigma_1 - \rho_{0V} * \sigma_0)$

$$M_1(p) = \frac{\varphi(\Phi^{-1}(p))}{p}$$

$$M_0(p) = \frac{-\varphi(\Phi^{-1}(p))}{[1 - p]}$$

tables demonstrate the greater generality of the control function approach. Even if the correlation between the observables and the unobservables (ρ_{jV}) is small, so that one might think that selection on unobservables is relatively unimportant, one still obtains substantial biases if one does not control for relevant omitted conditioning variables. Only for special values of the parameters can one avoid bias by matching. These examples also demonstrate that sensitivity analyses can be conducted for analysis based on control function methods even when they are not fully identified, as noted by Vijverberg (1993).

4.4.3. *Instrumental Variables*

Both the method of matching and the method of control functions work with $E(Y|X, Z, D)$ and $\Pr(D = 1|X, Z)$. The method of instrumental variables works with $E(Y|X, Z)$ and $\Pr(D = 1|X, Z)$. There are two versions of the method of instrumental variables: (1) conventional linear instrumental variables and (2) local instrumental variables (*LIV*) (Heckman and Vytlacil 1999, 2000, 2006b; Heckman 2001). *LIV* is equivalent to a semiparametric selection model (Vytlacil 2002; Heckman and Vytlacil 2005, 2006b). It is an alternative way to implement the principle of control functions. *LATE* (Imbens and Angrist 1994) is a special case of *LIV* under the conditions I specify below.

I first consider the conventional method of instrumental variables. In this framework, $P(X, Z)$ arises less naturally than it does in the matching and control function approaches. Z is the instrument and $P(X, Z)$ is a function of the instrument.

Using the model of equations (22b) and (22c), I obtain

$$
\begin{aligned}
Y &= D Y_1 + (1 - D) Y_0 \\
&= \mu_0(X) + (\mu_1(X) - \mu_0(X) + U_1 - U_0)D + U_0 \\
&= \mu_0(X) + \Delta(X)D + U_0,
\end{aligned}
$$

where $\Delta(X) = \mu_1(X) - \mu_0(X) + U_1 - U_0$. When $U_1 = U_0$, we obtain the conventional model to which *IV* is typically applied with

D correlated with U_0. Standard instrumental variable conditions apply and $P(X,Z)$ is a valid instrument if

$$E(U_0|P(X,Z), X) = E(U_0|X)^{87} \qquad \text{(IV-1)}$$

and

$$\Pr(D = 1|X, Z) \qquad \text{(IV-2)}$$

is a nontrivial function of Z for each X. When $U_1 \neq U_0$ but $D \perp\!\!\!\perp (U_1 - U_0)|X$ (or alternatively $U_V \perp\!\!\!\perp (U_1 - U_0)|X$), then the same two conditions identify (conditional on X):

$$\begin{aligned}
ATE\ (X) &= E(Y_1 - Y_0|X) = E(\Delta(X)|X) \\
TT\ (X) &= E(Y_1 - Y_0|X, D = 1) = E(Y_1 - Y_0|X) = E(\Delta(X) \mid X) \\
&= MTE(X)
\end{aligned}$$

and the marginal equals the average conditional on X and Z. The requirement that $D \perp\!\!\!\perp (U_1 - U_0)|X$ is strong and assumes that agents do not participate in the program on the basis of *any* information about unobservables in gross gains (Heckman and Robb 1985, 1986; Heckman 1997).[88]

How reasonable are the identifying assumptions of *IV*? An appeal to behavioral theory helps. Consider the use of draft lottery numbers as instruments (Z) for military service ($Z = 1$ if served in the army; $Z = 0$ otherwise). The question is how does military service affect earnings? (Angrist 1991). If agents participate in the military

---

[87]Observe that it is not required that $E(U_0|X) = 0$. We can write the *IV* estimator in the population as

$$\begin{aligned}
\Delta^{IV}(x) &= \frac{E(Y|P(X = x, Z = z) = p_z, X = x) - E(Y|P(X = x, Z = z') = p_{z'}, X = x)}{P(X = x, Z = z) - P(X = x, Z = z')} \\
&= \frac{[\mu_0(X) + \Delta(X)P(X = x, Z = z) + E(U_0|X) - \mu_0(X) + \Delta(X)P(X = x, Z = z) - E(U_0|X)]}{P(X = x, Z = z) - P(X = x, Z = z')} \\
&= \Delta(x)
\end{aligned}$$

Thus it is not necessary to assume that $E(U_0 \mid X) = 0$.

[88]We define *ATE* conditional on X as
$$E(Y_1 - Y_0|X = x) = \mu_1(X) - \mu_0(X) + E(U_1 - U_0|X = x).$$

based in part on the gain in the outcome measure (Y_1, Y_0) (e.g., the difference in earnings) and this is a nondegenerate random variable, then (IV-1) is violated and IV does not identify ATE. The validity of the estimator is conditional on an untestable behavioral assumption. Similar remarks apply to $LATE$ as developed by Imbens and Angrist (1994) and popularized by Angrist, Imbens, and Rubin (1996); see Heckman and Vytlacil (1999, 2000, 2005), and Vytlacil (2002) for more discussion of the implicit behavioral assumptions underlying $LATE$.

The more interesting case for many problems arises when $U_1 \neq U_0$ and D $(U_1 - U_0)$ so agents participate in a program based at least in part on factors not measured by the economist. To identify $ATE(X)$ using IV, it is required that

$$E(U_0 + D(U_1 - U_0)|P(X,Z), X) = E(U_0 + D(U_1 - U_0)|X) \quad \text{(IV-3)}$$

and condition (IV-2) (Heckman and Robb 1985, 1986; Heckman 1997). To identify $TT(X)$ using IV, it is required that

$$E(U_0 + D(U_1 - U_0) - E(U_0 + D(U_1 - U_0)|X)|P(X,Z), X)$$
$$= E(U_0 + D(U_1 - U_0) - E(U_0 + D(U_1 - U_0)|X)|X) \quad \text{(IV-4)}$$

and condition (IV-2). No simple conditions exist to identify the MTE using linear instrumental variables methods in the general case where D $(U_1 - U_0)|X, Z$. Heckman and Vytlacil (2001, 2005, 2006a,b) characterize what conventional IV estimates in terms of a weighted average of MTEs.

The conditions required to identify ATE using P as an instrument may be written in the following alternative form:

$$E(U_0|P(X,Z), X) + E(U_1 - U_0|D = 1, P(X,Z), X)P(X,Z)$$
$$= E(U_0|X) + E(U_1 - U_0|D = 1, X)P(X,Z).$$

If $U_1 = U_0$ (everyone with the same X responds to treatment in the same way) or $(U_1 - U_0) \perp\!\!\!\perp D|P(X,Z), X$ (people do not participate in treatment on the basis of unobserved gains), then these conditions are the standard instrumental variable conditions. In general, the conditions are not satisfied by economic choice models, except under special cancellations. If Z is a determinant of choices, and $U_1 - U_0$ is in the agent's choice set (or is only partly correlated with information in the agent's choice set), then this condition is not satisfied generically.

These identification conditions are fundamentally different from the conditions required to justify matching and control function methods. In matching, the essential condition for means (conditioning on X and $P(X, Z)$) is

$$E(U_0|X, D = 0, P(X,Z)) = E(U_0|X, P(X,Z))$$

and

$$E(U_1|X, D = 1, P(X,Z)) = E(U_1|X, P(X,Z)).$$

These conditions require that, conditional on $P(X, Z)$ and X, U_1, and U_0 are mean independent of U_V (or D). If (C-1) is invoked, $\mu_1(W)$ and $\mu_0(W)$ are the conditional means of Y_1 and Y_0 respectively, the two preceding expressions are zero. However, as I have stressed repeatedly, (C-1) is not strictly required in matching.

The method of control functions models and estimates the dependence of U_0 and U_1 on D rather than assuming that it vanishes like the method of matching. The method of linear instrumental variables requires that the composite error term $U_0 + D(U_1 - U_0)$ be mean independent of Z (or $P(X, Z)$), given X. Essentially, these conditions require that the dependence of U_0 and $D(U_1 - U_0)$ on Z vanish through conditioning on X. Matching requires that U_1 and U_0 are independent of D given (X, Z). These conditions are logically distinct. One set of conditions does not imply the other set (Heckman and Vytlacil 2006a,b). They are justified by different *a priori* assumptions. Hence the provisional nature of causal knowledge.

Assuming finite means, local instrumental variables methods developed by Heckman and Vytlacil (1999, 2001, 2005) estimate all three treatment parameters in the general case where $(U_1 - U_0) \not\perp D|(X, Z)$ under the following additional conditions

$\mu_D(Z)$ is a non-degenerate random variable given X (LIV-1)
         (exclusion restriction)

$$(U_0, U_1, U_V) \perp\!\!\!\perp Z|X \qquad \text{(LIV-2)}$$

$$0 < \Pr(D = 1|X) < 1 \qquad \text{(LIV-3)}$$

$$Supp\ P(D = 1|X, Z) = [0, 1]. \qquad \text{(LIV-4)}$$

Under these conditions

$$\frac{\partial E(Y|X, P(X, Z))}{\partial(P(X, Z))} = MTE(X, P(X, Z), V = 0).^{89}$$

Only (LIV-1)–(LIV-3) are required to identify this parameter locally. (LIV-4) is required to use the MTE to identify the standard treatment parameters.

As demonstrated by Heckman and Vytlacil (1999, 2000, 2005) and Heckman (2001), over the support of (X, Z), MTE can be used to construct (under LIV-4) or bound (in the case of partial support of $P(Z)$) ATE and TT. Policy-relevant treatment effects can be defined.

---

[89]Proof: From the law of iterated expectations,

$$
\begin{aligned}
E(Y|X, P(Z)) = {}& E(Y_1|D = 1, X, P(Z))P(Z) \\
& + E(Y_0|D = 0, X, P(Z))(1 - P(Z)) \\
= {}& \int_{-\infty}^{\infty} \int_{-P(Z)}^{\infty} y_1 f(y_1, U_V^*|X) dU_V^* dy_1 \\
& + \int_{-\infty}^{\infty} \int_{-\infty}^{-P(Z)} y_0 f(y_0, U_V^*|X) dU_V^* dy_0
\end{aligned}
$$

where $U_V^* = F_V(U_V)$. Thus

$$
\begin{aligned}
\frac{\partial E(Y|X, P(Z))}{\partial P(Z)} = {}& E(Y_1 - Y_0|X, U_V^* = -P(Z)) \\
= {}& MTE
\end{aligned}
$$

LATE is a special case of this method.[90] The *LIV* approach unifies matching, control functions, and classical instrumental variables under a common set of assumptions. Table 4 summarizes the alternative assumptions used in matching, control functions, and instrumental variables to identify treatment parameters identify conditional (on *X* or *X, Z*).

4.4.4. *Directed Acyclic Graphs and the Method of* g-*Computation*

Directed acyclic graphs (DAG) (Pearl 2000) or the *g*-computation algorithm (Robins 1989) have recently been advocated as mechanisms for causal discovery. These methods improve on the method of matching by making explicit *some* of the sources of the unobservables generating the outcomes and postulating their relationships to observables. My discussion is more brief and considers only one population-level causal effect. It is based on Freedman (2001).

Figure 2, patterned after Freedman (2001), shows the essence of the method. An unobserved confounder *A* is a determinant of outcome *F* and variable *B*.[91] We observe (*B*, *C*, *F*). Unobservables are denoted by '*U*'. Each of (*B*, *C*, *F*) is assumed to be a random variable produced in part from the variable preceding it in the triangle and from unobservables that are assumed to be mutually independent (hence the pattern of the arrows in Figure 2). Assume for simplicity that *A*, *B*, *C*, *F* are discrete random variables. Figure 2 describes a recursive model where $A = (U_A)$, *C* and U_F determine *F*; *B* and U_C determine *C* and U_B and $A = (U_A)$ determine *B*.

We seek to determine

$$\Pr(F = f | \text{set } B = b)$$

free of the unmeasured cofounder *A*, which affects both *B* and *F*. This is the probability of getting *F* when we set *B* = *b*. ("Set" is Pearl's (2000) "do" operation or Haavelmo's (1943) "fixing of the variables.") But there is confounding due to *A*. $A = U_A$ affects both *B* and *F*, so there may be no true causal *B* − *F* relationship. How can one control for *A*?

---

[90]Vytlacil (2002) establishes that *LATE* is a semiparametric version of a control function estimator.

[91]The symbols used in this subsection are not the same as those used in the previous sections of this paper.

82 HECKMAN

TABLE 4
Identifying Assumptions and Implicit Economic Assumptions Underlying the Four Methods Discussed in this Paper
Conditional on X and Z

Method	Exclusion Required?	Separability of Observables and Unobservables in Outcome Equations?	Functional Forms Required?	Marginal = Average? (Given X, Z)	Key Identification Condition for Means (assuming separability)
Matching*	No	No	No	Yes	$E(U_1\|X, D = 1, Z) = E(U_1\|X, Z)$ $E(U_0\|X, D = 0, Z) = E(U_0\|X, Z)$
Control Function**	Yes (for nonparametric identification)	Conventional, but not required	Conventional, but not required	No	$E(U_0\|X, D = 0, Z)$ and $E(U_1\|X, D = 1, Z)$ can be varied independently of $\mu_0(X)$ and $\mu_1(X)$, respectively and intercepts can be identified through limit arguments or symmetry assumptions
IV (conventional)	Yes	Yes	No	No (Yes in standard case)	$E(U_0 + D(U_1 - U_0)\|X, Z)$ $= E(U_0 + D(U_1 - U_0)\|X)$ (ATE) $E(U_0 + D(U_1 - U_0) - E(U_0 + D(U_1 - U_0)\|X)P(Z), X)$ $= E(U_0 + D(U_1 - U_0) - E(U_0 + D(U_1 - U_0)\|X)\|X)$ (TT)
LIV	Yes	No	No	No	$(U_0, U_1, U_v) \perp Z\|X$ $\Pr(D = 1\|Z, X)$ is a nontrivial function of Z for each X.

*For propensity score matching, (X, Z) are replaced with $P(X, Z)$ in defining parameters and conditioning sets.
**Conditions for writing the control function in terms of $P(X, Z)$ are given in the text.

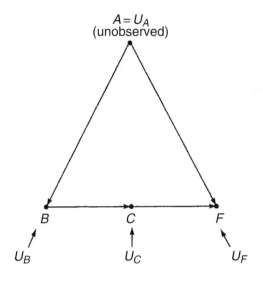

We know

$$\Pr(C=c \mid B=b)$$

$$\Pr(F=f \mid C=c) = \sum_a \Pr(F=f \mid A=a, C=c)\Pr(A=a)$$

and

$$\Pr(F=f \mid B=b) = \sum_c \Pr(F=f \mid C=c)\Pr(C=c \mid B=b)$$

FIGURE 2. DAG analysis. Adapted from Freedman (2001).

The *g*-computation algorithm operates by computing the following probabilities based on observables. From the data, we can compute $\Pr(C = c|B = b)$. We can also compute the left-hand side of

$$\Pr(F = f|C = c) = \sum_a \Pr(F = f|A = a, C = c)\Pr(A = a).$$

Hence we can identify the desired causal object using the following calculation:

$$\Pr(F = f|\text{set } B = b) = \sum_c \Pr(F = f|C = c)\Pr(C = c|B = b).$$

The ingredients on the right-hand side can be calculated from the available data (recall that A is not observed).

This very useful result breaks down entirely if we add an arrow like that shown in Figure 3, because in this case A also confounds C. The role of the *a priori* theory is to specify the arrows. No purely empirical algorithm can find causal effects in general models, a point emphasized by Freedman (2001). Figure 4 shows another case where the g-computation approach breaks down in nonrecursive simultaneous equations models. $F - C$ and $U_F - U_C$ interdependence create further problems ruled out in the DAG approach. These examples all illustrate the provisional nature of causal inference and the role of theory in justifying the estimators of causal effects.

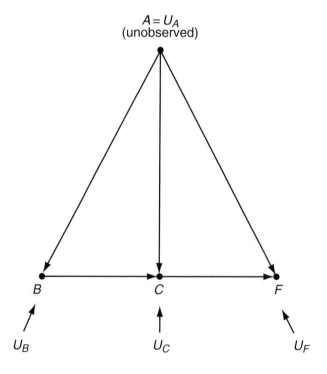

FIGURE 3. If another arrow is added to Figure 2, the argument breaks down. Where do arrows come from?

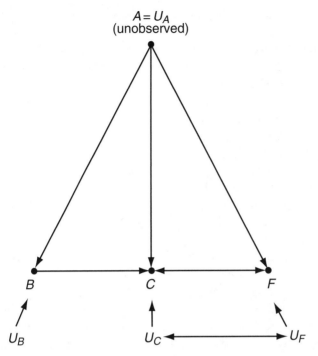

FIGURE 4. Nonrecursive. Argument breaks down. DAG is one estimation
scheme for one hypothetical model, not a general algorithm for
causal discovery.

5. SUMMARY AND CONCLUSIONS

This paper defines counterfactual models, causal parameters, and structural models and relates the parameters of the treatment effect literature to the parameters of structural econometrics and scientific causal
models. I distinguish counterfactuals from scientific causal models.
Counterfactuals are an ingredient of causal models. Scientific causal
models also specify a mechanism for selecting counterfactuals. I present
precise definitions of causal effects within structural models that are
inclusive of the specification of a mechanism (a formal model) by which
causal variables are externally manipulated (i.e., outcomes are selected).
Models of causality advocated in statistics are incomplete because they
do not specify the mechanisms of external variation that are central to
the definition of causality, nor do they specify the sources of randomness producing outcomes and the relationship between outcomes and

selection mechanisms. By not determining the causes of effects, or modeling the relationship between potential outcomes and assignment to treatment, statistical models of causality cannot be used to provide valid answers to the numerous counterfactual questions required for policy analysis. They do not exploit relationships among potential outcomes, assignment to treatment, and the variables causing potential outcomes that can be used to devise econometric evaluation estimators. The statistical approach does not model the choice of treatment mechanism and its relationship with outcome equations, whereas the scientific approach makes the choice of treatment equation a centerpiece of identification analysis. The statistical model does not apply to nonrecursive settings, whereas the econometric model can be readily adapted to handle both recursive and nonrecursive cases.

Statistical treatment effects are typically proposed to answer a more limited set of questions than are addressed by structural equation models and it is not surprising that they can do so under weaker conditions than are required to identify structural equations. At the same time, if treatment effects are used structurally—that is, to forecast the effect of a program on new populations or to forecast the effects of new programs—stronger assumptions are required of the sort used in standard structural econometrics (see Heckman 2001; Heckman and Vytlacil 2005, 2006b).

Table 5 compares scientific models with statistical "causal" models. Statistical causal models, in their current state, are not fully articulated models. Crucial assumptions about sources of randomness are kept implicit. The assumptions required to project treatment parameters to different populations are not specified. The scientific approach has no substitute for making out-of-sample predictions—that is, for answering policy questions P2 and P3. The scientific approach distinguishes derivation of a model as an abstract theoretical activity from the problem of identifying models from data.

APPENDIX: THE VALUE OF STRUCTURAL EQUATIONS IN MAKING POLICY FORECASTS

Structural equations are useful for three different purposes. First, the derivatives of such functions or finite changes generate the

TABLE 5
Econometric Versus Statistical Causal Models

	Statistical Causal Models	Econometric Models
Sources of randomness	Implicit	Explicit
Models of conditional counterfactuals	Implicit	Explicit
Mechanism of intervention for defining counterfactuals	Hypothetical randomization	Many mechanisms of hypothetical interventions including randomization; mechanism is explicitly modeled
Treatment of interdependence	Recursive	Recursive or simultaneous systems
Social/market interactions	Ignored	Modeled in general equilibrium frameworks
Projections to different populations?	Does not project	Projects
Parametric?	Nonparametric	Becoming nonparametric
Range of questions answered	One focused treatment effect	In principle, answers many possible questions

comparative statics *ceteris paribus* variations produced by scientific theory. For example, tests of economic theory and measurements of economic parameters (price elasticities, measurements of consumer surplus, etc.) are often based on structural equations.

Second, structural equations can be used to forecast the effects of policies evaluated in one population in other populations, provided that the parameters are invariant across populations and that support conditions are satisfied. However, a purely nonparametric structural equation determined on one support cannot be extrapolated to other populations with different supports.

Third, as emphasized by Marschak (1953), Marshallian causal functions and structural equations are one ingredient required to forecast the effect of a new policy, never previously implemented.

The problem of forecasting the effects of a policy evaluated on one population but applied to another population can be formulated in the following way. Let $Y(\omega) = \varphi(X(\omega), U(\omega))$, where $\varphi : \mathcal{D} \rightarrow \mathcal{Y}, \mathcal{D} \subseteq \mathbb{R}^J, \mathcal{Y} \subseteq \mathbb{R}$. φ is a structural equation determining outcome Y, and we assume that it is known only over $Supp(X(\omega), U(\omega)) = \mathcal{X} \times \mathcal{U}$. $X(\omega)$ and $U(\omega)$ are random input variables. The mean outcome conditional on $X(\omega) = x$ is

$$E_H(Y|X = x) = \int_{\mathcal{U}} \varphi(X = x, u) dF_H(u|X = x),$$

where $F_H(u|X)$ is the distribution of U in the historical data. We seek to forecast the outcome in a target population that may have a different support. The average outcome in the target population (T) is

$$E_T(Y|X = x) = \int_{\mathcal{U}^T} \varphi(X = x, u) dF_T(u|X = x)$$

where $\mathcal{U}^T$ is the support of U in the target population. Provided the support of (X, U) is the same in the source and the target populations, from knowledge of F_T it is possible to produce a correct value of $E_T(Y|X = x)$ on the target population. Otherwise, it is possible to evaluate this expectation only over the intersection set $Supp_T(X) \cap Supp_H(X)$, where $Supp_A(X)$ is the support of X in the A population. In order to extrapolate over the whole set $Supp_T(X)$, it is necessary to adopt some form of parametric or functional structure. Additive separability in φ simplifies the extrapolation problem. If φ is additively separable

$$Y = \varphi(X) + U,$$

$\varphi(X)$ applies to all populations for which we can condition on X. However, some structure may have to be imposed to extrapolate from $Supp_H(X)$ to $Supp_T(X)$ if $\varphi(X)$ on T is not determined nonparametrically from H.

The problem of forecasting the effect of a new policy, never previously experienced, is similar in character to the policy forecasting problem just discussed. It shares many elements in common with the problem of forecasting the demand for a new good, never previously consumed.[92] Without imposing some structure on this problem, it is impossible to solve. The literature in structural econometrics associated with the work of the Cowles Commission adopts the following five-step approach to this problem.

1. Structural functions are determined (e.g., $\varphi(X)$).
2. The new policy is characterized by an invertible mapping from observed random variables to the characteristics associated with the policy: $C = q(X)$, where c is the set of characteristics associated with the policy and q, $q: \mathbb{R}^J \to \mathbb{R}^J$, is a *known* invertible mapping.
3. $X = q^{-1}(C)$ is solved to associate characteristics that in principle can be observed with the policy. This places the characteristics of the new policy on the same footing as those of the old.
4. It is assumed that, in the historical data, $Supp(q^{-1}(C) \subseteq Supp(X))$. This ensures that the support of the new characteristics mapped into X space is contained in the support of X. If this condition is not met, some functional structure must be used to forecast the effects of the new policy, to extend it beyond the support of the source population.
5. The forecast effect of the policy on Y is $Y(C) = \varphi(q^{-1}(C))$.

---

[92]Quandt and Baumol (1966), Lancaster (1971), Gorman (1980), McFadden (1974), and Domencich and McFadden (1975) consider the problem of forecasting the demand for a new good. Marschak (1953) is the classic reference for evaluating the effect of a new policy; see Heckman (2001).

The leading example of this approach is Lancaster's method for estimating the demand for a new good (Lancaster 1971). New goods are viewed as bundles of old characteristics. McFadden's conditional logit scheme (1974) is based on a similar idea.[93]

Marschak's analysis of the effect of a new commodity tax is another example. Let $P(\omega)$ be the random variable denoting the price facing consumer ω. The tax changes the product price from $P(\omega)$ to $P(\omega)(1 + t)$, where t is the tax. With sufficient price variation so that the assumption in step 4 is satisfied so that the support of the price after tax, $Supp_{\text{post tax}}(P(\omega)(1 + t)) \subseteq Supp_{\text{pretax}}(P(\omega))$, it is possible to use reduced form demand functions fit on a pretax sample to forecast the effect of a tax never previously put in place. Marschak uses a linear structural equation to solve the problem of limited support. From linearity, determination of the structural equations over a small region determines it everywhere.

Marshallian or structural causal functions are an essential ingredient in constructing such forecasts because they explicitly model the relationship between U and X. The treatment effect approach does not explicitly model this relationship so that treatment parameters cannot be extrapolated in this fashion, unless the dependence of potential outcomes on U and X is specified, and the required support conditions are satisfied. The Rubin (1978)–Holland (1986) model does not specify the required relationships.

REFERENCES

Aakvik, A., J. J. Heckman, and E. J. Vytlacil. 1999. "Training Effects on Employment When the Training Effects are Heterogeneous: An Application

---

[93]McFadden's stochastic specification is different from Lancaster's specification. See Heckman and Snyder (1997) for a comparison of these two approaches. Lancaster assumes that the $U(\omega)$ are the same for each consumer in all choice settings. (They are preference parameters in his setting.) McFadden allows for $U(\omega)$ to be different for the same consumer across different choice settings but assumes that the $U(\omega)$ in each choice setting are draws from a common distribution that can be determined from the demand for old goods.

to Norwegian Vocational Rehabilitation Programs." University of Bergen Working Paper 0599.

———. 2005. "Estimating Treatment Effects for Discrete Outcomes When Responses to Treatment Vary: An Application to Norwegian Vocational Rehabilitation Programs." *Journal of Econometrics* 125(1–2):15–51.

Abadie, A. 2003. "Semiparametric Differences-in-Differences Estimators." Department of Economics, Harvard University, Unpublished manuscript.

Abadie, A., J. D. Angrist, and G. Imbens. 2002. "Instrumental Variables Estimates of the Effect of Subsidized Training on the Quantiles of Trainee Earnings." *Econometrica* 70(1):91–117.

Abbring, J. H., and G. J. Van Den Berg. 2003. "The Nonparametric Identification of Treatment Effects in Duration Models." *Econometrica* 71(5):1491–517.

Andrews, D. W., and M. M. Schafgans. 1998. "Semiparametric Estimation of the Intercept of a Sample Selection Model." *Review of Economic Studies* 65(3):497–517.

Angrist, J. D. 1991. "The Draft Lottery and Voluntary Enlistment in the Vietnam Era." *Journal of the American Statistical Association* 86(415):584–95.

Angrist, J. D., G. W. Imbens, and D. Rubin. 1996. "Identification of Causal Effects Using Instrumental Variables." *Journal of the American Statistical Association* 91:444–55.

Björklund, A., and R. Moffitt. 1987. "The Estimation of Wage Gains and Welfare Gains in Self-selection." *Review of Economics and Statistics* 69(1):42–49.

Boadway, R. W., and N. Bruce. 1984. *Welfare Economics*. New York: Blackwell Publishers.

Brock, W. A., and S. N. Durlauf 2001. "Interactions-based models." Pp. 3463–68 in *Handbook of Econometrics*, Vol. 5, edited by J. J. Heckman and E. Leamer. New York: North-Holland.

Cameron, S. V., and J. J. Heckman. 1998. "Life Cycle Schooling and Dynamic Selection Bias: Models and Evidence for Five Cohorts of American Males." *Journal of Political Economy* 106(2):262–333.

Campbell, D. T., and J. C. Stanley. 1963. *Experimental and Quasi-experimental Designs for Research*. Chicago: Rand McNally.

Carneiro, P. 2002. "Heterogeneity in the Returns to Schooling: Implications for Policy Evaluation." Ph. D. dissertation, University of Chicago.

Carneiro, P., K. Hansen, and J. J. Heckman. 2001. "Removing the Veil of Ignorance in Assessing the Distributional Impacts of Social Policies." *Swedish Economic Policy Review* 8(2):273–301.

———. 2003. "Estimating Distributions of Treatment Effects with an Application to the Returns to Schooling and Measurement of the Effects of Uncertainty on College Choice." 2001 Lawrence R. Klein Lecture. *International Economic Review* 44(2):361–422.

Carneiro, P., J. J. Heckman, and E. J. Vytlacil. 2005. "Understanding What Instrumental Variables Estimate: Estimating Marginal and Average Returns to Education." Department of Economics, University of Chicago. Unpublished manuscript.

Chen, S. 1999. "Distribution-free Estimation of the Random Coefficient Dummy Endogenous Variable Model." *Journal of Econometrics* 91(1):171–99.

Cox, D. 1958. *Planning of Experiments*. New York: Wiley.

———. 1992. "Causality: Some Statistical Aspects." *Journal of the Royal Statistical Society*, Series A, 155:291–301.

Cox, D., and N. Wermuth. 1996. *Multivariate Dependencies: Models, Analysis and Interpretation*. New York: Chapman and Hall.

Cunha, F., J. Heckman, and S. Navarro. 2005a. "Counterfactual Analysis of Inequality and Social Mobility." In *Income Inequality*, edited by M. Gretzky. Palo Alto: Stanford University Press. Forthcoming.

———. 2005b. "Separating Heterogeneity from Uncertainty in Modeling Schooling Choices." *Oxford Economic Papers* 57(2):191–261.

Dawid, A. 2000. "Causal Inference Without Counterfactuals." *Journal of the American Statistical Association* 95(450):407–24.

Domencich, T., and D. L. McFadden. 1975. *Urban Travel Demand: A Behavioral Analysis*. Amsterdam: North-Holland.

Fisher, R. A. 1966. *The Design of Experiments*. New York: Hafner.

Florens, J.-P., and J. J. Heckman. 2003. "Causality and Econometrics." Department of Economics, University of Chicago. Unpublished working paper.

Foster, J. E., and A. K. Sen. 1998. *On Economic Inequality*. New York: Oxford University Press.

Freedman, D. 2001. "On Specifying Graphical Models for Causation and the Identification Problem." Department of Statistics, University of California at Berkeley. Unpublished manuscript.

Gill, R. D., and J. M. Robins. 2001. "Causal Inference for Complex Longitudinal Data: The Continuous Case." *Annals of Statistics* 29(6):1785–1811.

Gorman, W. M. 1980. "A Possible Procedure for Analysing Quality Differentials in the Egg Market." *Review of Economic Studies* 47(5):843–56.

Haavelmo, T. 1943. "The Statistical Implications of a System of Simultaneous Equations." *Econometrica* 11(1):1–12.

———. 1944. "The Probability Approach in Econometrics." *Econometrica* 12(suppl.):iii–vi; 1–115.

Hahn, J. 1998. "On the Role of the Propensity Score in Efficient Semiparametric Estimation of Average Treatment Effects." *Econometrica* 66(2):315–31.

Harsanyi, J. C. 1955. "Cardinal Welfare, Individualistic Ethics and Interpersonal Comparisons of Utility." *Journal of Political Economy* 63(4):309–21.

———. 1975. "Can the Maximin Principle Serve as a Basis for Morality? A Critique of John Rawls's Theory." *American Political Science Review* 69(2):594–606.

Heckman, J. J. 1976. "Simultaneous Equation Models with Both Continuous and Discrete Endogenous Variables with and Without Structural Shift in the Equations." Pp. 235–72 in *Studies in Nonlinear Estimation*, edited by S. Goldfeld and R. Quandt. Cambridge, MA: Ballinger.

———. 1978. "Dummy Endogenous Variables in a Simultaneous Equation System." *Econometrica* 46(4):931–59.

————. 1980. "Sample Selection Bias as a Specification Error with an Application to the Estimation of Labor Supply Functions." Pp. 206–48 in *Female Labor Supply: Theory and Estimation*, edited by J. P. Smith. Princeton, NJ: Princeton University Press.

————. 1990. "Varieties of Selection Bias." *American Economic Review* 80(2), 313–18.

————. 1992. "Randomization and Social Policy Evaluation." Pp. 201–30 in *Evaluating Welfare and Training Programs*, edited by C. Manski and I. Garfinkel. Cambridge, MA: Harvard University Press.

————. 1997. "Instrumental Variables: A Study of Implicit Behavioral Assumptions Used in Making Program Evaluations." *Journal of Human Resources* 32(3):441–62.

————. 2000. "Causal Parameters and Policy Analysis in Economics: A Twentieth Century Retrospective." *Quarterly Journal of Economics* 115(1):45–97.

————. 2001. "Micro Data, Heterogeneity, and the Evaluation of Public Policy: Nobel Lecture." *Journal of Political Economy* 109(4):673–748.

————. 2006. *Evaluating Economic Policy*. Princeton, NJ: Princeton University Press.

Heckman, J. J., and B. E. Honoré. 1990. "The Empirical Content of the Roy Model." *Econometrica* 58(5):1121–49.

Heckman, J. J., and V. J. Hotz. 1989. "Choosing Among Alternative Nonexperimental Methods for Estimating the Impact of Social Programs: The Case of Manpower Training." *Journal of the American Statistical Association* 84(408):862–74.

Heckman, J. J., H. Ichimura, J. Smith, and P. E. Todd. 1998. "Characterizing Selection Bias Using Experimental Data." *Econometrica* 66(5):1017–98.

Heckman, J. J., H. Ichimura, and P. E. Todd. 1997. "Matching as an Econometric Evaluation Estimator: Evidence from Evaluating a Job Training Programme." *Review of Economic Studies* 64(4):605–54.

————. 1998. "Matching as an Econometric Evaluation Estimator." *Review of Economic Studies* 65(223):261–94.

Heckman, J. J., R. J. LaLonde, and J. A. Smith. 1999. "The Economics and Econometrics of Active Labor Market Programs." Pp. 1865–2097 in *Handbook of Labor Economics*, Vol. 3A, edited by O. Ashenfelter and D. Card. New York: North-Holland.

Heckman, J. J., and T. E. MaCurdy. 1985. "A Simultaneous Equations Linear Probability Model." *Canadian Journal of Economics* 18(1):28–37.

Heckman, J. J., and S. Navarro. 2004. "Using Matching, Instrumental Variables, and Control Functions to Estimate Economic Choice Models." *Review of Economics and Statistics* 86(1):30–57.

————. 2006. "Dynamic Discrete Choice and Dynamic Treatment Effects." *Journal of Econometrics*. Forthcoming.

Heckman, J. J., and R. Robb. 1985. "Alternative Methods for Evaluating the Impact of Interventions." Pp. 156–245 in *Longitudinal Analysis of Labor*

Market Data, Vol. 10, edited by J. Heckman and B. Singer. New York: Cambridge University Press.

————. 1986. "Alternative Methods for Solving the Problem of Selection Bias in Evaluating the Impact of Treatments on Outcomes." Pp. 63–107 in *Drawing Inferences from Self-Selected Samples*, edited by H. Wainer. New York: Springer-Verlag.

Heckman, J. J., and J. A. Smith. 1998. "Evaluating the Welfare State." Pp. 241–318 in *Econometrics and Economic Theory in the Twentieth Century: The Ragnar Frisch Centennial Symposium*, edited by S. Strom. New York: Cambridge University Press.

Heckman, J. J., J. Smith, and N. Clements. 1997. "Making the Most Out of Programme Evaluations and Social Experiments: Accounting for Heterogeneity in Programme Impacts." *Review of Economic Studies* 64(221):487–536.

Heckman, J. J., and J. M. Snyder Jr. 1997. "Linear Probability Models of the Demand for Attributes with an Empirical Application to Estimating the Preferences of Legislators" (Special issue). *RAND Journal of Economics* 28:S142.

Heckman, J. J., J. L. Tobias, and E. J. Vytlacil. 2001. "Four Parameters of Interest in the Evaluation of Social Programs." *Southern Economic Journal* 68(2):210–23.

————. 2003. "Simple Estimators for Treatment Parameters in a Latent Variable Framework." *Review of Economics and Statistics* 85(3):748–54.

Heckman, J. J., and E. J. Vytlacil. 1999. "Local Instrumental Variables and Latent Variable Models for Identifying and Bounding Treatment Effects." *Proceedings of the National Academy of Sciences* 96:4730–34.

————. 2000. "The Relationship Between Treatment Parameters Within a Latent Variable Framework." *Economics Letters* 66(1):33–39.

————. 2001. "Local Instrumental Variables." Pp. 1–46 in *Nonlinear Statistical Modeling: Proceedings of the Thirteenth International Symposium in Economic Theory and Econometrics: Essays in Honor of Takeshi Amemiya*, edited by C. Hsiao, K. Morimue, and J. L. Powell. New York: Cambridge University Press.

————. 2005. "Structural Equations, Treatment Effects and Econometric Policy Evaluation." *Econometrica* 73(3):669–738.

————. 2006a. "Econometric Evaluation of Social Programs," "Part I: Causal Models, Structural Models and Econometric Policy Evaluation." In J. Heckman and E. Leamer (Eds.), *Handbook of Econometrics, Volume 6.* Amsterdam: Elsevier, forthcoming.

————. 2006b. "Econometric Evaluation of Social Programs," "Part II: Using Economic Choice Theory and the Marginal Treatment Effect to Organize Alternative Econometric Estimators." In J. Heckman and E. Leamer (Eds.), *Handbook of Econometrics, Volume 6.* Amsterdam: Elsevier, forthcoming.

Holland, P. W. 1986. "Statistics and Causal Inference." *Journal of the American Statistical Association* 81(396):945–60.

————. 1988. "Causal Inference, Path Analysis, and Recursive Structural Equation Models." Pp. 449–84 in *Sociological Methodology*, Vol. 18, edited by C. Clogg and G. Arminger. Washington, DC: American Sociological Association.

Hurwicz, L. 1962. "On the Structural Form of Interdependent Systems." Pp. 232–39 in *Logic, Methodology and Philosophy of Science*, edited by E. Nagel, P. Suppes, and A. Tarski. Stanford, CA: Stanford University Press.

Imbens, G. W., and J. D. Angrist. 1994. "Identification and Estimation of Local Average Treatment Effects." *Econometrica* 62(2):467–75.

Katz, D., A. Gutek, R. Kahn, and E. Barton. 1975. *Bureaucratic Encounters: A Pilot Study in the Evaluation of Government Services*. Ann Arbor: Survey Research Center, Institute for Social Research, University of Michigan.

Knight, F. 1921. *Risk, Uncertainty and Profit*. New York: Houghton Mifflin.

Lancaster, K. J. 1971. *Consumer Demand: A New Approach*. New York: Columbia University Press.

Leamer, E. E. 1985. "Vector Autoregressions for Causal Inference?" *Carnegie-Rochester Conference Series on Public Policy* 22:255–303.

Lechner, M. 2004. "Sequential Matching Estimation of Dynamic Causal Models." Technical Report 2004, IZA Institute for the Study of Labor Discussion Paper.

Lewis, H. G. 1974. "Comments on Selectivity Biases in Wage Comparisons." *Journal of Political Economy* 82(6):1145–55.

Lucas, R. E., and T. J. Sargent. 1981. *Rational Expectations and Econometric Practice*. Minneapolis: University of Minnesota Press.

Marschak, J. 1953. "Economic Measurements for Policy and Prediction." Pp. 1–26 in *Studies in Econometric Method*, edited by W. Hood and T. Koopmans. New York: Wiley.

Marshall, A. 1890. *Principles of Economics*. New York: Macmillan.

Matzkin, R. 2003. "Nonparametric Estimation of Nonadditive Random Functions." *Econometrica* 71(5):1339–75.

————. 2004. "Unobserved Instruments." Department of Economics, Northwestern University, Evanston, IL. Unpublished manuscript.

————. 2006. "Nonparametric Identification." In *Handbook of Econometrics*, Vol. 6, edited by J. Heckman and E. Leamer. Amsterdam: Elsevier.

McFadden, D. 1974. "Conditional Logit Analysis of Qualitative Choice Behavior." In *Frontiers in Econometrics*, edited by P. Zarembka. New York: Academic Press.

————. 1981. "Econometric Models of Probabilistic Choice." In *Structural Analysis of Discrete Data with Econometric Applications*, edited by C. Manski and D. McFadden. Cambridge, MA: MIT Press.

Mill, J. S. 1848. *Principles of Political Economy with Some of Their Applications to Social Philosophy*. London: J. W. Parker.

Moulin, H. 1983. *The Strategy of Social Choice*. New York: North-Holland.

Neyman, J. 1923. "Statistical Problems in Agricultural Experiments." *Journal of the Royal Statistical Society* Series B (suppl.) (2):107–80.

Pearl, J. 2000. *Causality*. Cambridge, England: Cambridge University Press.

Powell, J. L. 1994. "Estimation of Semiparametric Models." Pp. 2443–521 in *Handbook of Econometrics*, Vol. 4, edited by R. Engle and D. McFadden. Amsterdam: Elsevier.

Quandt, R. E. 1958. "The Estimation of the Parameters of a Linear Regression System Obeying Two Separate Regimes." *Journal of the American Statistical Association* 53(284):873–80.

———. 1972. "A New Approach to Estimating Switching Regressions." *Journal of the American Statistical Association* 67(338):306–10.

———. 1974. "A Comparison of Methods for Testing Nonnested Hypotheses." *Review of Economics and Statistics* 56(1):92–99.

Quandt, R. E., and W. Baumol. 1966. "The Demand for Abstract Transport Modes: Theory and Measurement." *Journal of Regional Science* 6:13–26.

Rawls, J. 1971. *A Theory of Justice*. Cambridge, MA: Belknap.

Robins, J. M. 1989. "The Analysis of Randomized and Non-randomized AIDS Treatment Trials Using a New Approach to Causal Inference in Longitudinal Studies." Pp. 113–59 in *Health Services Research Methodology: A Focus on AIDS*, edited by L. Sechrest, H. Freeman, and A. Mulley. Rockville, MD: U.S. Department of Health and Human Services, National Center for Health Services Research and Health Care Technology Assessment.

———. (1997). "Causal Inference from Complex Longitudinal Data." Pp. 69–117 in *Latent Variable Modeling and Applications to Causality. Lecture Notes in Statistics*, edited by M. Berkane. New York: Springer-Verlag.

Rosenbaum, P. R. 1987. "Model-Based Direct Adjustment." *Journal of the American Statistical Association* 82(398):387–94.

———. 1995. *Observational Studies*. New York: Springer-Verlag.

Rosenbaum, P. R., and D. B. Rubin. 1983. "The Central Role of the Propensity Score in Observational Studies for Causal Effects." *Biometrika* 70(1):41–55.

Roy, A. 1951. "Some Thoughts on the Distribution of Earnings." *Oxford Economic Papers* 3(2):135–46.

Rubin, D. B. 1978. "Bayesian Inference for Causal Effects: The Role of Randomization." *Annals of Statistics* 6(1):34–58.

———. 1986. "Statistics and Casual Inference: Comment: Which Ifs Have Casual Answers." *Journal of the American Statistical Association* 81(396):961–62.

Rubin, D. B., and N. Thomas. 1992. "Characterizing the Effect of Matching Using Linear Propensity Score Methods with Normal Distributions." *Biometrika* 79(4):797–809.

Ruud, P. A. 2000. *An Introduction to Classical Econometric Theory*. New York: Oxford University Press.

Sen, A. K. 1999. "The Possibility of Social Choice." *American Economic Review* 89(3):349–78.

Sims, C. A. 1977. "Exogeneity and Casual Orderings in Macroeconomic Models." Pp. 23–43 in *New Methods in Business Cycle Research*. Minneapolis, MN: Federal Reserve Bank of Minneapolis.

Tamer, E. 2003. "Incomplete Simultaneous Discrete Response Model with Multiple Equilibria." *Review of Economic Studies* 70(1):147–65.

Thurstone, L. 1930. *The Fundamentals of Statistics*. New York: Macmillan.

Tukey, J. 1986. "Comments on Alternative Methods for Solving the Problem of Selection Bias in Evaluating the Impact of Treatments on Outcomes." Pp. 108–10 in *Drawing Inferences from Self-Selected Samples*, edited by H. Wainer. New York: Springer-Verlag.

Vickrey, W. 1945. "Measuring Marginal Utility by Reactions to Risk." *Econometrica* 13(4):319–33.

———. 1960. "Utility, Strategy, and Social Decision Rules." *Quarterly Journal of Economics* 74(4):507–35.

Vijverberg, W. P. M. 1993. "Measuring the Unidentified Parameter of the Extended Roy Model of Selectivity." *Journal of Econometrics* 57(1–3):69–89.

Vytlacil, E. J. 2002. "Independence, Monotonicity, and Latent Index Models: An Equivalence Result." *Econometrica* 70(1):331–41.

Wainer, H. (Ed.) 1986. *Drawing Inferences from Self-Selected Samples*. New York: Springer-Verlag (Reprinted in 2000, Mahwah, NJ: Lawrence Erlbaum Associates).

DISCUSSION: 'THE SCIENTIFIC MODEL OF CAUSALITY'

Michael E. Sobel*

1. INTRODUCTION

Heckman advocates an approach to causal inference that draws upon structural modeling of the outcome(s) of interest (which he calls scientific), and he contrasts this approach sharply with that arising out of the statistical literature on experimentation. Drawing extensively on several previous papers—for example, Heckman (1997, 2000, 2001) and Heckman and Navarro-Lozano (2004)—Heckman goes even further here, arguing that the statistical literature on causal inference is incomplete because it does not attempt to model the process by which subjects are selected into treatments (or what statisticians have called the "treatment assignment mechanism") and that this literature confounds the task of defining parameters with the tasks of identifying and estimating these parameters. I shall return to these points later.

But whereas Heckman distinguishes sharply between these approaches (and hence between certain literatures in economics and statistics), on balance I find the similarities in the approaches he discusses much more profound than the dissimilarities. To elaborate, while there has been and continues to be much philosophical

For financial support, I am grateful to the John D. and Catherine T. MacArthur Foundation. For helpful remarks, I am grateful to the members of the causal inference study group at Columbia University. Address all correspondence to Michael Sobel, 421 Fayerweather Hall, Columbia University, New York, NY, 10027 (or mes105@columbia.edu).

*Columbia University

disagreement about the nature of the causal relation, in both these literatures, there are strong similarities in the way that the word "cause" is used. In particular, a causal relation sustains a counterfactual conditional, while a noncausal relation need not do so. Second, causal effects are allowed to be heterogeneous across units, a point that both statisticians and Heckman have emphasized. Third, dovetailing with this shared perspective on the nature of the causal relation, the potential outcomes notation invented by Neyman (1923), widely used since by statisticians working on experimental design (see for example, the textbooks by Cox [1958] and Kempthorne [1952]), is now standard notation in both these literatures. This notation, adopted also by Heckman during the latter 1980s and since in a number of his papers (and here) nicely captures the idea that a causal relationship sustains a counterfactual conditional statement. To be sure, this idea can be represented in other ways (Robins and Greenland 2000), but the potential outcomes notation is very easy to work with and easy to use without leading oneself astray. The importance of good notation cannot be emphasized strongly enough. As Whitehead ([1911], 1958:39) pointed out, "By relieving the brain of all unnecessary work, a good notation sets it free to concentrate on more advanced problems, and in effect increases the power of the race." I would also propose that the use of a common notation encourages investigators to think similarly about a problem.

The incorporation of Neyman's notation into the modern literature on causal inference is due to Rubin (1974, 1977, 1978, 1980), who, using this notation, saw the applicability of the work from the statistical literature on experimental design to observational studies and gave explicit consideration to the key role of the treatment assignment mechanism in causal inference, thereby extending this work to observational studies. To be sure, previous workers in statistics and economics (and elsewhere) understood well in a less formal way the problems of making causal inferences in observational studies where respondents selected themselves into treatment groups, as evidenced, for example, by Cochran's work on matching and Heckman's work on sample selection bias. But Rubin's work was a critical breakthrough. The introduction of a suitable notation allowed in principle the clarification and formalization of the problem of making causal inferences with non-experimental data. Further, the use of this notation allowed the tasks of defining etimands to be separated from the tasks of identifying and estimating these. This separation enabled Rubin not only to pinpoint the key role of the treatment assignment mechanism but to state precise conditions under which this mechanism was "ignorable" or not. These conditions have been used by subsequent workers (including Heckman) to evaluate and clarify existing procedures for causal inference (for example, instrumental variables) and to develop new methods for estimating causal effects (for example, by creating matched samples using propensity scores).

And fourth, although Heckman criticizes the "treatment effects" literature for modeling the effects of causes, as opposed to modeling the causes of effects, the majority of his paper also focuses on modeling the effects of an intervention (cause) on an outcome of interest.

That said, some of the problems involved in making causal inferences about agents who are not (or cannot in practice be) subjected by an investigator to one or another treatment of interest will be somewhat different than those that typically arise when a treatment is applied or not to a plot of land in an agricultural experiment. In the latter case, where a randomized experiment can be conducted, the treatment assignment mechanism is essentially a (possibly biased) coin toss (or a coin toss within distinguishable types of plots). Causal inference is typically more straightforward in this case. However, in observational studies, individuals typically sort themselves into treatment groups and how they do so may also be of independent interest. Economists often argue that individuals make choices by behaving as if they are maximizing expected utility. When the utility associated with making particular choices is also related to the outcome under consideration, this may create problems when the agent uses more information than that available to the economist (or the economist simply does not know the treatment assignment mechanism). In this case, consideration of the available information may be inadequate for a "sufficient" description of the process by which agents allocate themselves to treatment groups. Here, the assignment mechanism cannot be treated as a coin toss (net of the available information). Thus, methods based on this premise are inadequate for this case. In other social and behavioral sciences, where notions of decision making may take on a different flavor, the above may or may not be problematic. In any event, the point is that even when the same notion of causation is under consideration, some variation by discipline in approaches to causal inference should be expected.

In addition, although assumptions are always present, investigators differ in the extent to which they are comfortable using these to make inferences. Heckman advocates herein what he has elsewhere (Heckman 2000) called a structural approach to estimating causal parameters. This model based approach can be very powerful and can be used as a basis for generating inferences that are sometimes much stronger and broader in scope than those typically made in the statistical literature Heckman criticizes. But the structural approach also typically features stronger assumptions. As Heckman (2000) documents, frustration with the seemingly arbitrary nature of the assumptions (for example, exclusion restrictions) used to identify structural models has led several generations of economists to eschew structural modeling in favor of other approaches, recently including experimentation (Heckman is quite critical of this "natural experiment movement;" for a nice treatment of the issues see Rosenzweig and Wolpin (2000)). As before, even when the same notion of causation is held, some differences in approaches to causal inference should be expected.

However, if one takes the view that statistical procedures should be tailored to address questions of interest to various constituencies (for example, different groups of scientists and policymakers), such differences should be regarded as both natural and desirable. Accordingly, I aim primarily to give a balanced overview of the issues.

To make my discussion as useful as possible for *Sociological Methodology* readers, I sometimes elaborate on material covered by Heckman in this or previous papers. Second (and primarily for the same reason), my remarks are organized around the following four themes in Heckman's paper: 1) the nature of the causal relation, 2) definitions of causal estimands, 3) policy evaluation and forecasting, and 4) the identification and estimation of causal effects. Although I do not find simultaneous equation models (and more generally, structural equation models) in their current form very useful for causal inference, I do not take up this subject here, in large measure because a thorough treatment would require substantially increasing the length of an already long discussion. For some previous and related discussions of causality in simultaneous equation models, the reader might also wish to consult Strotz and Wold (1960), Fisher (1970), and Sobel (1990).

To improve readability, in most instances, I include here the equations referred to, even if some of these already appear in Heckman's article. Whenever possible, I use notation similar or identical to Heckman's. In some instances, in order to retain consistency of style, minor deviations have been necessary.

2. THE CAUSAL RELATION

Heckman argues (page 2, this volume) that "Science is all about constructing models of the causes of effects" (vs. studying the effects of causes). He also argues that the notion of causality involves manipulating one or more variables and comparing the outcomes of these manipulations. Economists perform these (hypothetical) manipulations using models. And since models are mental constructs, Heckman concludes that causality resides in the mind. In addition, as different people think different thoughts and therefore construct different models, causes are "relative" (to use the language of Collingwood ([1940], 1972). That is, with equal legitimacy, different investigators may identify different factors as causes, while ignoring others. This is part of what Heckman refers to as the provisional nature of causal knowledge. The implications of this are further discussed in Sobel (1995), which readers may also wish to consult for more background on the causal relation.

Modeling the causes of effects is certainly an important scientific activity. But it should also be understood that many "scientific" questions are not causal. For example, NASA recently crashed a probe from the Deep Impact spacecraft into comet Tempel1 with the objective of learning more about the structure and composition of cometary nuclei. See Bunge (1979) for a discussion of the many kinds of noncausal questions that are of scientific interest. Further, studying the effects of causes is an important scientific activity: figuring out the causes of global warming would be considerably less important if the effects of global warming were inconsequential.

Next, the nature of the causal relation has consumed the attention of philosophers since well before Hume, without resolution. Regularity theories are one attempt to explicate the nature of causation. Here the cause (or causes of the effect) is (are) usually thought of as some set of necessary and/or sufficient antecedents for the effect. Regularity theories are both general and (typically) deterministic. In addition, contemporary regularity theories usually require that a causal statement sustain a counterfactual conditional. The foregoing ideas may be expressed mathematically using functions, as in an "all-causes" model:

$$y(s) = g_s(x, u), \tag{1}$$

where $y(s)$ is an outcome of interest depending on state s, g_s is a function of x, a vector of observables, and u, a vector of unobservables. By varying the components of g_s, effects of the arguments (which may be state specific) can be defined under suitable conditions. In other instances, attention focuses on the results of manipulating the states s, which might, for example, index a set of treatments that are to be applied.

The antecedents above are also held to have causal priority over the effect. Explicating the nature of this priority has proven to be a difficult task. Most philosophers hold to the view that there is more to causal priority than mere temporal order. Thus, some sequences are to be regarded as causal while others are not. Although manipulating a cause is one way to establish the priority of the cause over the effect, in many theories of causation, including regularity theories, manipulability is not regarded as essential.

On the other hand, manipulability theories of causation emphasize the ability of a human agent to manipulate a cause: "A cause is an event or state of things which it is in our power to produce or prevent, and by producing or preventing which we can produce or prevent that whose cause it is said to be" (Collingwood [1940], 1972: p. 296–97). Whereas regularity theories are theories about the causes of effects, manipulability theories are theories about the effects of causes. Such theories correspond more closely with the way an experimentalist thinks of causation. These theories are also readily combined with singular theories of the causal relation.

At first glance, it appears that manipulability theories are inherently at odds with regularity theories. Thus, it might be argued that the modern literatures on causal inference in both statistics and econometrics, because these literatures are typically concerned with the identification and estimation of the effect(s) of particular causes—for example, the effects of a policy intervention, as in Heckman's paper—are, from the scientific standpoint advocated by Heckman, misdirected. Importantly, this is not the case, and manipulability theories can be reconciled with regularity theories by noting that a manipulated cause is simply one component of (1) with u unknown (some components of u may be unknown and others simply not observed). To illustrate this point using (1), suppose the treatment variable s is 0 (no treatment) or 1 (treatment), $x \in \Omega_x$ and $u \in \Omega_u = \Omega_{0u} \cup \Omega_{1u}$, with $\Omega_{0u} \cap \Omega_{1u} = \emptyset$. Suppose that for $(x, u) \in \Omega_x \times \Omega_{0u}$, $g_0(x, u) = g_1(x, u) = 0$, while for $(x, u) \in \Omega_x \times \Omega_{1u}$, $g_0(x, u) = 0$, $g_1(x, u) = 1$. In a manipulability theory, the variable s is singled out for attention. If the investigator knows (s, x, u) and the functions g_s, the effect of s varies over x and u in a known (to the investigator) way. In practice, the investigator observes only s and x, in which case the effect of s (which the investigator may not be able to identify from data) varies over x in an apparently nondeterministic manner.

The relativity of causation (part of what Heckman calls the provisional nature of causal knowledge) is also easily illustrated. In (1) the treatment variable s may be singled out for attention and manipulated. The other arguments (x and u) remain in the causal background. A different investigator might identify one or more components of $x \equiv (x_1, x_2)$ as the cause and rewrite (1) as h_{x1} (x_2, u, s).

When the cause can be manipulated, each unit in a research study can receive any of the various levels of the cause (even though in practice a given unit is observed only at one level). In his presentation of what has come to be known in the statistical community as "Rubin's model for causal inference," Holland (1986), like Heckman, also emphasizes the importance of manipulating the cause, going so far as to coin the (unfortunate) phrase, "No causation without manipulation." Whereas Holland appears to insist on the actual ability of an investigator to manipulate the cause(s), many others, including Heckman, have argued that it is the idea of manipulating the cause, even if this can only be done hypothetically, that is key in defining causal relationships. If this point of view is taken (but not if not), Holland appears to be conflating the distinct problems of defining and identifying causal effects.

But perhaps the most controversial aspect of Heckman's brief treatment of causality is his claim that "causality is in the mind." This claim stems from (a) the fact that causal effects are defined as changes in outcomes when variables in a model are (hypothetically) manipulated and (b) the view that models are mental constructs made up by the scientist, "not empirical statements or descriptions of actual worlds" (page 3). While Heckman's conclusion is consistent with (a) and (b), and Heckman is certainly free to define causality in this fashion, I do not believe that most scientists (or philosophers) would subscribe to this view, and were they to do so, they would presumably have little further interest in causality (as science typically purports to be concerned with the real world).

In this vein, models (be they mathematical or of some other sort) are often constructed by scientists to represent causal processes (causal mechanisms) believed to be operating in the actual world (not just the mind). To be sure, the models have to be imagined and in this sense, our notion of the causal process(es) at play comes from the mind, but the processes (which we may or may not accurately model) are also believed to reside in the actual world. That is, the causal relation is typically held to describe a relation that is believed to exist in the real world.

3. DEFINING CAUSAL ESTIMANDS

In the statistical literature on causal inference, as in Heckman, assumptions (A-1) and (A-2) are typically made; Rubin (1980) has called this the stable unit treatment value assumption (SUTVA). When these assumptions are not made, the problem of defining causal estimands is more difficult, as is the problem of making inferences about these. In addition to Heckman, several others have worked on this problem (Halloran and Struchiner 1995; Sobel 2001, 2003). But this is fertile ground for social scientists, where interference due to social interactions and other constraints are the norm. Nevertheless, following Heckman, I shall hereafter assume SUTVA holds.

With (A-1) and (A-2) in hand, the response of unit ω to level s of the cause may be written as $Y_s(\omega)$; for the purposes at hand, assume that each unit can take on every level of the cause. Individual (unit) causal effects are then defined as an intra-unit, between-treatment comparison $h(Y_s(\omega), Y_{s'}(\omega))$. Because each study unit can actually be observed only under one treatment, it is not possible to observe unit causal effects. Holland (1986) refers to this fact as "the fundamental problem of causal inference."

Heckman focuses attention on three estimands in this paper, the average causal effect (ACE), the effect of treatment on the treated (TT), and the marginal treatment effect (MTE). Although the MTE can be useful for understanding other estimators, I do not discuss it further herein, as I believe sociologists will usually be more interested in the other two estimands. The local average treatment effect (LATE) will be discussed subsequently.

Let S denote a set of treatments of interest. The average causal effect of treatment s versus s' (ACE(s, s')) is defined as

$$E(Y_s - Y_{s'}), \tag{2}$$

in which $h(Y_s(\omega), Y_{s'}(\omega)) = (Y_s(\omega) - Y_{s'}(\omega))$. The ACE can also be defined conditionally on covariates W; as in Heckman, this is denoted ACE($s, s' \mid W$), and when it is obvious which treatments are being compared (as in the case where there is just one treatment compared to no treatment) simply ACE(W), or ACE in the case where there are no covariates. Since, following Heckman, $Y_s(\omega)$ is defined as the outcome of unit ω when treatment s is received, herein the ACE is the average difference when all units receive treatment s as versus s'. It is also (by virtue of assumptions (A-1) and (A-2)), the effect of receiving treatment s versus s' for a randomly selected person from the population.

The average effect of treatment s versus s' on the treated (TT(s, s')) is another parameter of longstanding interest:

$$E((Y_s - Y_{s'})|D = s), \tag{3}$$

where D is the random variable denoting which treatment in S is actually received. Thus, TT(s, s') is the average effect of treatment s versus s' for those units that actually take up treatment s.

To round out the discussion, I also want to consider a parameter that has received a great deal of attention from biostatisticians and the public health community, the so called "intent to treat" estimand (ITT(s, s')). For all $s \in S$, we define $\tilde{Y}_s(\omega)$ as the outcome of unit ω when assigned to treatment s. (The treatment to which a subject is assigned may differ from the treatment received because subjects will not always take up the treatment to which they are assigned; thus $\tilde{Y}_s(\omega) \neq Y_s(\omega)$ in general.) ITT(s, s') is then defined by (2) with $\tilde{Y}_s$ and $\tilde{Y}_{s'}$ replacing Y_s and $Y_{s'}$, respectively. Note that in the case where all subjects would take up their assignments, for any possible assignment, $\tilde{Y}_s(\omega) = Y_s(\omega)$ and ITT(s, s') = ACE(s, s').

There has been some controversy over which of the parameters above are of greatest interest. I take the view that it all depends on the problem at hand, the goals of the scientist(s) analyzing the data and the purposes of the person(s) making policy on the basis of the analysis. Some examples where one or more of the parameters above are of interest follow.

For policies with universal coverage and universal participation, the ACE is the obvious parameter of interest. For example, consider the effect of a specific currency devaluation (s = 0 if no devaluation, 1 otherwise) on household spending. Here $\tilde{Y}_s(\omega) = Y_s(\omega)$ for all ω, implying ACE = ITT. If the devaluation is implemented, ACE = TT as well (as every unit takes up the treatment).

For policies with universal coverage that do not require participation, some units may not take up the treatment. Because nonparticipating units will not obtain the benefits of participation, it might be argued that knowing the average effect of treatment for these units is irrelevant, suggesting TT is the parameter of interest. However, the untreated might take up treatment in the future if they believed the treatment were effective (for them). Thus, we might wish to also know the TUT (effect of treatment on the untreated). Alternatively, policymakers might want to know the effect for the nonparticipating units, for if this is deemed substantial, they will then want to make efforts to obtain the participation of such units. They will then also want to know the ACE, which is a weighted average of the TT and the effect of treatment on the untreated (TUT).

But some might argue instead that the effect that should be of interest is the effect of offering the program. For example, consider the case of a new contraceptive method. Whereas some scientists may be more interested in the ACE (or possibly the TT), which measures more directly the clinical effectiveness of the contraceptive, policymakers considering whether or not to widely distribute the contraceptive in a developing country are more concerned with the cost and the efficacy of the contraceptive in the field (where some people do not follow instructions). Consequently, they are more interested in the ITT.

Finally, it is worth noting that if receipt of treatment is independent of the potential outcomes, given a set of known covariates W (including the case of no covariates), TT(W) = TUT(W) = ACE(W).

Heckman also discusses a number of outcome measures that may be of interest to social scientists and economists but which are not discussed in the statistical literature he criticizes, where the outcomes $Y_s(\omega)$ are typically straightforward measures of the status of a unit—for example, the income of a family under treatment s or the survival time of a subject after surgery. In particular, Heckman considers outcomes $V(Y_s(\omega))$ where V is some function of the outcome—for example, the utility of $Y_s(\omega)$ to individual ω (or to a policymaker) under policy s. He then uses these to define various parameters comparing the benefit (welfare) associated with alternative policies. Although mathematically nothing new is involved here, this is useful, especially because it is possible that $E(V(Y_s) - V(Y_{s'})) \leq 0$ when (2) > 0, for example. Thus, if V were to measure a social planner's utility, the planner would not wish to choose policy s over s' even though the average causal effect is greater than 0. Choosing a policy is often not this simple, however; for some interesting recent work that applies decision theory to the problem of treatment choice, see Manski (2000, 2004).

The estimands above are differences between means. Because the integral is a linear operator, these estimands only require knowledge of the marginal distributions $F(y_s)$ and $F(y_{s'})$ of potential outcomes. Under some circumstances (discussed later), these distributions can be identified.

Heckman also discusses a number of other estimands $h(Y_s, Y'_s)$ of substantive interest that depend on the joint distribution $F(y_s, y'_s)$ of $(Y_s, Y_{s'})$. However, the fundamental problem of causal inference precludes the simultaneous observation of $Y_s(\omega)$ and $Y'_s(\omega)$, implying that it is not possible to know more than the marginal distributions. And while knowledge of the marginal distributions imposes some constraints on the joint distribution, these constraints often do not allow much useful information on the joint to be extracted (for example, if the marginals are normal with known means and variances, this is consistent with non-normal joint distributions, as well as a bivariate normal with any correlation between -1 and 1). Thus, much stronger assumptions will be required to point identify and estimate parameters depending on the joint distribution of potential outcomes than parameters depending only on the marginal distribution of the potential outcomes (for an example of this, see Carneiro, Hansen and Heckman 2003). Since the data impose few constraints (as discussed above) and the joint distribution of potential outcomes is not even an explicit auxiliary consideration in any substantive theory I can think of, the possibility that mathematical assumptions made primarily for the sake of convenience or tractability may be in large measure generating the "empirical" results seems especially strong here; sensitivity analyses should be a must.

4. POLICY EVALUATION AND FORECASTING

Drawing upon themes exposited at greater length in Heckman (2000, 2001) and several subsequent papers, Heckman emphasizes the value of the "scientific approach" (as exemplified by structural models) for policy evaluation and forecasting. He distinguishes three problems: (1) evaluating policies that have been implemented, (2) extrapolation of these to new environments, and (3) forecasting the effects of policies that have not been implemented to new environments. Heckman uses a structural equation model of the form $\phi(X(\omega), U(\omega))$ to examine this problem, writing the expectation of the observed outcome Y in the historical population, conditional on X as

$$E_H(Y|X = x) = \int_{\mathcal{U}} \phi(x, u) dF_H(u|x), \qquad (4)$$

where $F_H(u \mid x)$ is the conditional distribution of U given $X = x$ in the historical population. For problem 2, we want to know $E_T(Y \mid X = x)$. It is clear from equation (4) that this problem is easily solved if the distribution $F_T(u \mid X = x)$ is known in the new environment (target), assuming also the invariance of ϕ and the condition that the support of (X, U) in the target population is contained in the support of (X, U) in the historical population. Of course, the assumptions and information needed to solve this problem are very strong. The third problem can be dealt with in a similar fashion (see the appendix to Heckman's paper), although it is more complicated.

As Heckman points out, the statistical literature on causal inference has focused on estimating the impact of policies in a given environment and problems 2 and 3 have not received much explicit attention. But certainly problem 2 is easy to address within the usual "treatment effect" framework and perhaps this is why it has not been addressed explicitly; problem 3 I discuss momentarily.

I now proceed to discuss problem 2 within a "treatment effects" framework for several reasons. First, I want the reader to understand that the "treatment effects" framework and the "scientific" framework, despite apparent differences, often yield very similar answers to real questions. In particular, that must be the case when we see that the answers actually rest on similar assumptions, once these are exposited. Second, in comparing Heckman's structural approach with the alternative I exposit below, I believe that some researchers who might need to address this problem in their future substantive work may find it easier to think about this problem from the "treatment effects" perspective.

For the sake of concreteness, consider the problem of extrapolating the historical ACE $E_H(Y_1 - Y_0)$ to a new population T. The obvious thing to do is to think of a set of covariates Z such that the historical and target ACEs are identical, and to average the historical ACE over the marginal distribution of Z in the target population.

More formally (assuming Y_1 and Y_0 are real valued scalars), the conditional ACE in the target population is

$$E_T((Y_1 - Y_0)|Z = z) = \int_R y_1 dF_T(y_1|z) - \int_R y_0 dF_T(y_0|z). \quad (5)$$

Knowledge of the target distributions $F_T(y_0 \mid z)$ and $F_T(y_1 \mid z)$ is sufficient to determine the value of equation (5); of course, the problem is that target distributions are unknown and it might be very difficult to specify them. The simplest thing is to assume the historical and target distributions are the same (where these are both defined) $F_H(y_s \mid z) = F_T(y_s \mid z)$ for $s = 0, 1$. Alternatively, in this case, we might just as well assume the weaker condition $E_T((Y_1 - Y_0) \mid Z = z) = E_H((Y_1 - Y_0) \mid Z = z)$. Either of these is an invariance assumption and should not be lightly made. But this characterization of the problem seems to be one that is intuitively easy to understand, and this should allow an investigator to think reasonably about the necessary components of Z. Continuing, the target ACE is then $E_T(Y_1 - Y_0) = \int_R(E_H((Y_1 - Y_0) \mid z)dF_T(z)$. Of course, to average the integrand over the target distribution, it must be defined for all values (up to a set of probability measure 0) that Z takes on in the target population. This will be the case, for example, when the supports of (Y_s, Z) in the target population are contained in the supports of (Y_s, Z) in the historical population.

Now suppose Y_s is, as in Heckman, the invariant (over the historical and target population) structural equation; $Y_s = \phi_s(Z, U_s)$ for $s = 0, 1$, then

$$E_T(Y_s \mid Z = z) = \int_R \phi_s(z, u_s)dF_T(u_s \mid z). \tag{6}$$

Analogous to the case above, if the target distributions $F_T(u_0 \mid z)$ and $F_T(u_1 \mid z)$ are known, the value of (6) is known. If these are assumed to be identical to their historical counterparts, this implies $F_H(y_s \mid z) = F_T(y_s \mid z)$ for $s = 0, 1$; if some other assumption is made, this cannot be the case. Note also that $F_H(y_s \mid z) = F_T(y_s \mid z)$ for $s = 0, 1$ does not imply invariance of the structural equation model nor the conditional distributions of U_s. As before, the ACE is obtained by averaging over the marginal distribution of Z in the target population.

As for the second point, I at least find it easier to think about the distributions $F_T(y_s \mid z)$ (or the conditional ACE) than to think about invariant structural equations and the conditional distributions of the unobservables. (Of course, this does not invalidate a structural approach.)

Heckman is also very critical of the "treatment effects literature" for its failure to deal with problem P3, and he briefly (see some of Heckman's more recent work with Vytlacil for a more detailed treatment) considers this problem here, suggesting that treatments be viewed as a bundle of characteristics. The relationship between these characteristics (as versus just the treatments themselves) and the response (possibly with covariates) can then be modeled, and the relationship transported to the new environment, as per problem P2.

This idea is obvious (although its implementation can be difficult), which makes one wonder why statisticians have not addressed this topic. In that regard, several points are in order.

First, for more than 75 years, statisticians and applied workers have been using factorial experiments in conjunction with Fisher's analysis of variance (and more generally, response surface methodology) to both identify and estimate the effects of the factors (characteristics) comprising the treatment on the response, and to extrapolate these to conditions not actually experienced. A simple example is a partial factorial design, where higher order interactions are assumed to be 0, allowing extrapolation to combinations of the components not actually observed.

The solution above to problem P3 will be inadequate when the effects of the factors vary by covariates whose distributions are different in the historical and target population. In this case, it would be necessary to estimate the effects conditionally and then average over the distribution of these in the target population, as above. Conceptually, this is straightforward. Practically, the problem is to know what covariates to use and the relationship between the effects of the factors and the covariates. In the simplest case, where the investigator really does know what covariates to use and the covariates take on only a few levels, it may not be necessary to introduce (possibly arbitrary) modeling assumptions about the relationship between the effects of the factors and the covariates to make headway. But when there are many covariates and/or several continuous covariates, such assumptions become necessary.

There are two matters that make for additional complexity and the need for yet more assumptions. In observational studies, treatment assignment may not be ignorable. If it is ignorable, given known covariates, one can (in theory) proceed as above. If not, other avenues must be considered to achieve identification of parameters of interest.

Finally and perhaps critically, in contrast to the case in the experimental design literature, in most observational studies and social experiments, the number of characteristics an investigator would like to consider may far exceed the number of treatment groups. This will make for identification problems and point identification may end up resting on a number of assumptions that are difficult to substantively justify. For example, consider the case of an observational study where it is reasonable to assume treatment assignment is ignorable (without covariates) and the average effects do not depend on covariates whose distributions differ in the historical and target populations. In this case, transporting the relationship between the response and its components to the new environment is simple, once the relationship is determined. Suppose now there are 5 components, each having 2 values (i.e., there are 32 combinations of component values); to identify all the effects in the most general case, 32 treatment groups are needed. Even if many of the higher order interactions disappear, identification problems will remain if there are few treatment groups, as in the usual case. This may be the primary reason that the "treatment effects" literature has not explicitly unbundled the components of interventions and attempted to address problem P3 in its full generality. That said, it is unfortunate that social experiments are not usually designed to facilitate understanding the relationship between the components and the effect.

5. IDENTIFYING AND ESTIMATING CAUSAL EFFECTS

5.1. *Background*

Since the invention of randomization (generally attributed to Fisher [1925]), statisticians have emphasized the importance of study design for the estimation of causal effects. In a completely randomized experiment—assuming random sampling from the population of interest and (A-1) and (A-2)—the outcomes of subjects assigned to receive treatment s are a random sample from the distribution of $\tilde{Y}_s$; thus, this distribution can be consistently estimated from the data collected in the experiment.

Consequently, as previously noted, comparisons of potential outcomes that only require knowledge of the marginal distribution of outcomes can be made in randomized experiments. For example, statisticians have tested whether or not the outcome under treatment s is stochastically higher than the outcome under treatment s'. Another example is the ITT. Letting s denote treatment and s' the control treatment, statisticians have long known that when data are collected using randomized experiments, the difference between the treatment group mean and the control group mean on the outcome is an unbiased estimate of the ITT.

Under complete randomization the set of potential outcomes

$$(\{\tilde{Y}_s\}_{s\in S})\underline{\|}A, \tag{7}$$

where A is the treatment assignment variable and the notation is used to denote statistical independence. (Note that A refers to the treatment assigned, which may not be the treatment actually received.) Letting $\tilde{Y}$ denote the observed response, under (7), $E(\tilde{Y} \mid A = s) = E(\tilde{Y}_s \mid A = s) = E(\tilde{Y}_s)$; thus, the observable conditional expectations identify the parameter ITT(s, s').

The completely randomized experiment is a special case of the conditionally randomized experiment in which subjects are first grouped according to a set W of pretreatment covariates, and a completely randomized experiment is then conducted within the groups. Under conditional randomization, treatment assignment is "ignorable" given the covariates W:

$$(\{\tilde{Y}_s\}_{s\in S})\underline{\|}A|W. \tag{8}$$

Consequently, ITT$(s, s' \mid W)$ is identified from the observable conditional expectations:

$$E(\tilde{Y}_s - \tilde{Y}_{s'}|W) = E(\tilde{Y}|A = s, W) - E(\tilde{Y}|A = s', W). \tag{9}$$

Rubin (1977, 1978) saw that the conditionally randomized study provides a means to bridge the gap between experimental and observational studies. In observational studies, it is often not reasonable to believe the ignorability assumption:

$$(\{Y_s\}_{s\in S})\underline{\|}D. \tag{10}$$

However, if covariates W can be found that determine the treatment receipt process (in the sense that given these covariates, receipt of treatment does not depend on the potential outcomes), treatment assignment is ignorable, given the covariates (Barnow, Cain and Goldberger 1980 dubbed this "selection on observables"):[1]

---

[1]Editor's Note: This sentence is misprinted. The latter part of this sentence should read as follows: "... treatment assignment is ignorable, given the covariates (Barnow, Cain and Goldberger 1980). Heckman dubbed this 'selection on observables'):" After this page was typeset and finalized, it was discovered that the character string "). Heckman" was inadvertently omitted.

$$(\{Y_s\}_{s\in S})\underline{\parallel}D)|W. \tag{11}$$

Under (11), the conditional means for treatments s and s' identify ACE(s, $s' \mid W$):

$$E(Y_s - Y_{s'}|W) = E(Y|D = s, W) - E(Y|D = s', W). \tag{12}$$

The intuition behind (11) is straightforward and readily lends itself to use by empirical investigators. Within levels of W, treatment receipt is decided (in the binary case) by the toss of a (possibly biased) coin. If the parameter (2) is of interest, as versus (12), this is obtained by averaging over the marginal distribution of W. If the average effect is the same for all values of W, it is not necessary to know the distribution of W. Otherwise, it must be possible to estimate this distribution from the data or the distribution must be known; in practice, it may be that neither of these conditions is attainable.

By way of contrast, despite a longstanding interest in making causal statements, until more recently economists were less interested in experimental data than statisticians. In part, this is due to the fact that economists are interested in many questions that are not particularly amenable to experimentation.

Economists have also long recognized that human agents make choices and they use theories of rational decision making to characterize the manner in which agents choose among alternatives. That is, economists attempt to carefully consider one set of mechanisms that individuals might use to allocate themselves to treatments (how agents choose D). Further, this allocation process is often of intrinsic interest to economists.

Heckman characterizes the statistical literature as incomplete, in part because statisticians do not model the allocation process. An example of this is adjusting for covariates using regression analysis, long advocated by statisticians. Here modeling the conditional expectation $E(Y \mid W, D)$ alone leads to an estimate of (12). If interest resides solely in estimating (12) when (11) holds, there is no need to model the allocation process. But even when (11) holds, especially in an observational study where W may be a large vector, statisticians will often advocate modeling the allocation process to reduce the dimensionality of the estimation problem, a subject to which I shall return.

Nevertheless, the focus in the statistical literature is primarily on obtaining the best possible estimate of the causal parameter of interest.

From this point of view, all else being equal, given the choice between a randomized experiment and an observational study where units select their own treatment, the experiment is typically preferred (especially when ITT is the parameter of interest and/or ACE is the parameter of interest and subjects comply with their assignments (that is, for all ω and for all $s \in S$, subject ω takes up assignment s when assigned to s).

In general, the way in which units are allocated in the experiment will not reflect the real-world allocation mechanism where human agents are making choices, as studied by economists. As such, the opportunity to learn about this mechanism (at least from the experimental study) is given up. This is the price we pay to ensure (7) or (8).

In the observational study, however, we cannot be certain that all relevant covariates have been taken into account. If (11) holds and the regression function is modeled correctly, we can learn about both the allocation process and the causal parameter(s) of interest. But if one or more covariates have not been taken into account and (11) is assumed, credible estimates of causal parameters may not be obtained. As Heckman points out, individuals making decisions may have relevant information that is not accessible to the investigator and therefore such information cannot be included in the investigator's model of the agent's choice. In economic models of behavior, agents use this "hidden" information in computing the expected utility of different choices. The agent then makes the choice that maximizes expected utility. Since it is not unreasonable to suppose that utility is a monotone function of many of the types of outcomes (for example, earnings) studied by economists, in such circumstances (11) will in general not be satisfied for the set of pretreatment covariates accessible to the investigator, and (12) will then not hold. In this case, if (11) is (correctly) not assumed for a given set of available covariates W, credible estimates might be obtained using other methods—for example, fixed effects models (including differences in differences), control functions, instrumental variables. But if the assumptions underlying the use of these alternatives are incorrect in the application under consideration, then as before, credible estimates may not be obtained.

5.2. *Matching, Control Functions, and Instrumental Variables*

These are three approaches to estimating causal parameters. Interestingly, although the rationale and assumptions needed to justify these approaches differ, the propensity score (discussed below) figures prominently in all three.

In observational studies where it is believed that (11) holds, there still remains the problem of estimating $E(Y \mid W, D)$. When W is a high-dimensional vector and/or several components have many values, it may be difficult to specify the form of this function correctly, which can lead to faulty inferences. Matching will also be problematic in this case.

Let $S = \{0,1\}$. In a key paper, Rosenbaum and Rubin (1983) showed that when (11) holds and

$$0 < \Pr(D = 1 | W) < 1, \tag{13}$$

then

$$(\{Y_s\}_{s \in S}) \underline{\|} D) | P(W), \tag{14}$$

$$0 < \Pr(D = 1 | P(W)) < 1, \tag{15}$$

where $P(W) = \Pr(D = 1 \mid W)$ is the "so called" propensity score. Imbens (2000) generalizes the notion of a propensity score to the case of finitely many treatments. Imai and van Dyk (2004) extend the notion of a propensity score to the more general case where D may take on infinitely many values.

As a consequence of (15),

$$E(Y_1 - Y_0) | P(W)) = E(Y | D = 1, P(W)) - E(Y | D = 0, P(W)). \tag{16}$$

Equation (16) provides the mathematical justification for matching on the one-dimensional propensity score (as opposed to the multidimensional vector W, which may well be sparse), in which observations with the same values of $P(W)$—one with $D = 1$, the other with $D = 0$—are randomly paired, their difference providing an unbiased estimate of (16). An unbiased estimate of the parameter (2) can then be formed by taking the appropriate weighted average. Equation (16) can also be used to justify a related method called subclassification and to justify covariance adjustment using only D and $P(W)$ (as versus D and W). Other parameters (for example, TT) can also be estimated using these methods. At this point, there is a large statistical literature on matching and related methods. The interested reader might wish to consult Smith (1997) for a sociological application and Imbens (2004) for a nice overview of estimating average treatment effects under the assumption (11).

The beauty of matching is explained quite nicely by Heckman (page 65, this volume) and in Heckman and Navarro-Lozano (2004:33): matching "does not require separability of outcome or choice equations into observable and unobservable components, exogeneity of conditioning variables, exclusion restrictions or adoption of specific functional forms of outcome equations." Other methods of estimating causal effects, such as instrumental variables, fixed effects, and control functions, normally require one or more assumptions of the form above.

Nevertheless, Heckman is quite critical of matching on the propensity score. First, the method breaks down if $P(W) = 0$ or 1 for one or more values of W. In practice, even in less extreme cases, an investigator may encounter the case where the estimated $P(W)$ is close to, for example, 1 and there are no "good" matches from the control group. When such data are excluded, as is often the case, the causal parameter that is actually estimated (an average effect on a common support) may be of less interest. Second, when $P(W)$ is unknown (the typical case) and it is estimated nonparametrically, the dimensionality problem is simply transferred to this estimation problem.

Heckman also argues that it is often difficult to justify the use of (11) for some conditioning set W. According to him, this situation is exacerbated by the absence of an explicit model of treatment choice. Finally, he states that (11) is quite strong substantively, implying MTE(W) = ACE(W) = TT(W).

Of course, it can be argued that (14) may hold even if (11) does not. But it is difficult to think of substantive situations where we would want to argue that (14) holds and hence that (16) holds but (11) does not. We should note also that (12) may hold even if (11) does not hold, and that (16) can hold even if (14) does not. However, as above, it is difficult to think of instances where we would want to argue that one of the weaker conditions holds, but the stronger does not. Thus, I do not consider it worthwhile to further entertain arguments of this nature.

Heckman questions the value of assumption (11) in social contexts. He suggests that when agents have hunches about the values of the potential outcomes, and treatment choice is based on those hunches, assumption (11) will not hold. While often true, there may nevertheless be situations where an investigator knows and measures the covariates on which the agents' decisions are based, in which case (11) holds. See also Imbens (2004) for less trivial examples.

When investigators do not think carefully about the treatment assignment process in observational studies, they are likely to omit important covariates from consideration. That said, it is not the statistician's job to substantively justify a particular model of choice. Nor would it be correct to suggest that statisticians are ignorant of, or do not stress the importance of understanding the treatment assignment mechanism. Indeed, going back to Fisher (quoted in Cochran 1965) statisticians have long acknowledged the importance of having a good theory of the treatment assignment mechanism; see also Rosenbaum (2002, ch. 1), who pays a great deal of attention to this matter.) Rosenbaum and others (see Rosenbaum [2002] for further citations) have also studied the consequences due to the failure to adjust for relevant omitted covariates.

Nevertheless, even when an investigator pays very close attention to the treatment assignment mechanism, a covariate (set of covariates) known to be relevant may be missing from the data and/ or some relevant covariates are unknown to the investigator. This will be the case in some instances where treatment assignment is the result of an economic agent behaving rationally and in other instances where some other process describes the allocation to treatment groups. Unfortunately, assumption (11) is not directly testable, though it may be possible, by introducing auxiliary assumptions, to test this indirectly. Heckman's Tables 2 and 3 simply demonstrate what they should: if the assumptions underlying the use of matching are incorrect and the assumptions underlying Heckman's particular example of the use of control functions are correct, the observable parameters that also equal TT and ACE in the case where matching hold are now biased for TT and ACE. When it is suspected that (11) does not hold, an investigator can attempt to conduct sensitivity analyses (as statisticians have long advocated), construct bounds on the parameter(s) of interest—for example, Manski (1990) and Robins (1989)—or use some other approach—for example, fixed effects, instrumental variables, control functions—to estimate the causal parameter of interest.

Following Heckman, I now examine the method of control functions, expositing the additively separable case also considered by him. He assumes (his equations 22a–22c)

$$V = \mu_V(W) + U_V, \quad E(U_V|W) = 0, \tag{17}$$

$$Y_s = \mu_s(X) + U_s, \quad E(U_s|X = 0), \tag{18}$$

where $s = 0$ or 1 and $D = 1$ if and only if $V > 0$.

The observable conditional expectations ($Y = Y_1$ if $D = 1$, Y_0 if $D = 0$) are (using 18)

$$E(Y|X, Z, D = s) = \mu_s(X) + E(U_s|X, Z, D). \tag{19}$$

Under assumption (18), when (11) holds (with $(X, Z) = W$), $E(Y \mid X, Z, D = s) = E(Y_s \mid X, Z) = \mu_s(X)$. Note that the first equality follows from (11) and the second from the additional assumption (18); that is, the additional assumption (18) is not needed to justify matching on the propensity score. In the method of control functions, however, assumption (11) is not made and the components $E(U_s \mid X, Z, D = s)$ are modeled. Note that $E(U_1 \mid X, Z, D = 1) = E(U_1 \mid X, Z, V > 0) = E(U_1 \mid X, Z, U_V > -\mu_V(Z))$ by virtue of assumption (17); similarly, $E(U_0 \mid X, Z, D = 0) = E(U_0 \mid X, Z, V \leq 0)$. Thus, under (17) and (18), it might seem that the method of control functions is more general than matching. But modeling $E(U_s \mid X, Z, D = s)$ will require additional assumptions—for example, Heckman's assumption (C-1): $(U_1, U_0, U_V) \perp\!\!\!\perp (X, Z)$. Assumption (C-1) implies $(U_1, U_0 \perp\!\!\!\perp (X, Z) \mid U_V$, so that $E(U_s \mid X, Z, D = s)$ depends on X, Z only through the propensity score $P(X, Z)$. As in matching, a problem involving high dimensionality is now reduced to a one-dimensional problem through the use of the propensity score. It is worth noting that assumption [C-1] does not imply (11). Nor does (11) imply (C-1). Thus, even if (17) and (18) hold, it is not the case that "the control function approach is more general than the matching approach" (page 73, this volume). (Heckman points out that assumption (C-1) is not essential. Nevertheless, if this assumption is removed, others will have to be made.) The two approaches simply make different assumptions and will thus be useful in different circumstances.

One other point should be made. Heckman notes: "Without invoking parametric assumptions, the method of control functions requires an exclusion restriction (a variable in Z that is not in X) to achieve nonparametric identification." But he is far less critical of these assumptions (and others noted above) than he is of those required to justify matching and the use of instrumental variables. In that vein, Vella (1998, p. 131) points out the sensitivity to parametric assumptions of Heckman's original work: "As estimation relies heavily on the normality assumption, the estimates are inconsistent if normality fails." Vella (1998, p. 135) also notes that the exclusion restriction is "controversial" and he argues that many theoretical economic models of behavior, including the Roy model discussed by Heckman, explicitly impose $Z = X$.

Using instrumental variables is another way to estimate treatment effects in observational studies, and it makes assumptions that are different than those made in matching or the method of control functions. Social scientists have long used instrumental variables to estimate treatment effects when treatment choice is "endogenous." Traditionally, the technique is exposited as follows. Consider the regression

$$Y = \mu(X) + \tau D + \varepsilon, \tag{20}$$

where $D = 1$ if the treatment is received, 0 otherwise, τ is the desired treatment effect, and $E(\varepsilon \mid X) = 0$. The problem here is that D is correlated with ε, so in general $E(\varepsilon \mid X, D) \neq 0$ (equivalently, $E(Y \mid X, D) = \mu(X) + \tau D + E(\varepsilon \mid X, D)$). However, if a variable Z can be obtained that is associated with Y only through D, i.e., Z does not directly affect the outcome, $E(\varepsilon \mid X, Z) = E(\varepsilon \mid X) = 0$, in which case $E(Y \mid X, Z) = \mu(X) + \tau E(D \mid X, Z)$. Consequently (assuming $E(D \mid X, Z = 1) - E(D \mid X, Z = 0) \neq 0$),

$$\tau = \frac{E(Y|X, Z = 1) - E(Y|X, Z = 0)}{E(D|X, Z = 1) - E(D|X, Z = 0)}. \tag{21}$$

From a causal standpoint, the formulation above is quite vague. Heckman has helped to clarify the literature on instrumental variables. Angrist, Imbens, and Rubin (1996) is another paper that I find useful, and the approach taken there is somewhat different than Heckman's. Thus, I briefly exposit this approach and subsequently tie it to the exposition in Heckman; see also Vytlacil (2002).

I will focus on several parameters discussed by Heckman ($ACE(X)$), the local average treatment effect (hereafter $LATE(X)$), $TT(X)$, and I will also briefly discuss $ITT(X)$. Following Heckman, Z is the instrumental variable. It will also be taken to be binary, as in Angrist et al. (1996). (See Angrist and Imbens [1995] for some generalizations of the setup considered herein.) Let Z (previously denoted A) denote the treatment to which a subject is assigned (0 if assigned to the control group, 1 if assigned to the treatment group). Let $D(\omega)$ denote the observed choice of unit (ω) and let $D_z(\omega)$ denote the choice unit ω makes when assigned to treatment $z \in \{0, 1\}$. Similarly, let $Y_{(z,D_z)}(\omega)$ denote the response of unit ω when that unit is assigned to treatment z and chooses outcome $D_z(\omega)$. (Previously, $Y_{(z,D_z)}(\omega)$ was denoted $\tilde{Y}_z(\omega)$.) Let $Y_{zs}(\omega)$ denote the outcome of unit ω when that unit is assigned to treatment z and "takes up" treatment s, for $z = 0, 1$, $s = 0, 1$. Note that for each assignment, individuals take up only one treatment; nevertheless, as above, potential outcomes assuming they had taken up the treatment they did not take up can be defined.

To begin, it is useful to formalize the exclusion restriction— that is, the idea that the instrumental variable only affects the outcome by affecting D. This is the assumption (Holland 1988)

$$Y_{(0,s)}(\omega) = Y_{(1,s)}(\omega) \qquad (22)$$

for $s = 0, 1$ and all ω. Consequently, the potential outcomes may be written as $Y_s(\omega)$. The exclusion restriction is very strong, and it can be quite difficult to find instruments that satisfy this assumption.

The problem with estimating the effect of D (conditional on the covariates X) on the outcome is that (11) will not generally hold, because D is "endogenous"; thus, in general, $E(Y \mid D = s, X) \neq E(Y_s \mid X)$. However, if (8) holds (with Z in place of A), as would be the case in a randomized experiment,

$$E(Y|Z = 1, X) - E(Y|Z = 0, X) = E(Y_{1,D_1} - Y_{0,D_0}|X), \qquad (23)$$

that is, $ITT(X)$ is the numerator of the IV estimand (21). (Recall the previous discussion, which suggests that at least in some instances,

ITT(X) and/or *ITT* may be the parameter(s) of greatest interest to a policymaker.)

Continuing, *ITT(X)* may be broken down into the following four components:

$$E(Y_{1,D_1} - Y_{0,D_0}|X) = EE((Y_{1,D_1} - Y_{0,D_0})|D_0, D_1, X), \qquad (24)$$

where $(D_0, D_1) = (0, 0)$ or $(0, 1)$ or $(1, 0)$ or $(1, 1)$. By virtue of the exclusion restriction (22), units who always take up the treatment $(D_0(\omega) = D_1(\omega) = 1)$, hereafter called "always takers," or never take up the treatment $(D_0(\omega) = D_1(\omega) = 0)$, hereafter called "never takers," contribute nothing to (24). Angrist et al. (1996) call subjects with $D_1 = 1$, $D_0 = 0$ compliers and subjects with $D_1 = 0$, $D_0 = 1$ defiers; only these two types of units contribute to (24) under the exclusion restriction.

Angrist et al. (1996) also assume there are no defiers (the monotonicity assumption), in which case

$$ITT(X) = E((Y_{1,D_1} - Y_{0,D_0})|D_0=0, D_1=1, X)\Pr(D_0=0, D_1=1|X). \quad (25)$$

Dividing *ITT(X)* by the compliance probability (assuming this is greater than 0) gives the parameter *LATE(X)*, the average treatment effect for the compliers (at *X*). The compliance probability $\Pr(D_1 = 1, D_0 = 0 \mid X) > 0$ may also be written (under the assumptions here) as $E((D_1 - D_0) \mid X)$. But this is equal to $E(D \mid X, Z = 1) - E(D \mid X, Z = 0)$ when treatment assignment (*Z*) is ignorable, given *X*, as here. Thus, under the assumptions above, $LATE(X) = IV(X)$. Note also that the compliance probability may be written as $\Pr(D_1 = 1 \mid X) - \Pr(D_0 = 1 \mid X) = P(X, 1) - P(X, 0)$, which makes the connection with the propensity score evident.

The parameter *LATE(X)* (or *LATE* when there are no covariates *X*) will not always have policy implications of interest. To begin, the compliers constitute a latent subpopulation. So, even if we wanted to administer the treatment only to the compliers and it was politically feasible to do so, it is not possible to identify these individuals (in practice, we could model the probability of being a complier and administer the program to those deemed "most likely" to be compliers). Second, when the compliers are a "small" fraction of the population, it may be difficult to argue that the results are of great interest. For example, the question addressed by Angrist et al. (1996) is the excess civilian mortality (between 1974 and 1983) resulting from service in the Vietnam War (not the excess mortality among compliers). For men born in 1950, the compliers constitute only 15.9 percent of the population; technically, *LATE* only applies to this fraction of the population. In some applications, however, even if the compliers are a small fraction of the population, *LATE* (or *LATE(X)*) is nevertheless a parameter of great interest. This would be the case when it could be argued that the noncompliers, had they complied, would experience the same benefits as the compliers. I return to this subject momentarily. Third, Heckman (1997) has also pointed out that *LATE (LATE(X))* is an unusual parameter, insofar as its very definition depends on the instrumental variable chosen. Thus, in some cases, *LATE(X)* and/or *LATE* may identify a parameter with policy relevance (as when Z represents assignment under a particular policy of interest), and in other cases it may not. For further discussion of *LATE* and other possible parameters of interest, see the discussion following Angrist et al. (1996) and Heckman (1997).

Although the parameters *LATE* and *LATE(X)* may not always be of great substantive interest, the methodological point is that the meaning of the IV estimand has been clarified (which has great substantive implications). In particular, a basis is provided that makes it very easy to ask if *IV(X)* identifies other parameters of possibly greater interest, such as *TT(X)* and *ACE(X)*.

To see this, consider the parameter *TT(X)*, which conditions on receipt of treatment ($D = 1$). The units receiving treatment are the compliers in the treatment group and the always takers (still assuming there are no defiers). It follows from the foregoing results that *IV(X) $\neq$ TT(X)* in general, and that *IV(X) = TT(X)* if and only if the average effect of receiving treatment for the always takers (assuming the probability of being an always taker is greater than 0) and compliers is the same. Put this way, an analyst can ask whether the equality of treatment effects across these two groups is a reasonable assumption to make. If the analyst suspects, for example, that the always takers know that (even after conditioning on X) they will benefit by taking up the treatment (or have higher gains than others by so doing), he or she will not want to assume equality across groups and hence that *IV(X) = TT(X)*.

It is also easy to see that there is one important case where $IV(X)$ must equal $TT(X)$. If the treatment cannot be obtained in the control group, as in many social programs, it is not possible to be an always taker. In this case, $LATE(X) = TT(X)$ (without it being necessary to assume that the average effects of receiving treatment are the same for compliers and always takers), hence $IV(X) = TT(X)$.

Similarly, if the average effect of D on the response is the same for compliers, always takers, and never takers, $IV(X) = LATE(X) = TT(X) = ACE(X)$. If it is not possible to be an always taker, $LATE(X) = TT(X)$ (as above) and $LATE(X) = ACE(X)$ (hence $IV(X) = ACE(X)$) when it is assumed that the average effects of receiving treatment are identical for never takers and compliers. In cases where it is impossible to be a never taker (programs with universal coverage and participation), $LATE(X) = ACE(X)$ if it is assumed that the average effects of D on Y are identical for always takers and compliers.

In the case where the unit effects of D on Y are the same for all ω, the average effects of receiving treatment must be the same for all units, hence all groups, implying $IV = TT = ACE$. Of course, the assumption of constant effect is quite strong and not likely to be substantively reasonable in most social science applications.

Finally, if the probability of being a defier is nonzero, in general $IV(X) \neq LATE(X)$; but in the special case where the average effect of receiving treatment for compliers and defiers is the same, $IV(X) = LATE(X)$. Angrist et al. (1996) also discuss the consequences of violating the exclusion restriction, and there is some literature on estimating complier average causal effects in the absence of this restriction (for example, see, Jo [2002]).

Heckman approaches this subject somewhat differently. He imposes the additively separable model (18) on the potential outcomes. He then writes the observed outcome Y in terms of the potential outcomes as

$$Y = \mu_0(X) + (\mu_1(X) - \mu_0(X) + U_1 - U_0)D + U_0, \qquad (26)$$

expresses the parameters $TT(X)$ and $ACE(X)$ in terms of (26), and states identifiability conditions in terms of D, U_0, and U_1.

The assumption of a constant effect holds ($Y_1 - Y_0$ is the same for all units) if $U_0 = U_1 \equiv U$. In this case, the instrumental variable Z

needs to satisfy the condition $E(U \mid X, Z) = E(U \mid X) = 0$ (equivalently, under (18) $E(Y_s \mid X, Z) = E(Y_s \mid X)$ for $s = 0, 1$)). As above, a sufficient condition for this is $Y_s \| Z \mid X$ for $s = 0, 1$, and as above, assuming $P(X, 1) - P(X, 0) \neq 0$, $\overline{IV}(X) = LATE(X) = TT(X) = ACE(X)$.

When the constant effect assumption fails but $E(U_1 - U_0 \mid X, D = 1) = 0$, Heckman (1997) shows that $TT(X) = ACE(X)$. A sufficient condition for this is

$$(U_1 - U_0) \| D \mid X \tag{27}$$

(or more generally $(Y_1 - Y_0)D \mid X$). Though weaker than the condition (11), which was not presumed to hold, Heckman points out that the sufficient condition above is nevertheless quite strong, requiring that receipt of treatment not depend, given X, on gains anticipated by subjects. That is, in general, we should not expect $TT(X) = ACE(X)$. We can also see this from the results above, where it was established that if there are no defiers, and the average effect of D on the response is identical for compliers and always takers, $LATE(X) = TT(X) = ACE(X)$. Similarly, if there are defiers and the average effect of receiving treatment is identical for defiers and compliers, and for compliers and always takers, $LATE(X) = TT(X) = ACE(X)$.

Heckman also gives general conditions under which $IV(X) = TT(X)$ and $IV(X) = ACE(X)$. As in the simpler case above, and for the same reasons, Heckman argues that these conditions are quite strong. Again, this argument seems most compelling when the analyst does not have access to data that the decision maker is using to make his decision and this information is predictive of the potential outcomes. For further details, the reader may consult Heckman (1997) or his paper in this volume.

6. CONCLUSION

Heckman argues for the use of an approach to causal inference in which structural models play a central role. It is worth remembering that these models are often powerful in part because they make strong assumptions. When these assumptions are correct, powerful (and correct) inferences may be obtained. Such inferences are likely to be stronger than those that would be made by advocates of randomized experiments. For example, using a structural model in an observational study, we might learn about the treatment assignment mechanism and various average effects, and we might extrapolate the results to a new policy in a new environment. But when the assumptions are arbitrarily invoked in applications or require the use of knowledge that the investigator does not have, as seems often the case, so are the inferences derived from such modeling exercises. Thus, an investigator might well prefer to stick with simple estimators from randomized experiments, whenever possible. In such a case (presuming the experiment did not get botched and subjects complied with experimental protocols), the investigator can have greater confidence in his or her estimates of parameters such as ITT and ACE, for example.

But I do not want to argue that structural modeling is not useful, nor do I want to suggest that methodologists should bear complete responsibility for the use of the tools they have fashioned. To my mind, both structural modeling and approaches that feature weaker assumptions have their place, and in some circumstances, one will be more appropriate than the other. Which approach is more reasonable in a particular case will often depend on the feasibility of conducting a randomized study, what we can actually say about the reasonableness of invoking various assumptions, as well as the question facing the investigator (which might be dictated by a third party, such as a policymaker). An investigator's tastes and preferences may also come into play. A cautious and risk-averse investigator may care primarily about being right, even if this limits the conclusions he or she draws, whereas another investigator who wants (or is required) to address a bigger question may have (or need to have) a greater tolerance for uncertainty about the validity of his or her conclusions.

In his introductory section, Heckman claims to make two major points: (1) that "causality is a property of a model of hypotheticals" (page 2), and (2) that statisticians have conflated the distinct tasks of defining parameters of interest, identification, and estimation. I have already discussed the first point. I conclude with a discussion of the second. With respect to this point, Heckman writes (page 5): "This emphasis on randomization or its surrogates (like matching) rules out a variety of alternative channels of identification of counterfactuals from population or sample data. It has practical consequences because of the conflation of step one with steps two and three in Table 1. Since randomization is used to define the parameters of interest, this practice sometimes leads to the confusion that randomization is the only way—or at least the best way—to identify causal parameters from real data."

Heckman appears to be arguing here that statisticians are putting the cart before the horse by focusing interest on average causal effects that do not depend on the joint distribution of potential outcomes and emphasizing identification conditions in observational studies that parallel random assignment, thus justifying estimation methods such as matching and even randomization itself. While it is impossible to assess such a claim, it is worth noting that average causal effects such as the ACE and ITT have been of great interest in public health, for example, for many years. These parameters can and have been used to address policy questions that are of great interest. Recall also that both the potential outcomes notation and the ACE (Neyman 1923) preceded randomization.

Of course, Heckman is certainly correct to note that there are interesting estimands that depend on the joint distribution and that here, randomization is of considerably less help. In addition, as he and many others have pointed out, when it is impossible for the investigator to obtain a sufficiently rich set of covariates to condition on, other methods of identifying, and estimating causal effects (including the usual effects that do not depend on joint distributions of potential outcomes) must be used.

But Heckman goes much further, arguing that statisticians have confounded the tasks of defining, identifying, and estimating causal parameters and, as above, even use randomization to define parameters of interest. By and large (except for some minor quibbles one might have about the way some authors have defined $LATE$), I would argue the opposite. One of the key contributions that statisticians have made is to unconfound these issues, paving the way for (1) the assessment of conditions under which valid causal inferences are permitted and (2) the development of appropriate methods for making valid causal inferences.

Consider the claim that randomization is used to define causal parameters of interest. In the introduction, I stressed the importance of good notation. By using the potential outcomes notation, statisticians (recall Neyman 1923 and later Rubin) were able to define causal estimands that mirrored their thinking on the counterfactual nature of the causal relation and that were different from the usual descriptive (observable) parameters.

Once such estimands have been defined, it can then be asked under what conditions various observable parameters are equal to (identify) these estimands. Randomization is a device for assigning subjects to treatments that makes the ignorability assumptions (conditions) (8) and/or (11) plausible. When these conditions hold, various observable parameters also equal the causal estimands. These conditions may also be met when randomization has not been used. This demonstrates the logical independence between the ignorability conditions and randomization. And clearly, these conditions are also logically independent of the definitions of causal estimands such as the ITT, ACE, and TT. (Readers might also want to look directly at the definition of these parameters and note that no mention of randomization is made.)

More generally, defining causal estimands independently of the conditions that must be met in order to identify them allows for the development of appropriate procedures (including randomization, matching, IV, control functions, etc.) for identifying (and then estimating) the causal parameters. This is the approach taken in both the "treatment effects" literature and recent econometric literatures, and it is also the approach that Heckman takes. It is a big step forward.

Another way to see the utility of making the definitions of causal effects logically independent of the conditions needed to identify them is to consider the usual approach to regression analysis (or structural equation models) which is typically taken (both in the past and often even now) by many social scientists. The parameters of a regression are certainly interpretable in a descriptive sense, but social scientists often impart a causal interpretation to one or more (often to all) parameters, which are typically interpreted as "effects" in this counterfactual sense (see Sobel [1990] for more on this point). Justifications for such interpretations have included the notion that the model is well specified and/or that important confounders have been controlled and/or that the causal ordering is correct. All of these justifications are extra-mathematical and virtually impossible to evaluate, insofar as a target (i.e., a well-defined estimand) has not even been defined. Using an appropriate notation allows the researcher to clearly define the estimand of interest independently of the regression parameter(s), enabling the analyst to give conditions under which the regression parameter(s) actually identify the target(s) of interest.

Although I disagree with him on this point and a number of others, Heckman, in conjunction with his collaborators, has made useful contributions to the literature on causal inference. I hope the next generation of researchers will cooperate and incorporate the various literatures on causal inference, including the statistical and econometric literatures, under one umbrella. Science will be better served when this is the case.

REFERENCES

Angrist, Joshua D., and Guido W. Imbens. 1995. "Two Stage Least squares Estimation of Average Causal Effects in Models with Variable Treatment Intensity." *Journal of the American Statistical Association* 90:431–42.

Angrist, Joshua D., Guido W. Imbens, and Donald B. Rubin. 1996. "Identification of Causal Effects Using Instrumental Variables" (with discussion). *Journal of the American Statistical Association* 91:444–72.

Barnow, Bert S., Cain, Glenn C., and Arthur S. Goldberger. 1980. "Issues in the Analysis of Selectivity Bias." Pp. 43–59 in *Evaluation Studies Review Annual*, 5, edited by E. Stromsdorfer and G. Farkas. Beverly Hills: Sage.

Bunge, Mario. 1979. *Causality and Modern Science*. 3d ed. New York: Dover.

Carneiro, Piedro, Hansen, Karsten T., and James J. Heckman. 2003 "Estimating Distributions of Treatment Effects With an Application to the Returns to Schooling and Measurement of the Effects of Uncertainty on College Choice." *International Economic Review* 44:361–432.

Cochran, William G. 1965. "The Planning of Observational Studies of Human Populations." *Journal of the Royal Statistical Society*, Series. A, 128:234–55.

Collingwood, Robin G. 1940: 1972. *An Essay on Metaphysics*. Chicago, IL.: Henrey Regnery Company.

Cox, David R. 1958. *The Planning of Experiments*. New York: Wiley.

Fisher, Franklin M. 1970. "A Correspondence Principle for Simultaneous Equation Models." *Econometrica* 38:73–92.

Fisher, Ronald A. 1925. *Statistical Methods for Research Workers*. Edinburgh, Scotland: Olive and Boyd.

Halloran, M. E., and C. J. Struchiner. 1995. "Causal Inference in Infectious Diseases." *Epidemiology*, 6:142–51.

Heckman, James J. 1997. "Instrumental Variables: A Study of Implicit Behavioral Assumptions Used in Making Program Evaluations." *Journal of Human Resources* 32:441–62.

———. 2000. "Causal Parameters and Policy Analysis in Economics: A Twentieth Century Retrospective." *Quarterly Journal of Economics* 115:45–97.

———. 2001. "Micro Data, Heterogeneity, and the Evaluation of Public Policy: Nobel Lecture." *Journal of Political Economy* 109:673–748.

Heckman, James J., and Salvador Navarro-Lozano. 2004. "Using Matching, Instrumental Variables, and Control Functions to Estimate Economic Choice Models." *Review of Economics and Statistics* 86:30–57.

Holland, Paul W. 1986. "Statistics and Causal Inference" (with discussion). *Journal of the American Statistical Association* 81:941–70.

———. 1988. "Causal Inference, Path Analysis, and Recursive Structural Equations Models." (with discussion). Pp. 449–493 in *Sociological Methodology*, edited by C. C. Clogg. Washington, D.C: American Sociological Association.

Imbens, Guido W. 2000. "The Role of the Propensity Score in Estimating Dose-Response Functions." *Biometrika* 87:706–10.

———. 2004. "Nonparametric Estimation of Average Treatment Effects Under Exogeneity: A Review." *Review of Economics and Statistics* 86:4–29.

Imai, Kosuke, and David A. van Dyk. 2004. "Causal Inference with General Treatment Regimes: Generalizing the Propensity Score." *Journal of the American Statistical Association* 99:854–66.

Jo, Booil. 2002. "Estimation of Intervention Effects with Noncompliane: Alternative Model Specifications" (with discussion). *Journal of Educational and Behavioral Statistics* 27:385–420.

Kempthorne, Oscar. 1952. *The Design and Analysis of Experiments*. New York: Wiley.

Manski, Charles F. 1990. "Nonparametric Bounds on Treatment Effects." *American Economic Review Papers and Proceedings* 80:319–23.

———. 2000. "Identification Problems and Decisions Under Ambiguity: Empirical Analysis of Treatment Response and Normative Choice of Treatment Choice." *Journal of Econometrics* 95:415–42.

———. 2004. "Statistical Treatment Rules for Heterogeneous Populations." *Econometrica* 72:1221–46.

Neyman, Jerzy S. 1923: 1990. "On the Application of Probability Theory to Agri-Cultural Experiments. Essay on Principles. Section 9" (with discussion). *Statistical Science* 4:465–80.

Pearl, Judea. 2000. *Causality*. Cambridge, England: Cambridge University Press.

Robins, James M. 1989. "The Analysis of Randomized and Non-Randomized AIDS Trials Using a New Approach to Causal Inference in Longitudinal Studies." Pp. 113–59 in *Health Service Research Methodology: A Focus on AIDS*, edited by Lee Sechrest, Howard Freeman, and Albert Mulley. Washington, DC: U.S. Public Health Service, National Center for Health Services Research.

Robins, James M., and Sander Greenland. 2000. "Comment on 'Causal Inference without Counterfactuals,' by A. Philip Dawid." *Journal of the American Statistical Association* 95:431–35.

Rosenbaum, Paul R. 2002. *Observational Studies*. 2d ed. New York: Springer.

Rosenbaum, Paul R., and Donald B. Rubin. 1983. "The Central Role of the Propensity Score in Observational Studies for Causal Effects." *Biometrika* 70:41–55.

Rosenzweig, Mark R., and Kenneth I. Wolpin. 2000. "Natural 'Natural Experiments' in Economics." *Journal of Economic Literature* 38:827–874.

Rubin, D. B. 1974. "Estimating Causal Effects of Treatments in Randomized and Nonrandomized Studies." *Journal of Educational Psychology* 66:688–701.

———. 1977. "Assignment to Treatment Groups on the Basis of a Covariate." *Journal of Educational Statistics* 2:1–26.

———. 1978. "Bayesian Inference for Causal Effects: The Role of Randomization." *Annals of Statistics* 6:34–58.

———. 1980. "Comment on 'Randomization Analysis of Experimental Data: The Fisher Randomization Test,' by D. Basu." *Journal of the American Statistical Association* 75:591–93.

Smith, Herbert L. 1997. "Matching with Multiple Controls to Estimate Treatment Effects in Observational Studies." Pp. 325–53 in *Sociological Methodology*, vol. 27, edited by Adrian E. Raftery. Boston, MA: Blackwell Publishing.

Sobel, Michael E. 1990. "Effect Analysis and Causation in Linear Structural Equation Models." *Psychometrika* 55:495–515.

———. 1995. "Causal Inference in the Social and Behavioral Sciences." Pp. 1–38 in *Handbook of Statistical Modeling for the Social and Behavioral Sciences*, edited by G. Arminger, C. C. Clogg, and M. E. Sobel. New York: Plenum Press.

———. 2001. "Spatial Concentration and Social Stratification. Does the Clustering of Disadvantage 'Beget' Bad Outcomes?" Forthcoming in *Poverty Traps*, edited by S. Bowles, S. N. Durlauf, and K. Hoff. New York: Russel Sage Foundation.

———. 2003. "What Do Randomized Studies of Housing Mobility Demonstrate: Causal Inference in the Face of Interference." Unpublished manuscript, Columbia University.

Strotz, Robert H., and Herman O. A. Wold. 1960. "Recursive vs. Nonrecursive Systems: An Attempt at Synthesis (Part 1)." *Econometrica* 28:417–27.

Vella, Francis. 1998. "Estimating Models with Sample Selection Bias: A Survey." *Journal of Human Resources* 33: 127–169.

Vytlacil, Edward. 2002. "Independence, Monotonicity, and Latent Index Models: An Equivalence Result." *Econometrica* 70:331–41.

Whitehead, Alfred N. [1911] 1958. *An Introduction to Mathematics*. New York: Oxford University Press.

REJOINDER: RESPONSE TO SOBEL*

James J. Heckman[†]

"The term 'cause' is highly unspecific. It commits us to nothing about the kind of causality involved nor about how the causes operate. Recognizing this should make us more cautious about investing in the quest for universal methods for causal inference." Cartwright, 1999, Chapter 5.

Sobel claims to disagree with many of the points made in my paper. He also claims that much if not all of what I say is already in the statistical treatment effect literature. He treats my Section 4 as a literature review rather than an illustration of the basic principles made in Sections 1–3 of the paper, as I intended it to be. In joint work with Edward Vytlacil, I present a comprehensive literature review (Heckman and Vytlacil 2006a,b).

The primary objective of my paper is to present a general and coherent view of causality as it applies to social science. As part of my analysis, I address the approach to causality popularized in statistics by Donald Rubin, Paul Holland and other statisticians. This is an approach to which Sobel subscribes. As my essay documents, the statistical approach suffers from many limitations and in many fundamental respects is a recapitulation of older approaches in econometrics, well understood by economists, that have been enhanced and developed further by contemporary econometricians. I am disappointed that, rather than addressing my arguments, Sobel restates misleading arguments made in the statistics literature. In

*This research was supported by NSF-SES-0241858 and NIH-R01-HDO43411. I thank Jennifer Boobar, Steve Durlauf and Hanna Lee for comments on this rejoinder.
†University of Chicago and the American Bar Foundation

responding to Sobel, I am in essence responding to Rubin, Holland and other statisticians whose views are reiterated by Sobel in his commentary.

1. WHAT MY PAPER IS ABOUT

My paper moves discussions of causal inference away from vague philosophical discussions about what "really" constitutes causality to a precise discussion of three prototypical policy problems.[1] In my interpretation, causal models are tools for policy analysis. Different policy problems place different demands on models and data. I articulate the econometric approach that (a) defines the problems of interest precisely; (b) describes the environments, outcomes and choices of the agents being studied precisely and (c) presents conditions on data and models under which the policy problems can be solved. The objective of my paper is not to attack statistics but rather to attack serious policy problems. Sobel attacks the explicit approach developed in econometrics and confuses clearly formulated abstract models for outcomes and selection of outcomes with assumptions made within the context of the explicit models that are maintained in particular applications of the models.

Building on my previous analysis (Heckman 2001), I reconcile the statistical treatment effect literature and the econometrics literature by noting that the wider set of questions addressed by the latter entails considering more ambitious models. Whether the particular assumptions required for identifying a parameter are satisfied is a different problem than the problem of determining conditions under which a question can in principle be answered. I draw on Marschak (1953) and later economists to note that for certain narrowly focused policy questions, it is often possible to get by with much weaker assumptions and data requirements when crafting acceptable answers.

---

[1]Cartwright (2005) provides an illuminating discussion of alternative and often inconsistent uses of the term "causality."

My essay is about all three policy questions, P1–P3, and not solely about P1. Sobel, however, largely focuses on P1. He briefly touches on P2 and considers a special case of an exogenous conditioning set. His discussion of problem P3 is about extrapolation from factorial experiments instead of a careful discussion of how to forecast new programs with new characteristics as discussed in my paper and in Heckman and Vytlacil (2005, 2006b). His discussion is defensive and does not grapple with the larger aims of my paper.

The careful reader of my paper, Sobel's discussion and the recent literature on causal inference in econometrics and statistics will recognize that Sobel ignores major points that are developed in the econometrics literature and are absent in the statistical treatment effect literature. These are:

1. Development of an explicit framework for outcomes, measurements and the choice of outcomes where the role of unobservables ("missing variables") in creating selection problems and justifying estimators is developed.
2. The analysis of subjective evaluations of outcomes and the use of choice data to infer them.
3. The analysis of *ex ante* and *ex post* realizations and evaluations of treatments. This analysis enables analysts to model and identify regret and anticipation by agents. Developments 2 and 3 introduce human decision making into the treatment effect literature.
4. Development of models for identifying entire distributions of treatment effects (*ex ante* and *ex post*) rather than just the traditional mean parameters focused on by statisticians. These distributions enable analysts to determine the proportion of people who benefit from treatment, something not attempted in the literature Sobel draws on.
5. Development and identification of distributional criteria allowing for analysis of alternative social welfare functions for outcome distributions comparing different treatment states.
6. Models for simultaneous causality relaxing the recursive frameworks adopted by Rubin (1978) and Holland (1986).
7. Definitions of parameters made without appeals to hypothetical experimental manipulations.

8.   Demonstration of the need for invariance of parameters with respect to classes of manipulations to answer classes of questions.[2]

One theme developed in my paper is that major limitations hamper the statistical treatment effect literature in answering important social science questions. These limitations are not surprising since the statistical treatment effect literature is an offshoot of the experimental design literature in biostatistics. My essay shows that "technical" assumptions invoked in the statistical treatment effect literature have unappealing implications for social science.

Two cornerstone assumptions: *SUTVA* and *Strong Ignorability* (*SI*) are especially unappealing. *SUTVA* is a version of an invariance assumption developed in econometrics some 40–50 years ago and formalized in the Hurwicz (1962) paper I cite. In the form advocated by Sobel and many other statisticians, it precludes social interactions and general equilibrium effects, and so precludes the evaluation of large scale social programs. The *SI* assumption, by ruling out any role for unobservables in self selection, justifies matching by assuming away any interesting behavior of the agents being studied. While Sobel criticizes econometrics for making various assumptions, he ignores the fact that the approach that he favors makes implicit assumptions that are stronger and less tenable. The econometric approach is explicit about its assumptions.

Sobel does not acknowledge any intellectual priority for early work by economists that precedes the "Rubin model" as exposited by Holland (1986). Selection models defined over potential outcomes with explicit treatment assignment mechanisms were presented by Gronau (1974) and Heckman (1974, 1976, 1978) in the economics literature. The econometric discrete choice literature (McFadden 1974, 1981) used counterfactual utilities as did its parent literature in mathematical psychology (Thurstone 1927, 1959). Unlike the Rubin model, these models do not start with the experiment as an ideal point of departure, but they start with well-posed, clearly

---

[2]This notion is in the early Cowles Commission work. See Marschak (1953) and Koopmans, Rubin, and Leipnik (1950). It is formalized in Hurwicz (1962) as cited in my paper. Rubin's *SUTVA* is a special case of the invariance condition formalized by Hurwicz.

articulated models for outcome and treatment choice derived from behavioral theory where the unobservables that underlie the selection and evaluation problem are made explicit.

Rubin's 1978 model of treatment choice came later and only implicitly accounts for the unobservables that drive the selection problem. His point of departure is randomization and the analysis of his 1976 and 1978 papers is a dichotomy between randomization (ignorability) and nonrandomization, not an explicit treatment of particular selection mechanisms in the nonrandomized case as developed in the econometrics literature.

Sobel dismisses the value of making clear the assumptions about model unobservables that produce selection and evaluation problems when he dismisses "structural" models. In this regard he follows Angrist, Imbens, and Rubin (1996) and Holland (1986). Sobel equates structural models (economic models) with *LISREL* type models and standard simultaneous equations models despite the greater generality of the structural models (see, e.g., Matzkin 2006).

Structural models do not "make strong assumptions." They make explicit the assumptions required to identify parameters in any particular problem. The treatment effect literature does not make fewer assumptions; it is just much less explicit about its assumptions. Like many statisticians, Sobel prefers to be implicit about many of his assumptions. This approach begs serious questions about the best way to model the severe problems that arise in making sound policy evaluations.

My essay is about:

1. Clearly defining the policy problem being addressed;
2. Asking what parameter is required to answer the problem;
3. Discussing minimal identification conditions; and
4. Analyzing the properties of various estimators.

While Sobel's discussion claims to show that there are dimensions along which the econometric literature is lacking relative to the statistical literature on treatment effects, his arguments are based on misstatements and misunderstandings of the econometrics literature that are prevalent in the statistical treatment effect literature. For example, he makes the claim, like Rubin and many other statisticians, that econometric selection models depend on normality.[3] He claims that economists, and I in particular, "adopted the Rubin model" in the 1980s. This repeats a claim made by Rubin.[4] Sobel clearly has not read or understood the work published in econometrics in 1974–1976 which presented models of potential outcomes and treatment assignment rules long before Rubin's 1978 paper.[5] My 1974–1976 papers are not "informal" and they present precise discussions of potential outcomes (e.g., market and nonmarket wages) and outcome selection mechanisms. The switching regression model of Quandt (1958, 1972) describes a model of potential outcomes and develops various regime (potential outcome) selection rules. Detached readers would be advised to compare the level of formality in these papers with the relative informality of Rubin's papers, especially his informal 1974 paper which Sobel cites. In that paper, there is no systematic discussion of treatment assignment rules whereas, by 1974, the econometric literature had systematically developed and analyzed such rules.

The early econometric work clearly separates the definition of parameters from their identification in a fashion not found in the statistics literature. Heckman and Robb (1985, 1986) present comprehensive analyses of outcome equations, selection mechanisms and unobservables using economic theory. We had no need to draw on the "Rubin Model" which was a special case of economic models that were formulated prior to Rubin's work. A more accurate description of Rubin's contribution is that he exposited aspects of econometric models to statisticians.

2. WHAT IS NEW IN MY PAPER AND NOT DISCUSSED BY SOBEL

Sobel does not discuss my extension of the treatment effect literature to the identification of non-recursive systems. The literature on

---

[3]Heckman (1980, 1990), Heckman and Robb (1985, 1986), Heckman and Honoré (1990), Ahn and Powell (1993), and Powell (1994), among many others, have relaxed the normality assumption made in the early 1970's literature. See Heckman and Vytlacil (2005, 2006b) for a survey. It is far from clear that in practice normality is a poor assumption in many applications. See Heckman (2001).

[4]Rubin (2000).

[5]The Roy model (1951) is a clear predecessor as are the switching models of Quandt (1958, 1972).

causality in statistics is recursive and rules out simultaneous causality. My Section 2.5 is standard econometrics but new statistics that reveals the power of the econometric approach over "frontier" methods in statistics like directed acyclic graphs (see Pearl 2000) that are recursive. Given long-standing interest in social interactions by sociologists (see also Durlauf and Young 2001) it is unfortunate that Sobel dismisses out of hand this contribution of my essay that allows sociologists to define and identify models of social interactions that are ruled out in the Rubin (1978)–Holland (1986, 1988) approach that he espouses.

Sobel misses another main contribution of my paper: to make the literature on causality specific by addressing real problems. Abstract discussions of causality with appeals to philosophy, "closest worlds," "regularity," and the like sound profound but in fact are superficial since they have no operational content and do not address policy problems. Most empirical social scientists are not concerned with philosophy *per se*, but instead they want honest answers to clearly stated problems.

My essay is organized around the theme of addressing three policy evaluation questions that arise in everyday practice. Problem P1 is what statisticians focus on. Problems P2 and P3 are new problems that can be answered using the econometric approach. Sobel's attempt to address P2—the extrapolation problem—demonstrates the *ad hoc* nature of current statistical approaches and the power of the econometric approach. By keeping the unobservables implicit, he disguises an implicit exogeneity assumption for the conditioning variables in the approach he advocates. Heckman and Vytlacil (2005, 2006b) consider extrapolation under more general conditions.

An alternative approach discussed in Heckman and Vytlacil (2005, 2006b) is to model the dependence between the conditioning variables and the unobservables, but since Sobel (like Rubin and Holland) does not like to make unobservables explicit, this route is denied him. He implicitly agrees that the literature in statistics does not address P3 and his discussion of it confuses problem P2 with problem P3.

He offers a discussion of factorial experiments as a substitute for a clear discussion of P3. Since he will not make explicit statements about unobservables, he begs a central question addressed in the econometrics literature of how to predict the effects of new programs never previously observed. His version of P3 is a simple extrapolation exercise and hence a version of P2. He does not offer a general treatment of P3 as I do in the paper and in Heckman and Vytlacil (2005, 2006b).

Our approach goes well beyond the interpolation and extrapolation advocated by Sobel to consider predictions of programs with features never previously observed.[6] Making predictions about new programs and policies is an essential task of social science. If these predictions are not made in a cautious, principled, explicit way, plenty of "causal inference experts" stand waiting to fill the vacuum and provide less credible estimates. By discussing hard problems clearly, analysts can pinpoint limits to knowledge that raise the standards of evidence.

In failing to present a serious discussion of problem P3, which is a central focus of my essay, Sobel echoes the conventional statistical approach that ignores this policy evaluation problem. Had he carefully considered my analysis of this problem in this paper and in my work with Vytlacil, his claims about close "agreement" between the econometric approach and the statistical approach would vanish.

Sobel misses another major theme of my essay and the entire econometric evaluation literature: that treatment effects should be defined relative to the problem being analyzed (Marschak 1953; Heckman 2001; Heckman and Vytlacil 2001b, 2006a,b). The econometric literature develops the point that the choice of an estimator cannot be separated from the choice of the question being addressed by the investigator and the *a priori* assumptions made by the investigator.

Thus, although *ACE*, *ITT* or *TT* may be traditional parameters, they do not address many specific policy questions. My work with Vytlacil (2001b, 2005, 2006b) discusses specific policy questions and devises estimators that address them. Manski (2000, 2004), in his interesting work, derives treatment assignment rules for particular loss functions.

3. IS CAUSALITY IN THE MIND?

Sobel, evidently influenced by my exchange with Tukey (in Wainer 1986, reprinted 2000), sharply attacks me for claiming that "causality

---

[6]His approach is based on arbitrary functional form assumptions whereas we present a general analysis guided by theory.

is in the mind" and that causal knowledge is provisional. Then, throughout the rest of his discussion, he demonstrates the validity of my point by offering a series of unsupported opinions and assertions about what is "reasonable" and what is not. His opinions and value judgements are his expressions of intuitive models in his mind that he never formalizes or makes explicit, but introduces casually using rhetorical devices. Sobel is typical of many statisticians who keep crucial assumptions implicit.

My claim is not intended as a defense of solipsism, post-modernist relativism or the notion that analysts are free to make up any crazy model they like. Instead, I am saying that all scientific activity is predicated on assumptions.

A clearly formulated causal model should (a) define the rules or theories that generate the counterfactuals being studied, including specification of the variables known to the agents being studied as well as the properties of the unobservables of the model where the unobservables are not known to the analyst but may be partly known by the agent; (b) define how a particular counterfactual (or potential outcome) is chosen; (c) make clear the assumptions used to identify the model (or to address the policy questions being considered); and (d) justify the properties of estimators under the maintained assumptions and under alternative assumptions. These are tasks 1 (corresponding to a and b), 2 (corresponding to c) and 3 (corresponding to d) in my Table 1. These ingredients are the hallmark of the selection model as analyzed in Heckman (1974, 1976, 1979), Gronau (1974), Roy (1951), Willis and Rosen (1979) and numerous other papers in the econometrics literature. Understanding the relationship between the unobservables generating choice of treatment and the unobservables generating outcomes is the key to understanding the properties of various evaluation estimators, a point first made in Heckman and Robb (1985, 1986, reprinted 2000).

One will look in vain in the papers of Neyman, Cox, Kempthorne, Rubin or Holland for the specification of precise treatment assignment rules that have been the hallmark of econometric selection models since 1974. Sobel's claim that Rubin (1978) or any other statistician has systematically developed treatment assignment mechanisms is false. Rubin (1976, 1978) contrasts randomization with nonrandomization and does not develop the structure of nonrandomized selection rules in the fashion pioneered and developed in econometrics.[7]

The act of defining a model is a purely mental activity. It may draw on preexisting theory (which is itself derived from earlier mental acts), interpretations of data (which involve a mental act using models for the phenomenon being studied and models of statistical inference) and the rules of logic. There is no purely empirical process for discovering or defining causality. All causal knowledge is conditional on maintained assumptions.[8]

Sobel (p. 106) dismisses the conditional nature of causality, writing that "I do not believe that most scientists (or philosophers) would subscribe to this view and were they to do so they would presumably have little further interest in causality." This claim runs contrary to a large body of thought in philosophy associated with Kant and Hume, among others.

Indeed, "causality" is not a central issue in fields with well-formulated models where it usually emerges as an automatic by-product and not as the main feature of a scientific investigation. Moreover, intuitive notions about causality have been dropped in pursuit of a rigorous physical theory. As I note in my essay with Abbring (2006), Richard Feyman in his work on quantum electro-dynamics allowed the future to cause the past in pursuit of a scientifically rigorous model even though it violated "common sense" causal principles. The less clearly developed is a field of inquiry, the more likely is it to rely on vague notions like causality rather than explicitly formulated models.

Most scholars intend to describe the real world with their models. Certainly, in addressing P1–P3, I am referring to real world problems. However, any empirical or theoretical analysis rests on assumptions. The clearer analysts are about these assumptions and the more they are able to test them, the more clearly stated are the sources of agreement or disagreement among analysts. Such clarity determines the next steps in the scientific process of constructing

---

[7]When Sobel writes that $TT = ACE = TUT$ when treatment decisions do not depend on potential outcomes, he presents a garbled version of a precise result established in my 1974 and 1976 papers.

[8]Indeed all knowledge is conditional in this sense. For example, much of modern mathematics is predicated on the Axiom of Choice.

better models and better data to narrow down the zones of disagreement among analysts.

Although Sobel objects to my assertion about the importance of maintained assumptions and *a priori* beliefs in the causality enterprise, he proceeds, like many statisticians, to pass judgements about what is and is not good practice. Unlike the econometric approach, Sobel adopts the statistical approach which often hides key assumptions by invoking slogans instead of science.

Each of Sobel's judgements is based on maintained assumptions and beliefs "in his mind." They involve his implicit assumptions and value judgements. Statisticians like him who are not explicit do not convey their private thoughts in an objective, publicly interpretable way. Like many statisticians working in the field of causal inference, he is not clear about many of his crucial implicit assumptions. Implicit assumptions are entailed in writing down the arguments of causal relationship (1) (his notation) and characterizing its properties.

Sobel writes "the focus of the statistical literature is primarily on obtaining the best possible estimate of the causal parameter of interest" without defining "best possible," the basis for the choice of the "parameter of interest" or the question being addressed.[9] In his defense of matching, he appeals to conditional independence assumption (11) (in the notation of his paper) as " straightforward" and that it "readily lends itself to use by empirical investigators." Some statisticians often use the phrase "it works well in practice" without defining "works well." Another common slogan used to justify matching is that "my clients understand it." In these and numerous other instances, Sobel and a large statistical community implicitly appeal to a variety of conventions rather than presenting explicit rigorous models and assumptions. The credo "let sleeping dogs lie" is good for sales, but it is bad for science. Instead of invoking slogans as a solution to problems, the structural approach emphasizes understanding the underlying mechanisms producing outcomes and selection rules.

As an application of the scientific approach, my discussion of matching develops the point that (i) there is no rigorous basis for picking the set or sets of conditioning variables that make the method

---

[9]The "best possible estimate" is defined precisely in Bayesian and Wald decision theories. See, e.g., the discussion in Manski (2000).

"work." Heckman and Navarro (2004) show how the conventional model selection rules for picking the conditioning variables W in a set of data can produce badly biased estimates of the average causal effect and other parameters. (ii) The method assumes that the analyst has as much relevant information as the agent being studied (see, e.g., Heckman and Navarro 2004, for a precise definition of "relevant" information). If the agent knows more than the analyst and acts on it, matching breaks down. (iii) The analyst assumes that people at the margin of being attracted into a program are the same (have same outcomes on average) as average participants. Matching is just non-parametric regression analysis. It is more careful than Ordinary Least Squares (OLS) in accounting for empirical support problems but it assumes that the conditioning variables that the analyst has at his disposal fortuitously solve selection problems.[10]

To take another point, like many statisticians, Sobel resolutely defends randomization. The Rubin (1978)–Holland (1986) papers take as their benchmark randomized trials where treatments are selected by a hypothetical randomization. As I point out in my essay, even under ideal conditions, unaided randomization cannot answer some very basic questions such as what fraction of a population benefits from a program.[11] And in practice, contamination and cross over effects make randomization a far from sure-fire solution even for constructing ATE or ACE (see the evidence on disruption bias and contamination bias arising in randomized trials that is presented in Heckman, LaLonde, and Smith 1999; Heckman, Hohmann, Smith, and Khoo 2000). Sobel makes a series of implicit assumptions about what questions should be answered, the effects of randomization on participants and the like.

Sobel also disagrees with my claim that statisticians conflate the three tasks shown in my Table 1. The analysis of Holland (1986, 1988) is a good illustration of my point. It also illustrates the central

---

[10]In one of his many attributional errors, he echoes Imbens (2004) and credits Barnow, Cain, and Goldberger (1980) with the phrase "selection on observables" to describe matching. The term originates in Heckman and Robb (1985) and is not to be found in Barnow, Cain, and Goldberger.

[11]See Carneiro, Hansen, and Heckman (2001, 2003), where this parameter is identified using choice data and/or supplementary proxy measures. See also Cunha and Heckman (2006a,b) and Cunha, Heckman, and Navarro (2005, 2006).

role of the randomized trial to the Holland-Rubin analysis. After explicating what he calls the "Rubin model," Holland gives a very revealing illustration of how the first two tasks of Table 1 are conflated by one leading figure in the statistical treatment effect literature. Holland claims that there can be no causal effect of gender on earnings. Why? Because we cannot randomly assign gender. This confused statement conflates the act of definition of the causal effect (a purely mental act) with empirical difficulties in estimating it (Steps 1 and 2 in my Table 1). This type of reasoning is prevalent in statistics.[12]

As another example of the same point, Rubin (1978, p. 39) denies that it is possible to define a causal effect of sex on intelligence because a randomization cannot *in principle* be performed.[13] In this and many other passages in the statistics literature, a causal effect is defined by a randomization. Issues of definition and identification are confused. A recent paper shows that this fallacy is alive and well in statistics. A paper by Berk, Li, and Hickman (2005) makes the same error as Rubin and Holland. Sobel is correct in saying that population treatment parameters can be defined abstractly. However, that point was not made in the statistical treatment effect literature. It is made in econometrics.[14]

I agree with Sobel that the act of definition is logically separate from the acts of identification and inference. That is a main point of my paper. We both agree that a purely mental act can define a causal effect of gender. That is a separate task from identifying it. What is odd is that he states his agreement with my position and that of the econometrics literature as a disagreement. And he fails to accurately

---

[12]Parenthetically, my title "Scientific Causality" was motivated by Holland's contrast between models of science that attempt to probe deeply and understand the "causes of effects" and the statistical treatment effect literature. Understanding the causes of effects is an essential activity for prediction and forecasting—problems P2 and P3 in my paper.

[13]"Without treatment definitions that specify actions to be performed on experimental units, we cannot unambiguously discuss causal effects of treatments." (Rubin 1978, p. 39).

[14]The *LATE* parameter of Imbens and Angrist (1994) is defined by an instrument and conflates task 1 and 2 (definition and identification). Heckman and Vytlacil (2001b, 2005, 2006b) define the *LATE* parameter abstractly and separate issues of definition of parameters from issues of identification. Imbens and Angrist (1994) use instrumental variables as surrogates for randomization.

represent a pervasive point of view among statisticians that gives rise to the myth that causality can only be determined by randomization, and that glorifies randomization as the "gold standard" of causal inference.[15]

4. THE ROY MODEL, THE SWITCHING MODEL AND THE RUBIN MODEL

Sobel repeats an assertion made by Rubin: that I, and other economists, "started using the Rubin model in the 1980s."[16] Sobel has clearly not studied the econometrics literature with any care. The "Rubin model" is in fact a version of an econometric model developed by Roy (1951). It is also a version of the switching regression model of Quandt (1958, 1972). That model contains both a framework for potential outcomes (Y_0, Y_1) and also a choice of treatment rule.[17] There was no explicit discussion of the treatment assignment rule in any of the Rubin papers that Sobel cites or in the statistics literature until very recently.[18]

Heckman and Honoré (1990) present a comprehensive analysis of the Roy model. Heckman (1990) and Heckman and Smith (1998) extend it (see also Heckman 2001, and Heckman and Vytlacil 2006a,b). Unlike the statisticians, Pearl (2000) is forthright about his own debt to the economics literature in the distinction between "fixing" and "conditioning," which is central to his work on causality. See Haavelmo (1943) for the source of Pearl's "do" operator.[19]

[15]As noted in my essay, and in Heckman (1992), self selection provides information on agent-subjective evaluations of programs.

[16]See Rubin (2000).

[17]One cannot find any explicit analysis of treatment selection rules in the statistical literature (Neyman 1923; Rubin 1978; Holland 1986; Rubin 1986) other than the randomized-nonrandomized dichotomy previously discussed.

[18]Sobel cites Rosenbaum (2002) for use of such rules. As previously noted, Rubin does develop the dichotomy "randomized vs. nonrandomized." He does not go deeper, nor does he consider how the form of the treatment assignment rule affects the choice of an appropriate estimator. That point is developed in Heckman and Robb (1985, 1986).

[19]Lewis (1963) is an early pioneering analysis of counterfactuals in economics that also considers the problems raised by self selection and general equilibrium effects.

The simplest form of the Roy model has two potential outcomes and a decision rule (treatment assignment rule). In its simplest version, the treatment indicator variable is $D = \mathbf{1}(Y_1 \geq Y_0)$, where $\mathbf{1}(\cdot) = 1$ if the argument is true and is zero otherwise. Thus a doctor might assign treatment on the basis of which therapy has the best outcome. A student may decide to go to college vs. stopping at high school based on which option has the highest income. The Roy model is a version of the competing risks model of biostatistics.[20] This model of potential outcomes and treatment selection predates Cox and Rubin, as does the Thurstone (1927) model of counterfactual utilities of choices developed in mathematical psychology.

More general versions of this model developed in econometrics allow agents to be partially informed about (Y_1, Y_0) when they make their decisions and to allow for more general costs. In the generalized Roy model, $D = \mathbf{1}(E(g(Y_1, Y_0, C)|\mathcal{I}) > 0)$ where $\mathcal{I}$ is the agent's information set, C is the cost of moving from "0" to "1" where "0" is the initial state, and g is a general preference function for the agent making the treatment decision. In the original Roy model $C = 0$, $\mathcal{I} = (Y_1, Y_0)$ and $g = (Y_1 - Y_0)$. The general form of this model allows analysts to distinguish objective from subjective evaluations of treatments and *ex ante* and *ex post* versions of both. See Carneiro, Hansen, and Heckman (2001, 2003), Cunha and Heckman (2006a), Cunha, Heckman, and Navarro (2005, 2006), Heckman and Vytlacil (2006b) and Heckman and Navarro (2006) for more general analyses.

In my 1974 paper, Y_1 is the market wage of a woman. Y_0 is her nonmarket wage (her value in home production). Her decision rule is to work ($D = 1$) if the market wage is greater than the reservation wage $D = \mathbf{1}(Y_1 \geq Y_0)$.[21] Otherwise, she does not work. I also develop a model for hours of work. Willis and Rosen (1979) use this model when Y_1 is college earnings and Y_0 is high school earnings. They allow for costs C. $D = 1$ (a person goes to college) if $Y_1 - Y_0 - C > 0$ $(D = \mathbf{1}(Y_1 - Y_0 - C \geq 0))$.[22] There is a huge literature starting in economics long before the "Rubin model" became popularized in

---

[20]See Heckman (1987) where this link is established. Versions of the competing risks model go back to early Twentieth Century work by Danish actuaries.

[21]See Gronau (1974) for a closely related model.

[22]They assume perfect certainty. See Cunha and Heckman (2006a) for a version of this model with uncertainty as well as additional features.

statistics and it is this literature that influences econometric analyses of causal models.

The "Rubin model" is thus a version of this classical econometric model without explicit specification of the decision model for choice of treatment. Sobel claims that statisticians such as Rosenbaum (2002) are now using the framework developed by economists some 30 years before. If true, this is a welcome acquisition from economics by statistics.

As previously noted, Sobel also claims that Rubin explicitly discusses treatment assignment rules. In fact, Rubin relies on the crutch of randomization to define his models and only vaguely describes other assignment rules as "not randomized."[23] One needs to look to Gronau (1974) and Heckman (1974, 1976, 1979, 1978) for explicit development of selection models with explicit treatment assignment and selection rules. Had Rubin understood the general selection model, he would not have advocated matching or balancing to overcome nonrandomized assignment as he does in his 1974 and 1978 papers. Heckman and Navarro (2004), Heckman and Vytlacil (2006b), and Heckman, Urzua, and Vytlacil (2006) show the bias that arises from using matching when a general selection rule characterizes treatment choice.

5. COMPARISON OF ESTIMATORS

My analysis in Section 4 was only intended to illustrate the basic point that each evaluation estimator makes assumptions. Sobel misinterprets this section as my attempt to write an exhaustive survey instead of my attempt to illustrate some points from the earlier part of the paper. In Section 4, I focus attention on certain mean treatment effect parameters because of their familiarity and simplicity. Heckman, LaLonde, and Smith (1999) and Heckman and Vytlacil (2006b) present comprehensive surveys of the econometric approach.

Sobel confines his discussion to a few mean treatment parameters, ignoring the range of parameters introduced in the earlier

---

[23]Rubin (1978) discusses the distribution of treatment assignment rules in a general way but never develops their properties in the systemic, formal way it is developed in economics.

sections of my essay. His discussion is selective and he seizes on small points to make objections to my paper. He misses key developments in the econometrics literature that show that in models with hetero-geneous responses, *IV* and selection models are closely related (Heckman and Vytlacil 2005; Heckman, Urzua, and Vytlacil 2006).

I use separability in my analysis of selection models in Section 4 only to simplify the exposition. Matzkin (2006) presents a compre-hensive discussion of nonparametric identifiability in nonseparable selection (and other) models.

His contrast between matching and control functions on this issue is specious and ignores an entire recent semiparametric literature in econometrics (see Heckman and Vytlacil 2006a; Matzkin 2006). Selection models do not require normality, separability or standard exclusion restrictions in order to be identified.

He takes out of context my claim that control functions are more general than matching. That claim is made under a series of assumptions about the separable selection model and was not intended as a general characterization.

The recent semiparametric literature by Heckman (1980, 1990), Powell (1994) and Carneiro, Hansen, and Heckman (2003) does not rely on normality or functional form assumptions. On this point Sobel inaccurately characterizes the econometrics literature. Even in the absence of distributional assumptions, no exclusions are needed to identify the Roy model, contrary to his claims. In his notation, a model with $Z = X$ can be identified using curvature restrictions with-out any exclusion of variables. See Heckman and Honoré (1990).[24]

The key idea underlying the control function approach intro-duced in Heckman (1980) and in Heckman and Robb (1985, 1986) is to model the relationship between the unobservables in the treatment choice equation and the unobservables in the outcome equations rather than to assume they are independent given a specified set of variables as is done in the matching literature. Sobel inaccurately compares matching and selection estimators in terms of the number of assumptions invoked by each method and not in terms of their strong implications.

---

[24]Sobel relies on a flawed survey by Vella (1998) which does not accu-rately portray the econometric selection literature.

Matching assumes that, on average, the marginal person and average person with the same observed conditioning variables respond the same to treatment ($TT = ATE = TUT$). It assumes that the analyst knows the right conditioning set and uses it. Selection models allow for variables that produce conditional independence invoked in matching to be unobserved by the analyst (see Carneiro, Hansen, and Heckman 2003). Sobel's analysis of IV also ignores the entire body of recent econometric work which establishes what instrumental variables estimate in the general nonseparable case (see Heckman and Vytlacil 1999, 2001a, 2006b). I now turn to that work.

6. THE UNIFYING ROLE OF THE MARGINAL TREATMENT EFFECT

Sobel has evidently not read my 2001 Nobel Lecture or my work with Vytlacil (1999, 2001a,b, 2005, 2006a,b). Had he done so he would not claim that "sociologists will usually be more interested in Treatment on the Treated (TT) or ACE (Average Causal Effect) than the Marginal Treatment Effect (MTE)." In rereading my essay, I now realize it was a mistake for me not to discuss my work with Vytlacil in my paper.

Vytlacil and I establish that the marginal treatment effect (MTE) is a device that unifies the evaluation literature. From knowledge of the MTE, analysts can interpret what IV estimates as well as the commonly used treatment effects, OLS and matching estimators as a different weighted average of the marginal treatment effect. Under the assumptions clearly stated in our papers, we establish that all treatment effects and all estimands (probability limits of IV, matching, OLS, control function estimators) can be expressed as weighted averages of the MTE with known weights, i.e., weights that can be estimated from the sample data. Letting $MTE(x, u)$ be the MTE for a given value of $X = x$ (observables) and $U = u$ (unobservables), we may write the estimand or treatment effect j given x, $\Delta^j(x)$ as

$$\Delta^j(x) = \int_b^a MTE(x, u)\omega^j(x, u)du \qquad (1)$$

where $\omega^j(x, u)$ is a weight for estimand or effect j that can be empirically determined and the limits (a, b) are known in any application. We can generate *LATE* as a special case of this formula. When the model has limited support (regions where *MTE* can be identified), the estimator automatically adjusts for it.[25]

Bounds for the treatment parameters are presented in Heckman and Vytlacil (2006b). Different instruments produce different weights and these weights are generally not the weights required to define the standard treatment effects. Our approach is far more general than the piecemeal type of analysis of what *IV* estimates of the sort presented by Sobel in his comments on the statistical literature. Each of his special cases drops out from our general analysis. The *MTE* approach presents a nonparametric control function analysis where the propensity score plays a conceptually distinct role from the role it plays in matching models (Heckman and Vytlacil 2006b). Our analysis is not to be found in the statistics literature.

Sobel is clearly a fan of the *LATE* approach. Therefore, he has to be a fan of *MTE*. The Imbens-Angrist (1994) *LATE* parameter is a discrete version of the Björklund-Moffitt (1987) marginal gain parameter introduced into the evaluation literature in a selection model framework. The Björklund-Moffitt parameter is the mean gain to participants induced into the program by an instrument. They identify the parameter in a selection framework. Imbens-Angrist show how *IV* can approximate it. Heckman and Vytlacil (1999) show how local instrumental variables (*LIV*) identify it. Heckman, Urzua, and Vytlacil (2006) and Heckman and Vytlacil (2006b) show that *IV* and selection models are closely related. *IV* and its extension Local *IV* (*LIV*) estimate the slopes of the models estimated by selection models in levels.

As pointed out in Heckman, Urzua, and Vytlacil (2006) and Heckman and Vytlacil (2005), the "monotonicity" assumptions made in the *LATE* literature are not innocuous. If, in response to a change in an instrument, some people go into treatment and others drop out, instrumental variables do not identify any treatment effect but they do identify a weighted average of two way flows (Heckman and

---

[25]Software for estimating *MTE* and generating all of the treatment parameters is available from Heckman, Urzua, Vytlacil (2006). See the website http://jenni.uchicago.edu/underiv.

Vytlacil 2005, 2006b; Heckman, Urzua, and Vytlacil 2006). The recent *IV* literature is asymmetric. Outcomes are permitted to be heterogeneous among persons in a general way. Choices of treatment are not permitted to be heterogeneous in a general way.

7. POLICY RELEVANT TREATMENT PARAMETERS

The Policy Relevant Treatment Effect (*PRTE*) introduced in Heckman and Vytlacil (2001a) and elaborated in Heckman and Vytlacil (2005, 2006a,b) is a good example of the benefits of the econometric approach. It is defined by stating a policy problem— estimating the effect of a policy on mean outcomes—and showing that this treatment effect can be generated as a weighted average of the marginal treatment effect with known weights using formula (1) presented in the preceding section. Standard *IV* and matching estimators do not, in general, identify this parameter.

Policy problems dictate the identification and estimation strategy in our approach. As shown in Heckman (2001), Heckman and Vytlacil (2001a, 2005, 2006b), Heckman, Urzua, and Vytlacil (2006) and Carneiro, Heckman, and Vytlacil (2005), the weights on *MTE* required to form the *PRTE* parameter are generally not the same as the weights for *OLS*, matching or *IV*, although an *IV* estimator can be devised to identify the *PRTE*.

Heckman and Vytlacil (2005) develop an algorithm for defining causal effects that answer specific policy problems from a general list of possible problems rather than relying exclusively on the standard set of causal effects discussed by Sobel in his Section 3 that answer only a few narrowly selected policy problems.[26] Sobel ignores parameters like the *PRTE* and fails to recognize that the standard treatment estimators do not identify this parameter. Heckman and Vytlacil develop estimators for specific well-posed policy problems

[26]In his defense of *ACE*, Sobel makes a familiar error. In defending *ACE* as estimating the effect of a policy with universal coverage compared to the effect with no coverage, he fails to account for the effects of large scale programs on potential outcomes—what economists call "general equilibrium" effects. Heckman, Lochner, and Taber (1998a,b) show that these are empirically important in the analysis of education policies. These effects violate the *SUTVA* assumption of Holland (1986) or the invariance assumption of Hurwicz (1962).

rather than hope that a favored estimator just happens to hit the selected target. This is a large advance over the existing literature in statistics. Just compare Sobel's discussion of *IV* with our own.

8. ESTIMATING THE PROPORTION OF PEOPLE WHO BENEFIT FROM A PROGRAM

Sobel's discussion of the benefits of randomization illustrates all of the problems with the *ad hoc* statistical approach he favors. Randomized trials cannot identify $\Pr(Y_1 > Y_0)$. In a large sample, this is the proportion of the population that benefits from a program.[27] See Heckman (1992). This is because randomized trials produce Y_1 or Y_0 but not both for each person. The parameter $\Pr(Y_1 > Y_0)$ is not even contemplated in the Neyman (1923)–Rubin (1978) setup. Using the Roy model (Heckman and Honoré 1989) or more general models (Carneiro, Hansen, and Heckman 2001, 2003; Cunha, Heckman, and Navarro 2005, 2006; Cunha and Heckman 2006a,b; Heckman, Lochner, and Todd 2006) it is possible to estimate this proportion. Modeling the unobservables and their relationship with the treatment selection rule and any related measurement equations plays an important role in their analysis. The statistical treatment effect literature is silent on this crucial parameter. Modeling the dependence among the unobservables in choice, outcome and auxiliary measurement equations, is the key to identifying this proportion.

Sobel says that "much stronger assumptions" are required to estimate this parameter. In any specific case, this claim is not true. The assumptions required to justify randomization (no randomization bias; no contamination or crossover effects; see Heckman, LaLonde, and Smith 1999) are *different* and not weaker or stronger than the assumptions used to identify the Roy model and its extensions. Indeed when randomization breaks down, Roy models and their generalizations can exploit the attrition and self selection information to identify $\Pr(Y_1 > Y_0)$. See Heckman (1992) and Heckman and Vytlacil (2006a,b).

---

[27]I keep the conditioning on covariates implicit. I assume a heterogeneous response model.

9. SENSITIVITY ANALYSIS

If the purpose of my essay had been a comprehensive review of econometric evaluation estimators, I would have discussed bounds and sensitivity analysis. See Heckman and Vytlacil (2006b) for such a discussion using the *MTE* as an organizing device for an entire literature. Vijverberg (1993) is a good reference for sensitivity analysis in a Roy model. Peterson (1976) is an early example of bounds for the competing risks model which is a version of the Roy model.[28]

10. POLICY FORECASTING

Sobel explores a few special cases of my analysis of problem P2. This section of his discussion abounds with personal opinions like "intuitively easy" and "think reasonably." These assertions are his excuse for begging the general problems considered in my paper. If he does not like unobservables, he can use standard change of variable arguments to substitute out unobservables from my equations and recast my argument into observables to solve identification problems.

My argument uses structural models directly because they are interpretable in terms of theory and they explicitly recognize missing variables ("unobservables"). They also provide the machinery for integrating information on auxiliary measures into analyses to help overcome problems with missing variables.

His analysis makes implicit exogeneity assumptions. See Heckman and Vytlacil (2005, 2006b) for a general analysis of the extrapolation problem based on the *MTE* which explicitly discusses the role of exogeneity assumptions in policy forecasts.

11. THE ROLE OF UNOBSERVABLES

Sobel, like many statisticians, says he does not like unobservables. Neither do I. I wish all important variables were observed. But it is the unobservables in the outcome equations and the outcomes in the treatment choice

---

[28]See Heckman and Honoré (1989, 1990).

equation that give rise to selection and evaluation problems. One can be implicit about them and their properties, as are Sobel and most statisticians, or explicit, as is common in the econometric approach.

Implicit in all statistical analyses are unobservables that generate outcomes given the observables. Matching assumes that all unobservables in outcome equations are random with respect to the unobservables in the treatment choice equation given the matching variables. The *LATE* estimator that Sobel implicitly espouses assumes a latent unobserved variable with a special structure.[29] By being clear and objective, the econometric approach allows analysts to pinpoint their differences in assumptions about the unobservables and explore the role of assumptions in producing any differences in conclusions.

12. TOWARDS CONVERGENCE

I applaud Sobel's desire to see the emergence of a literature that combines the best features of the econometric and statistical treatment effect literatures. For that synthesis to occur, statisticians like Sobel should carefully read the econometrics literature and its genuine pioneering contributions and more carefully note the publication dates of key ideas before dismissing 30 years of econometric research as the application of an incompletely formulated statistical model.

REFERENCES

Abbring, J. H., and J. J. Heckman. 2006. "Dynamic Policy Analysis." In *The Econometrics of Panel Data*, edited by L. Matyas and P. Sevestre. Kluwer Academic Publishers. Forthcoming.

Ahn, H., and J. Powell. 1993. "Semiparametric Estimation of Censored Selection Models with a Nonparametric Selection Mechanism." *Journal of Econometrics* 58(1–2):3–29.

Angrist, J. D., G. W. Imbens, and D. Rubin. 1996. "Identification of Causal Effects Using Instrumental Variables." *Journal of the American Statistical Association* 91(434):444–55.

---

[29]Vytlacil (2002) explicitly develops the latent variable model implicitly assumed by Imbens and Angrist (1994) and Angrist, Imbens, and Rubin (1996).

Barnow, B. S., G. G. Cain, and A. S. Goldberger. 1980. "Issues in the Analysis of Selectivity Bias." Pp. 42–59 in *Evaluation Studies*, vol. 5, edited by E. Stromsdorfer and G. Farkas. Beverly Hill, CA: Sage Publications.

Berk, R., A. Li, and L. Hickman. 2005. "Statistical Difficulties in Determining the Role of Race in Capital Cases: A Re-Analysis of Data from the State of Maryland." *Journal of Quantitative Criminology* 21(4):365–90.

Björklund, A., and R. Moffitt. 1987. "The Estimation of Wage Gains and Welfare Gains in Self-Selection." *Review of Economics and Statistics* 69(1):42–49.

Carneiro, P., K. Hansen, and J. J. Heckman. 2001. "Removing the Veil of Ignorance in Assessing the Distributional Impacts of Social Policies." *Swedish Economic Policy Review* 8(2):273–301.

———. 2003. "Estimating Distributions of Treatment Effects with an Application to the Returns to Schooling and Measurement of the Effects of Uncertainty on College Choice." 2001 Lawrence R. Klein Lecture. *International Economic Review* 44(2):361–422.

Carneiro, P., J. J. Heckman, and E. J. Vytlacil. 2005. "Understanding What Instrumental Variables Estimate: Estimating Marginal and Average Returns to Education." Presented at Harvard University, 2001. Under review.

Cartwright, N. 1999. *The Dappled World: A Study of the Boundaries of Science.* Cambridge, UK: Cambridge University Press.

———. 2005. "Causation: One Word Many Things." Unpublished manuscript, London School of Economics, Centre for Philosophy of Natural and Social Science.

Cunha, F., and J. J. Heckman. 2006a. "The Evolution of Earnings Risk in the US Economy." Presented at the 9th World Congress of the Econometric Society, London.

———. 2006b. "A Framework for the Analysis of Inequality." *Journal of Macroeconomics*, forthcoming.

Cunha, F., J. J. Heckman, and S. Navarro. 2005. "Separating Uncertainty from Heterogeneity in Life Cycle Earnings." 2004 Hicks Lecture. *Oxford Economic Papers* 57(2):191–261.

———. 2006. "Counterfactual Analysis of Inequality and Social Mobility." In *Mobility and Inequality: Frontiers of Research from Sociology and Economics*, ch. 4, edited by S. L. Morgan, D. B. Grusky, and G. S. Fields. Palo Alto, CA: Stanford University Press.

Durlauf, S. N., and H. P. Young. 2001. *Social Dynamics.* Cambridge, MA: MIT Press.

Gronau, R. 1974. "Wage Comparisons—A Selectivity Bias." *Journal of Political Economy* 82(6):1119–43.

Haavelmo, T. 1943. "The Statistical Implications of a System of Simultaneous Equations." *Econometrica* 11(1):1–12.

Heckman, J. J. 1974. "Shadow Prices, Market Wages, and Labor Supply." *Econometrica* 42(4):679–94.

———. 1976. "The Common Structure of Statistical Models of Truncation, Sample Selection and Limited Dependent Variables and a Simple Estimator for Such Models." *Annals of Economic and Social Measurement* 5(4):475–92.

———. 1978. "Dummy Endogenous Variables in a Simultaneous Equation System." *Econometrica* 46(4):931–59.

———. 1979. "Sample Selection Bias as a Specification Error." *Econometrica* 47(1):153–62.

———. 1980. "Addendum to Sample Selection Bias as a Specification Error." In *Evaluation Studies Review Annual*, vol. 5, edited by E. Stromsdorfer and G. Farkas. Beverly Hills, CA: Sage Publications.

———. 1987. "Selection Bias and Self-Selection." Pp. 287–97 in *The New Palgrave: A Dictionary of Economics*, edited by J. Eatwell, M. Milgate, and P. Newman. London: Palgrave Macmillan Press.

———. 1990. "Varieties of Selection Bias." *American Economic Review* 80(2):313–18.

———. 1992. "Randomization and Social Policy Evaluation." Pp. 201–30 in *Evaluating Welfare and Training Programs*, edited by C. Manski and I. Garfinkel. Cambridge, MA: Harvard University Press.

———. 2001. "Micro Data, Heterogeneity, and the Evaluation of Public Policy: Nobel Lecture." *Journal of Political Economy* 109(4):673–748.

Heckman, J. J., N. Hohmann, J. Smith, and M. Khoo. 2000. "Substitution and Dropout Bias in Social Experiments: A Study of an Influential Social Experiment." *Quarterly Journal of Economics* 115(2):651–94.

Heckman, J. J., and B. E. Honoré. 1989. "The Identifiability of the Competing Risks Model." *Biometrika* 76(2):325–30.

———. 1990. "The Empirical Content of the Roy Model." *Econometrica* 58(5):1121–49.

Heckman, J. J., R. J. LaLonde, and J. A. Smith. 1999. "The Economics and Econometrics of Active Labor Market Programs." Pp. 1865–2097 in *Handbook of Labor Economics*, vol. 3A, edited by O. Ashenfelter and D. Card. New York: North-Holland.

Heckman, J. J., L. J. Lochner, and C. Taber. 1998a. "Explaining Rising Wage Inequality: Explorations with a Dynamic General Equilibrium Model of Labor Earnings with Heterogeneous Agents." *Review of Economic Dynamics* 1(1):1–58.

———. 1998b. "General-Equilibrium Treatment Effects: A Study of Tuition Policy." *American Economic Review* 88(2):381–86.

Heckman, J. J., L. J. Lochner, and P. E. Todd. 2006. "Earnings Equations and Rates of Return: The Mincer Equation and Beyond." In *Handbook of the Economics of Education*, edited by E. A. Hanushek and F. Welch. Amsterdam: North-Holland. Forthcoming.

Heckman, J. J., and S. Navarro. 2004. "Using Matching, Instrumental Variables, and Control Functions to Estimate Economic Choice Models." *Review of Economics and Statistics* 86(1):30–57.

————. 2006. "Dynamic Discrete Choice and Dynamic Treatment Effects." *Journal of Econometrics*. Forthcoming.

Heckman, J. J., and R. Robb. 1985. "Alternative Methods for Evaluating the Impact of Interventions." Pp. 156–245 in *Longitudinal Analysis of Labor Market Data*, vol. 10, edited by J. Heckman and B. Singer. New York: Cambridge University Press.

————. 1986. "Alternative Methods for Solving the Problem of Selection Bias in Evaluating the Impact of Treatments on Outcomes." Pp. 63–107 in *Drawing Inferences from Self-Selected Samples*, edited by H. Wainer. New York: Springer-Verlag. Reprinted in 2000, Mahwah, NJ: Lawrence Erlbaum.

Heckman, J. J., and J. A. Smith. 1998. "Evaluating the Welfare State." Pp. 241–318 in *Econometrics and Economic Theory in the Twentieth Century: The Ragnar Frisch Centennial Symposium*, edited by S. Strom. New York: Cambridge University Press.

Heckman, J. J., S. Urzua, and E. J. Vytlacil. 2006. "Understanding Instrumental Variables in Models with Essential Heterogeneity." *Review of Economics and Statistics*. Forthcoming.

Heckman, J. J., and E. J. Vytlacil. 1999. "Local Instrumental Variables and Latent Variable Models for Identifying and Bounding Treatment Effects." *Proceedings of the National Academy of Sciences* 96:4730–34.

————. 2001a. "Local Instrumental Variables." Pp. 1–46 in *Nonlinear Statistical Modeling: Proceedings of the Thirteenth International Symposium in Economic Theory and Econometrics: Essays in Honor of Takeshi Amemiya*, edited by C. Hsiao, K. Morimune, and J. L. Powell. New York: Cambridge University Press.

————. 2001b. "Policy-Relevant Treatment Effects." *American Economic Review* 91(2):107–111.

————. 2005. "Structural Equations, Treatment Effects, and Econometric Policy Evaluation." *Econometrica* 73(3):669–738.

————. 2006a. "Econometric Evaluation of Social Programs, Part I: Causal Models, Structural Models and Econometric Policy Evaluation." In *Handbook of Econometrics*, vol. 6, edited by J. Heckman and E. Leamer. Amsterdam: Elsevier, forthcoming.

————. 2006b. "Econometric Evaluation of Social Programs, Part II: Using the Marginal Treatment Effect to Organize Alternative Economic Estimators to Evaluate Social Programs and to Forecast Their Effects in New Environments." In *Handbook of Econometrics*, vol. 6, edited by J. Heckman and E. Leamer, Amsterdam: Elsevier, forthcoming.

Holland, P. W. 1986. "Statistics and Causal Inference." *Journal of the American Statistical Association* 81(396):945–60.

————. 1988. "Causal Inference, Path Analysis, and Recursive Structural Equation Models." Pp. 449–84 in *Sociological Methodology*, edited by C. Clogg and G. Arminger. Washington, DC: American Sociological Association.

Hurwicz, L. 1962. "On the Structural Form of Interdependent Systems." Pp. 232–39 in *Logic, Methodology and Philosophy of Science*, edited by E. Nagel, P. Suppes, and A. Tarski. Stanford, CA: Stanford University Press.

Imbens, G. W. 2004. "Nonparametric Estimation of Average Treatment Effects under Exogeneity: A Review." *Review of Economics and Statistics* 86(1):4–29.

Imbens, G. W., and J. D. Angrist. 1994. "Identification and Estimation of Local Average Treatment Effects." *Econometrica* 62(2):467–75.

Koopmans, T. C., H. Rubin, and R. B. Leipnik. 1950. "Measuring the Equation Systems of Dynamic Economics." Pp. 53–237 in *Statistical Inference in Dynamic Economic Models*, no. 10, ch. 2 in Cowles Commission Monograph, edited by T. C. Koopmans. New York: John Wiley & Sons.

Lewis, H. G. 1963. *Unionism and Relative Wages in the United States: An Empirical Inquiry*. Chicago: University of Chicago Press.

Manski, C. F. 2000. "Identification Problems and Decisions under Ambiguity: Empirical Treatment of Response and Normative Analysis of Treatment Choice." *Journal of Econometrics* 95(2):415–42.

———. 2004. "Statistical Treatment Rules for Heterogeneous Populations." *Econometrica* 72(4):1221–46.

Marschak, J. 1953. "Economic Measurements for Policy and Prediction." Pp. 1–26 in *Studies in Econometric Method*, edited by W. Hood and T. Koopmans. New York: Wiley.

Matzkin, R. L. 2006. "Nonparametric Identification." In *Handbook of Econometrics*, vol. 6, edited by J. Heckman and E. Leamer. Amsterdam: Elsevier.

McFadden, D. 1974. "Conditional Logit Analysis of Qualitative Choice Behavior." In *Frontiers in Econometrics*, edited by P. Zarembka. New York: Academic Press.

———. 1981. "Econometric Models of Probabilistic Choice." In *Structural Analysis of Discrete Data with Econometric Applications*, edited by C. Manski and D. McFadden. Cambridge, MA: MIT Press.

Neyman, J. 1923. "On the Application of Probability Theory to Agricultural Experiments. Essay on Principles." *Roczniki Nauk Rolniczych* 10:1–51. In Polish; edited and translated version of Section 9 by D. M. Dabrowska and T. P. Speed. Statistical Science 5:465–72.

Pearl, J. 2000. *Causality*. Cambridge, UK: Cambridge University Press.

Peterson, A. V. 1976. "Bounds for a Joint Distribution Function with Fixed Sub-distribution Functions: Application to Competing Risks." *Proceedings of the National Academy of Sciences of the United States of America* 73(1):11–13.

Powell, J. L. 1994. "Estimation of Semiparametric Models." Pp. 2443–2521 in *Handbook of Econometrics*, vol. 4, edited by R. Engle and D. McFadden. Amsterdam: Elsevier.

Quandt, R. E. 1958. "The Estimation of the Parameters of a Linear Regression System Obeying Two Separate Regimes." *Journal of the American Statistical Association* 53(284):873–80.

———. 1972. "A New Approach to Estimating Switching Regressions." *Journal of the American Statistical Association* 67(338):306–10.

Rosenbaum, P. R. 2002. *Observational Studies* (2d ed.), Series in Statistics. New York: Springer-Verlag.

Roy, A. 1951. "Some Thoughts on the Distribution of Earnings." *Oxford Economic Papers* 3(2):135–46.

Rubin, D. B. 1974. "Estimating Causal Effects of Treatments in Randomized and Nonrandomized Studies." *Journal of Educational Psychology* 66(5):688–701.

———. 1976. "Inference and Missing Data." *Biometrika* 63(3):581–92.

———. 1978. "Bayesian Inference for Causal Effects: The Role of Randomization." *Annals of Statistics* 6(1):34–58.

———. 1986. "Statistics and Causal Inference: Comment: Which Ifs Have Causal Answers." *Journal of the American Statistical Association* 81(396):961–62.

———. 2000. "Comment on 'Causal Inference Without Counterfactuals.'" *Journal of the American Statistical Association* 95(450):435–38.

Thurstone, L. 1927. "A Law of Comparative Judgement." *Psychological Review* 34:273–86.

———. 1959. *The Measurement of Values.* Chicago, IL: University of Chicago Press.

Vella, F. 1998. "Estimating Models with Sample Selection Bias: A Survey." *Journal of Human Resources* 33(1):127–69.

Vijverberg, W. P. M. 1993. "Measuring the Unidentified Parameter of the Extended Roy Model of Selectivity." *Journal of Econometrics* 57(1–3):69–89.

Vytlacil, E. J. 2002. "Independence, Monotonicity, and Latent Index Models: An Equivalence Result." *Econometrica* 70(1):331–41.

Wainer, H., ed. 1986. *Drawing Inferences from Self-Selected Samples.* Papers from a conference sponsored by Educational Testing Service. Originally published by Springer-Verlag. Reprinted in 2000, Mahwah, NJ: Lawrence Erlbaum Associates.

Willis, R. J., and S. Rosen. 1979. "Education and Self-Selection." *Journal of Political Economy* 87(5, part 2):S7–S36.

❧ 2 ❧

PRETESTING EXPERIMENTAL INSTRUCTIONS

*Lisa Slattery Rashotte**
*Murray Webster Jr.**
*Joseph M. Whitmeyer**

Laboratory experiments, well established in sociology and social psychology, are alternate realities constructed for assessing derivations from theories. Experiments instantiate a theory's scope and initial conditions, and that information is usually delivered through instructions to participants. Because experiments often use video and computer technology and often test very precise predictions of new theories, we suggest developing objective means to assess information delivery. We illustrate these points by reference to a widely used standard experiment to assess theories of status processes. We first describe elements of good experimental design with their justifications. Next, we describe new techniques we have developed and illustrate their usefulness, showing results of a first use of the new techniques. While the assessment still relies somewhat on judgments, we find the technique useful and suggest further developments that might improve it for experimental and other research uses.

NSF award SES 9911135 supported research and preparation of this report. Cortney Hedman and Stephanie Southworth-Brown were research assistants. Stuart Hysom and Cathryn Johnson provided the outside instructions tape. Suggestions from two reviewers and the editor improved the organization and phrasing. We gratefully acknowledge all.

*University of North Carolina – Charlotte

1. INTRODUCTION AND OVERVIEW

Appropriately used, laboratory experiments offer sociologists a strong method to develop and test many kinds of theories. Experiments permit simplification of natural settings to focus on a few theoretically relevant variables; their results often are less susceptible to alternate interpretations than other kinds of data; they also permit devising situations where effects and measurement are clearly visible and relatively uncontaminated by extraneous effects.

At the same time, creating experimental situations appropriately is a complex achievement. Many factors are involved in successfully instantiating independent variables, scope conditions and initial conditions; and in measuring dependent variables. They involve both theoretical and operational concerns. When poorly realized, an experiment becomes irrelevant to theory testing. While no design ever manages theoretical and operational issues perfectly, good design involves attending to questions of translating abstract theories to operational experimental methods.

A significant part of an experiment is the way information is transmitted to participants, often called "experimental instructions." Everything about a design—from definition of the situation to roles and to possible behaviors and the meanings they convey—must be transmitted through instructions. Because of the significance of experimental instructions, systematic assessment of them is desirable for knowing and standardizing effects, and for understanding how participants interpret information that experimenters provide.

In this chapter, we begin with a consideration of relations between theories and experimental design and focus on types of information an experiment should communicate. We next describe a standard experiment that has been used for almost 50 years for sequential studies of status processes, showing changes allowed by video and computer technology. Finally, we present a new tool we have developed to assess information provided by technology in the standard experiment, and we show some preliminary results that confirm the usefulness of this assessment.

2. SOME FEATURES OF EXPERIMENTAL SOCIOLOGY

Experiments create situations for testing derivations from theories. An experiment, like a theory, is a simplification of natural complexity, permitting investigators to focus on elements of nature within manageable limits of number, size, and variation. Ideally, an experiment would contain *all* and *only* the theoretically relevant aspects of a social situation. Theoretical foundations of an experiment appear in derived hypotheses for testing, containing independent variables to be controlled and dependent variables to be measured. An experiment must also create a situation that fits the scope conditions of the theory, and it must include initial conditions of structure and interaction that allow predicted outcomes to occur, or not to occur.

Experimental design means creating an alternate reality that volunteer participants will inhabit for a time. Experiments generally should not approximate natural settings, for if a natural setting is available that offers something close to the situation needed for testing hypotheses, an investigator would be wise to use that instead of working to create an experiment. Experiments depend on uniformity and standardization; so far as possible, every participant in a condition ought to experience it in the same way. Subtlety, complexity, nuance, and ambiguity are out of place; everything should be obvious and unmistakable.

Whatever the design of an experiment, it is communicated to participants through instructions delivered by experimenters. All relevant aspects of a situation must appear in ways participants understand so that they can cognitively enter the situation described in the theory under test. This is not an easy task. Some decades ago, investigators identified "experimenter effects" that can systematically bias results (Rosenthal 1963), and contemporary experimental methods include ways to discover, measure, or control unintended biasing effects of experimenters' behavior. More recently, other investigators have begun to identify and document effects of aspects of experiments such as video and computer technology (e.g., Cohen 1988; Kiesler, Siegel, and McGuire 1984; Troyer 2001, 2002). In this more recent work, the concern is not with biasing results in favor of or against hypotheses but rather with adequately creating required elements of a situation so that theoretical derivations may receive test.

Successful experimental designs instantiate *scope conditions* of a theory and *initial conditions* of a group interaction situation. Scope conditions are abstract statements of classes of situations to which a theory claims to apply; they constrain the applicability of theories. For instance, a theory of group processes may take as its scope all groups whose members are *task focused* and *collectively oriented*. The first condition means that members' primary motivation in interaction is to solve a problem; the second means they consider it legitimate and necessary for every individual to contribute to the problem solving. Thus a jury is within the scope of such a theory, while a fraternity party or a group of students taking a final exam are not (the party is not task focused; the students are not supposed to share information). Confirmatory results in situations meeting a theory's scope conditions increase confidence in the theory, and disconfirmation decreases confidence. However, for situations not meeting a theory's scope, any empirical results are irrelevant to that theory's confirmation status.[1]

Initial conditions describe features of a situation that an experiment must create. These include operational instances of independent and dependent variables of hypotheses, and other conditions describing structural and interaction conditions of a particular experiment. For instance, an independent variable in a particular experimental condition might require placing a participant in a position of status advantage compared to his or her partner. If participants are told that their partners are younger (using an operational presumption that age functions as a status characteristic for this population), an initial condition here is that such participants believe they have a status advantage in this group. If participants work on a joint task in which every disagreement must be resolved before completing their work, an initial condition is that they recognize the disagreements (and, if the disagreements are contrived by an experimenter, the participants treat them as real).

In the following section, we illustrate and expand this discussion of desirable features of experimental design with an established theoretical and experimental research tradition into how status processes affect group interaction.

3. STATUS, EXPECTATIONS, AND OBSERVABLE BEHAVIOR

Among sociologists who study group processes, a well-established research tradition is the study of status organizing processes. This

---

[1]Foschi (1997) and Walker and Cohen (1985) describe scope conditions and their functions in sociological theories. Walker and Cohen discuss the logical status of scope conditions, and Foschi considers ways to assess whether they have been met in particular cases.

approach originated with Joseph Berger (Berger and Snell 1961) and he and many other scholars have developed it cumulatively. Recent summaries are available in Wagner and Berger (1993, 2002).

Status organizing theories are concerned with understanding the emergence and maintenance of structural and behavioral inequalities in groups whose members work together to solve a problem or a set of problems. Such groups include committees, juries, sports teams, and Bales-type discussion groups. Virtually all these groups show behavioral inequality among members. It appears in participation rates, evaluations, influence, perceived ability, perceived helpfulness, votes for honorific positions such as foreperson, and other manifestations. The different inequalities tend to correlate highly with each other, and together they constitute the *power and prestige structure* of a group.

Given the scope conditions *task focus* and *collective orientation* of group members, the core theory of status organizing claims that the power and prestige structure is the observable result of an underlying structure of *performance expectation states* associated with group members. Expectations are anticipations of the likely quality of each individual's future performance attempts.[2] For instance, if I hold high expectations for Sally, that fact predisposes me to grant a positive evaluation ("I think that's right") to Sally's next problem-solving attempt; and the converse is true for low expectations. More complete expositions of the theory are available in Berger et al. (1977); Webster and Foschi (1988); and Wagner and Berger (1993).

Two general sources of expectations have been identified: social structure and social interaction. Structural sources include the

---

[2]Performance expectations are theoretical constructs, and are not necessarily in the realm of conscious awareness (Berger et al. 1966:33, 40; Ridgeway and Walker 1995:288; Skvoretz, Webster, and Whitmeyer 1999:201). Theoretically, expectations affect behavior whether or not an actor thinks about them. In other words, someone does not need to think, "I am a woman and he is a man and therefore he probably understands this task better than I do" before she defers to another's suggestion. Expectations are dispositions, and their manifestations depend on how they get activated in a particular setting. They may be moved into awareness by direct questions, for instance. However, their behavioral manifestations do not (according to the theory) require intervening steps of motivation or planning. Men are often unaware they talk more than women in committees, and women are often unaware that they accept more suggestions from men than vice-versa.

status characteristics that individuals "carry" with them into an interaction situation, such as skin color. Interaction sources include hesi-
tation, repeated behavior patterns, and expressed status claims. Those
factors, and others, activate performance expectations, which in turn
affect group power and prestige behaviors.

4. THE STANDARD EXPERIMENT AND CHANGING TECHNOLOGY

Cumulative theory development in this area has been fostered by a
basic experimental design often referred to as "the standard experiment"—(for instance, in Berger et al. 1977:43–48). The standard
experiment creates the simplest case to which status organizing theories apply, and it allows measurement of performance expectations
produced in different kinds of situations. Because the theory deals
with inequality and interaction, the smallest size group to which it can
apply is usually two (larger in some cases, such as those involving
conflicting evaluators of an individual). The power and prestige component that most reliably measures relative expectations is interac-
tants' relative likelihoods of resolving task-related disagreements in
favor of themselves. The clearest and simplest kind of problem over
which to disagree is binary, having only two possible answers. Finally,
disagreements, which are essential to generate the data of the experiment, are created experimentally and, for efficiency, are nearly
continual.

The standard experiment has two phases or parts; roughly,
these correspond to independent and dependent variables. Phase I
introduces theoretical scope conditions, independent variables, and
general features of interaction (the initial conditions); and Phase II
collects data on the dependent variable, influence. Phase I is usually
accomplished by two experimenters who present instructions and
information to participants. One is presented as a sociologist expert
and guides participants through the task they will be performing; the
other is said to be an expert in scoring performance.

The dependent variable, influence, is a measure of relative
expectations, and it is measured in Phase II as group members work
together at a series of binary problems. Each participant studies a
slide, makes an "initial choice" and sees the partner's initial choice;

then, after further consideration, each participant makes a "final decision" as to correct answer. Feedback generally is controlled such that each person receives nearly continuous disagreements from the partner, and thus is forced to resolve many disagreements in favor of self or other (usually 20 to 40 critical trials). The proportion of disagreements resolved in favor of self, $P(s)$, varies directly with the expectations held for self, relative to those held for other.

Standard means of creating status inequality employ either diffuse status characteristics (such as age, gender, or skin color), or specific status characteristics (such as different ability scores). Each has advantages and disadvantages. Briefly, most group participants understand diffuse characteristics readily, but the most powerful characteristics—gender and skin color—have only "advantaged" and "disadvantaged" states. That makes it impossible to place individuals from the same subject pool into both relatively high and relatively low positions in different conditions of an experiment. The diffuse characteristic age does permit placement into either high or low positions; for instance, a college student can be either relatively advantaged if the purported partner is a high school student or relatively disadvantaged if the partner is an older adult. However not all college students automatically feel advantaged compared to high school students, and not all of them feel disadvantaged compared to adults. Specific characteristics, such as reading ability or ability at an unfamiliar experimental task, permit easy placement. On the other hand, an experimenter must make the "test" of the characteristic plausible enough to overcome any general suspicion of the reliability of test results (e.g., "I never [or always] do well at tests").

For measuring predicted effects on expectation states, computer programs present a standard criterion task, Contrast Sensitivity.[3] Each participant faces a computer terminal that presents pairs of

[3]Moore (1968) created the contrast sensitivity task, originally presented from 35 mm slides using a slide projector. Webster and Driskell (1978) first used tape to present the slides. Foschi (1996; also Foschi et al. 1990) first used a computer-mediated presentation of the contrast sensitivity task. Troyer (1999; Troyer and Younts 1997) modified several aspects of Foschi's program to make its presentation closer to the presentation of slides. Troyer (2002) describes changes in the administration of contrast sensitivity and their effects on the $P(s)$ measure. Our programs are similar to Troyer's, though developed independently.

patterns composed of black and white rectangles. For each trial, the task is to determine whether the top or the bottom pattern contains more white area. Actually, the patterns have identical amounts of white. This removes sensory bases of decisions, leaving social bases such as influence processes most visible. After study, each participant receives a prompt to make an "initial choice." When he or she makes it, that choice is supposedly exchanged with the partner, but actually, the computer shows a disagreement on all but three of the 23 trials. After further study, all participants receive a prompt to make a "final decision." They do not see each other's final decisions. The computer records initial choices and final decisions, and it calculates $P(s)$ for every participant.

As noted earlier, theoretical development has been greatly assisted by the use of a standard experimental design, modified appropriately to assess new theoretical developments. If different investigators use different designs, comparing results and developing knowledge cumulatively are much more difficult. Any meta-analyses designed to summarize the state of knowledge would be faced with difficulties from diversity of interaction conditions, tasks, independent and dependent variables, and operationalizations of all aspects of the design.

A body of experiments using a standard design generally permits comparisons across different experiments, and when drawn from similar subject pools, conditions of one experiment may serve as control conditions for a second experiment. Focusing on a series of related experiments deals with problems of population uniqueness, measurement unreliability, and artifact interpretations that plague any one-time designs. Cohen (1989:385–86) discusses these and other benefits of successive uses of a standard design.

More intuitively, investigators using a standard design often develop "rules of thumb" about operations and measures that can be useful to assess operational modifications. For instance, in the standard design, $P(s)$ values normally appear in the range .40–.80. While individual outcomes outside that range certainly occur, if many participants display extreme data, an experimenter should look for evidence of processes other than status-expectation processes. Very high $P(s)$ values may appear if a design causes participants to feel anger toward their partners; very low values may appear if something about the design triggers preexisting low expectations, such as reminding a participant of a particularly difficult test situation.

Experimental studies of status processes have developed and changed since the experiments of the 1960s and 1970s. We have come to think of the standard experiment as evolving through three "generations," each incorporating new technology and operational changes. The first generation was used for experiments conducted between 1958 and 1977; in it, two experimenters in the same room with participants present all instructions and monitor progress of the experiment. The second generation appeared in 1978; the main change was to present information on closed-circuit television through experimenters on tape. The third generation appeared around 1995; data collection for this experiment, including behavioral $P(s)$ and questionnaires, takes place using computer programs. Current research uses second- or third-generation designs.[4]

5. REQUIREMENTS, OPERATIONS, AND POTENTIAL PROBLEMS IN EXPERIMENTAL DESIGN

Imagine an experiment in which two participants, p and o, are distinguished by a single diffuse status characteristic, gender, that gives p an advantage (i.e., p is male and o is female). According to the core theory of status organizing, both p and o will form higher performance expectations for p, and those will place p above o in the dyad's power and prestige structure. The status advantage of the o will appear in $P(s)$ differences in the standard experiment, such that $p > o$.

It is useful to examine implicit steps in that argument. First, in simplified form, we are using several theoretical statements that may be stated in the form of material implication. Here is one example:

---

[4]Most early experiments used the simplest situation in which inequality is manifest, that of two participants, and only two actual participants are included in each group. Second-generation and third-generation designs allow running more than two actual participants at a time, though each of them is told she or he is in a two-person group, with only one "partner." Among the benefits are efficiency from running as many as six participants at a time; and the ability to conduct a "group" even if only one participant can be scheduled for a time, or only one shows up to keep the appointment. Troyer (2002) discusses technological changes and their effects in the standard experiment for studying status processes.

1. Status advantage → expectation advantage.
2. Expectation advantage → power and prestige advantage.

Statements (1) and (2) could be combined to yield a derivation.

3. Status advantage → power and prestige advantage.

The concepts *status, expectations,* and *power and prestige* all are abstract and thus they are not directly observable.[5] We might take gender as an operational instance of status. Doing that uses an operational rule that says gender is a status characteristic for the individuals involved; that is, they recognize it as a socially meaningful difference and they believe males have an advantage. We take $P(s)$ as an operational measure of power and prestige position because influence is one component of that concept. If we did that, we would have this operational hypothesis for test:

H1. Gender advantage → $P(s)$ advantage.

Empirically, gender is an independent variable and $P(s)$ is a dependent variable. Operational definitions, of course, are chosen largely for convenience, and if they are chosen mistakenly, results of a hypothesis test tell nothing about the theory from which this hypothesis was derived.

A second issue in experimental design is to instantiate a theory's scope conditions—in this case, that individuals are *task focused* and *collectively oriented.* If scope conditions are not met, results of a test have no implications for the theory. A third and final issue is to instantiate initial conditions of independent variables, and many conditions of interaction and structure. For instance, participants work on a unitary task requiring a single kind of skill; they interact under conditions of nearly continuous disagreement; they must be motivated to try to get the best possible answers to the task; and they should have no prior performance expectations for how well they and their partner will do at the task.

---

[5]Willer and Webster (1970) discuss uses of theoretical and observable concepts in sociology.

Walker and Cohen (1985) have shown that, though they are often unstated, scope conditions and initial conditions function as part of the deductive apparatus of any theory test. That is, antecedents in the above syllogism include conditions that must be true or else the test is meaningless. Those include operational definitions, scope conditions of the theory, and initial conditions of the interaction situation. While a theorist bears responsibility to identify scope limitations of a theory, an experimenter bears responsibility to incorporate scope and initial conditions, and to choose appropriate operational definitions. Experimental pretests can help to assess the adequacy of new parts of a standard design.

The standard experiment includes several features developed to ensure compliance with those three considerations:

- *Standard written instructions*: Since the earliest days of the first-generation designs, experimenters present all information from a rigid script. The script presents information in a sequence that participants can understand and retain. It includes all crucial information and avoids extraneous distractions.
- *Repetition*: Every crucial piece of information is presented three times (in slightly different wording). For some, the repetition can seem tedious, but that is preferable to having some participants miss something crucial.
- *Multiple measures*: While the theory predicts behavior, not cognitions, participants typically complete questionnaires that ask their perceptions of relative ability. Answers they give may identify potential problems for further examination in an interview. Questionnaires also help assess whether participants remember initial conditions such as partner's gender and whether gender carries status value in their eyes.
- *Postsession interview*: Every participant receives an individual interview, typically lasting 45 minutes or so, at the end of the session. The interviewer is concerned to learn as much as possible about how the participant understood and interpreted the situation. For instance, a participant who did not believe the disagreements actually came from the partner would not have been resolving disagreements and his or her $P(s)$ data would not therefore reflect accepting or rejecting influence. Equally important, the interview is used to explain and correct any deceptions in the

experiment, such as the disagreement operations and any false information about the partner.

6. RATIONALE FOR DIRECTLY ASSESSING VIDEO PRESENTATIONS

This section focuses on a technological change introduced at the second generation and now universally adopted, with tape used to present instructions on the situation.

The advantages of using tapes instead of live experimenters include the following:

- *Ease, simplicity*: It is much easier to start a tape than to read instructions to participants for an experiment that may take an hour or more to complete, and that may be repeated three or four times each day. Experimenters are able to monitor other aspects of the experiment more closely, and often they are more alert for the interviews.
- *Standardization*: Tapes ensure that every individual in a given condition receives virtually the same treatment. Any effects that might occur due to fatigue of experimenters or to subtle changes in their delivery from increasing familiarity with the material are eliminated. When experimental conditions differ only by inclusion or exclusion of some information, that part of a tape may be edited, leaving other parts unchanged from tapes used in other conditions. Thus, all participants hearing recorded experimental instructions experience virtually the same situation, to a far greater extent than is possible with live administration.

Improved standardization of instructions is probably the most important improvement of design at the second generation. However, it also entails potential problems. Any flaws in the tapes will affect every participant, rather than simply causing variance by influencing a few groups out of an entire design as happens when live experimenters make mistakes. Put this way, it might seem obvious that the tapes themselves require heightened scrutiny, and we describe our experience assessing recorded instructions.

7. METHODS

Among the many concerns in developing an experimental design, the following factors have more to do with paraverbal and nonverbal presentation styles of the experimenters than with content of the scripts.

1. Do participants treat the situation seriously, and are they motivated to do the best they can? This is important for instantiating the scope condition *task focus.*
2. Do participants understand the collective nature of the task—for instance, that their initial choices are not counted toward team scores and that only final decisions count? This is important for the scope condition *collective orientation.*
3. Do participants understand how they will go about working on the task, including using the computer terminal and the television monitor? This is important to create some *initial conditions* of the interaction situation.
4. Do participants accept and believe the status manipulation—for instance, knowing the characteristics possessed by self and others? This is important for an *initial condition,* and it requires that experimenters convey an air of authority.
5. Do participants hold status beliefs associated with the operational characteristic—for instance, believing they are different from and superior to a middle school child who is their partner? This is important for an *operational definition* of a status characteristic.
6. Are the presentations reasonably free of distractions? Distracting mannerisms of the recorded experimenters may cause some participants to overlook significant facts or lose task focus.
7. Can participants form minimal bonds to the experimenters so that they wish to follow the instructions and do well at the task? The experimenters should be likeable enough that participants undertake the interaction task, though not so likeable that participants want them for friends.

The first step in our work was to adapt scripts that our experimenters would read in the tape. These scripts were based on years of experience with these tasks and with experimental procedures. The instructions lay out all of the key points of technical instruction (initial conditions such as how to use the equipment), and encouraged participants to be task-focused and collectively oriented (scope conditions for the theory). All key points in the instructions were repeated at least three times, a practice we have come to believe is essential for uniform communication of a message. As noted earlier, decades of experience with the standard experiment have shown that the scripts themselves are excellent at conveying information. However, scripts are delivered by human actors, and their paraverbal and nonverbal behavior may affect the quality of the information delivered.

The script included two experimenters: a Host, Dr. Philip Gordon, and a Boardman, Ms. Lynn Mason. Dr. Gordon is a scholar who has dedicated his life to understanding group interaction processes. Ms. Mason is an expert in the scoring and interpreting of scores on the tests to be used in these groups.

Next, we began production of the video. To play Dr. Gordon, we hired an actor who looked scholarly—at least in our estimation: a graying, serious-looking man wearing glasses and a suit. (He is, in fact, an accountant, and his manner reflects many aspects of that occupation.) Ms. Mason was a graduate student research assistant involved in the project. They rehearsed for the roles on their own and also with supervision and guidance from the research staff.

The video was produced in a campus classroom using a single camera and a professional camera operator. Props included a television monitor and control panel facing Dr. Gordon, and a lab coat and clipboard for Ms. Mason and several charts showing supposed "standards" for the test scores. Some portions of the script were recorded more than once to correct misspoken lines, technical difficulties, and last-minute script changes.

Postproduction editing selected the best takes of each portion of the script. Minor misspeaking was retained in the tape to preserve an appearance of live instructions. When it was impossible for the video and audio portions of the tape to be matched exactly, the editor inserted footage of the other experimenter listening and nodding. The final tape flowed well yet still had an appearance of being live-action.

Our concern in pretesting was not so much with whether the scripts were clear and understandable, for the scripts have stood the test of time in this kind of research. We were, however, concerned with the styles of the actors, whether they were *clear, authoritative, serious*, and *free of distracting mannerisms* of speech and action. To assess those qualities, we developed a paper and pencil questionnaire consisting of 40 adjectives presented as opposites with a response scale between them, as in this sample:

Ignorant ... ... Knowledgeable

The data tables below contain complete lists of the items.

We do not know all the characteristics that are important in effective delivery of experimental instructions, and we see this exercise as a preliminary attempt to develop objective assessments of experimental instructions. In the discussion section below, we note some shortcomings that appeared after data analysis, and suggest some improvements for this method. For this preliminary assessment, however, the following concerns seemed to be especially worthwhile assessing.

- *Authority and competence*: This appears to be the highest priority, for experimenters must be believable sources of all the information in the experiment. If these properties are weak, all experimental conditions—scope, initial conditions, and procedures—may be jeopardized. We measured authority and competence with 16 items: knowledgeable/ignorant, believable/not believable, well prepared/unprepared, perceptive/dull-witted, convincing/unconvincing, competent/incompetent, excellent/poor vocabulary, professional/unprofessional, experienced/inexperienced, capable/incapable, highly educated/uneducated, clever/dumb, expert/novice, strong/weak, attractive/unattractive, and confident/uncertain.
- *Absence of distractions*: Experimenters must establish at least minimal ties to participants to motivate cooperation and willingness to attend to the task situation presented. Mannerisms that distract from the material presented may lower task focus, or cause participants to ignore or forget crucial information. We measured this with 15 items: friendly/unfriendly, to the point/wordy, flexible/rigid, exciting/boring, genuine/phony, pleasant/irritating, zealous/indifferent, respectful/condescending, too old/too young, easy to understand/hard to understand, comfortable/awkward, melodramatic/matter of fact, enjoyable/frustrating, likeable/dislikeable, overbearing/meek, and interesting/boring.
- *Clarity*: While clarity is obviously important, we used fewer items to assess it because of the repetition of crucial parts and because

the scripts have been used and improved for decades in the standard experiment. We used six items for clarity, emphasizing paraverbal characteristics of the experimenters: not enough repetition/ too much repetition, excellent pronunciation/poor pronunciation, too fast/too slow, meaningful/nonsensical, logical/illogical, and excellent grammar/poor grammar.

- *Serious manner*: Finally, to reinforce task focus, the experimenters should communicate that the session deserves a serious approach. Three items focus on paraverbal behaviors, for the script is serious in content: reliable/unreliable, thorough/careless, and zealous/ indifferent.

Each semantic differential item was rated on a seven-point Likert-style scale. A final open-ended question asked for any additional comments respondents wished to make. For some of the items, such as "knowledgeable/ignorant," the most desirable response is at one pole (either 1 or 7, in this case 7); for others, such as "too fast/too slow," the most desirable response is in the middle of the scale (4).

In order to judge the adequacy of the actors' performances, of course we need comparisons. We were fortunate to secure a tape developed by researchers at another university for a different, though similar, project that we could assess along with ours. Thus we could compare Dr. Gordon in our tape to the host in the other tape. (The other tape uses the Host's real name.)

The first pretest was conducted with 56 students in two upper-level sociology classes. Students were told participation was voluntary and there were no course-related benefits or repercussions for participating or not participating. Students in these two classes may not have represented the student body of the university in all respects, but they were quite similar to those who volunteered from other social science classes to participate in the actual experiments.

Each class viewed a 10-minute segment of both tapes taken from near the beginning of the experiment. One class saw our initial tape first and the other class saw the outside tape first. Our initial tape included both the fictional Dr. Gordon and his fictional assistant, Ms. Mason. The outside tape portrayed only the Host. After viewing each segment, students completed the questionnaires.

Table 1 compares the Host Experimenter in our tape ("Initial Tape Mean" shown in column 3) to the Host in the outside tape

TABLE 1
Comparison of Host on Initial Tape to Host on the Outside Tape

Variable	Ideal	Initial Tape Mean	Outside Tape Mean	Difference Between Initial and Outside Tape Means
Too fast/Too slow	4	5.36	4.44	.92**
Ignorant/Knowledgeable	7	4.07	5.29	1.22**
Friendly/Unfriendly	4	3.74	2.87	.87**
Not believable/Believable	7	4.13	5.16	1.03**
Well prepared/Unprepared	1	4.66	2.30	2.36**
Reliable/Unreliable	1	3.94	3.08	.86**
Perceptive/Dull-witted	1	4.65	3.08	1.57**
Nonsensical/Meaningful	7	3.89	5.02	1.13**
Convincing/Unconvincing	1	4.53	2.96	1.57**
Competent/Incompetent	1	4.13	2.44	1.69**
Poor/Excellent vocabulary	7	4.02	5.25	1.23**
To the point/Wordy	1	4.63	3.64	.99**
Logical/Illogical	1	3.52	2.78	.74**
Professional/Unprofessional	1	3.82	2.49	1.33**
Careless/Thorough	7	4.41	5.69	1.28**
Inexperienced/Experienced	7	3.33	5.31	1.98**
Capable/Incapable	1	4.05	2.68	1.37**
Highly educated/Uneducated	1	3.53	2.40	1.13**
Clever/Dumb	1	4.11	2.96	1.15**
Flexible/Rigid	4	4.89	3.80	1.09**
Boring/Exciting	4	2.07	3.79	1.72**
Phony/Genuine	7	3.39	4.25	.86**
Irritating/Pleasant	7	3.25	4.23	.98**
Zealous/Indifferent	1	4.50	3.55	.95**
Expert/Novice	1	4.27	2.92	1.35**
Condescending/Respectful	7	4.57	4.67	.10
Strong/Weak	1	4.46	2.96	1.50**
Too old/Too young	4	3.50	4.06	.56**
Easy/Hard to understand	1	4.05	2.43	1.58**
Comfortable/Awkward	1	4.93	2.69	2.24**
Melodramatic/Matter of fact	7	4.93	4.49	.44
Frustrating/Enjoyable	7	3.28	4.23	.95**
Dislikeable/Likeable	4	3.75	4.67	.92**
Attractive/Unattractive	4	4.62	3.58	1.04**
Poor/Excellent grammar	7	3.84	5.38	1.54**
Meek/Overbearing	4	3.56	3.98	.42
Interesting/Boring	1	5.89	3.79	2.10**
Too repetitious/Not enough	4	3.41	3.55	.14
Uncertain/Confident	7	3.09	5.52	2.43**
Excellent/Poor pronunciation	1	4.84	2.70	2.14**

$*p < .05$ $**p < .01$

("Outside Tape Mean" shown in column 4). To facilitate comparisons, ideal scores are presented as well, in column 2.

We performed independent-samples t-tests for each item. For 36 of the 40 items, tests show significant differences between the two tapes. All but two of those differences favored the outside tape. In other words, for 34 of the 40 items, the outside tape was significantly closer to the ideal than was our initial tape. The two items on which our initial tape was significantly closer to the ideal than the outside tape both relate to absence of distracting manner: friendly/unfriendly and dislikeable/likeable. The four items for which there was no significant difference between the two tapes were condescending/respectful, melodramatic/matter of fact, meek/overbearing, and too repetitious/not repetitious enough. Three of those have to do with distracting manner; the fourth, with clarity.

Those findings prompted us to redo our tape, this time hiring the host from the outside tape to replace our initial actor. We also made a few slight modifications to the script, and produced and pretested the new tape.

We conducted a second pretest comparison using data from two additional undergraduate classes, a sociology course and an anthropology course. These classes also enroll students of the population pool for experimental participants, though they may not be completely typical of all students at the university. Forty-two students participated in this comparison. As before, participation was voluntary and uncompensated. Again, each saw two 10-minute segments with the order of viewing reversed for the second class. Ms. Mason's portion of the tape had not changed and thus was not viewed by these students or rerated. Students completed the questionnaires containing the semantic differentials after watching each segment. We again solicited open-ended comments.

Results in Table 2 compare the new tape to the initial tape that we had produced. Table 2 compares the Host Experimenter in our tape ("Initial Tape Mean" in column 3) to the Host in our revised tape ("Final Tape Mean" in column 4).

The final tape showed significant improvement on 15 of the 40 measures. On an additional 21 measures, the final tape appears to have been improved, although those changes are not statistically significant. On no measure did the final tape get significantly worse, and on only four items—friendly/unfriendly, condescending/

TABLE 2
Comparison of Host on Initial Tape to Host on the Final Tape

Variable	Ideal	Initial Tape Mean	Final Tape Mean	Difference Between Initial and Final Tape Means
Too fast/Too slow	4	4.83	4.40	.43
Ignorant/Knowledgeable	7	4.37	4.71	.34
Friendly/Unfriendly	4	3.83	3.48	.35
Not believable/Believable	7	4.22	4.71	.49
Well prepared/Unprepared	1	4.10	3.71	.39
Reliable/Unreliable	1	3.85	3.45	.40
Perceptive/Dull-witted	1	4.37	3.40	.97**
Nonsensical/Meaningful	7	4.08	4.88	.80*
Convincing/Unconvincing	1	4.29	3.52	.77*
Competent/Incompetent	1	4.05	3.19	.86**
Poor/Excellent vocabulary	7	3.95	4.48	.53
To the point/Wordy	1	4.49	4.02	.47
Logical/Illogical	1	3.68	3.19	.49
Professional/Unprofessional	1	3.56	3.31	.25
Careless/Thorough	7	4.54	5.33	.79*
Inexperienced/Experienced	7	3.76	4.45	.69*
Capable/Incapable	1	3.70	3.36	.34
Highly educated/Uneducated	1	3.54	3.14	.40
Clever/Dumb	1	4.00	3.83	.17
Flexible/Rigid	4	4.73	4.29	.44
Boring/Exciting	4	2.66	3.07	.41
Phony/Genuine	7	3.63	4.31	.68*
Irritating/Pleasant	7	3.15	3.43	.28
Zealous/Indifferent	1	4.93	4.07	.86**
Expert/Novice	1	5.93	3.69	2.24
Condescending/Respectful	7	4.51	4.50	.01
Strong/Weak	1	4.29	3.71	.58
Too old/Too young	4	3.20	3.86	.66**
Easy/Hard to understand	1	4.22	3.52	.70
Comfortable/Awkward	1	4.80	3.98	.82*
Melodramatic/Matter of fact	7	4.80	4.50	.30
Frustrating/Enjoyable	7	3.22	3.68	.46
Dislikeable/Likeable	4	3.63	3.76	.13
Attractive/Unattractive	4	4.70	4.10	.60*
Poor grammar/Excellent grammar	7	3.73	4.52	.79**
Meek/Overbearing	4	3.85	4.12	.27
Interesting/Boring	1	5.37	4.21	1.16**
Too repetitious/Not enough	4	3.63	3.31	.32
Uncertain/Confident	7	3.24	4.07	.83*
Excellent/Poor pronunciation	1	4.59	3.73	.86*

*p < .05   **p < .01

respectful, melodramatic/matter of fact, and too repetitious/not enough repetition—was the final tape any worse at all. We conclude that our portrayal of Dr. Gordon is significantly better in the new ("final") tape than in the first tape.

Finally, we assess both Dr. Gordon in the new tape and Ms. Mason, to be sure that both actors are conveying about the same impressions to participants. We cannot decide in any absolute sense whether the final tape is "good enough" using tests of significance. It would be nearly impossible for means actually to meet the ideal values when those ideas are endpoints of a scale (1 or 7). Adequacy is therefore relative to other tapes (our first tape and the outside tape), and other judgments are facilitated by inspection of values. Table 3 presents the means for Dr. Gordon and Ms. Mason on the final tape. Once again, the table presents ideal scores, and in many cases, the means for both individuals approach ideal scores. Dr. Gordon may be more "irritating," "boring," and "frustrating" than would be ideal. Whether those defects are effects of the detail and repetition in the script or are correctable through modifying his behavior, we cannot tell at this point. Ms. Mason may be a bit "boring" and "indifferent." Again, whether those effects come from the script or from her behavior is not clear from these data.

8. DISCUSSION AND CONCLUSIONS

A laboratory experiment is a complicated social situation. It requires experimenters to create and sustain an alternate reality for some period, one in which participants respond to features of that reality in ways that an experimenter can measure. Creating such a situation is difficult, and we believe sociologists are wise to adapt proven experimental designs when possible, rather than designing a new experiment for each new investigation.

Experiments have some features that are analogous to stage performances. In both, actors must portray certain texts using certain styles, and an experimenter, like a stage director, is responsible for guiding and shaping their behavior. Also like a stage director, an experimenter may find it possible to communicate what outcome she or he desires, but may not always be capable of conveying that to an actor, and an actor may not always be capable of delivering the

TABLE 3
Dr. Gordon and Ms. Mason in Final Tape

Variable	Ideal	Dr. Gordon Mean	Ms. Mason Mean
Too fast/Too slow	4	4.40	4.46
Ignorant/Knowledgeable	7	4.71	5.07
Friendly/Unfriendly	4	3.48	3.20
Not believable/Believable	7	4.71	5.15
Well prepared/Unprepared	1	3.71	2.70
Reliable/Unreliable	1	3.45	2.90
Perceptive/Dull witted	1	3.40	2.98
Nonsensical/Meaningful	7	4.88	4.74
Convincing/Unconvincing	1	3.52	2.81
Competent/Incompetent	1	3.19	2.74
Poor/Excellent vocabulary	7	4.48	5.15
To the point/Wordy	1	4.02	3.91
Logical/Illogical	1	3.19	2.91
Professional/Unprofessional	1	3.31	2.89
Careless/Thorough	7	5.33	5.43
Inexperienced/Experienced	7	4.45	4.72
Capable/Incapable	1	3.36	2.91
Highly educated/Uneducated	1	3.14	2.98
Clever/Dumb	1	3.83	3.39
Flexible/Rigid	4	4.29	3.72
Boring/Exciting	4	3.07	4.22
Phony/Genuine	7	4.31	4.09
Irritating/Pleasant	7	3.43	4.42
Zealous/Indifferent	1	4.07	4.96
Expert/Novice	1	3.69	4.04
Condescending/Respectful	7	4.50	4.53
Strong/Weak	1	3.71	3.60
Too old/Too young	4	3.86	4.35
Easy/Hard to understand	1	3.52	2.49
Comfortable/Awkward	1	3.98	3.13
Melodramatic/Matter of fact	7	4.50	4.51
Frustrating/Enjoyable	7	3.68	4.43
Dislikeable/Likeable	4	3.76	4.70
Attractive/Unattractive	4	4.10	3.02
Poor grammar/Excellent grammar	7	4.52	5.13
Meek/Overbearing	4	4.12	3.94
Interesting/Boring	1	4.21	4.31
Too repetitious/Not enough	4	3.31	2.76
Uncertain/Confident	7	4.07	5.26
Excellent/Poor pronunciation	1	3.73	3.02

behavior that is called for. Unlike a stage director, however, an experimenter does not welcome individuality or spontaneity; indeed, the opposite is usually called for. Experiments are not entertainment, and in an ideal world, every actor would portray a role such as Dr. Gordon or Ms. Mason in exactly the same fashion.

Pretesting is crucial to check on success of the design and operations at creating the situation needed. With theoretical development, experiments often test derivations that require complex social situations with subtle differences between conditions. Such advances make pretesting especially important, and thus we hope to see it become more a standard part of procedure than it has been in the past. Certainly, theories of status generalization are now developed sufficiently that new work is likely to require complex experiments or subtle differences between conditions, or both.

Most contemporary experimental research makes some provision for pretesting of designs (for instance, to be sure that materials are appropriate and the equipment functions), and many experimenters assess how participants interpret situations through questionnaires at the end of each session. Questionnaires, however, often tap only a small part of the information that a thorough pretest could provide, and sometimes they use only a single item to assess important information. Pretesting using multiple measures of significant facts would improve those designs.

Here we reported a preliminary investigation of a tool to improve pretest assessments of design modifications and instantiation. Our results showed that it is possible to compare tapes for presence and absence of desirable and undesirable properties, respectively.

A worthwhile next step to develop this method of pretesting tapes would be to construct assessments more systematically than we did here. We were guided by theoretical considerations of what is important to create in the experiment, and by our experience in knowing what kinds of things can go wrong. Future work might benefit from more rigorous scale construction using psychometric techniques such as factor analysis in conjunction with theoretical considerations. That work might also address ways to decide whether a particular tape is adequate using statistical tests that address the truncation problem when ideal ratings are at the endpoints of scales.

Pretesting may be particularly important when information is delivered through only one medium, such as printed instructions participants are asked to read, and which may not include repetition of key points. Unless pretesting is employed that asks respondents, for instance, to repeat the information they are supposed to have noted, we have no objective way to be confident that an experiment actually does create the situation needed. Our data here do not bear on this kind of information; designs would be stronger if they did provide such information.

The second kind of information pretests can provide is what we report here. In experiments, we are concerned about introducing unintended messages and information, and thus activating unwanted social processes that might interfere with the crucial processes of theoretical interest. If behavior of the actors undercuts their authority, participants might not believe some of the information required to create the situation—for example, the importance of doing well at the task, or the instruction that their prior experiences are irrelevant for predicting how well they are likely to perform at it. Similarly, if unintended behavior distracts participants, or makes them less serious about paying attention to the experiment, that undercuts visibility of the theoretical processes of interest. Worse, it might even set up competing processes that obscure effects of expectations on the dependent measure of these experiments. In our experiment, if participants are angry, their $P(s)$ may rise for reasons that have nothing to do with performance expectations. If participants feel excessive sympathy for their partners, their $P(s)$ may fall, again for reasons outside the focus of the study. Neither effect has anything to do with the theory under test, but because they produce the same sorts of empirical consequences, we could be misled in interpreting the data from these experiments.

Though successful experimental design probably will always involve art as well as science, our results show it is possible to assess interpretations of presentations. Pretesting is, we believe, essential in creating good experiments. To pretest "dry runs," we suggest adding assessments of success at creating the sorts of reality the experiment calls for, and we recommend tape pretesting as a useful tool.

In summary, we offer the following conclusions:

- Pretesting of tapes is important in producing the sorts of effects called for by an experimental design, and we have developed one method for doing such pretesting.

- Because our initial tape was produced using the best intuitions of all of us, and because data later showed it to be far from ideal, we believe pretesting is essential, even for materials that appear adequate, in researchers' judgments.
- Several kinds of pretests are desirable. Ours involves how information was conveyed. Another kind of pretest would check to see whether respondents actually understand and remember key parts of the instructions.

We hope that our methods and these results are useful to others, and that more extensive pretesting will become a common feature of laboratory experiments.

REFERENCES

Berger, Joseph, Bernard P. Cohen, and Morris Zelditch Jr. 1966. "Status Characteristics and Expectation States." Pp. 29–46 in *Sociological Theories in Progress*, Vol. 1, edited by Joseph Berger, Morris Zelditch Jr., and Bo Anderson. Boston: Houghton Mifflin.

Berger, Joseph, Hamit Fisek, Robert Z. Norman, and Morris Zelditch Jr. 1977. *Status Characteristics and Social Influence: A Status Characteristics Approach.* New York: Elsevier Scientific.

Berger, Joseph, and J. Laurie Snell. 1961. "A Stochastic Theory for Self-Other Expectations." Technical Report No. 1, Laboratory for Social Research, Stanford University.

Cohen, Bernard P. 1988. "A New Experimental Situation Using Microcomputers." Pp. 383–98 in *Status Generalization: New Theory and Research*, edited by Murray Webster Jr. and Martha Foschi. Stanford, CA: Stanford University Press.

———. 1989. *Developing Sociological Knowledge: Theory and Method.* Chicago: Nelson-Hall.

Foschi, Martha. 1996. "Double Standards in the Evaluation of Men and Women." *Social Psychology Quarterly* 59:237–54.

———. 1997. "On Scope Conditions." *Small Group Research* 28:535–55.

Foschi, Martha, Kirsten Sigerson, Larissa Lai, and Ricardo Foschi. 1990. "A Computerized Setting for Expectation States Research." Presented at the West Coast Conference for Small Group Research, Portland, OR, April 27–28.

Kiesler, S., J. Siegel, and T. W. McGuire. 1984. "Social Psychological Aspects of Computer-Mediated Communication." *American Psychologist* 39:1123–34.

Moore, James C. Jr. 1968. "Status and Influence in Small Group Interactions." *Sociometry* 31:47–63.

Ridgeway, Cecilia L., and Henry A. Walker. 1995. "Status Structures." Pp. 281–310 in *Sociological Perspectives on Social Psychology*, edited by Karen S. Cook, Gary Alan Fine, and James S. House. Boston: Allyn and Bacon.

Rosenthal, Robert. 1963. "On the Social Psychology of the Psychological Experiment: The Experimenter's Hypothesis as Unintended Determinant of the Experimental Results." *American Scientist* 51:268–83.

Skvoretz, John, Murray Webster Jr., and Joseph M. Whitmeyer. 1999. "Status Orders in Task Discussion Groups." Pp. 199–218 in *Advances in Group Processes*, Vol. 16, edited by Shane R. Thye, Edward J. Lawler, Michael W. Macy, and Henry A. Walker. Stamford, CT: JAI.

Troyer, Lisa. 1999. "MacSES version 5.0." Unpublished software manual, Department of Sociology, University of Iowa.

———. 2001. "Effects of Protocol Differences on the Study of Status and Social Influence." *Current Research in Social Psychology* 16:182–204. http://www.uiowa.edu/~grpproc.

———. 2002. "The Relation Between Experimental Standardization and Theoretical Development in Group Processes Research." Pp. 131–47 in *The Growth of Social Knowledge: Theory, Simulation, and Empirical Research in Group Processes*, edited by Jacek Szmatka, Michael Lovaglia, and Kinga Wysienska. Westport, CT: Praeger.

Troyer, Lisa, and C. Wesley Younts. 1997. "Whose Expectations Matter? The Relative Power of First-Order and Second-Order Expectations in Determining Social Influence." *American Journal of Sociology* 103:692–732.

Wagner, David G., and Joseph Berger. 1993. "Status Characteristics Theory: The Growth of a Program." Pp. 23–63 in *Theoretical Research Programs: Studies in the Growth of Theory*, edited by Joseph Berger and Morris Zelditch Jr. Stanford CA: Stanford University Press.

———. 2002. "Expectation States Theory." Pp. 41–46 in *New Directions in Contemporary Sociological Theory*, Joseph Berger and Morris Zelditch Jr. Lanham, MD: Rowman and Littlefield.

Walker, Henry A., and Bernard P. Cohen. 1985. "Scope Statements: Imperatives for Evaluating Theory." *American Sociological Review* 50:288–301.

Webster, Murray Jr., and James E. Driskell, Jr. 1978. "Status Generalization: A Review and Some New Data." *American Sociological Review* 43:220–36.

Webster, Murray Jr., and Martha Foschi. 1988. *Status Generalization: New Theory and Research*. Stanford, CA: Stanford University Press.

Willer, David, and Murray Webster Jr. 1970. "Theoretical Concepts and Observables." *American Sociological Review* 35:748–57.

A NEW APPROACH TO ESTIMATING LIFE TABLES WITH COVARIATES AND CONSTRUCTING INTERVAL ESTIMATES OF LIFE TABLE QUANTITIES

Scott M. Lynch*
J. Scott Brown[†]

Extant approaches to constructing life tables generally rely on the use of population data, and differences between groups defined by discrete characteristics are examined by disaggregating the data before estimation. When sample data are used, few researchers have attempted to include covariates directly in the process of estimation, and fewer still have attempted to construct interval estimates for state expectancies when covariates are used. In this paper, we present a Bayesian approach that is useful for producing interval estimates for single-decrement, multiple-decrement, and multistate life tables. The method involves (1) estimating a hazard or survival model using Bayesian Markov chain Monte

Scott M. Lynch is an assistant professor of sociology and a faculty associate of the Office of Population Research at Princeton University. J. Scott Brown is an assistant professor of sociology and gerontology at Miami University and was supported by National Institute on Aging training grant T32 AG00155 at the University of North Carolina at Chapel Hill. Direct correspondence to Scott M. Lynch, Department of Sociology, Princeton University, Princeton, NJ 08544; email: slynch@princeton.edu.

*Princeton University
[†]Department of Sociology and Gerontology, Miami University (Oxford, OH)

Carlo (MCMC) methods to produce a sample from the posterior distribution for the parameters of the model; (2) generating distributions of transition probabilities for selected values of covariates using the sample of model parameters; (3) using these distributions of transition probabilities as inputs for life table construction; and (4) summarizing the distribution of life table quantities. We illustrate the method on data simulated from the Berkeley Mortality Database, data from the National Health and Nutrition Examination Survey (and follow-ups), and data from the National Long Term Care Survey, and we show how the results can be used for hypothesis testing.

Life tables have been used in mortality research for centuries. More recently, life table methods have become popular in examining other time-dependent phenomena. For example, Pettit and Western (2001) used multiple decrement life tables to examine the cumulative probability of incarceration for black low-skill males, while simultaneously considering mortality as a competing risk to incarceration. Land and Hough (1989) used increment-decrement (multistate) life tables to determine the expected number of years individuals will spend in school over their lifetime. Menken et al. (1981) constructed single decrement life tables from proportional hazard models for predicting marital dissolution.

Researchers have increasingly used event-history/hazard models for modeling time-dependence (Allison 1984), in part because these models enable the use of multiple covariates and allow for hypothesis testing on parameters of interest. In comparison, including covariates in life tables, especially multiple decrement and multistate tables, is not a straightforward task. Furthermore, constructing interval estimates for life expectancies (or other life table quantities) for hypothesis testing is even more difficult. Indeed, discussion of the inclusion of covariates, coupled with interval estimation of life table quantities, is virtually nonexistent in the life table methodology literature.

In this paper, we present a Bayesian technique that enables both the inclusion of covariates and the construction of interval estimates in single-decrement, multiple-decrement, and increment-decrement (multistate) life tables. Our approach enables us to answer questions that require life table quantities, and estimates of uncertainty in them, that traditionally have not been easy, or in some cases possible, to compute. For example, is there a difference between the number of years black and white women can expect to remain unmarried, and does the answer depend on level of education? Do white men and women with advanced degrees differ in their remaining life expectancy? Is the active life expectancy for a black college-educated female greater than that for a white male with a high school diploma?

1. BACKGROUND

Existing approaches to generating life tables typically rely on the use of population data, with construction of the life table being a mechanical process of applying flow equations to population rates (see Preston, Heuveline, and Guillot 2001; Schoen 1988). Alternative approaches to estimating single-decrement life tables have been derived when (1) the data are from a sample rather than a population or (2) the processes of decrement are at least considered stochastic. Chiang (1960, 1961) and Keyfitz (1968) each show how variances of life table quantities can be derived so as to capture uncertainty in single-decrement table quantities. Yet their works do not show how to incorporate covariates into estimation. On the other hand, a number of authors have described how to generate life tables when inclusion of covariates is desired (e.g., Menken et al. 1981; Trussell and Hammerslough 1983). Specifically, research has shown how standard hazard models can be used to estimate transition probabilities for input into single-decrement life tables. However, such work has not shown how to obtain interval estimates for life table quantities when covariates are used.

In terms of multistate life tables, little research to date has attempted to compute state expectancies for multistate models with covariates, and even less research has attempted to construct interval estimates for quantities in such models. Paralleling the single-decrement life table literature, some research has shown how to incorporate covariates into the estimation process, and some has shown how to construct interval estimates, but strikingly little research has sought to do both. For example, Land, Guralnik, and Blazer (1994) show how covariates can be included by using log-linear models to construct smoothed transition rates for inputs in multistate tables with relatively simple state spaces. Additionally, Manton and Stallard (1994) show how covariates can be included in hazard models to produce multistate life tables with highly complex state spaces. However, neither show how interval estimates can be obtained from such models. On the other hand, Molla, Wagener, and Madans (2001) show how standard errors for life table quantities can be obtained when using Sullivan's method for estimating active/healthy life expectancy. However, they do not show how covariates can be incorporated into estimation via Sullivan's method.

To date, we can find only two approaches in the literature to combining the inclusion of covariates with the construction of interval estimates in multistate models. The method advanced by Hayward, Rendall, and Crimmins (1999) involves (1) bootstrapping hazard regression model estimates and (2) constructing life tables from parameters derived from each bootstrap sample. The method advanced by Laditka and Wolf (1998) involves (1) estimating a discrete time Markov chain model for generating transition probabilities and (2) using microsimulation to simulate life histories for individuals based on these transition probabilities. The results of the simulation can then be used to construct interval estimates of life table quantities.

The bootstrapping approach is similar to the approach we present here, differing primarily in interpretation of the results. Specifically, bootstrapping yields the sampling distribution for a parameter/quantity of interest, and so standard classical interpretation of the intervals produced from this approach applies. On the other hand, our Bayesian approach allows for probabilitistic interpretation of results (see below). The microsimulation approach, on the other hand, differs considerably from the approach we discuss here. Under that approach, only point estimates for parameters are obtained, and then life histories based on these point estimates are simulated under an assumption regarding the frequencies of transitioning between states (monthly in Laditka and Wolf 1998). Widths of intervals for state expectancies are highly dependent on this frequency assumption, so that the more frequently transitions are allowed to occur, the wider the intervals that are produced. Thus, while the microsimulation approach is more realistic and flexible in terms of the handling of time intervals between transitions, it produces widely varying interval widths under different (and possibly untestable) assumptions regarding the (unobservable) frequency of transitions.

The inclusion of covariates and the construction of confidence intervals are important for life table construction for two reasons.

First, the traditional approach to including covariates—disaggregation and separate estimation—is inefficient and can be restrictive because of small sample sizes, especially when disaggregating data across a continuous covariate and especially in multistate tables with high-dimensional state spaces (Land, Guralnik, and Blazer 1994). Second, although historically demographers have used population data to construct life tables, much current research using life table methods constructs tables based on microlevel sample data. Indeed, the questions presented above would almost certainly require sample data. Sampling error, therefore, is a concern that should be taken into account when estimating life table quantities from such data.

The approach we develop here enables construction of interval estimates for state expectancies from models with covariates. Using our approach, comparisons can be made between groups that differ on multiple covariates, something that would be very difficult, if not impossible, with conventional approaches. We demonstrate the approach for single-decrement, multiple-decrement, and multistate life tables.

2. A BAYESIAN APPROACH TO LIFE TABLES

The method we discuss involves a hybrid of traditional modeling techniques (e.g., hazard models) with Bayesian Markov chain Monte Carlo (MCMC) estimation methods. The models we present are commonly used in life course research (see Allison 1984; Yamaguchi 1991), and the methods that we use to estimate them have been used extensively in Bayesian statistics over the last decade (see Gilks, Richardson, and Spiegelhalter 1996). However, we have found no literature to date, methodological or substantive, that has combined these models with these methods for the purpose of constructing life tables and for capturing uncertainty in life table quantities.

The key advantages to using a Bayesian approach include the following: (1) MCMC estimation allows for relatively simple construction of interval estimates, something that cannot be done with a maximum likelihood approach that generates only point estimates for standard errors; and (2) the Bayesian perspective on probability allows for greater flexibility in conducting formal hypothesis tests, something that other approaches do not offer.

Our approach follows four steps[1]:

1. Determine a model for predicting transition probabilities or hazard rates.
2. Estimate the model via MCMC methods to obtain simulated draws (called "iterates") from the posterior densities for the parameters of the model.
3. After discarding some early iterates prior to the algorithm's convergence, construct life tables using each simulated set of parameters applied to whatever covariate combination is desired.
4. Order the resulting life table quantities and take the appropriate percentile cutpoints for the desired confidence level on any desired life table quantity.

The first step is straightforward. For example, some have used Cox regression or other hazard/survival modeling approaches to generate life tables (e.g., Hayward, Crimmins, and Saito 1998; Manton and Land 2000; Menken et al. 1981; Trussel and Hammerslough 1983; see also Cox 1972). In the examples presented in this research, we use a discrete-time probit for generating single-decrement tables, a discrete-time multinomial probit for generating multiple-decrement tables, and a discrete-time multinomial probit with the starting state as a covariate for generating multistate tables (see Allison 1984 or Yamaguchi 1991 for discussion of discrete-time hazard models). We choose these particular models because most sample data are collected in discrete time intervals, and these models are quite common in the literature. However, although we use discrete-time models, *it is important to note that any type of probability or hazard model may be used.* For example, one could use gamma-Gompertz, gamma-Makeham, or even more complex models (see Horiuchi and Wilmoth 1998) to estimate mortality hazards or transition probabilities. We recommend that one explore the age (or time) dependence of the event of interest and choose an appropriate model or parameterization of age or time.

---

[1]We use a combination of unix-based C programs written by the authors to perform all the MCMC estimation discussed in this paper. We use a combination of C programs and SAS programs/macros to generate the life tables and descriptive statistics. All of these programs can be obtained from the authors.

The second step is to estimate the model via Bayesian MCMC methods. Bayes theorem states that

$$p(B|A) = \frac{p(A|B)p(B)}{p(A)}.$$

(1)

While this equation applies specifically to probabilities, Bayesians apply the theorem to probability distributions and use the following version:

$$\text{Posterior} \propto \text{Likelihood} \times \text{Prior}.$$

(2)

This version says that a posterior distribution for parameters is proportional to the multiple of the sampling density for the data, given the parameters (also called the likelihood function), and a prior distribution representing *a priori* uncertainty about the true values of the parameters. Bayesian analysis has been criticized for injecting subjectivity into modeling via the inclusion of the prior (an empirically testable proposition), and for treating parameters as random quantities to which a probability distribution can be attached (a philosophical/paradigmatic dispute). We believe these arguments tend to be straw-man arguments that are easily countered. For example, subjectivity permeates all statistical analyses (e.g., consider the determination of a "significant" p-value), priors often matter little asymptotically (and some priors are relatively noninformative regardless of sample size), Bayesian analysis directly allows for tests of the validity of priors, and ML estimation is simply a special case of the Bayesian approach. For further discussion of Bayesian theory, see Box and Tiao (1973), Gelman et al. (1995), or Lee (1989).

In the models we present in this paper, we discuss the likelihood functions for each, but we do not discuss the priors: In all cases, we used a reference prior for the multivariate normal distribution $(1/|\Sigma|)$ (univariate normal—$1/\sigma^2$—in the single decrement example). Additional analyses using uniform priors (making the posterior distribution proportional to the likelihood function) yielded virtually identical results, largely because the sample sizes used here overwhelm the prior (see Gelman et al. 1995 for a discussion of priors).

Assuming one has decided to undertake a Bayesian analysis, the difficult task is model estimation. In likelihood analysis, one differentiates the likelihood function with respect to each parameter, sets the resulting system of equations equal to 0, and uses some optimization technique to find values of the parameters that maximize the probability of the data. Standard errors for parameters are found by deriving the matrix of second partial derivatives of the log of the likelihood function (the Hessian matrix), finding the negative expectation of this matrix (the information matrix), and inverting this matrix to obtain the asymptotic covariance matrix of parameters. Taking the square root of the diagonal elements of this matrix and evaluating the result at the MLE for the parameters yields the standard errors.

In contrast, in the Bayesian paradigm the goal is not to maximize the likelihood function but rather to integrate the posterior density over the data (which are treated as fixed) to obtain marginal distributions for the parameters. Thus the goal is to obtain a probability distribution for the parameters that describes posterior uncertainty regarding the parameters' true values. Such multivariate integration is often analytically impossible, and hence Bayesians often use methods for simulating from the posterior distribution, obtaining enough simulated values to produce summaries of the distribution that are essentially the same as would be obtained by analytical integration.

MCMC methods constitute one class of methods for conducting such simulation (see Gilks, Richardson, and Spiegelhalter 1996). At the end of a run of an MCMC algorithm, one has a set of parameter values, with the set containing values in proportion to their posterior probability. We describe such algorithms specifically in our examples below. It should be noted that, if priors are uniform on all parameters in the model, the results approximate those obtained via maximum-likelihood estimation. For example, the mode of the posterior distribution will equal the MLE, and the standard deviation computed from the distribution of sampled parameters will approximate the standard error that would be obtained via maximum-likelihood estimation. In that sense, Bayesian analysis is often simpler than standard likelihood analysis, because posterior standard deviations are simple by-products of estimation and thus need not be derived using complex multivariable differential calculus.

The important feature of MCMC estimation is that it yields more than point estimates of the variability in the posterior density for parameters: It produces samples from the posterior density, and it is these samples that allow the construction of interval estimates. Once these simulated parameter values are obtained, one can use functions of them to generate distributions for quantities of interest that are a function of the model parameters (e.g., life expectancies). For example, in a simple linear regression model, one could compute $X_i'\beta$ for each individual i, using each sequence of simulated parameters to obtain a distribution of predicted scores (rather than a point estimate) for each individual. For our purposes, we can use each simulated parameter vector to compute a life table, yielding a distribution of life table quantities.

The resulting distribution of each life table quantity can then be sorted in ascending order, and the empirical 2.5 percentile and 97.5 percentile cutpoints of the distribution can be used as estimates of the lower and upper bounds (respectively) for a 95 percent empirical confidence interval on the quantity of interest. We note that Bayesians generally refer to these intervals as either *credible intervals* or *empirical probability intervals*, but we use the more familiar term *empirical confidence intervals* or just *confidence intervals* throughout the paper. It is important to note, however, that the Bayesian intervals differ in interpretation. From a Bayesian perspective, the true parameter of interest falls within this interval with probability .95. This is an important interpretation to bear in mind, because under this interpretation the comparison of Bayesian intervals can lead to statements regarding the probability that one group's life expectancy (or other quantity) is greater than another's.

Our primary focus in this paper is methodological and not substantive. Nonetheless, we ground our examples in terms of black-white differences in health and mortality across the life course. Specifically, we evaluate the double-jeopardy hypothesis in medical sociology and demography in terms of general mortality, cause-specific mortality, and active life expectancy. The double-jeopardy hypothesis (see Ferraro 1987) claims that aging and minority status present a double threat to health, such that the health gap between blacks and whites widens in late life. Empirical research to date has produced mixed results, with most research finding evidence for mortality (and often, health) crossovers (see Nam 1995): health and mortality rates tend to converge across age to produce a black health *advantage* at the oldest ages. As Nam (1995) notes, there is considerable debate regarding the underlying cause of the observed crossover. Some demographers suggest that the crossover is the result of age misreporting by African-Americans (e.g., Mason and Cope 1987; Preston et al. 1996). Others, however, argue that higher mortality rates for African-Americans at younger ages reduce the frailest portion of this racial group, leaving a robust group in old age with a mortality advantage over whites (e.g., Coale and Kisker 1986; Horiuchi and Wilmoth 1998). Recent research suggests that both camps are probably correct, given that adjusting for African-American data quality significantly affects the age at which a crossover is observed while not eliminating the observed crossover entirely (e.g., Lynch, Brown, and Harmsen 2003).

Ferraro (1987) has argued that subjective health measures most likely obscure support for the double jeopardy hypothesis because self-rated health is age-sensitive: elders tend to report their health relative to peers, whereas young persons tend to report their health relative to a "gold standard" for health. Thus, health measured subjectively tends not to decline across age as rapidly as would be expected, and few between-group differences can be found. Here, we test the hypothesis using mortality and physical disability, which are fairly objective measures of health. In the single-decrement example, we compare blacks and whites, controlling on sex (constructing separate life expectancy intervals for men and women), to determine whether life expectancies converge or diverge across age between races. In the multiple-decrement example, we compare blacks and whites in terms of differences in causes of death. For this example, we include a number of covariates and compare blacks and whites fixed at specific values of other covariates to determine whether black and white mortality probabilities diverge or converge for two different classes of causes of death. In the multistate example, we compare blacks and whites, controlling again on sex, to determine whether active, disabled, and total life expectancies converge or diverge across age for the two racial groups.

We note at the outset that tests of the double-jeopardy hypothesis typically involve including an interaction between race and age in regression models. While our single decrement example does include a black-by-age interaction, our multiple decrement and multistate examples do not, for two reasons: (1) in the models we use (probits), all covariates are multiplicatively related; and (2) the transformation of model parameters into life table quantities is a nonlinear process as well. Certainly, age-by-race interactions could be included within these models (as in the single decrement example), and substantive research investigating this hypothesis should do so at least as a sensitivity test.

3. SINGLE-DECREMENT LIFE TABLES

A standard approach to constructing a single-decrement life table is to convert population rates into transition probabilities using an assumption about the distribution of transitions across time within an age interval (see Preston, Heuveline, and Guillot 2001; Schoen 1988). Once transition probabilities are derived, they are then systematically applied to a radix population to obtain counts of transitions by age. Another assumption is then made to determine the number of person-years lived in the interval between two ages. Finally, life expectancies are calculated by taking the number of persons remaining in the population at a given age and dividing into the number of person-years lived from that age forward. When using a sample, we can model the hazard rate using hazard models like Cox regression or some fully parametric model (e.g., exponential, Gompertz, Weibull, etc.), or we can model the transition probabilities directly. We take the latter approach.

Assume that individuals have latent propensities to transition to death in an interval of time, and that these propensities are distributed normally with a mean of $X_i'\beta$ and standard deviation 1. With a person-year data set, this distributional assumption produces a discrete time probit model, whose likelihood appears as

$$L(\beta|y) \propto \prod_{i=1}^{n} \Phi(X_i'\beta)^{y_i}(1 - \Phi(X_i'\beta))^{1-y_i}, \tag{3}$$

where Φ is the cumulative standard normal distribution function, y_i is the observed indicator of mortality for individual i, X is a matrix of covariates, and β is a vector of parameters.

Latent propensities can be brought directly into the model estimation process when using an MCMC algorithm. Such an algorithm can be established in two steps (see Johnson and Albert 1999):

1. Simulate latent propensities, z, from truncated normal distributions: $z_i \sim TN(X_i\beta, 1)$, $\forall i$. The point of truncation is defined by the observed transition and the threshold 0. An individual i who transitions to death ($y_i = 1$) gets z_i: $z > 0$; a person who survives ($y_i = 0$) gets z_i: $z \leq 0$.
2. Given a vector of latent normally distributed propensities, the parameters can be simulated from a normal distribution, as in OLS regression: $\beta \sim MVN((X'X)^{-1}(X'Z), (X'X)^{-1})$

3. Return to step 1 and repeat the process until "enough" draws of β are obtained.

The prescribed algorithm is called a *Gibbs sampler*, because all the parameters are drawn from their full conditional distributions (see Gilks 1996; Gilks, Richardson, and Spiegelhalter 1996). Step 2 can be modified if necessary so that each β parameter can be simulated sequentially if deriving the conditional distributions for the parameters is not straightforward. We discuss such an approach in the subsequent examples.

MCMC algorithms require a number of iterations before converging on the posterior distribution for the parameters. After convergence, a number of additional iterations should be performed in order to obtain a sample size adequate to fully summarize the posterior distribution (at least 500 to 1000 unique draws are generally sufficient to summarize a distribution). After discarding the initial iterations prior to the algorithm converging to the correct distribution (the "burn-in"), we will have a set of J simulated parameter values that can be transformed into transition probabilities. We can then construct life tables from these transition probabilities using the following steps:

1. Compute transition probabilities for a given set of values for X, and a set of ages a, for each of the J parameter samples:

$$p(y = 1 | age = a, iteration = j) = \int_{-\infty}^{X\beta^j} N(0,1), \forall a, \, j.$$

2. Use each of the J sets of transition probabilities by age for a given vector of covariates to compute a life table. Each life table may have the form found in Table 1, a standard life table format, although we emphasize that the assumptions regarding the person years lived within an age interval is entirely flexible. Here, we use the linear assumption, as the L_a column indicates.

3. Once these life tables are computed, we have a distribution of life expectancies, e_a, at each age a, which can be summarized via simple descriptive statistics. Quantities of interest include both point estimates and interval estimates. Regarding point estimates, we may be interested in the expected value of life expectancy. The mean for a given age a can be computed as

TABLE 1
Single-Decrement Life Table for Iteration J

Age	l_a	p_a	L_a	e_a^j
20	1	p_{20}	$\frac{l_{20}+l_{21}}{2}$	$\frac{\sum_{a=20}^{\omega} L_a}{l_{20}}$
21	$(1-p_{20})$	p_{21}	$\frac{l_{21}+l_{22}}{2}$	$\frac{\sum_{a=21}^{\omega} L_a}{l_{21}}$
22	$(1-p_{20})(1-p_{21})$	p_{22}	$\frac{l_{22}+l_{23}}{2}$	$\frac{\sum_{a=22}^{\omega} L_a}{l_{22}}$
$\vdots$	$\vdots$	$\vdots$	$\vdots$	$\vdots$
k	$\prod_{a=20}^{k-1}(1-p_a)$	p_k	$\frac{l_k+l_{k+1}}{2}$	$\frac{\sum_{a=k}^{\omega} L_a}{l_k}$
$\vdots$	$\vdots$	$\vdots$	$\vdots$	$\vdots$

Note: The L_a column indicates we are using the linear approximation in estimating person-years lived in the interval. Other approaches could be used.

$$\bar{e}_a = \frac{\sum_{j=1}^{J} e_a^j}{J}.$$

Alternatively, we may be interested in the median or mode of the life expectancy distribution (or, still yet, we may be interested in evaluating the symmetry of the distribution by comparing these quantities). Regarding interval estimates, the bounds on a $(1-\alpha)$ percent empirical confidence interval for age a can be constructed by ordering the distribution of life expectancies at age a and taking:

$$[e_a(l) : F(e_a(l)) = \frac{\alpha}{2}, e_a(u) : F(e_a(u)) = 1 - \frac{\alpha}{2}],$$

where l and u reference the lower and upper bounds on the interval, $F()$ represents the empirical cumulative distribution function for e, and $1 - \alpha$ is the desired confidence level. In other words, we take the empirical values of e such that 2.5 percent fall below $e(l)$ and 97.5 percent fall below $e(u)$, if we want a 95 percent interval.

In order to demonstrate this approach, we use 1992 U.S. data from the Berkeley Mortality Database (BMD, see http://www.demog. berkeley.edu/wilmoth/mortality). The BMD reports life expectancies as well as the population data from which they were computed. For our demonstration, we generated a sample from the U.S. 1992 original data that were used to generate the BMD life tables, by expanding the population counts and death counts into a massive rectangular data file ordered by age, sex, race, and death indicator (without knowing anything more about individuals' characteristics beyond their age, sex, and race, all deaths are exchangeable). Using this massive data set, we sampled observations systematically to obtain a sample of $n = 20,001$ individuals (9176 white females/102 deaths; 8510 white males/110 deaths; 1260 black females/19 deaths; and 1055 black males/16 deaths).

Our model for this example contains age and age^2, sex (male = 1), race (black = 1), an interaction between age and sex, and an interaction between age and race, in order to capture nonproportional hazards across age by race and sex. In general, the probit model here seems to provide an appropriate functional form for mortality across age, because mortality probabilities decelerate across age (Horiuchi and Wilmoth 1998; Lynch and Brown 2001; see Thatcher, Kannisto, and Vaupel 1998, for a discussion of the excellent fit of the logistic model; see also Beard 1971 for a discussion of the origination of the logistic model for mortality), but some examination of model fit and retesting suggested that including a quadratic age term produced a better fit than including age alone.

Figure 1 contains trace plots (left column) and histograms (right column) for the intercept, age, sex, and race parameters from the probit model. The x-axis in the trace plots reflects the iteration of the algorithm, while the y-axis reflects the sampled parameter value at a given iteration. As the figure reveals, the algorithm converged very quickly: for example, for the intercept, observe how the trace plot "drops" from the starting value of 0 to the region around -3.5 within very few iterations and remains in that region throughout the remainder of the 10,000-iteration run. After discarding all but the last 1000 iterations of the MCMC run, a histogram for the marginal distribution of each parameter can be obtained. Heuristically, one can imagine turning the trace plot on its right edge, allowing the "ink" to fall to the right edge and "pile-up" into a histogram. Such histograms are presented in the right column of the figure.

Table 2 displays the results of the probit model, after discarding all but the last 1000 iterates. We present both Bayesian and maximum-likelihood estimates. The Bayesian estimates are posterior means and standard deviations computed using standard techniques for computing

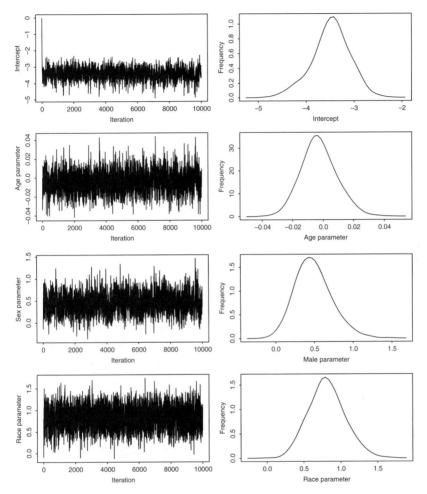

FIGURE 1. Trace plot and histograms of parameters estimated with the Gibbs sampler for the single-decrement life table.

descriptive statistics for a sample. The maximum-likelihood estimates are those produced by a standard software package (SAS), as are the estimates of the standard errors. Given the noninformative prior used here, the Bayesian results are virtually identical to those obtained using maximum-likelihood estimation. The intercept reveals that the baseline hazard of death is very small. The age and age^2 coefficients indicate a net increase in the hazard for each year of age. The coefficients for sex and race indicate a significant difference between

TABLE 2
Probit Model Results: Effects of Covariates on Probability of Death

Covariate	Bayesian Estimates Parameter(S.D.)	Maximum Likelihood Estimates Parameter(Estimated S.E.)
Intercept[a]	−3.49(.39)***	−3.40(.35)***
Age	−.003(.01)	−.005(.01)
Age^2	.0003(.00009)***	.0003(.00008)***
Male	.49(.23)**	.45(.22)*
Black	.81(.24)***	.81(.24)***
Age*Male	−.004(.003)	−.003(.003)
Age*Black	−.009(.004)*	−.009(.004)*

[a] The p-values for the Bayesian estimates are the empirical probability that the parameter is either >0 or <0, depending on the sign of the parameter. These values are found by computing the proportion of the simulated parameter values that exceed 0 (either positively or negatively). The p-values reported are classified into the ranges represented by the asterisks.

#$p < .1$, *$p < .05$, **$p < .01$, ***$p < .001$.

male and female and black and white mortality probabilities, with females and whites evidencing the advantage. Both the gender and race gaps, however, diminish across age, although only the race gap diminishes significantly.

Using each of the 1000 iterates from the Gibbs run as discussed above, life tables can be computed, something that could not be done using the estimated standard errors from maximum-likelihood results. Figure 2 shows the process of moving from the model parameters through the calculation of transition probabilities, to the subsequent calculations of the columns of the life table (all for white females). Once again, the left column of the figure presents trace plots of the life table quantities, while the right column shows the histogram of the distribution of these quantities. The first trace plot shows the distribution of mortality probabilities at age 65 (for white females). The second shows the distribution for the population surviving at the beginning of the interval (l_x column of the life table) at age 65. The third shows the distribution for the person-years lived in the 65–66 year age interval. The fourth shows life expectancy at age 65.

Figure 3 is a plot of the empirical confidence intervals for all four sex-race groups derived from the model. Again, these intervals were constructed by computing the model-predicted scores after fixing

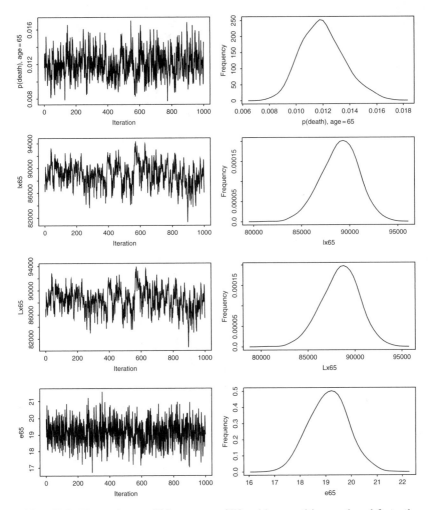

FIGURE 2. Trace plots and histograms of life table quantities produced from the Gibbs sampler for the single-decrement life table (white females).

the covariates at their desired values, converting these predicted scores into probabilities and completing the table with each distribution of probabilities. The dashed lines in the figure represent the BMD life expectancies. As the figure reveals, the confidence intervals squarely capture the BMD life expectancies for all sex-race aggregates, and the intervals appear to be centered over the BMD estimates for all but the youngest ages for black males.

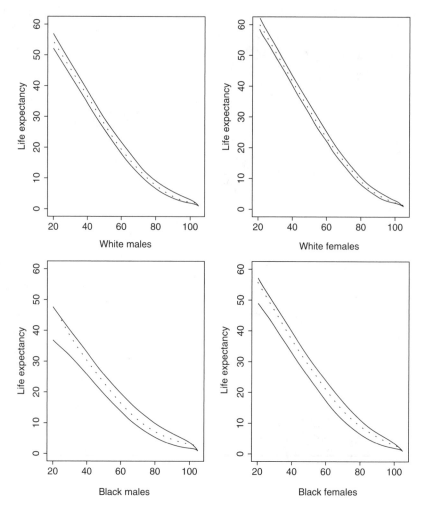

FIGURE 3. Empirical confidence intervals for life expectancy across age by gender and race estimated from the single-decrement model. The dashed lines are the Berkeley Mortality Database life expectancies.

We display these results in tabular form as well. Table 3 shows the estimated posterior mean by age (for every 10 years of age) and the empirical confidence intervals for all four groups. The point estimates (means) reflect differences that are commonly found. For example, white men (at age 20) can expect to live approximately six fewer years than women, and the race gap is even greater. After considering uncertainty in these estimates, however, it appears that

TABLE 3
Posterior Means and Empirical Confidence Intervals for Life Expectancy from
Single-Decrement Table by Race and Sex for Selected Ages

| | Male | | Female | |
| | Black | White | Black | White |
Age	Pmean [C.I.]	PMean [CI]	PMean [CI]	PMean [CI]
20	42.4 [37.0 , 47.6]	54.4 [52.1 , 56.8]	53.3 [49.0 , 57.4]	60.8 [58.8 , 62.8]
30	36.0 [31.9 , 40.1]	45.2 [43.2 , 47.3]	44.8 [41.3 , 48.4]	51.1 [49.2 , 53.0]
40	29.3 [25.8 , 32.8]	36.2 [34.3 , 38.2]	36.4 [32.9 , 39.8]	41.5 [39.7 , 43.3]
50	22.7 [19.6 , 26.0]	27.5 [25.8 , 29.5]	28.2 [24.9 , 31.7]	32.1 [30.4 , 33.8]
60	16.6 [13.9 , 19.7]	19.6 [18.0 , 21.4]	20.6 [17.6 , 23.9]	23.2 [21.7 , 24.8]
70	11.4 [9.1 , 14.4]	12.8 [11.5 , 14.5]	14.0 [11.3 , 17.3]	15.4 [14.0 , 16.8]
80	7.4 [5.5 , 10.1]	7.7 [6.6 , 9.2]	8.8 [6.6 , 11.5]	9.2 [8.0 , 10.3]
90	4.6 [3.2 , 6.8]	4.4 [3.6 , 5.6]	5.2 [3.7 , 7.4]	5.0 [4.2 , 5.9]
100	2.7 [1.9 , 3.7]	2.6 [2.0 , 3.1]	2.8 [2.1 , 3.8]	2.6 [2.2 , 3.1]

the greatest differences in life expectancy exist between white females and black males, at least up to age 80.

We can make this comparison more formal by examining the probability that black male life expectancy is less than white female life expectancy. This probability is computed simply as the proportion of the black male life expectancy values that are lower than the minimum white female value for a specified age. In this example, the probability that black male life expectancy is less than white female life expectancy is 1 at age 20, remains so until age 60, and then declines steadily through age 100. These results do not lend support for the double-jeopardy hypothesis, even when comparing the groups with the greatest differential in life expectancy at age 20.

Before turning to our multiple-decrement and multistate examples, a note is in order regarding the width of our intervals. The intervals produced are seemingly wide, at least at the youngest ages. For example, we computed confidence intervals based on Chiang's method (1960) and obtained intervals for white females that ranged from 59.2 to 59.72 at age 20 (width of .52 years versus 4.0 years under our method), 30.45 to 30.89 at age 50 (width of .44 years versus 3.4 years under our method), and 8.04 to 8.21 at age 80 (width of .17 years versus 2.3 years under our method). Although our interval widths are considerably wider, there are a number of reasons for this. First, Chiang's method cannot be applied when the observed mortality probabilities are 0; thus we applied Chiang's method to our model-predicted probabilities. Hence, Chiang's approach ignores uncertainty in the estimation of these probabilities. Second, and relatedly, our method is based on a parametric specification of the age-dependence of transition probabilities. Thus parametric uncertainty in the estimation of age-dependence also expands our intervals relative to the nonparametric approach to which Chiang's method is applicable. For that matter, there is considerable parametric uncertainty via the inclusion of covariates when the model specification does not perfectly reproduce the observed probabilities (e.g., suppose the model predicts the appropriate pattern of mortality probabilities across age for one group but not another). For example, the widths of our intervals vary across the sex-race aggregates, with the widest intervals being observed for black males, and the narrowest intervals being observed for white females. Part of this cross-group difference in interval widths is attributable to differences in the shape of the age-dependence of mortality probabilities across subgroups and the inability of the model itself to perfectly capture these differences.

In addition to this parametric uncertainty, sampling error is affected by differences in subsample sizes and differences in the magnitude of mortality probabilities, because the standard deviation of a proportion is a function of the proportion itself (it reaches a maximum when the proportion is at .5). In additional work (not reported here) we found that the interval widths change as expected with changes in sample size (by a factor of $\sqrt{n}$,) and that the relative interval widths indeed are proportional to a function of the proportion of deaths in each subsample and each subsample's size. Finally, standard errors are affected by multicollinearity in the hazard model. It is well known that multicollinearity tends to inflate standard errors, and inflated standard errors, of course, increase interval widths. In this example, we have two interaction terms; without the interaction terms, the interval widths are considerably narrower, although less accurate. This is not a shortcoming of the method, but rather a reflection of the importance of specifying an appropriate model.

4. MULTIPLE-DECREMENT LIFE TABLES

It is often useful to disaggregate death (or other exiting transitions) into various causes. When multiple types of exits are possible, we can construct multiple-decrement life tables. From a modeling standpoint, we often term methods that model these processes "competing risk models." A standard approach to estimating such models is to construct a discrete-time data file for each possible outcome and to estimate the models separately (see Allison 1984). Individuals who exit via transition m at age a are treated as censored observations at a in the model for all other outcomes ($-m$). This approach to estimation is inefficient in the sense that the outcome variable is really a multinomial variable of dimension $k-1$, with each dimension of the multinomial being a binary outcome (did or did not experience transition). The "competition" between outcomes can be captured via the matrix of error correlations between outcomes in the multinomial space.

A model for obtaining transition probabilities for a multiple-decrement table is a simple extension of the univariate probit model constructed above for single-decrement tables. Rather than considering the outcome a scalar quantity, we now consider the outcome a vector quantity representing each possible exit. For example, suppose we are interested in two possible outcomes—death due to circulatory system diseases (CSD) versus death due to other causes (OCD). This gives rise to a multinomial probit model if the outcomes are mutually exclusive (if not, then it would be considered a multivariate probit). In the case of these two outcomes, we can assume individuals have two-dimensional propensities ($Z_i = [Z_{i,1}, Z_{i,2}]$) to exit one way or another. These propensities are truncated as in the univariate case, but now in two dimensions, based on the observed transition the individual experienced:

$$Z_i \sim \text{TruncatedMVN}(\mu_i, \Sigma) \qquad (4)$$

In this case, the truncation point is a vector of zeros, with individuals' propensities drawn from the appropriate region in the multinomial space. For example, if CSDs are represented by the first dimension, and OCDs are represented by the second, then the latent propensities for an individual who dies from CSD are sampled such that $z_{i,1} > 0$ and $z_{i,2} < 0$. We determine μ_i via a regression on covariates—e.g., for dimension/equation k: $\mu_i(k) = X_i(k)'\beta(k)$, $\forall_i$, k, where the dimensionality of the regression vector (and its corresponding coefficients) may vary across equations.

These propensities are related to each other via the covariance matrix, Σ, which allows error correlations between the propensities that are not accounted for by the regression model. These correlations will likely be highly negative because of the structural aspect of the model that renders an outcome with multiple exits impossible.

If we have a complete set of multivariate propensities to replace the observed multinomial variable, then the augmented likelihood function for the parameters can be viewed as a multivariate normal likelihood, similar to the univariate probit example

$$L(\beta, \Sigma | Z) \propto \prod_{i=1}^{n} |\Sigma|^{-1/2} \exp(\omega' \Sigma^{-1} \omega), \qquad (5)$$

where the vector, $\omega = [\omega_{i,1} \ldots \omega_{i,k-1}]$, $\omega_{i,1}$ is the residual for the ith individual and the first equation/outcome, and β and Σ are the regression coefficients and error covariances, respectively.

Estimation of this model is similar to that for the univariate probit, but slightly more complicated because the full conditional distributions for the parameters are not as simple to derive. Thus we modify the Gibbs sampler from the univariate example, by including "Metropolis-Hastings" steps to update parameters one-by-one:

1. Simulate latent Z from the TruncMVN distribution as discussed above and in the univariate probit example. An individual Z vector is drawn until it satisfies the truncation requirements.
2. Given the latent data, simulate the parameters of the model, including regression coefficients and elements of the error covariance matrix using Metropolis-Hastings steps:

    a. Sample a "candidate" parameter, β^c, from a "proposal" density (say a $N(0,d)$), so that $\beta^c = \beta^{j-1} + N(0,d)$, where j references the iteration, and d is the variance of the proposal density (chosen to produce a candidate acceptance rate that is acceptable—generally between 25 percent and 75 percent; see Gilks, Richardson, and Speigelhalter 1996).[2]

---

[2]Technically, centering the proposal density over the previous value of the parameter makes this algorithm a "random walk metropolis" algorithm. It is not necessary to center the proposal, but if one does not, the latter half of the ratio R becomes more important.

b. Compute the posterior density $p()$ at β^c and β^{j-1} and form the ratio

$$R = \frac{p(\beta^c)p(\beta^{j-1}|\beta^c)}{p(\beta^{j-1})p(\beta^c|\beta^{j-1})}.$$

c. Compare R to $u \sim U(0,1)$. If $R > u$ then set $\beta^j = \beta^c$ (i.e., update); otherwise, set $\beta^j = \beta^{j-1}$ (i.e., reject candidate).

d. Repeat these substeps for additional parameters if necessary.

3. Return to step 1.

The subsequence in step 2, a series of Metropolis-Hastings (MH) steps, can be used to update parameters one at a time. The steps differ from a Gibbs sampler in that not all candidate values will be accepted; hence it tends to converge and mix more slowly than a Gibbs sampler. In step 2(a), "candidate" parameters are simulated from a density from which simulating is easy (a "proposal"), rather than from their full conditionals as in the Gibbs sampler. For example, as mentioned in step 2(a), we may choose to simulate a candidate parameter by taking the previous value of the parameter and adding a mean 0, variance d normal random draw. Alternatively, other distributions could be used for simulating candidates (e.g., uniform, gamma, etc.).

In step 2(b), a ratio is computed that quantifies the relative preference of the candidate parameter over the previously sampled value (the first part of the ratio), while compensating for possible asymmetry in the densities used to propose the candidates (the latter half of the ratio—$p(a|b)$ is the probability that a would be proposed when the chain is in state b). For example, suppose that the proposal density is a uniform density centered over the previous parameter value, and suppose that the parameter of interest is bounded at 0 (e.g., like a variance parameter). Whenever the Markov chain "wanders" close to the boundary so that some regions of the uniform proposal are not usable, the proposal density loses its symmetry, making the algorithm more likely to select candidates away from the boundary. This ratio helps adjust for this tendency to overselect/underselect particular values.

Step 2c determines whether the candidate is accepted or rejected. A candidate with greater posterior probability than the previous one will always be accepted (because R will be greater than 1 in that case, at least with symmetric proposal densities), while one with less posterior probability will occasionally be accepted. MCMC theory indicates that such candidates will be accepted in proportion to their probability under the density of interest (see Tierney 1996). See the appendix for a simple example of a generic Metropolis-Hastings algorithm.

As before, once distributions of parameters have been obtained, we can compute transition probabilities. Such probabilities are slightly more complicated in the multiple-decrement setting, because the transition probabilities require integrating multivariate (or in this case, bivariate) normal densities. Thus the probability of experiencing transition m at age a is

$$
p_a^m = \int_{X\beta(-m)}^{\infty} \cdots \int_{\infty}^{X\beta(m)} MVN(0, \Sigma) d_m \ldots d_{-m}, \tag{6}
$$

where the "$\ldots$" and "$-m$" refer to the collection of transitions other than m, and the probabilities must be computed at all ages (by modifying the part of X that contains a).

Also as before, a distribution of these transition probabilities can be obtained for any combination of covariates using the sampled parameters from the algorithm outlined above. Multiple-decrement life table quantities can then be computed using the formulas displayed in Table 4, and distributions of these quantities can be obtained as in the single-decrement example.

TABLE 4
Multiple-Decrement Life Table for Iteration J

Age	p_a^m	p_a^{-m}	l_a	d_a^m	d_a^{-m}	l_a^m	l_a^{-m}
20	p_{20}^m	p_{20}^{-m}	1	$p_{20}^m \times l_{20}$	$p_{20}^{-m} \times l_{20}$	$\sum_{a=20}^{\infty} d_{20}^m$	$\sum_{a=20}^{\infty} d_{20}^{-m}$
21	p_{21}^m	p_{21}^{-m}	$(1 - (p_{20}^m + p_{20}^{-m}))$	$p_{21}^m \times l_{21}$	$p_{21}^{-m} \times l_{21}$	$\sum_{a=21}^{\infty} d_{21}^m$	$\sum_{a=20}^{\infty} d_{21}^{-m}$
⋮	⋮	⋮	⋮	⋮	⋮	⋮	⋮
k	p_k^m	p_k^{-m}	$\prod_{a=20}^{k-1}(1 - (p_a^m + p_a^{-m}))$	$p_k^m \times l_k$	$p_k^{-m} \times l_k$	$\sum_{a=k}^{\infty} d_k^m$	$\sum_{a=k}^{\infty} d_k^{-m}$
⋮	⋮	⋮	⋮	⋮	⋮	⋮	⋮

Note: m refers to cause m, while $-m$ refers to a competing cause. More than two causes could be included. We do not include life expectancies, although total life expectancies can easily be computed from the l_a column as in the single-decrement table. Furthermore, we do not show an important quantity derived from this table—the proportion of individuals alive at age a who can expect to die from cause m. This quantity is easily computed using $\frac{l_a^m}{l_a}$.

Our example of multiple-decrement tables uses a model of cause of death. We use data from the National Health and Nutrition Examination Survey (NHANES) and its followups. The baseline sample of 34,000 persons ages 25–74 were surveyed in 1971. Of these, 6913 individuals who were administered a detailed medical exam and a health care supplement were followed up in 1982, 1987, and 1992. For the purposes of this example, we use only persons who were 65 years of age or over at baseline. At the end of the survey period, a vital and tracing status file was compiled that included date and cause of death as well as final interview status. We excluded 29 (2.4 percent) individuals who did not have a final interview and whose final status was unknown, leaving us with 1202 respondents measured across 22 years. We constructed a person-year file from these data ($n = 18,005$). Individuals who survived beyond 1992 were treated as censored, while those who died ($n = 909$) were coded as dying from either CSD ($n = 497$) or OCD ($n = 412$), based on ICD9 codes from their death certificates. CSDs include cardiovascular and cerbrovascular problems and events, as well as other defects (congenital or other) of the heart and problems induced by heart conditions. The majority of these deaths cluster around ischemic heart disease and stroke.

We include age (baseline $\bar{x} = 68.98$, s.d. $= 2.82$, range $= 25$–77), sex (male $= 1$, 48.7 percent), race (nonwhite $= 1$, 15.3 percent), southern residence (south $= 1$, 31.3 percent), baseline marital status (married $= 1$, 63.9 percent), smoking history ($0 =$ nonsmoker, 51 percent, $1 =$ former smoker, 29.0 percent, $2 =$ current smoker, 20 percent), and education (in years, $\bar{x} = 9.43$, s.d. $= 3.6$, range $= 1 - 17+$) as covariates predicting both outcomes.

The results of these analyses (point estimates and estimated posterior standard deviations of the parameters) can be found in Table 5. The results are consistent with social epidemiologic and demographic research on mortality: Age, being male, being nonwhite, being from the south, and smoking each increase the probability of death from both causes, while greater education and marriage reduce the probability.

From the samples from the distribution of parameters from the model, we generated multiple-decrement life tables. Figure 4 shows examples of the progression from the modeling parameters, through the computation of transition probabilities, to the computation of life expectancies. The figure contains three trace plots. The first is a trace

TABLE 5

Bivariate Probit Model Results: Effects of Covariates on Death Due to Circulatory System Diseases and Death Due to Other Causes

Covariate	Outcome Death Due to CSD	Death Due to OCD
Intercept[a]	−6.22(.17)***	−4.92(.16)***
Age	.05(.002)***	.04(.002)***
Male	.23(.05)***	.14(.05)***
Nonwhite	.05(.06)	.13(.06)*
South	.07(.04)#	−.02(.05)
Married	−.13(.05)**	−.08(.05)#
Smoking	.10(.03)***	.13(.03)***
Education	−.009(.006)#	−.01(.006)*
ρ_e	−.84(.10)***	

[a] The p-values are the empirical probability that the parameter is either >0 or <0,
depending on the sign of the parameter. These values are found by computing the proportion of the simulated parameter values that exceed 0 (either positively or negatively). The
p-values reported are classified into the ranges represented by the asterisks.

$\#p < .1, *p < .05, **p < .01, ***p < .001.$

plot of the intercept parameter for the equation predicting CSDs. The
second is a trace plot of the mortality probability for dying from CSD
between ages 65 and 66, for married, nonsmoking, nonwhite females
from the south with 12 years of education. The third is a trace plot of
remaining life expectancy at age 65 for this subpopulation. All three
plots reveal stability in the MCMC algorithm: the iterates appear to
remain in a narrow region around the mean estimate and evidence
no trending. We do not include figures for all parameters, nor all
probabilities, but the figure we present shows how variability in the
parameter estimates translates into variability around estimates for
probabilities, and ultimately, life expectancies.

For the purposes of this example, we chose four covariate combinations for which the life expectancies would be difficult to compare
using traditional methods. We compare white females from the South to
white females from the non-South, nonwhite females from the South,
and nonwhite females from the non-South, in order to test the double-
jeopardy hypothesis in the context of competing causes of death. We
acknowledge at least one key problem with testing the hypothesis:
selective mortality. If the health gap between whites and blacks is

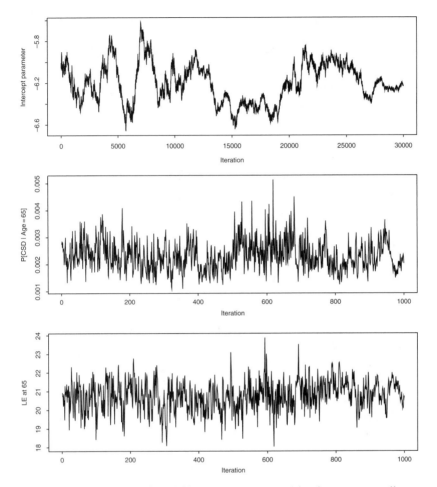

FIGURE 4. Trace plots of model intercept parameter (circulatory system disease [CSD] outcome), transition probability for CSD at age 65, and life expectancy at age 65, produced from the multinomial probit model for causes of death.

considerable, we might then expect mortality to select out the frailest members of the nonwhite population and ultimately lead to convergence in mortality rates between nonwhites and whites at the very oldest ages. This problem has been generally discussed elsewhere in terms of hetero-geneity (e.g., Vaupel and Yashin 1985; see also Beard 1971) and speci-fically in the black-white mortality crossover literature (e.g., Markides and Black 1996; Nam 1995). Thus we limit our analyses to females, because females have lower mortality rates at most ages than males (reducing the impact of selective mortality). We also differentiate the subpopulations by region, because southerners tend to have worse health than persons from other regions, because blacks are disproportionately represented in the south, and because causes of death vary by region (e.g., possibly in part due to diet differences). In terms of the other covariates, we fix them so that the women are married nonsmokers with 12 years of education (the modal categories for these other variables).

Tables 6(a) through 6(d) present the multiple-decrement table results for the four groups at three-year intervals, following the form found in Table 4. The tables contain only the posterior mean estimates for the quantities, but they provide for an initial comparison of the groups. White females have greater overall expected survival probabilities than nonwhite females, and southerners of both racial groups tend to have higher risk of death from CSDs than nonsoutherners. On the other hand, nonsoutherners tend to have higher risk of death from OCDs than southerners. Finally, a crossover exists in the conditional probabilities of death due to one set of causes versus the others. At the younger ages, the risk of death due to OCDs is stronger than the risk of death from CSDs, but the relative magnitudes of these probabilities reverse as age increases.

Other interesting comparisons can be made between the four groups, based on the total number of deaths expected by cause (or proportions of them, i.e., l_a^m / l_a—which are not reported in this table).

TABLE 6(a)

Posterior Means for Multiple-Decrement Life Table Quantities: White Female Nonsoutherners

Age	p^{CSD}	p^{OCD}	l	d^{CSD}	d^{OCD}	f^{CSD}	f^{OCD}
65	.0016	.0033	100000	157	334	42231	35278
68	.0026	.0046	98324	257	455	41670	34163
71	.0043	.0064	95902	408	610	40761	32650
74	.0068	.0086	92464	627	798	39334	30639
77	.0105	.0115	87705	919	1009	37176	28038
80	.0159	.0153	81339	1288	1242	34068	24780
83	.0235	.0201	73100	1715	1465	29784	20825
86	.0340	.0261	62935	2138	1639	24205	16238
89	.0482	.0336	51148	2457	1712	17437	11220
92	.0667	.0427	38514	2559	1639	9903	6121

TABLE 6(b)
Posterior Means for Multiple-Decrement Life Table Quantities: White Female
Southerners

Age	p^{CSD}	p^{OCD}	l	d^{CSD}	d^{OCD}	l^{CSD}	l^{OCD}
65	.0019	.0032	100000	195	317	47028	32708
68	.0032	.0044	98246	316	433	46334	31647
71	.0052	.0061	95696	496	580	45222	30209
74	.0082	.0082	92060	751	758	43497	28298
77	.0125	.0110	87021	1084	958	40929	25828
80	.0187	.0146	80283	1500	1172	37278	22742
83	.0275	.0193	71599	1962	1375	32319	19015
86	.0394	.0251	60974	2394	1523	25983	14726
89	.0553	.0323	48813	2685	1569	18464	10084
92	.0758	.0412	36018	2712	1474	10314	5439

For example, at 65, a larger proportion of nonwhite nonsoutherners
are expected to die from OCDs than CSDs, but survivors to age 71
have a greater probability of dying from CSDs than OCDs. This
pattern is not consistent with those of the other three groups.

Regarding the double-jeopardy hypothesis, these results provide
conflicting evidence. On the one hand, mortality probabilities for both
causes appear to diverge across age, with nonwhites from both regions
evidencing a more rapid increase in mortality probabilities than whites
from both regions, thus supporting the hypothesis. The total survival

TABLE 6(c)
Posterior Means for Multiple-Decrement Life Table Quantities: Nonwhite
Female Nonsoutherners

Age	p^{CSD}	p^{OCD}	l	d^{CSD}	d^{OCD}	l^{CSD}	l^{OCD}
65	.0019	.0049	100000	187	493	41289	42412
68	.0031	.0067	97698	303	658	40622	40776
71	.0050	.0091	94466	472	859	39558	38608
74	.0079	.0121	90026	710	1090	37919	35807
77	.0121	.0161	84086	1014	1345	35501	32285
80	.0182	.0210	76394	1382	1599	33102	27992
83	.0267	.0273	66830	1775	1810	27560	22970
86	.0383	.0350	55566	2116	1927	21872	17394
89	.0539	.0444	43193	2305	1897	15289	11605
92	.0740	.0558	30749	2246	1692	8371	6078

TABLE 6(d)
Posterior Means for Multiple-Decrement Life Table Quantities: Nonwhite
Female Southerners

Age	p^{CSD}	p^{OCD}	l	d^{CSD}	d^{OCD}	T^{CSD}	T^{OCD}
65	.0023	.0047	100000	231	469	45947	39447
68	.0038	.0064	97625	369	626	45128	37891
71	.0061	.0087	94269	570	818	43836	35827
74	.0094	.0116	89634	844	1037	41868	33160
77	.0143	.0154	83424	1191	1276	39006	29812
80	.0213	.0202	75382	1601	1511	35033	25743
83	.0310	.0262	65416	2020	1700	29805	21005
86	.0442	.0336	53771	2358	1792	23379	15786
89	.0614	.0428	41139	2503	1739	16104	10428
92	.0837	.0538	28665	2366	1520	8664	5395

curves also diverge (see the "l" column), but this is less informative because it is attributable to both earlier mortality among nonwhites as well as the divergence in the conditional mortality probabilities.

On the other hand, if we construct the T^{cause} columns (not in table) and examine the expected proportion dying from each cause from age a to age 95, an interesting story emerges. A racial crossover exists between these proportions for CSDs across both regions, with the proportion of non-whites succumbing to CSD being *smaller* than that for whites until age 80. No such crossover exists in OCDs, where the black proportions are higher at all ages than the white proportions, but the two converge across age.

These results suggest that we may need to refine the double-jeopardy hypothesis beyond the subjective versus objective distinction that Ferraro (1987) and Ferraro and Farmer (1996) make. That is, if we test the hypothesis using health measures that are more likely to capture aspects of health that may be related to CSDs, we may find evidence in support of the hypothesis (but see Nam 1995 for discussion of the role of CSDs in producing a mortality crossover). On the other hand, if we test the hypothesis using measures that capture aspects of health related to other causes, we may disconfirm it.

The above results are suggestive; however, they do not constitute formal hypothesis tests. A traditional approach to estimating multiple-decrement tables would limit us in our ability to construct these tables in the first place (for example, recall that we fixed education, smoking status, and marital status to be constant across these groupings), but it would also limit our ability to test hypotheses about quantities of interest. Here, we have distributions of all the quantities in the table, plus other quantities not included in the table, from which we can construct confidence intervals (or other statistics) for formal testing.

In Table 7, we present intervals for total life expectancy produced from the table results and demonstrate how our results can be used for testing. Although most of the intervals in the table appear to overlap, the largest difference in life expectancies can be observed between nonwhite southerners and white nonsoutherners. Figure 5(a) displays the intervals for these groups. Despite the differences in the point estimates presented in the tables above, the figure indicates a considerable amount of overlap in the life expectancy intervals for these two groups. Figure 5(b) shows the probability that life expectancy for nonwhite southerners is less than that for white nonsoutherners across age. As this figure indicates, there is a tendency for this probability to increase across age, lending perhaps some slight support for the double-jeopardy hypothesis regarding all cause mortality. However, the evidence is weak, because, after considering sampling variability in the estimates for life expectancy, there is no clear difference in life expectancies between these groups at any age above 65. Furthermore, while Figure 5(b) reveals an increasing trend in the probabilities that nonwhite life expectancy is less than that for whites, this trend is trivial—the probabilities only increase from about .60 to .66 across age.

TABLE 7

Confidence Intervals for Total Life Expectancies Derived from a Multiple-Decrement Life Table

| | Whites | | Nonwhites | |
Age	Non-South	South	Non-South	South
65	[21.6 , 23.4]	[21.0 , 23.1]	[19.6 , 22.6]	[19.1 , 22.3]
68	[19.0 , 20.7]	[18.4 , 20.4]	[17.2 , 19.9]	[16.7 , 19.6]
71	[16.5 , 18.1]	[16.0 , 17.9]	[14.8 , 17.3]	[14.5 , 17.1]
74	[14.2 , 15.6]	[13.7 , 15.4]	[12.7 , 14.9]	[12.3 , 14.7]
77	[12.0 , 13.2]	[11.5 , 13.0]	[10.7 , 12.7]	[10.4 , 12.4]
80	[10.0 , 11.0]	[9.6 , 10.9]	[8.9 , 10.5]	[8.6 , 10.3]
83	[8.1 , 8.9]	[7.8 , 8.8]	[7.2 , 8.5]	[7.0 , 8.4]
86	[6.3 , 6.9]	[6.1 , 6.8]	[5.7 , 6.6]	[5.5 , 6.5]
89	[4.6 , 5.0]	[4.4 , 4.9]	[4.2 , 4.8]	[4.1 , 4.7]
92	[2.8 , 2.9]	[2.7 , 2.9]	[2.6 , 2.9]	[2.6 , 2.8]

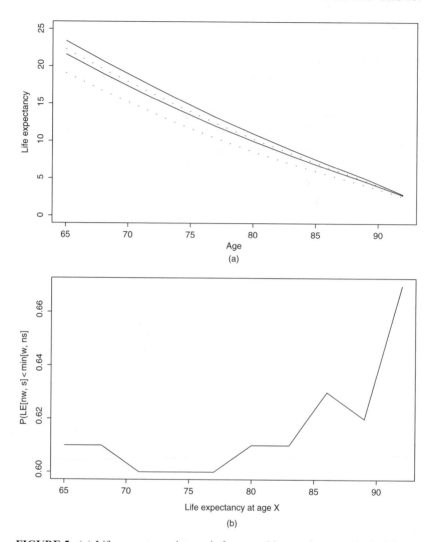

FIGURE 5. (a) Life expectancy intervals for nonwhite southerners (dashed lines) and white nonsoutherners (solid lines) and (b) empirical probabilities that life expectancy for nonwhites from the south is less than that for white nonsoutherners.

In sum, although we have not presented a lengthy discussion of the results, it should be apparent that our approach allows for numerous tests beyond the simple, nonstatistical comparison of point estimates, across any covariate combinations of interest.

5. INCREMENT-DECREMENT (MULTISTATE) LIFE TABLES

Multistate life tables are a generalization of the multiple-decrement table in which multiple and reverse transitions are possible, but so too are reverse transitions. A primary difficulty with constructing a multistate table is that we now have to consider reverse transitions in our modeling strategy, which makes parameterization of duration-dependence more difficult. For example, while it may be reasonable to assume that transitions toward death follow an S-shaped pattern across age, it may not be reasonable to assume that transitions from being disabled to being healthy follow the same shape across age. We can compensate for this problem by estimating age-dependence nonparametrically (i.e., by using dummy variables for age categories) or by allowing the effect of age to vary across groups defined by starting state.

We can construct a single model predicting the outcome state, using the starting state as a predictor. Consider three outcome states—healthy, disabled, and deceased—and two starting states—healthy and disabled. Once again, we can use a multinomial probit model, with the dichotomous outcomes disabled versus not and deceased versus not being the two outcome variables modeled. A $(0, 0)$ vector of responses indicates a healthy outcome state; a $(1, 0)$ vector indicates a disabled outcome state; and a $(0, 1)$ vector indicates a deceased outcome state. The likelihood function is thus identical to that presented in equation (5), with starting state (represented with dummy variables), as well as interactions between the starting state variables and age—to allow duration dependence to vary across starting states—included as predictors.

After estimating the model, we can again compute transition probabilities using multivariate normal integrals as in equation (6). Table 8 provides a depiction of the structure of these transition probabilities for a single iteration of the MCMC algorithm. The matrix of transition probabilities for our three state model appears as

$$
\begin{bmatrix}
p_a^{hh} & p_a^{hd} & p_a^{hx} \\
p_a^{dh} & p_a^{dd} & p_a^{dx} \\
p_a^{xh} & p_a^{xd} & p_a^{xx}
\end{bmatrix},
\tag{7}
$$

where the subscript denotes a particular age, the first superscript denotes the starting state (h = healthy; d = disabled; x = deceased),

TABLE 8
Transition Probabilities Used as Inputs for Multistate Life Table Construction
for Iteration J

Starting State → Transition →	Healthy (0)			Disabled (1)		
Age	Healthy	Disabled	Dead	Healthy	Disabled	Dead (2)
20	p_{20}^{00}	p_{20}^{01}	p_{20}^{02}	p_{20}^{10}	p_{20}^{11}	p_{20}^{12}
21	p_{21}^{00}	p_{21}^{01}	p_{21}^{02}	p_{21}^{10}	p_{21}^{11}	p_{21}^{12}
$\vdots$	$\vdots$	$\vdots$	$\vdots$	$\vdots$	$\vdots$	$\vdots$
k	p_k^{00}	p_k^{01}	p_k^{02}	p_k^{10}	p_k^{11}	p_k^{12}
$\vdots$	$\vdots$	$\vdots$	$\vdots$	$\vdots$	$\vdots$	$\vdots$

Note: For additional transitions, the table of probabilities would need to be expanded column-wise.

and the second superscript denotes the ending state. The bottom row of the matrix consists of zeros, given that no one can enter the survey deceased. The remaining probabilities can be computed via multivariate normal integrals or via subtraction. For example, since the outcomes modeled include "disabled" and "deceased," and starting state is included as a covariate in the model, the probability of transitioning from healthy to disabled (p^{hd}) can be computed as $\int_{-\infty}^{X\beta} \int_{Z\gamma}^{\infty} MVN(0, \Sigma)d_d d_x$, where part of the X and Z vectors are set equal to 0 for a healthy starting state, and each integral must be computed for every age. The integral is from $-\infty$ to $X\beta$ in the disability dimension of the equation, and from $Z\gamma$ to ∞ in the deceased dimension to indicate the probability of being disabled and not deceased. The limits of integration are reversed to compute the probability of transitioning from healthy to deceased, and the probability of remaining healthy is computed via subtraction, given that the rows must sum to 1 (see Schoen 1988). The probabilities for the second row are computed identically, except that the starting state covariate is set to 1 to indicate a disabled starting state.

From these transition probabilities, we can then construct the multistate life table, using calculations such as those in Tables 9(a) and (b). The general equation for transfers in and out of state m is

$$l_{a+1}^m = l_a^m - \sum_{n \neq m} p_a^{mn} \times l_a^m + \sum_{n \neq m} p_a^{nm} \times l_a^n, \tag{8}$$

TABLE 9(a)
Multistate Life Table for Iteration J, Healthy Starting State

Age	l_a^0	L_a^0	e_a^0
20	$\frac{N^0}{N}$	$\frac{l_{20}^0 + l_{21}^0}{2}$	$\frac{\sum_{a=20}^{\omega} L_a^0}{l_{20}^0}$
21	$l_{20}^0 - \sum_{m \neq 0} p_{20}^{0m} \times l_{20}^0 + \sum_{m \neq 0} p_{20}^{m0} \times l_{20}^m$	$\frac{l_{21}^0 + l_{22}^0}{2}$	$\frac{\sum_{a=21}^{\omega} L_a^0}{l_{21}^0}$
⋮	⋮	⋮	⋮
k	$l_{k-1}^0 - \sum_{m \neq 0} p_{k-1}^{0m} \times l_{k-1}^0 + \sum_{m \neq 0} p_{k-1}^{m0} \times l_{k-1}^m$	$\frac{l_k^0 + l_{k+1}^0}{2}$	$\frac{\sum_{a=k}^{\omega} L_a^0}{l_k^0}$
⋮	⋮	⋮	⋮

where l refers to the number of persons in a given state at a given age, *a* represents age, and *n* represents states other than *m*, and the person-years and additional calculations follow from these equations (see Tables 9[a] and [b]).

For this example, we use data from the 1989 and 1994 National Long Term Care Survey analytic files. The NLTCS is a panel study whose members are drawn from a list frame consisting of all Medicare beneficiaries, conducted in 1982, 1984, 1989, 1994, and 1999. Persons reaching age 65 are screened into the sample on the basis of showing

TABLE 9(b)
Multistate Life Table for Iteration J, Disabled Starting State

Age	l_a^1	L_a^1	e_a^1
20	$\frac{N^1}{N}$	$\frac{l_{20}^1 + l_{21}^1}{2}$	$\frac{\sum_{a=20}^{\omega} L_a^1}{l_{20}^1}$
21	$l_{20}^1 - \sum_{m \neq 1} p_{20}^{1m} \times l_{20}^1 + \sum_{m \neq 1} p_{20}^{m1} \times l_{20}^m$	$\frac{l_{21}^1 + l_{22}^1}{2}$	$\frac{\sum_{a=21}^{\omega} L_a^1}{l_{21}^1}$
⋮	⋮	⋮	⋮
k	$l_{k-1}^1 - \sum_{m \neq 1} p_{k-1}^{1m} \times l_{k-1}^1 + \sum_{m \neq 1} p_{k-1}^{m1} \times l_{k-1}^m$	$\frac{l_k^1 + l_{k+1}^1}{2}$	$\frac{\sum_{a=k}^{\omega} L_a^1}{l_k^1}$
⋮	⋮	⋮	⋮

Note: Table 9(a) reports the quantities for starting state 0 (healthy); Table 9(b) reports the quantities for starting state 1 (disabled). State *m* in each case refers generally to the states other than the one of interest. The L_a column indicates we are using the linear approximation in estimating person-years lived in the interval that begins at age *a*. Other approaches could be used.

any limitation on a number of disability items. A subset of persons in 1989 who were not disabled were screened into the sample and followed up in 1994. We use the 1989 and 1994 data, excluding decedents prior to 1989 and persons who are institutionalized in either 1989 or 1994. After deleting missing observations (5.7 percent), we were left with 9733 sample members.

We include age (a five-category variable: $0 = 65–69$, $1 = 70–74$, $2 = 75–79$, $3 = 80–84$, $4 = 85+$), sex (37.9 percent male), race (9 percent nonwhite), starting state, and an interaction between age and starting state as covariates in the model. As mentioned above, we use two starting states—healthy and disabled. Individuals are considered disabled if they have at least one physical limitation on the Katz ADL scale, which consists of six items that are necessary for independent living (ability to bathe self, dress self, feed self, move around the house, get in and out of bed, use the toilet). We note that even with few covariates, as here, traditional sex-race disaggregation would yield sample sizes too small to compute stable transition probabilities. For example, there are only a total of 41 nonwhite males in the oldest age category, and of these, only 18 start the interval healthy.

The results for the model can be found in Table 10. These results are generally as expected. Persons who start healthy are less

TABLE 10

Bivariate Probit Model Results: Effects of Covariates on Transitions to Disability and Death

Covariate	Outcome Category	
	Disabled	Deceased
Intercept[a]	.05(.04)	−.46(.02)***
Age	−.20(.01)***	.28(.01)***
Male	−.26(.03)***	.28(.04)***
Nonwhite	−.07(.02)**	.06(.03)*
Start healthy	−1.45(.03)***	−1.70(.03)***
Age × Start	.43(.02)***	.05(.02)***
ρ_e	−.998(.001)***	

[a] The p-values are the empirical probability that the parameter is either >0 or <0, depending on the sign of the parameter. These values are found by computing the proportion of the simulated parameter values that exceed 0 (either positively or negatively). The p-values reported are classified into the ranges represented by the asterisks.

$\#p < .1$, $*p < .05$, $**p < .01$, $***p < .001$.

likely to become disabled or die than those who start disabled. Age leads to an increased risk of death, but, interestingly, not an increase in the risk of becoming disabled. The interaction between starting state and age explains part of this finding: for individuals who start healthy, age has a positive effect on becoming disabled. However, for individuals who start disabled, age has a negative effect on remaining disabled. Rather, they are perhaps more likely to transition to death. Nonwhites are slightly less likely to become disabled, but more likely to die, than whites. Males are much less likely to become disabled, but much more likely to die, than females (following the old adage: women get sick, men die). In general, these results reveal much larger gender differences in downward transitions than racial differences.

Given the model parameters, we next constructed multistate life tables from the results. We continue with our discussion of the double-jeopardy hypothesis, but now we examine gender and racial differences in active, disabled, and total life expectancy (ALE, DLE, and TLE, respectively). For the sake of space, we do not present the life tables themselves, but in Table 11 we present the confidence intervals for state expectancies obtained from these tables.

The results show that male ALE for both racial groups exceeds that of females, although the gender gap is considerably smaller for nonwhites than for whites. On the other hand, TLE is greater for females than for males for both races. However, the gender gap is smaller and closes across age for nonwhites, while the gender gap does not close across age for whites. The racial gap in ALE narrows across age for both genders. Finally, the racial gap in TLE also narrows for both genders across age. Figures 6 and 7 present these results graphically. Figure 6 shows confidence intervals for ALE. Plot (a) shows the intervals for white males versus white females; plot (b) shows the intervals for nonwhite males versus nonwhite females; plot (c) presents the intervals for white versus nonwhite males; plot (d) presents the intervals for white versus nonwhite females. Figure 7 presents the identical graphs for TLE. Both figures show an increasing overlap in the 95 percent intervals across age for both ALE and TLE between races and between genders.

Figure 8 specifically addresses the double-jeopardy hypothesis. The figure contains four plots of the probability that the state expectancy for nonwhites is less than that for whites across age. All four plots follow the same general pattern: as age increases, the racial gap in both ALE

TABLE 11

Confidence Intervals for Active, Disabled, and Total Life Expectancies Derived from Multistate Life Table

	Whites		Nonwhites	
Age	Males	Females	Males	Females
Active Life Expectancy				
65–69	[14.6 , 15.4]	[13.8 , 14.5]	[12.9 , 13.8]	[12.1 , 13.0]
70–74	[11.5 , 12.3]	[10.7 , 11.4]	[10.7 , 11.5]	[9.7 , 10.7]
75–79	[8.3 , 9.0]	[7.7 , 8.3]	[8.0 , 8.7]	[7.1 , 7.9]
80–84	[5.4 , 5.9]	[4.9 , 5.4]	[5.2 , 5.8]	[4.6 , 5.2]
85+	[2.7 , 3.1]	[2.4 , 2.7]	[2.6 , 3.0]	[2.3 , 2.6]
Disabled Life Expectancy				
65–69	[2.2 , 2.6]	[3.7 , 4.1]	[2.9 , 3.4]	[4.4 , 5.0]
70–74	[1.9 , 2.2]	[3.1 , 3.5]	[2.2 , 2.8]	[3.5 , 4.2]
75–79	[1.6 , 1.9]	[2.6 , 3.0]	[1.8 , 2.3]	[2.9 , 3.5]
80–84	[1.3 , 1.6]	[2.1 , 2.4]	[1.5 , 1.9]	[2.3 , 2.7]
85+	[.92 , 1.2]	[1.4 , 1.6]	[1.0 , 1.3]	[1.4 , 1.7]
Total Life Expectancy				
65–69	[17.1 , 17.8]	[17.7 , 18.4]	[16.0 , 16.9]	[17.0 , 17.5]
70–74	[13.6 , 14.3]	[14.1 , 14.7]	[13.2 , 14.0]	[13.8 , 14.3]
75–79	[10.1 , 10.7]	[10.6 , 11.0]	[10.0 , 10.7]	[10.5 , 10.9]
80–84	[6.9 , 7.3]	[7.2 , 7.5]	[6.9 , 7.3]	[7.2 , 7.5]
85+	[3.8 , 4.0]	[4.0 , 4.1]	[3.9 , 4.1]	[4.0 , 4.1]

and TLE narrow, so that by the oldest ages, the confidence intervals are indistinguishable between nonwhites and whites within gender. In sum, the multistate life table results reveal no support for the double-jeopardy hypothesis, because both ALE and TLE are comparable for whites and nonwhites and become increasingly more so across age.

Before closing this section, we pause to compare the results from the multiple-decrement and multistate tables. There are several differences between the results. For example, the total life expectancies are higher in the multiple-decrement table than in the multistate table. This is attributable to several factors. First, the results were obtained from very different samples. One sample is a long-term panel, while the other is a short-term panel. The data used in the multiple-decrement table constitute only a few birth cohorts, whereas

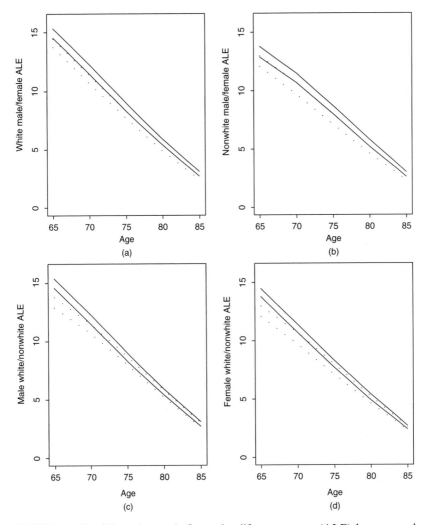

FIGURE 6. Confidence intervals for active life expectancy (ALE) by race and gender. (Dashed lines = males in parts [a] and [b] or nonwhites in parts [c] and [d]).

the data in the multistate example produce a table that is more similar to a period life table. Life expectancies obtained from period versus cohort data tend to differ, especially when mortality rates are changing rapidly across birth cohorts, and such has certainly been the case over the time period studied. Second, we fixed certain covariates in

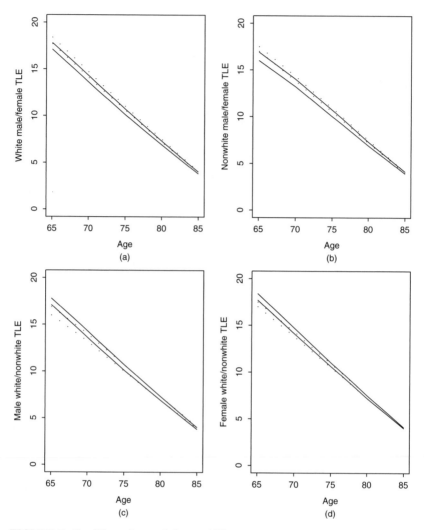

FIGURE 7. Confidence intervals for total life expectancy (TLE) by race and gender. (Dashed lines = males in parts [a] and [b] or nonwhites in parts [c] and [d]).

the multiple-decrement tables: We estimated the table for nonsmoking married women with a high school education. This education level is considerably higher than the mean educational attainment found in the NLTCS, not all NLTCS sample members are nonsmokers, and marriage protects health. All three factors influence mortality rates

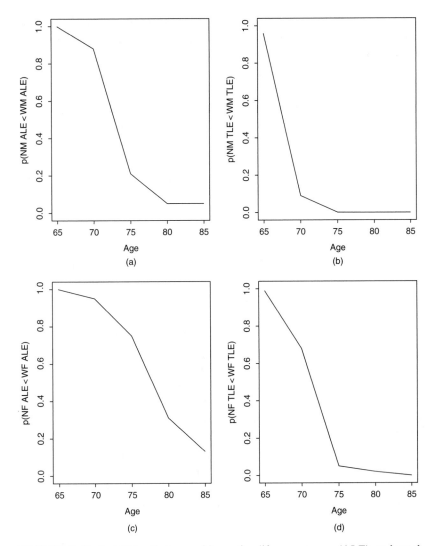

FIGURE 8. Probabilities that nonwhite active life expectancy (ALE) and total life expectancy (TLE) is less than that for whites by sex and age. (N = nonwhite, M = male, W = white, F = female)

and account for the differences in our estimates. Third, although both models used were multinomial probit models, their structures were quite different. In the multistate model we used a categorical measurement for age, and we included the starting state in the model. We also used far more covariates in the multiple-decrement model. These differences affect not only the life expectancy estimates but also the relative widths of the confidence intervals we obtained.

It is difficult to compare our multiple decrement and multistate results with the results of other published studies, given our use of optimal values of covariates in the multiple decrement example, and given the differing definitions of disability used in research estimating ALE using multistate methods. For example, Manton, Stallard, and Corder (1997), using the 1982, 1984, and 1989 waves of the NLTCS, estimated ALE to be approximately 18.6 for females at age 65, while Crimmins, Saito, and Ingegneri (1997) estimate ALE to be 9.8 years for the same subpopulation in 1990. In another study, Laditka and Wolf (1998) estimate 11 years of ALE for women at age 70, an estimate that is greater than that obtained by Crimmins et al. (1997) for women 5 years younger. To that extent, our estimated range of 12.1–14.5 for women ages 65–69 and 9.70–11.4 for women ages 70–74 (taking the lower limit for nonwhites and the upper limit for whites) is similar to Laditka and Wolf's estimate (1998), lower than that of Manton et al. (1997), but higher than Crimmins et al. (1997).

Comparison of population total life expectancy estimates is possible and more straightforward. For this purpose, as in the single-decrement example, we use life expectancy estimates from the BMD. Our estimates in the multiple decrement example tend to be a little higher than those the BMD reports. For example, at age 65 in 1992, the BMD reports a life expectancy of 15.99 for blacks. Our corresponding estimates range from 19.1 to 22.6 (see again Table 7, which is disaggregated by region). The three-year difference may be explained by our use of optimal values for covariates (married, nonsmoking females with high school education). For instance, the BMD estimate for black females is 17.76, accounting for about half of the difference between our estimate and the BMD estimate for the total population.

In terms of the multistate example, the BMD estimate for white females ages 65–69 (1991–1992) is 19.12, while our interval at the same age is [17.7,18.4]. Thus, our estimate is less than a year different. This difference may be attributable to the fact that our sample excluded institutionalized individuals, or it may be attributable to general differences between the use of a panel data set spanning a five-year period and the use of population level data spanning a two-year period. Finally, it may be simply attributable to differences in calculation. For example, we used the linear approach to estimating person-years lived in our age intervals, while the BMD may have used an alternate approach. As stated throughout the paper, other choices for life table calculations could be used.

6. CONCLUSION

Our goal in this paper was to demonstrate a Bayesian approach to constructing life tables. In our brief exposition, we have attempted to demonstrate some of the flexibility of the approach. We chose to provide examples of the types of tests that can be performed and the comparisons that can be made using this method for all three primary types of life tables, rather than providing an in-depth exposition of just one. There are many more aspects of this approach than we were able to demonstrate in a single paper. As we mentioned throughout the paper, there are distributions for all quantities in the life tables, and additional distributions could be constructed. For example, in the multistate table, it may be of interest to construct a distribution of the ratio of active life expectancy to total life expectancy. In the multiple-decrement table, it may be of interest to construct a distribution of the ratio of individuals expected to die from one cause versus another. Both of these extrapolations are straightforward.

We have also focused in this exposition on one type of data: health and mortality data from panel surveys. In the single-decrement example, we constructed a simple one-year panel for persons of different ages. In the multiple decrement example, we used cause of death data collected on a panel across approximately 20 years. For the multi-state example, we used two waves of a panel study with five years between waves. In all three examples, we constructed period life tables by treating members of multiple cohorts as a single synthetic cohort. Of course, cohort life tables could be constructed with this method also. For example, if we were interested in constructing a cohort (possibly multistate) life table and had data on a single birth cohort collected across numerous waves, a multiple failure time model could be estimated. A cohort table could then be constructed from the estimated age-specific transition probabilities. Other types of data could be used as well. For example, if we had data on transitions between regions by age, a multinomial probit (or logit) model could be constructed with region as the outcome and with age (and other variables) included as covariates. Transition probabilities between regions could be generated from the model parameters, and life tables could be constructed from the transition probabilities. In short, if a statistical model can be constructed for the data at hand, and matrices of transition probabilities can be generated from the model, this method can be applied.

Throughout the paper, we have stated that this is *a* Bayesian approach, and not *the* Bayesian approach. Other models could be used than the ones we chose here (e.g., survival models). Additionally, other approaches to generating the intervals could be used (e.g., based on posterior predictive distributions), although such approaches would still most likely require MCMC sampling methods. The real power of a Bayesian approach lay not in model development, but in (1) the theoretical framework that allows us to attach probability distributions to parameters and (2) MCMC estimation methods. Bayesian theory provides for very simple tests of hypotheses, as we have demonstrated. MCMC methods make such tests possible in relatively complicated multistep modeling processes such as construction of life tables.

APPENDIX: METROPOLIS-HASTINGS ALGORITHMS

This appendix will briefly demonstrate the workings of a generic Metropolis-Hastings (MH) algorithm (technically, it is a random walk Metropolis algorithm; see footnote 2). We demonstrate the algorithm by showing how normal random draws—from an $N(0,1)$ distribution—can be simulated using a uniform proposal density ($U(0,1)$). We emphasize that MCMC algorithms can be used to simulate draws from virtually any distribution; we choose the normal for its simplicity. Furthermore, we note that we generally would use an MH algorithm to simulate draws from the distribution of the *parameters given the data*; here, we are simulating draws from the distribution of the *data given the parameters*. From a Bayesian perspective, both parameters and data have comparable status as random variables, and so the application of an MH algorithm for generating values from parameter distributions is a straightforward transition from what we present.

In the section of the paper on multiple-decrement life tables, we show how MH steps can be included in an MCMC algorithm along with a Gibbs sampling step (the drawing of latent propensities). A more generic MH algorithm consists of the following steps:

1. Establish a starting value for the quantity of interest, $x^{j=0}$, and set $j = 1$.
2. Sample a "candidate" quantity, x^c, from a "proposal" density (here, say a $U(0,1)$), so that $x^c = x^{j-1} + U(0,1) - .5$, where j references the iteration, and .5 is subtracted so that the uniform proposal density is centered over the previous value of x.
3. Compute the probability density function $p()$ at x^c and x^{j-1} and form the ratio

$$R = \frac{p(x^c)p(x^{j-1}|x^c)}{p(x^{j-1})p(x^c|x^{j-1})}.$$

4. Compare R to $u \sim U(0,1)$. If $R > u$ then set $x^j = x^c$ (i.e., update); otherwise, set $x^j = x^{j-1}$ (i.e., reject candidate).
5. Repeat these steps for additional parameters if necessary (incrementing j at each iteration).

The density function for the $N(0,1)$ distribution is

$$p(x|\mu = 0, \sigma = 1) \propto \exp\left\{\frac{-x^2}{2}\right\}.$$

Suppose, in step 1 of the MH algorithm, we choose a starting value of -3 for the first data point in the distribution (so, $x^0 = -3$). In step 2, we generate a candidate value, x^c, from the $U(0,1)$ distribution centered over x^0. In other words, x^c can fall anywhere in the interval $[-3.5, -2.5]$ with equal probability. Suppose that we draw $x^c = -3.2$. In step 3, we construct the ratio $R = \frac{p(x^c)p(x^0|x^c)}{p(x^0)p(x^c|x^0)}$. In this case, because the uniform density is symmetric, the latter half of this ratio is unity, and we need to calculate only the first half. Furthermore, we presented the density of the $N(0,1)$ distribution above as being proportional to $\exp\left\{\frac{-x^2}{2}\right\}$: we need not include the constant $\frac{1}{\sqrt{2\pi}}$, because the constant cancels in the numerator and denominator of R. Thus

$$R = \frac{\exp\frac{-3.2^2}{2}}{\exp\frac{-3^2}{2}} = \frac{.005976}{.011109} = .5379.$$

This ratio indicates that the value of the candidate is less probable than the previous value, which we know to be true because x^c is further out in the tail of the standard normal distribution than is x^0. In step 4, we compare R to a uniform deviate $u \sim U(0,1)$ to determine whether to accept the candidate. Suppose we draw $u = .7$. In that case, we would reject the candidate (because $R < u$) and so $x^1 = -3$ (x remains at -3). On the other hand, suppose we draw $u = .4$. In that case, $x^1 = -3.2$. In either case, we then return to step 2 and draw a new candidate and repeat the process. If the candidate of -3.2 had been accepted, the proposal in the next iteration would be centered over -3.2; if the candidate had been rejected, the proposal would remain centered over -3.0.

Suppose that, instead of drawing -3.2 as our candidate, we had drawn -2.8. In that case, R would have been

$$R = \frac{\exp\frac{-2.8^2}{2}}{\exp\frac{-3^2}{2}} = \frac{.01984}{.011109} = 1.786.$$

Because this value for R is greater than 1, the draw would have automatically been accepted (so $x^1 = -2.8$).

Figure A1 consists of three graphs depicting a run of such an MH algorithm. Plot (a) is a trace plot of the first 200 iterations of the algorithm (starting value of $x^0 = -3$). Plot (b) shows the entire run of 5000 iterations. Observe from plot (a) how the algorithm "walks" from -3, a region of very low density in an $N(0,1)$ distribution, toward 0 (the center of the distribution) and then begins to "wander" around 0. Plot (b) shows the entire run; once again, observe how the algorithm converged from -3 to concentrate primarily in the region $[-2,2]$. Finally, plot (c) shows the distribution of the last 4000 iterates, with the $N(0,1)$ density function superimposed over the sampled values. There is a close fit between the MCMC sampled values and the true $N(0,1)$ density, although, as with any finite simulation, there is some error.

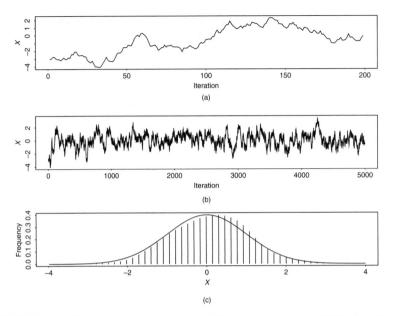

(a)

(b)

(c)

FIGURE A1. Trace plot of (a) the first 200 iterations of an MH algorithm simulating from an $N(0,1)$ distribution, (b) all 5000 iterations of the algorithm, (c) the histogram of the last 4000 iterates with an $N(0,1)$ pdf superimposed.

REFERENCES

Allison, Paul D. 1984. *Event History Analysis: Regression for Longitudinal Event Data.* Sage University Paper series on Quantitative Applications in the Social Sciences, 07–046. Beverly Hills, CA: Sage.

Beard, Robert E. 1971. "Some Aspects of Theories of Mortality, Cause of Death Analysis, Forecasting and Stochastic Processes." Pp. 57–68 in *Biological Aspects of Demography*, edited by W. Brass. London: Taylor and Francis.

Box, George E. P., and George C. Tiao. 1973. *Bayesian Inference in Statistical Analysis.* Reading, MA: Addison-Wesley.

Chiang, C. L. 1960. "A Stochastic Study of the Life Table and Its Applications: II. Sample Variance of the Observed Expectation of Life and Other Biometric Functions." *Human Biology* 32(3):221–38.

———. 1961. "Standard Error of the Age-Adjusted Death Rate." *Vital Statistics— Special Reports* 47(9):275–83.

Coale, Ansley J., and Ellen Eliason Kisker. 1986. "Mortality Crossovers: Reality or Bad Data?" *Population Studies* 40:389–401.

Cox, D. R. 1972. "Regression Models and Life Tables" (with discussion). *Journal of the Royal Statistical Society*, Series B34:187–220.

Crimmins, E. M., Y. Saito, and D. Ingegneri. 1997. "Trends in Disability-Free Life Expectancy in the United States, 1970–90." *Population and Development Review* 23(3):555–72.

Ferraro, Kenneth F. 1987. "Double Jeopardy to Health for Black Older Adults?" *Journal of Gerontology* 42:528–33.

Ferraro, Kenneth F., and Melissa M. Farmer. 1996. "Double Jeopardy to Health Hypothesis for African Americans: Analysis and Critique." *Journal of Health and Social Behavior* 37(1):27–43.

Gelman, Andrew, John B. Carlin, Hal S. Stern, and Donald B. Rubin. 1995. *Bayesian Data Analysis*. London: Chapman and Hall.

Gilks, Walter R. 1996. "Introduction to General State-Space Markov Chain Theory." Pp. 59–74 in *Markov Chain Monte Carlo in Practice*, edited by Walter R. Gilks, S. Richardson, and D. J. Spiegelhalter. Boca Raton, FL: Chapman and Hall/CRC.

Gilks, Walter R., S. Richardson, and D. J. Spiegelhalter. 1996. *Markov Chain Monte Carlo in Practice*. Boca Raton, FL: Chapman and Hall/CRC.

Hayward, Mark D., Eileen M. Crimmins, and Yasuhiko Saito. 1998. "Cause of Death and Active Life Expectancy in the Older Population of the United States." *Journal of Aging and Health* 10(2):192–213.

Hayward, Mark D., Michael Rendall, and Eileen Crimmins. 1999. "Evaluating Group Differences in Healthy Life Expectancy: The Estimation of Confidence Intervals for Multistate Life Table Expectancies." Presented at the annual meeting of the Gerontological Society of America, San Francisco.

Horiuchi, Shiro, and John R. Wilmoth. 1998. "Deceleration in the Age Pattern of Mortality at Older Ages." *Demography* 35:391–412.

Johnson, Valen E., and James H. Albert. 1999. *Ordinal Data Modeling*. New York: Springer.

Keyfitz, N. 1968. *Introduction to the Mathematics of Population*. Reading, MA: Addison-Wesley.

Laditka, Sarah B., and Douglas A. Wolf. 1998. "New Methods for Analyzing Active Life Expectancy." *Journal of Aging and Health* 10(2):214–41.

Land, Kenneth C., Jack M. Guralnik, and Dan G. Blazer. 1994. "Estimating Increment-Decrement Life Tables with Multiple Covariates from Panel Data: The Case of Active Life Expectancy." *Demography* 31(2):297–319.

Land, Kenneth C., and George C. Hough, Jr. 1989. "New Methods for Tables of School Life, with Applications to U.S. Data from Recent School Years." *Journal of the American Statistical Association* 84(405):63–75.

Lee, Peter M. 1989. *Bayesian Statistics: An Introduction*. New York: Oxford University Press.

Lynch, Scott M., and J. Scott Brown. 2001. "Reconsidering Mortality Compression and Deceleration: An Alternative Model of Mortality Rates." *Demography* 38(1):79–95.

Lynch, Scott M., J. Scott Brown, and Katherine G. Harmsen. 2003. "Black-White Differences in Mortality Deceleration and Compression and the Mortality Crossover Reconsidered." *Research on Aging* 25(5):456–83.

Manton, Kenneth G., and Kenneth C. Land. 2000. "Active Life Expectancy Estimates for the US Elderly Population: A Multidimensional Continuous-Mixture Model of Functional Change Applied to Completed Cohorts, 1982–1996." *Demography* 37(3):253–65.

Manton, K. G., and E. Stallard. 1994. "Medical Demography: Interaction of Disability Dynamics and Mortality." Pp. 217–78 in *Demography of Aging*, edited by L. G. Martin and S. H. Preston. Washington, DC: National Academy Press.

Manton, K. G., E. Stallard, and L. Corder. 1997. "Changes in the Age Dependence of Mortality and Disability: Cohort and Other Determinants." *Demography* 34(1):135–57.

Markides, Kyriakos S., and Sandra A. Black. 1996. "Race, Ethnicity and Aging: The Impact of Inequality." Pp. 153–170 in *Handbook of Aging in the Social Sciences*, 4th ed., edited by R. H. Binstock and L. K. George. San Diego, CA: Academic Press.

Mason, Karen C., and Lisa G. Cope. 1987. "Sources of Age and Date-of-Birth Misreporting in the 1900 U.S. Census." *Demography* 24: 563–73.

Menken, Jane, James Trussell, Debra Stempel, and Ozer Babakol. 1981. "Proportional Hazards Life Table Models: An Illustrative Analysis of Socio-Demographic Influences on Marriage Dissolution in the United States." *Demography* 18(2):181–200.

Molla, Michael T., D. K. Wagener, and J. H. Madans. 2001. "Summary Measures of Population Health: Methods for Calculating Healthy Life Expectancy." *Healthy People Statistical Notes, no. 21*. Hyattsville, MD: National Center for Health Statistics.

Nam, Charles B. 1995. "Another Look at Mortality Crossovers." *Social Biology* 42(1–2):133–142.

Pettit, Becky, and Bruce Western. 2001. "Inequality in Lifetime Risks of Imprisonment." Presented at the annual meeting of the Population Association of America, Washington, DC.

Preston, S. H., I. T. Elo, I. Rosenwaike, and M. Hill. 1996. "African-American Mortality at Older Ages: Results of a Matching Study." *Demography* 33: 193–209.

Preston, Samuel H., Patrick Heuveline, and Michel Guillot. 2001. *Demography: Measuring and Modeling Social Processes*. Oxford, England: Blackwell.

Schoen, Robert. 1988. *Modeling Multigroup Populations*. New York: Plenum.

Thatcher, A. R., V. Kannisto, and J. W. Vaupel. 1998. *The Force of Mortality at Ages 80 to 120*. Odense, Denmark: Odense University Press.

Tierney, Luke. 1996. "Full Conditional Distributions." Pp. 75–88 in *Markov Chain Monte Carlo in Practice*, edited by Walter R. Gilks, S. Richardson, and D. J. Spiegelhalter. Boca Raton, FL: Chapman and Hall/CRC.

Trussell, James, and Charles Hammerslough. 1983. "A Hazards-Model Analysis of the Covariates of Infant and Child Mortality in Sri Lanka." *Demography* 20(1):1–26.

Vaupel, James W., and Anatoli I. Yashin. 1985. "Heterogeneity's Ruses: Some Surprising Effects of Selection on Population Dynamics." *The American Statistician* 39(3):176–85.

Yamaguchi, Kazuo. 1991. *Event History Analysis*. Newbury Park, CA: Sage.

ROBUST SPATIAL ANALYSIS OF RARE CRIMES: AN INFORMATION-THEORETIC APPROACH

*Avinash Singh Bhati**

In this paper we describe a semiparametric information-theoretic framework for modeling the determinants of rare events aggregated at intracity areal units while allowing for various forms of error correlation structures. The approach is applied to an examination of the effects of socioeconomic and demographic macro-characteristics of communities on the amount of violence they experience. We investigate and find evidence of some instability in these processes across types of violence and level of areal aggregation. However, we also find evidence of a stable predictor—resource deprivation—for all the types of violence analyzed and at both levels of areal aggregation considered. In addition, we find evidence of a spillover effect of a community's

This research was supported by grant 2002-IJ-CX-0006 from the Mapping and Analysis for Public Safety (MAPS) program of the National Institute of Justice (NIJ), Office of Justice Programs, U.S. Department of Justice. Points of view in this document are those of the author and do not represent the official positions or policies of the U.S. Department of Justice, nor of the Urban Institute, its trustees or its funders. I thank Dr. Robert Sampson for providing me with the information needed for mapping Chicago's census tracts to its neighborhood clusters. I thank Dr. Amos Golan for his guidance and valuable contributions that have helped shape the analysis reported here. All remaining errors are mine.

Direct correspondence to Avinash Singh Bhati, Research Associate, Justice Policy Center, The Urban Institute, 2100 M Street, NW, Washington, DC 20037. Email: abhati@ui.urban.org.

*Justice Policy Center, The Urban Institute

239

resource deprivation on the level of violence its neighboring areas can expect. We discuss our findings in light of their substantive, methodological, and practical implications.

1. INTRODUCTION

Multivariate regression analysis is a common technique researchers use to explain observed patterns in outcomes—the dependent variables—with theoretically motivated predictors—the independent variables. Despite heavy reliance on this approach by researchers and its ubiquitous use as a tool to inform policy, the approach is built on several strong assumptions which, in practice, may not hold true. One such assumption is that the *unexplained* variation in the outcome, as captured by the regression residuals or errors, should be devoid of any structure. When modeling patterns of crime across geographic space—where the observational units are linked in meaningful ways—this assumption is very likely to be violated. To the extent that it is, and we proceed as if it were not, the resulting inferences may be misleading and hence a poor foundation on which to base policy.

Major advances have been made in estimating regression models in the presence of spatially autocorrelated errors when the dependent variable is continuous (Anselin 1988; Anselin and Bera 1998). But doing so when the criterion (or outcome) measure is discrete has proved to be more difficult and is currently an area of active research. This focus is important because when rates or counts of relatively rare events are analyzed at local (intracity) levels of areal aggregation, such as census tracts or neighborhoods, discrete outcomes are usually the norm. This paper describes and applies an information-theoretic method that allows for the incorporation of spatially dependent error structures in regression models of discrete outcomes.

1.1. *Background*

The homicide rate is an example of an outcome that qualifies as being "rare," or one that is discrete in nature, when it is measured at local (intracity) levels of aggregation. By discrete we mean that the observed outcomes are typically low non-negative integer values (e.g., 0, 1, 2, ...).

Researchers have attempted to explain observed cross-sectional variations in homicide rates using macrostructural covariates at various levels of areal aggregation. These include nations (Braithwaite and Braithwaite 1980), states (Kennedy, Silverman, and Forde 1991), counties (Land, McCall, and Cohen 1990), Metropolitan Statistical Areas (Balkwell 1990), cities (Williams and Flewelling 1988), and neighborhoods (Baller et al. 2001; Kubrin 2003). Motivated primarily by social disorganization, strain, and social capital theories of crime, researchers typically seek to establish links between the structural, economic, and social conditions in areal units with the rates or counts of homicide observed there. See, among others, Land, McCall, and Cohen (1990) and Reiss and Roth (1994) for comprehensive reviews.

In addition, to isolate and identify the macroprocesses leading to different *types* of violence, researchers sometimes estimate models with disaggregated homicide rates with varying bases for the disaggregation. These include disaggregation by race (Cubbin, Pickle, and Fingerhut 2000; Parker and McCall 1999), intimacy (Avakame 1998), gender within intimate partner homicides (Felson and Messner 1998), and homicide types (Williams and Flewelling 1988; Rosenfeld, Bray, and Egley 1999; Kubrin 2003).

At higher levels of areal aggregation (e.g., counties or states), when the number of homicides is sufficiently large and nonzero events are observed in most of the sampled units, the outcome may be considered continuous, and traditional spatial analytical methods can be, and have been, applied (Messner et al. 1999; Baller et al. 2001).

As the unit of analysis becomes smaller, however, four things can be expected. First, the number of outcomes observed in each sampled unit decreases, thereby discretizing the criterion variable (i.e., the variable approaches a count measure with a highly skewed distribution). Second, the number of units with zero counts increases, thereby inflating the outcome's distribution at zero. Third, differences in the number of outcomes (e.g., homicides) that could have been observed in sampled units, simply because of differences in the populations-at-risk of experiencing the event, become more pronounced. Finally, explanatory macrocharacteristics of areal units like neighborhoods, census tracts, etc., may be more volatile over time than those for larger aggregations such as counties and states. Therefore, increasing the counts of the rare crimes at neighborhood or local levels by simply counting over extended periods of time may lead to distorted inferences and may mask true data-generating processes.

Of course, the problems noted above relate to any rare events. In these instances, Poisson-based regression models are usually more appropriate to employ (Osgood 2000). However, the existing spatial analytical toolkit readily available to researchers is not directly applicable to these types of nonlinear models. In order to study the processes that generate spatial distributions of rare crimes such as homicide, therefore, researchers often aggregate over larger areal units, across several types of homicides, or over longer time periods, and they rely on spatial analytical methods developed for continuous criterion measures. Even when the discrete nature of the criterion measure is explicitly recognized, researchers are often forced to rely on a two-stage approach—(1) convert this measure into an *approximately* continuous variable, and (2) apply traditional spatial analytical methods. Inferences derived from these models, however, could be misleading as they rely on *ad hoc* transformations based, more often than not, on mathematically convenient assumptions rather than a conservative incorporation of only the limited knowledge that researchers typically have about the underlying data-generating processes.

1.2. *Areal Analysis of Rare Crimes*

The incorporation of a spatial dimension in applied work is now a fairly routine component of homicide research (Messner and Anselin 2004). Although the theoretical basis for linking crime to place can be derived from several well-established sociological and ecological perspectives on crime, deviance, and victimization, a proliferation of user-friendly software and geocoded crime data has sparked this recent shift in applied work (Anselin et al. 2000). Borrowing insights from applied research in other fields involving spatially "labeled" data, researchers analyzing violent crime are now well aware that the assumption of independence across geographic space is questionable. Irrespective of whether the notion of space is used for exploratory spatial data analysis (ESDA), for studying spatial diffusion processes and spillover effects, or simply for addressing inefficiencies introduced by error-dependence across space, spatial econometric methods have proved useful in clarifying the links between macrocovariates and homicide rates (Baller et al. 2001; Morenoff, Sampson, and Raudenbush 2001) or in modeling other rare crimes (Smith, Frazee, and Davison 2000). As such, they are indispensable tools for the applied researcher interested in studying and explaining the spatial patterning of crime.

With the wealth of geocoded data increasingly becoming available at local levels both from census sources and from primary data collection efforts, researchers analyzing homicides as well as other rare crimes are more frequently confronted with the need to apply spatial econometric methods to data that are discrete by nature. This proves challenging for several reasons.

Currently, there are no well-established and universally accepted (or available) estimation methods for such models. For example, to analyze binomial or multinomial choice outcomes researchers have proposed several likelihood-based estimators (Besag 1974; Case 1992; McMillen 1992; Bolduc, Fortin, and Gordon 1997; Heagerty and Lele 1998) as well as a generalized method of moments estimator, making use of the concept of a generalized residual (Pinske and Slade 1998). To analyze count data, researchers rely mainly on Bayes, empirical Bayes, or maximum-likelihood estimators of the so-called Poisson "auto-models" (Besag 1974; Clayton and Kaldor 1987; Cressie and Read 1989; Cressie and Chan 1989; Kaiser and Cressie 1997; Waller et al. 1997). Simulation-based estimators are an attractive alternative and are an area of active research (LeSage 1999).

Unfortunately, fully parametric methods that rely on a likelihood function, including traditional Bayesian methods, need to invoke some form of strong distributional assumption *a priori*. In nonexperimental settings, such as the social sciences, true underlying data-generating processes are seldom, if ever, known *a priori*. Hence, model estimates and inferences derived from them can be sensitive to distributional assumptions. Moreover, the small-sample properties of many of these approaches are either unknown or not desirable. When dealing with intracity areal units such as neighborhoods, researchers may be restricted to less than a hundred or a few hundred observations that are spatially dependent. Such sample sizes, coupled with highly collinear (ill-conditioned) data, reduce the efficiency of estimates.

In practice, researchers typically resort to the two-stage approach described above whereby the criterion variable is first converted into an approximately continuous measure and then traditional spatial analytical techniques are applied to it. Though usually feasible, it is unclear whether these transformations always yield their desired corrections (Bailey and Gartell 1995:277). When analyzing rare crimes like homicides, for example, logarithmic, rate, or Freeman-Tukey type transformations may not yield the desired Gaussian criterion measures. This is especially true when rare events such as homicides are measured at local levels of areal aggregation and the number of units with zero counts may be large.

Alternatively, proxy measures—estimated using first-stage nonspatial models—are sometimes used to either redefine the criterion measure directly (Morenoff, Sampson, and Raudenbush 2001) or to statistically "control" for spatial dependence in the second stage (Kubrin 2003). In finite samples, however, there is no guarantee that the first-stage estimates used in such two-step approaches have the assumed desirable properties. These proxy measures must, by definition, inherit any good/bad properties from a misspecified first stage.

Consequently, given researchers' ignorance about data sampling processes, model functional forms, and error-correlation structures, as well as the potential sensitivity of inferences to *ad hoc* and convenient transformations, it seems reasonable to seek alternative estimation and inference frameworks that do *not* force the analyst to commit to assumptions about some or all of these features in order to proceed with the recovery of information from a nonexperimental sample.

The generalized cross entropy (GCE) method applied in this paper is one such flexible, semiparametric approach that avoids strong parametric distributional assumptions. In addition, rather than parameterize the spatial error-dependence in terms of a few autoregressive parameters, the methodology uses knowledge of the relative spatial positioning or contiguity of the sampled units to guide the structure in the errors—each of which is individually estimated. Despite the simultaneous estimation of the realized errors and the expected outcomes in one step, however, the *complexity* of the information-recovery problem does not increase in the sense that the number of unknowns that need to be estimated remains fixed. Finally, the approach is not very resource-intensive to implement as it does not require high-dimensional integration of marginal probabilities nor does it require the inversion of the spatial weight matrix.

1.3. *Overview*

The main goal of this paper is to describe an analytical framework that can be used for robust analysis of rare crimes that are typically observed at local (intracity) levels of areal aggregation. As described above, real-world problems such as discrete outcomes, finite samples, ill-conditioned data, spatial clustering, and ill-measured regressors all preclude a simple adoption of the standard ordinary least squares (OLS) framework with its associated spatial-analytical toolkit. Section 2 provides a detailed description of the alternate semi-parametric information-theoretic framework. This paper does *not* aim to compare the proposed analytical framework with other fully parametric ones. Rather, it aims to explain and apply it. Detailed analytical and empirical (simulation-based) comparisons are left for future work.

To demonstrate the application of this analytical framework to a real-world issue, a second stated goal of this paper is to report the extent to which structural and socioeconomic determinants of different kinds of violence (the disaggregated homicide types) may be distinct, and whether these findings persist at different (intracity) levels of areal aggregation. More specifically, this paper aims to examine the following questions:

- How do the socioeconomic and demographic characteristics in an area affect the amount of violence that a community can expect to experience?
- Are the links violence-type-specific?
- Is there evidence of a modifiable areal unit problem (MAUP)? In other words, are inferences sensitive to the areal unit of aggregation?

Given the explicit spatial nature of the data needed, these questions need to be examined in the presence of possibly spatially dependent errors for which the information-theoretic approach described next is used. A related question, hence, is whether the inferences derived from the analysis would have been *qualitatively* different had the possible spatial structure in the errors been ignored and traditional nonspatial modeling strategies been used. The data that are used to examine all these issues are described in Section 3, with findings discussed in

Section 4. Finally, Section 5 discusses implications of this research effort, lists promising extensions of the proposed analytical framework, and enumerates the merits and drawbacks of the approach.

2. METHODOLOGY

This section describes the information-theoretic method used in this paper. It first explains one application of the generalized cross entropy (GCE) framework, introduced in Golan, Judge, and Miller (1996), that may be used for modeling count outcomes under ideal and asymptotic conditions and then explains its finite sample version. Next, it describes how the framework may be extended to allow for spatially dependent and/or heteroskedastic errors and suggests how the appropriateness of various specifications may be gauged. It concludes with a discussion of substantive spatial dependence and how the current formulations may be extended to model it.

Consider, as a point of departure, the basic identity

$$y_n = s_n + e_n \qquad \forall n = 1, 2, \ldots, N, \tag{1}$$

where y_n is an observed outcome, s_n is the expected outcome or a pure emitted signal, and e_n is a random noise term that distorts the signal into the observed outcome. The observed outcome may be a binary choice, a non-negative integer, or the more traditional continuous outcome. The signal and noise terms are both unknowns and the challenge for researchers is to use all available knowledge to recover information about them.

Knowledge about the process that is available to the researcher includes a set of exogenous predictors, as suggested by theory, as well as the relative spatial positioning of the observations in the sample. For the former, let us assume that a set of K characteristics exists for each of the n sampled units, recorded as x_{kn}, which are hypothesized to influence the signal. For the latter, we may have knowledge about the spatial proximity of observations to each other—i.e., a measure of the spatial structure in the sample. Let this knowledge be available in the form of a full $N \times N$ matrix. For example, we may have actual measures of the Euclidean distance, or some other measures like social or economic distance, between all units in the sample. Or we may simply have knowledge about the contiguity of these observations. Ignoring knowledge of the spatial structure in the sample when it is available is therefore an inefficient way of recovering information from the sample.

Observed spatial patterns in the outcomes (y_n) result from patterns in the signals (s_n) that are modeled by researchers. Bad, incomplete, or inappropriate model specifications, however, often yield residuals (e_n) with spatial patterns. Excluding important predictors, for example, will result in the spatial pattern in the outcomes being inherited by the regression residuals. Including regressors that are badly measured, or measured at inappropriate areal units, will have the same effect. Irrespective of its cause(s), the resulting spatial dependence in the errors proves to be a "nuisance" (Anselin and Bera 1998) when the primary goal is to recover the signals accurately. In what follows, we explain one way to tackle this problem from an information-theoretic perspective building on the generalized cross entropy (GCE) framework introduced in Golan, Judge, and Miller (1996).

2.1. The Generalized Cross Entropy (GCE) Approach

2.1.1. Setting Up the Basic Problem

First consider the case where we may have no knowledge about the spatial positioning of the sampled units—i.e., we have available only the observed outcomes and an exogenous set of possible predictors. We wish to use these data to estimate the signal in order to assess how the hypothesized predictors influence it. To do so within the information-theoretic framework, we first need to reparameterize all unknowns (i.e., the signal and noise terms) into well-defined probabilities. For example, we can define each signal as

$$s_n = \mathbf{z}'\mathbf{p}_n = z_1 p_{1n} + z_2 p_{2n} + \ldots + z_L p_{Ln} \qquad \forall n, \qquad (2)$$

where $\mathbf{z} = (z_1, z_2, \ldots, z_L)'$ is a column vector of real numbers that spans the range of possible values that the signal can take (with $z_1 < z_2 < \ldots < z_L$) and $'$ represents a vector or matrix transpose. Knowledge about bounds on the signal is typically available to the researcher based on knowledge of the dependent variable. For example, the range of possibilities of a binary choice outcome is $s_n \in (0, 1)$; that of a count outcome is $s_n \in (0, +T)$; and for traditional unlimited continuous outcomes, it is $s_n \in \pm T$. Here T is a *sufficiently* large number—one that contains the true signal. If its value is unknown, we may assume a value for T large enough so that it contains, at the very least, the observed outcomes in the sample. The points in z need to be equally spaced unless prior knowledge to the contrary is available to the researcher. This sequence of support points constitutes an L-dimensional *signal support space*. To these support points are applied a set of proper probabilities that, once estimated, will yield the expected outcome of interest—the signal. By *proper* we mean that these probabilities are non-negative—i.e., $p_{in} > 0$ $\forall n$, l—and that they sum to unity—i.e., $\Sigma_l p_{nl} = 1$ $\forall n$.

The reparameterization of the noise term can be carried out in a similar way. That is, we can define each error as

$$e_n = \mathbf{v}'\mathbf{w}_n = v_1 w_{1n} + v_2 w_{2n} + \ldots + v_M w_{Mn} \qquad \forall n \qquad (3)$$

where v is an M-dimensional *error support space* that is defined as being symmetric about zero and the probabilities applied to it are proper. Choosing bounds on the error support requires sample-specific consideration that will be discussed in more detail later. Unless specific knowledge exists to the contrary, the error support points are equally spaced and symmetrical about 0. These definitions allow us to write a reparameterized version of (1) as

$$y_n = \mathbf{z}'\mathbf{p}_n + \mathbf{v}'\mathbf{w}_n \qquad \forall n = 1, 2, \ldots, N \qquad (4)$$

where no assumptions are made about the probabilities of interest other than that they are proper in the sense described above.

Next, we wish to use the available data in constraining the values that these probabilities can take. In the current setting, a natural method of introducing exogenous information is through the formulation of moments. Suppose we premultiply both sides of (4) by x_{kn} and then sum the resulting products over the entire sample. This would yield the following K moment equations

$$\sum_n x_{kn} y_n = \sum_n x_{kn} \mathbf{z}' \mathbf{p}_n + \sum_n x_{kn} \mathbf{v}' \mathbf{w}_n \qquad \forall k = 1, 2, \ldots, K \qquad (5)$$

along with the N adding-up constraints that we would like to impose on each set of proper probabilities

$$\sum_l p_{ln} = \sum_m w_{mn} = 1 \qquad \forall n = 1, 2, \ldots, N. \qquad (6)$$

So far we have only reparameterized the unknowns into proper probabilities and have imposed moment restrictions on them using all the available predictors we have. Under *ideal* experimental conditions—where it may be reasonable to assume that the errors have no structure to them, that the regressors are measured without error, and that the model is well-specified—it may be reasonable to assume that the regressors $\{x_{kn}\}$ are completely uncorrelated with the errors e_n. If so, it may then be reasonable to make the strong orthogonality assumptions of

$$\sum_n x_{kn} e_n = \sum_n x_{kn} \mathbf{v}' \mathbf{w}_n = 0 \qquad \forall k = 1, 2, \ldots, K \qquad (7)$$

so that the moment constraints of (5) are reduced to

$$\sum_n x_{kn} y_n = \sum_n x_{kn} \mathbf{z}' \mathbf{p}_n \qquad \forall k = 1, 2, \ldots, K. \qquad (8)$$

2.1.2. *Estimation*

Having restricted the moment constraints to be pure (noiseless), where the observed (sample) moments are *exactly* matched to the expected (population) moments, we see that the only unknowns remaining in the problem are the probabilities $\mathbf{p}_n$. Now we have a set of K moment equations (8) and a set of N adding-up equations (6) constraining a set of $N \times L$ probabilities. This is an ill-posed inversion problem (Levine 1980) with more unknowns than equations linking them, which means that an infinite number of solutions can satisfy the constraints. How do we select one solution out of these infinite possibilities? Faced with such a problem in statistical mechanics, Jaynes (1957a, 1957b) proposed maximizing the uncertainty implied by the probabilities as a means of selecting an optimal solution. In other words, from all the probability vectors that satisfy the moment and adding-up constraints, Jaynes proposed selecting the one that implies maximum uncertainty. That way the recovered information will be as conservative as the data allow it to be. Put another way, the optimal solution chosen should be the one that only "just" satisfies the constraints required of it.

The next obvious question then is, "How does one measure (quantify) uncertainty?" In the context of a problem in communication theory, Shannon (1948) had defined the uncertainty contained in a message with J mutually exclusive and exhaustive outcomes as $H(\mathbf{p}) = -\Sigma_j \, p_j \ln p_j$. This quantity, termed *information entropy* by Shannon, is maximized when all possibilities are equally likely (probable)—i.e., when $p_j = 1/J \; \forall \, j$—and it is at a minimum of 0 when any one of the possibilities is certain—i.e., when $p_j = 1$ for some j and zero for the rest. Entropy derived from two sources of uncertainty are additive *only* if they are independent sources of uncertainty (Shannon 1948). In what came to be known as maximum entropy formalism, Edwin Jaynes proposed to use this measure—entropy—as the criterion function to maximize, subject to all available constraints, in order to derive conservative inferences from a sample. Building on this view of data analysis, there is a rapidly accumulating information and entropy econometrics literature. Golan (2002) and other authors contributing to that special issue of the *Journal of Econometrics* provide a good review of recent theoretic and applied work in this field.

Applying this principle to our pure moment constraints case, the resulting information-recovery task is formulated as a constrained optimization problem that can be written as

$$\max_{\mathbf{p}} \quad H(\mathbf{p}) = -\mathbf{p}' \ln \mathbf{p} = -\sum_{ln} p_{ln} \ln p_{ln} \tag{9}$$

subject to (8) and (6) where $\mathbf{p} = (\mathbf{p}_1', \mathbf{p}_2', \ldots, \mathbf{p}_N')'$. Since entropy is additive only for independent sources of uncertainty, an implicit assumption in (9) is that the signals are independent across sample units.

If, in addition to the moment constraints, we have some nonsample information about the signals in the form of prior probabilities $\{p_{nl}^0\}$ that have the same dimension and are defined on the same space as the posteriors $\{p_{nl}\}$, then an equivalent problem is to minimize the informational distance between the prior and the posterior probabilities. Unlike the maximum entropy (ME) approach, where we maximize uncertainty implied by the probabilities, in the minimum cross entropy formalism, we minimize the cross entropy (CE), or the Kullback-Leibler (KL) informational distance (Kullback 1959), between the posterior probabilities and their priors. For a message with J mutually exclusive and exhaustive outcomes with prior probabilities p_j^0, the KL informational distance or the CE is defined as $CE = \sum_j p_j \ln(p_j/p_j^0)$. Therefore, given prior probabilities $\mathbf{p}^0$, the resulting constrained optimization problem is to

$$\min_{\mathbf{p}} \quad CE(\mathbf{p}; \mathbf{p}^0) = \mathbf{p}' \ln(\mathbf{p}/\mathbf{p}^0) = \sum_{ln} p_{ln} \ln(p_{ln}/p_{ln}^0) \tag{10}$$

subject to (8) and (6).

The ME formulation is a special case of the minimum CE problem when the prior probabilities in the latter formulation are forced to be uniform. Therefore, in what follows we will restrict our derivations and explanations to only the minimum CE formulations.

The CE problem is a constrained minimization problem that can be solved analytically using the Lagrange method. The primal Lagrangian ($\mathcal{L}_{CE}^P$) for this problem is set up as

$$\mathcal{L}_{CE}^P = \sum_n \mathbf{p}_n' \ln(\mathbf{p}_n/\mathbf{p}_n^0) + \sum_k \lambda_k \left\{ \sum_n x_{kn} y_n - \sum_n x_{kn} \mathbf{z}' \mathbf{p}_n \right\}$$
$$+ \sum_n \mu_n \{1 - \mathbf{1}' \mathbf{p}_n\}, \tag{11}$$

where $\{\lambda_k\}$ and $\{\mu_n\}$ are the sets of Lagrange multipliers corresponding to the imposed constraints.

Solving the first-order conditions for this optimization problem analytically, we obtain optimal solutions for the probabilities of interest as

$$\hat{p}_{ln} = \frac{p_{ln}^0 \exp(z_l \sum_k x_{kn} \hat{\lambda}_k)}{\sum_l p_{ln}^0 \exp(z_l \sum_k x_{kn} \hat{\lambda}_k)} = \frac{p_{ln}^0 \exp(z_l \mathbf{x}_n' \hat{\boldsymbol{\lambda}})}{\Omega_n} \qquad \forall n, l, \tag{12}$$

where $\hat{\boldsymbol{\lambda}} = (\hat{\lambda}_1, \hat{\lambda}_2, \ldots, \hat{\lambda}_K)'$ are the optimum Lagrange multipliers corresponding to the K data constraints, $\mathbf{x}_n = (x_{n1}, x_{n2}, \ldots, x_{nK})'$ is a vector of K covariates for the nth observation, and the partition function (Ω_n) ensures that the probabilities sum to one. Inserting these optimum solutions back into the primal constrained optimization problem of (11), we can derive a dual unconstrained version of the optimization problem, where the dual objective is a function of the Lagrange multipliers, as

$$\mathcal{L}_{CE}^D = \sum_{kn} x_{kn} y_n \lambda_k - \sum_n \ln \Omega_n. \tag{13}$$

This dual unconstrained *maximization* problem typically does not have an analytical solution, but a numerical one can be obtained using optimization techniques available in a variety of software. Once we obtain optimum values for the Lagrange multipliers, we can then recover the signals, or expected outcomes, using (12) and (2).

2.1.3. *Noisy Moment Constraints*
In the optimization problem derived above, strong assumptions were made regarding the exact matching of the observed (sample) moments and the expected (population) moments. In most real-world non-experimental settings—e.g., in almost all of social science research—the sample moments may not be perfect analogs of the population moments being estimated. Hence, making strong assumptions when they are possibly violated may yield inferior results. In order to impose less restrictive constraints than those implied by (8), we need to allow some flexibility in the formulation of the moment constraints. Rather than force $\Sigma_n x_{kn} e_n = 0 \ \forall k$ as in (7), one way to allow this flexibility is to require only that the cross products *shrink* to 0 as the sample size increases. Following the traditional consistency requirement, $\operatorname{plim} \frac{1}{N} \sum_n x_{kn} e_n \rightarrow 0 \quad \forall k$, which underlies most likelihood-based estimators, we use N as a shrinkage factor explicitly in our formulation. That is, we replace the pure (noiseless) moment constraints of (8) with

$$\sum_n x_{kn} y_n = \sum_n x_{kn} \mathbf{z}' \mathbf{p}_n + \frac{1}{N} \sum_n x_{kn} \mathbf{v}' \mathbf{w}_n \qquad \forall k = 1, 2, \ldots, K. \tag{14}$$

This formulation implies that, in any finite sample, we do not force the moments to hold exactly. The amount of flexibility *allowed* in the constraints depends on the sample size and the specification of **v**. The amount of flexibility *used* by the estimator, however, depends on the observed data. The trivial solution $w_{mn} = 1/M$ $\forall n$, m or $e_n = 0$ $\forall n$ is within the allowable solutions for the unknown error terms. That is, if the sample is close to being *ideal*, then it should only help reduce uncertainty about the signal and $e_n \approx 0$, $\forall n$. If the sample is *imperfect* in any sense, then by allowing some flexibility in the constraints we allow for a more stable solution to the optimization problem. In other words, loosening the constraints does not *force*, but rather *allows*, the solutions to be different from those obtained by exactly matching the observed and expected moments. The solutions will be different to the extent that the observed data do not strictly conform to the assumption of $\Sigma_n x_{kn} e_n = 0$ $\forall k$.

Unlike the pure (noiseless) moment constraints cases of the previous section, the problem is now defined in terms of two sources of uncertainty—relating to $\mathbf{p}_n$ and $\mathbf{w}_n$. Following the maximum entropy or cross entropy formalisms as described above, we can now set up a more *generalized* information recovery problem. This approach, termed the generalized maximum entropy (GME) or the generalized cross entropy (GCE) method, was introduced by Golan, Judge, and Miller (1996). As before, the GME formulation is but a special case of the GCE when the prior probabilities for $\mathbf{p}_n$ as well as $\mathbf{w}_n$ are forced to be uniform. The primal constrained optimization problem now is to

$$\min_{\mathbf{p},\mathbf{w}} \quad CE(\mathbf{p}, \mathbf{w}; \mathbf{p}^0, \mathbf{w}^0) = \mathbf{p}' \ln(\mathbf{p}/\mathbf{p}^0) + \mathbf{w}' \ln(\mathbf{w}/\mathbf{w}^0), \qquad (15)$$

subject to the flexible moment constraints of (14) and the adding-up constraints of (6). Note that despite the flexible constraints, the assumption of independence between the signal and noise terms and across sample units must be maintained in order for the cross entropy from each of these sources of uncertainty to be additive. Following through with the optimization, we obtain

$$\hat{p}_{ln} = \frac{p_{ln}^0 \exp(z_l \sum_k x_{kn} \hat{\lambda}_k)}{\sum_l p_{ln}^0 \exp(z_l \sum_k x_{kn} \hat{\lambda}_k)} = \frac{p_{ln}^0 \exp(z_l \mathbf{x}_n' \hat{\boldsymbol{\lambda}})}{\Omega_n} \qquad \forall n, l \qquad (16)$$

and

$$\hat{w}_{mn} = \frac{w_{mn}^0 \exp(v_m^* \sum_k x_{kn} \hat{\lambda}_k)}{\sum_m w_{mn}^0 \exp(v_m^* \sum_k x_{kn} \hat{\lambda}_k)} = \frac{w_{mn}^0 \exp(v_m^* \mathbf{x}_n' \hat{\boldsymbol{\lambda}})}{\Psi_n} \qquad \forall n, m \qquad (17)$$

as the optimum solutions for the probabilities of interest, where $v_m^* = v_m/N$. Once again, these solutions may be used along with the primal Lagrangian function to derive a dual unconstrained optimization problem in the unknown Lagrange multipliers as

$$\mathcal{L}_{GCE}^D = \sum_{kn} x_{kn} y_n \lambda_k - \sum_n \ln \Omega_n - \sum_n \ln \Psi_n, \qquad (18)$$

where Ω_n and Ψ_n are the partition functions for the two sets of probabilities.

2.2. Nonspherical Errors

In the preceding sections we described how the noiseless moment constraints can be relaxed for any finite sample and how these constraints, along with the ME/CE principle, can be used to recover information from a sample of observed data. The resulting flexibility, however, still relies on the assumption that the errors are uncorrelated or that they are determined independently of one another. To the extent that we believe there to be some structure in the errors, we need to explicitly use this knowledge in recovering information from the sample.

Consider the case where this structure is explicitly known—i.e., where the *known* error covariance matrix is denoted as $\sigma^2 \boldsymbol{\Phi}$ with $\boldsymbol{\Phi}$ a $N \times N$ positive definite matrix. Then, writing the identity (1) in matrix notation as

$$\mathbf{y} = \mathbf{s} + \mathbf{e}$$

and setting $\mathbf{e} = \boldsymbol{\Phi} \mathbf{u}$, we obtain a new identity

$$\mathbf{y} = \mathbf{s} + \boldsymbol{\Phi} \mathbf{u}, \qquad (19)$$

where $\mathbf{y} = (y_1, y_2, \ldots, y_N)'$ and $\mathbf{s} = (s_1, s_2, \ldots, s_N)'$ are as defined before. The new set of errors ($\mathbf{u}$) are now assumed to be completely devoid of structure, although they combine with each other in a systematic way (coded in Φ) to create signal distortion. Even with this knowledge, we are unable to use the exogenous data $\mathbf{X} = (\mathbf{x}_1, \mathbf{x}_2, \ldots, \mathbf{x}_N)'$ to create exact moment constraints because

$$\mathbf{X'y} = \mathbf{X's} + \mathbf{X'\Phi u} \qquad (20)$$

and even if we can assume that $\mathbf{X'u} = \mathbf{0}$ this does not imply $\mathbf{X'\Phi u} = \mathbf{0}$. Therefore, we typically first transform the problem by premultiplying both sides of the equality (19) by Φ^{-1} to get

$$\Phi^{-1}\mathbf{y} = \Phi^{-1}\mathbf{s} + \mathbf{u} \qquad (21)$$

and then, using the orthogonality assumption of $\mathbf{X'u} = \mathbf{0}$, we obtain noiseless moment constraints:

$$\mathbf{X'}\Phi^{-1}\mathbf{y} = \mathbf{X'}\Phi^{-1}\mathbf{s}. \qquad (22)$$

If we make the general linear model assumption of $\mathbf{s} = \mathbf{X\beta}$, then the above moments yield the generalized least squares estimates of β (Judge et al. 1988:330). If Φ^{-1} is unknown but can be consistently estimated in the first of a two-stage procedure, then this results in the feasible or estimated generalized least squares estimator. Nothing precludes us from applying this approach in the nonlinear case (see Mittelhammer, Judge, and Miller [2000:361–68]- or the case where the signal is left unspecified as in our formulation. However, there are several practical difficulties in applying this approach. First, the error covariance structure Φ is seldom, if ever, known. Second, even if we use a two-stage procedure, there is no guarantee that the estimated $\hat{\Phi}$ will be a positive definite matrix and therefore invertible. Creative assumptions often need to be made to ensure that it is invertible. The most common approach, of course, is to explicitly parameterize the entire error structure in terms of a few parameters and to estimate them simultaneously with the signals. This fully parametric framework, though well developed for the linear model, is less tractable when estimating nonlinear models like binary choices or count outcomes.

In what follows, the GCE framework of the previous section is extended to allow for errors that may be heteroskedastic and/or autocorrelated across space.

2.2.1. GCE with Heteroskedastic Errors

In the GCE formulation of the last section, fixed weights of $1/N$ were applied to each of the observations in the sample while formulating the flexible moment constraints of (14). To allow for heteroskedasticity of an unspecified form, we can replace the fixed weights of $1/N$ by an unknown weight π_n that is allowed to vary across the cross-sectional units. The π_n are now an additional set of proper probabilities that need to be estimated. Again, by proper we mean that $\pi_n > 0 \; \forall n$ and $\Sigma_n \pi_n = 1$.

If the observed sample supports *equal* weighting of the errors, then we should obtain estimates of $\hat{\pi}_n \approx 1/N \; \forall n$. On the other hand, if the data support *unequal* weighting of the sample errors, then $\hat{\pi}_n$ should be different for some or all n. The resulting GCE estimates will, therefore, be consistent with "optimally reweighted errors" and can hence be considered heteroskedastic-consistent. This approach is similar to the optimal reweighting of estimating equations allowed in exponential tilting and empirical likelihood approaches discussed, among others, by Imbens, Spady, and Johnson (1998).

The resulting heteroskedastic-consistent flexible moment constraints can be written as

$$\sum_n x_{kn} y_n = \sum_n x_{kn} \mathbf{z}' \mathbf{p}_n + \sum_n x_{kn} \pi_n \mathbf{v}' \mathbf{w}_n \qquad \forall k = 1, 2, \ldots, K. \qquad (23)$$

with the added requirement that $\Sigma_n \pi_n = 1$. These constraints are similar to the flexible constraints of (20) with $\boldsymbol{\Phi}$ defined as a diagonal square matrix with π_n as its nth diagonal element. To proceed, note first that, assuming independence between π_n and w_{mn}, we can define an auxiliary joint probability measure $q_{mn} = w_{mn} \cdot \pi_n$ so that $\pi_n = \Sigma_m q_{mn} \; \forall n$ and $w_{mn} = q_{mn}/\Sigma_m q_{mn} \; \forall m, n$ are marginal and conditional probabilities (respectively) derivable from q_{mn}. In addition, since $\Sigma_n \pi_n = 1$ and $\Sigma_m w_{mn} = 1 \; \forall n$, then $\Sigma_{mn} q_{mn} = 1$ over all m and n. Finally, given the above definition of q_{mn}, we may specify its associated priors as $q_{mn}^0 = \pi_n^0 \cdot w_{mn}^0$. Unless knowledge to the contrary is available to the researcher, these priors are defined as being uniform and therefore $q_{mn}^0 = 1/(M \cdot N)$.

Reformulating the task from one of recovering $\mathbf{p}$, $\boldsymbol{\pi}$, and $\mathbf{w}$ into one of recovering $\mathbf{p}$ and $\mathbf{q}$, the resulting constrained optimization problem that incorporates all available knowledge is

$$\min_{\mathbf{p} \cdot \mathbf{q}} \quad CE(\mathbf{p}, \mathbf{q}; \mathbf{p}^0, \mathbf{q}^0) = \mathbf{p}' \ln(\mathbf{p}/\mathbf{p}^0) + \mathbf{q}' \ln(\mathbf{q}/\mathbf{q}^0) \tag{24}$$

subject to the flexible moment constraints

$$\mathbf{X}'\mathbf{y} = \mathbf{X}'\mathbf{Z}\mathbf{p} + \mathbf{X}'\mathbf{V}\mathbf{q} \tag{25}$$

and the adding-up constraints of $\Sigma_l p_{ln} = 1$ $\forall n$ and $\Sigma_{mn} q_{mn} = 1$. The matrices of the signal and error supports are defined as

$$\mathbf{Z} = (\mathbf{I} \otimes \mathbf{z}') = \begin{pmatrix} \mathbf{z}' & & & \\ & \mathbf{z}' & & \\ & & \ddots & \\ & & & \mathbf{z}' \end{pmatrix} \quad \text{and}$$

$$\mathbf{V} = (\mathbf{I} \otimes \mathbf{v}') = \begin{pmatrix} \mathbf{v}' & & & \\ & \mathbf{v}' & & \\ & & \ddots & \\ & & & \mathbf{v}' \end{pmatrix}$$

where $\mathbf{I}$ is an identity matrix and $\otimes$ denotes the Kronecker product.

As before, we obtain optimal solutions for $\mathbf{p}$ and $\mathbf{q}$ by setting up the primal Lagrange function and following through with the optimization. The optimal solution for $\mathbf{p}$ is as given in (16) and that for $\mathbf{q}$ is

$$\hat{q}_{mn} = \frac{q_{mn}^0 \exp(v_m \sum_k x_{kn} \hat{\lambda}_k)}{\sum_{mn} q_{mn}^0 \exp(v_m \sum_k x_{kn} \hat{\lambda}_k)} = \frac{q_{mn}^0 \exp(v_m \mathbf{x}_n' \hat{\boldsymbol{\lambda}})}{\Gamma} \qquad \forall n, m. \tag{26}$$

Note the distinction between this solution and the optimal solution for $\hat{\mathbf{w}}$ given in (17). Unlike the solution for $\hat{\mathbf{w}}$, where the fixed weights $1/N$ were applied directly to the support space $\mathbf{v}$, here the support space for each error is not shrunk directly. Rather, the partition function Γ is defined over the entire sample and, as such, allows for an observation specific rate of shrinkage. Using the obtained solutions back in the primal, as before, we may derive an unconstrained dual optimization problem that can be solved in a variety of software. The heteroskedastic consistent GCE dual problem is

$$\mathcal{L}_{GCE}^{D} = \sum_{kn} x_{kn} y_n \lambda_k - \sum_{n} \ln \Omega_n - \ln \Gamma. \qquad (27)$$

2.2.2. GCE with Autocorrelated Errors

The heteroskedastic consistent formulation of the GCE problem derived above can be seen as a special case of a more general formulation that not only allows error shrinkage rates to be determined endogenously, but also allows the optimally reweighted errors to combine with each other in order to create signal distortion. That is, the moment constraints of (25) can be seen as a special case of the constraints

$$\sum_{n} x_{kn} y_n = \sum_{n} x_{kn} \mathbf{z}' \mathbf{p}_n + \sum_{n} x_{kn} \sum_{j} a_{nj} \pi_j \mathbf{v}' \mathbf{w}_j \qquad \forall k = 1, 2, \ldots, K$$

or, in matrix notation

$$\mathbf{X}' \mathbf{y} = \mathbf{X}' \mathbf{Z} \mathbf{p} + \mathbf{X}' \mathbf{A} \mathbf{V} \mathbf{q}, \qquad (28)$$

where $\mathbf{A}$ is a row-standardized hypothesized error structure matrix such that (25) is obtained by setting $\mathbf{A} = \mathbf{I}$. The introduction of a row-standardized weight matrix means that the noise terms that distort the signals are now *smoothed* versions of the optimally reweighted errors. For a similar smoothing of moment-generating functions in an empirical likelihood framework, see Kitamura (1997) and Kitamura and Stutzer (1997).

The resulting optimization problem is very similar to the hetero-skedastic case above. The addition of the link matrix alters only the definition of Γ in the optimal solution and, therefore, in the derivation of the dual objective function. Now, the optimal solution for $\mathbf{q}$ is

$$\hat{q}_{mn} = \frac{q_{mn}^0 \exp(v_m \sum_k \tilde{x}_{kn} \hat{\lambda}_k)}{\sum_{mn} q_{mn}^0 \exp(v_m \sum_k \tilde{x}_{kn} \hat{\lambda}_k)} = \frac{q_{mn}^0 \exp(v_m \tilde{\mathbf{x}}_n' \hat{\boldsymbol{\lambda}})}{\tilde{\Gamma}} \qquad \forall n, m, \qquad (29)$$

where $\tilde{\mathbf{x}}_n$ is the nth row from the matrix $\tilde{\mathbf{X}} = \mathbf{A}' \mathbf{X}$ and $\tilde{\Gamma}$ is the partition function that is based on $\tilde{\mathbf{X}}$. The resulting dual objective function is derived in an identical fashion to the heteroskedastic case, with the exception that Γ is replaced with $\tilde{\Gamma}$.

To the extent that the off-diagonal elements in **A** are allowed to be nonzero, the optimally reweighted errors are permitted to combine while distorting the signal. The matrix **A** is a row-standardized version of a spatial link matrix, say **A***, which can be specified in a number of different ways. As stated above, if the desire is to allow for only heteroskedasticity, then $\mathbf{A}^* \equiv \mathbf{I}_n$ or

$$
a_{nj}^* = \begin{cases} 1 & \forall j = n \\ 0 & \forall j \neq n. \end{cases}
$$

To code heteroskedasticity as well as local first-order autocorrelation, we can define $\mathbf{A}^* = \mathbf{I} + \mathbf{C}$, where **C** is a first-order spatial contiguity matrix. That is,

$$
a_{nj}^* = \begin{cases} 1 & \forall j = n \\ 1 & \forall j \in J_n \\ 0 & \text{for all other } j, \end{cases}
$$

where $j \in J_n$ is taken to read "all j units within the neighborhood of the nth unit." In order to include distance-based dependence for local neighbors (based on contiguity alone), we can define this matrix as $\mathbf{A}^* = \mathbf{I} + \exp(-\mathbf{D}) \odot \mathbf{C}$, where $\odot$ represents an element-by-element matrix multiplication, **D** represents an $N \times N$ matrix of distances between all pairs of data points, and **C** is as defined above. Finally, allowing global dependence, albeit with some distance-based decay, can be represented by setting $\mathbf{A}^* = \exp(-\mathbf{D})$. Row-standardizing **A*** generally yields an asymmetric matrix—i.e., $\mathbf{A}' \neq \mathbf{A}$.

2.3. *Specifying the Support Space*

So far the flexibility allowed in the moment constraints and the estimation implications derived thereof have been discussed for abstractly defined signal and noise supports. If natural bounds exist for these unknowns, then that knowledge may be used directly in specifying the supports. If they do not exist, then specifying the supports requires careful sample-specific considerations. Below we discuss the specification for two examples—binary choice and count outcomes—that are relevant to this paper.

2.3.1. *Binary Choice Outcomes*

In the case of binary choices, there exist natural bounds for both the signal as well as the noise terms: the observed and expected outcomes in this case can exist only between 0 and 1. This means the signals are naturally bounded by 0 and 1—i.e., $z_l \in (0, 1)$. A simple specification would be $\mathbf{z} = (0, 1)'$. Now, if we observe an outcome (i.e., $y_n = 1$) but predict it as being nearly impossible (i.e., $\hat{s}_n \approx 0$), then the error can be as high as $+1$. Or, if the binary choice is not observed (i.e., $y_n = 0$) but we predict it with near certainty (i.e., $\hat{s}_n \approx 1$), then the error can be as low as -1. In other words, the errors are also naturally bounded between ± 1—i.e., $v_m \in \pm 1$—and a simple specification would be $\mathbf{v} = (-1, +1)'$.

If we specify the support spaces as described above and create noiseless moment constraints of (8), then the resulting maximum entropy solutions are identical to the logit parameters. In fact, under this specification the maximum entropy dual objective function turns out to be identical to the logit log-likelihood function. As such, all inferences derived from it, including the parameter estimates and their covariance matrix, are identical to those that would be recovered from the logit model. The GME/GCE specification results in loosened constraints and, in finite samples, yields more conservative but superior (i.e., more stable) parameter estimates. The asymptotic equivalence of the GME/GCE model to the maximum-likelihood logit model is explicitly demonstrated in Golan, Judge, and Perloff (1996).

2.3.2. *Count Outcomes*

Count outcomes can be thought of as a summation over a large but finite sequence of independent and identical binary choices. That is, the motivation underlying a binomial distribution and the Poisson distribution is in fact obtained at the limit when the number of binary choices in the sequence approach infinity. Suppose, then, that we define the count outcome as T times the signal and noise terms in each of the T individual binary choices. That is, we let

$$\mathbf{y} = T\{\mathbf{s} + \mathbf{e}\},$$

where the underlying signal and noise supports ($\mathbf{z}$ and $\mathbf{v}$) are as defined for the binary choice outcome. The resulting expected count would now be $\in (0, T)$. However, since there are T different sources of signal and noise uncertainty for each sampled unit, the entropy

function must be appropriately scaled. The flexible moment constraints for the count outcome case therefore get redefined as

$$\sum_n x_{kn} y_n = T \left\{ \sum_n x_{kn} \mathbf{z}' \mathbf{p}_n + \frac{1}{N} \sum_n x_{kn} \mathbf{v}' \mathbf{w}_n \right\} \qquad \forall k = 1, 2, \ldots, K \quad (30)$$

and the objective function is accordingly redefined as

$$\min_{\mathbf{p} \cdot \mathbf{w}} \quad CE(\mathbf{p}, \mathbf{w}; \mathbf{p}^0, \mathbf{w}^0) = T \left\{ \mathbf{p}' \ln(\mathbf{p}/\mathbf{p}^0) + \mathbf{w}' \ln(\mathbf{w}/\mathbf{w}^0) \right\}. \quad (31)$$

Given the close connection between this formulation and the binary
choice outcome case (i.e., the count outcome information-recovery
problem is simply one of recovering information about the sum of T
independent binary choices), it may be conjectured that the asymptotic properties of the count outcome CCE estimator are similar to
those derived for the multinomial choice GME/GCE problem in
Golan, Judge, and Perloff (1996).

All derivations and extensions (for heteroskedastic and/or
autocorrelated errors) from the previous sections follow exactly as
explained in Section 2.2 with a scaling factor T appropriately
included. The final dual objective function for a GCE model for
count outcomes with potentially heteroskedastic and spatially autocorrelated errors is defined as

$$\mathcal{L}^D_{GCE} = \sum_{kn} x_{kn} y_n \lambda_k - T \sum_n \ln \Omega_n - T \ln \tilde{\Gamma} \quad (32)$$

where all terms have been defined before. The only remaining issue is a
choice for the value of T. Here we use knowledge of the empirical
distribution of y_n as a guiding factor. For example, if we observe counts
only as high as 10, then it is unlikely that the underlying expected count
may be much higher than that. Therefore, as a conservative rule of
thumb, we use $3 \times \max(y)$ in any sample as the fixed value for T.

2.4. Hypothesis and Specification Tests

2.4.1. Hypothesis Concerning Parameters
If a solution exists, then the optimization problems described above
yield estimates of the Lagrange multipliers ($\hat{\lambda}$) that can be used to

recover the probabilities of interest ($\hat{\mathbf{p}}_n$, $\hat{\mathbf{w}}_n$, $\hat{\mathbf{q}}_n$, or $\hat{\boldsymbol{\pi}}_n$) as well as the corresponding signals ($\hat{s}_n$) and realized error terms ($\hat{e}_n$), and ultimately to derive marginal effects ($\partial \hat{s}_n / \partial x_{kn}$) and other inferential quantities as needed. Underlying all these quantities, however, is the set of Lagrange multipliers ($\hat{\boldsymbol{\lambda}}$).

The dual versions of the information-recovery tasks are nonlinear unconstrained optimization problems in the K Lagrange multipliers. Therefore, in addition to estimating these parameters, we can use the dual objective function to estimate a covariance matrix for $\hat{\boldsymbol{\lambda}}$. This can be used to conduct hypothesis tests on the Lagrange multipliers of interest or any derivatives thereof. A discussion of the *sample*-theoretic properties of the Lagrange multipliers is given in the appendix to this paper. As shown there, the covariance matrix for the Lagrange multipliers ($\boldsymbol{\Sigma}_\lambda$) may be approximated by the inverse negative Hessian of the dual objective function evaluated at the optimal Lagrange multipliers:

$$\hat{\boldsymbol{\Sigma}}_\lambda = \left\{ -\frac{\partial^2 \mathcal{L}_{GCE}^D}{\partial \hat{\boldsymbol{\lambda}} \partial \hat{\boldsymbol{\lambda}}'} \right\}^{-1} \tag{33}$$

This may be either computed analytically or retrieved from the numeric routine that is used to solve the optimization problem. In either case, the square root of the diagonal elements of this matrix may be used as approximate standard errors for the Lagrange multipliers. This yields a measure of the stability of the Lagrange multipliers and, consequently, a means of performing hypothesis tests on any inferential quantity based on them (e.g., using the χ^2, z, or t tests).

One quantity that is usually of interest is the marginal effect of the independent variables on the signal—i.e., $\partial \hat{s}_n / \partial x_{kn}$. As in all other nonlinear models, this quantity must be evaluated at some data point (which is usually the sample means of the predictors). Let $\mathbf{x}_*$ represent a generic point of evaluation and let $\hat{p}_{l*}$ represent the probability computed at that point. Then, in our semiparametric formulation of the signal, the marginal effects are computed as

$$\hat{\gamma}_k = \frac{\partial \hat{s}_*}{\partial x_{k*}} = \hat{\lambda}_k \left\{ \sum_l z_l^2 \hat{p}_{l*} - \left(\sum_l z_l \hat{p}_{l*} \right)^2 \right\}$$

or, in matrix notation, as

$$\hat{\gamma} = \frac{\partial \hat{s}_*}{\partial \mathbf{x}_*} = \hat{\lambda} \left\{ \mathbf{z}^{2'} \hat{\mathbf{p}}_* - (\mathbf{z}' \hat{\mathbf{p}}_*)^2 \right\} \tag{34}$$

which are nonlinear functions of the underlying Lagrange multipliers (because $\hat{\mathbf{p}}_*$ are functions of $\hat{\lambda}$). In order to convert the estimated covariance matrix of $\hat{\lambda}$ into an estimate of the covariance among $\hat{\gamma}$, we make use of the delta-method (Greene 2000: 357). That is,

$$\hat{\boldsymbol{\Sigma}}_\gamma = \left(\frac{\partial \hat{\gamma}}{\partial \hat{\lambda}'} \right) \hat{\Sigma}_\lambda \left(\frac{\partial \hat{\gamma}}{\partial \hat{\lambda}'} \right)', \tag{35}$$

where, given the definition of $\hat{\gamma}$ above, we have

$$\frac{\partial \hat{\gamma}}{\partial \hat{\lambda}'} = \left\{ \mathbf{z}^{2'} \hat{\mathbf{p}}_* - (\mathbf{z}' \hat{\mathbf{p}}_*)^2 \right\} \cdot \mathbf{I}$$
$$+ \left\{ \mathbf{z}^{2'} \hat{\mathbf{p}}_* + (\mathbf{z}^{2'} \hat{\mathbf{p}}_*)(\mathbf{z}' \hat{\mathbf{p}}_*) - 2(\mathbf{z}' \hat{\mathbf{p}}_*)^3 \right\} \cdot \hat{\lambda} \mathbf{x}_*' \tag{36}$$

In small samples, rather than use a single point of evaluation, researchers may compute the average marginal effects (over all sample points) and approximate the covariance matrix of these marginals instead. Alternately, as suggested by a reviewer, in some instances it may be more desirable to evaluate these marginal effects at various data points and study variations, if any, in derived inferences.

2.4.2. Hypothesis Concerning Specification

Although several structures can be hypothesized for the spatial error correlation, in the information-theoretic framework described above they all lead to nonnested models. Since the correlation in the errors is not imposed by means of explicit data constraints, resulting in corresponding Lagrange multipliers, it cannot be tested using the framework described above. Therefore, we need some other criterion to choose among the alternate error structures.

Once we have estimated a model, or more precisely the Lagrange multipliers, we may use them to recover all the probabilities in the model. In the GCE models with heteroskedasticity and/or autocorrelation, this means both $\hat{\mathbf{p}}$ and $\hat{\mathbf{q}}$. Using these estimated probabilities, we can construct the entropy measures for each of the sources of uncertainty in the model. The entropy of a probability vector is a measure of the amount of uncertainty it implies. Uncertainty, on the other hand, is an inverse measure of information (Soofi 1994). The more uncertain we are about the outcome, the less information the model conveys about it. Therefore, we should be able to combine the computed entropy measures from these distinct sources of uncertainty for a pair of models to yield a criterion for selecting between them. Additionally, we should be able to use these measures to choose among several nonnested models. Below we describe one way of doing so.

Consider a pair of models $\mathcal{M}_0$ and $\mathcal{M}_1$ where $\mathcal{M}_0$ is encompassed by $\mathcal{M}_1$. That is, even though $\mathcal{M}_0$ is not nested within $\mathcal{M}_1$ parametrically, $\mathcal{M}_1$ allows within it all the specifications in $\mathcal{M}_0$. For example, a model with $\mathbf{A}^* = \mathbf{I}$ is encompassed by the model that defines $\mathbf{A}^* = \mathbf{I} + \mathbf{C}$ if everything else in the model remains fixed. That is, a model that permits *only* heteroskedasticity is encompassed within a model that permits heteroskedasticity *and* first-order spatial error-correlation. In fact, all the specifications of $\mathbf{A}^*$ described above (except when $\mathbf{A}^* = \mathbf{0}$) encompass the heteroskedastic consistent model where $\mathbf{A}^* = \mathbf{I}$. In a similar manner, the heteroskedastic-consistent model encompasses the ME/CE models, which may be obtained by setting $\mathbf{A}^* = \mathbf{0}$. Therefore, logically, all models that permit heteroskedasticity as well as autocorrelation encompass the pure ME/CE models.

The GCE models described above all have one thing in common: they are all attempts at capturing the structure in the errors nonparametrically. If the structure hypothesized in $\mathbf{A}$ is a good approximation of reality, then this must help us gain information about the error structure *without* giving up too much information about the signals. Of course, if it helps us gain information about the signals, all the better. Therefore, if we define entropy measures $H(\hat{\mathbf{p}}_0)$ and $H(\hat{\mathbf{q}}_0)$ as quantifying our uncertainty about the signal and noise terms in model $\mathcal{M}_0$, and $H(\hat{\mathbf{p}}_1)$ and $H(\hat{\mathbf{q}}_1)$ as quantifying our uncertainty about the corresponding measures in model $\mathcal{M}_1$, then we may define the relative *gain* in error information as

$$\mathcal{H}_e = H(\hat{\mathbf{q}}_0)/H(\hat{\mathbf{q}}_1)$$

and the relative *loss* in signal information as

$$\mathcal{H}_s = H(\hat{\mathbf{p}}_1)/H(\hat{\mathbf{p}}_0).$$

These quantities may be defined equivalently in terms of the normalized entropy measures $S(\hat{\mathbf{p}}) = H(\hat{\mathbf{p}})/H(\hat{\mathbf{p}}^0)$ (Golan, Judge, and Miller 1996:27). Since the prior probabilities in each pair of competing models is the same, the normalizing constants cancel each other out, and we obtain the definitions given above.

To see if the flexibility provided in a given model $\mathcal{M}_1$ over that provided in model $\mathcal{M}_0$ is worthwhile, we can compare these two measures. To do so, we define a composite ratio of these measures as

$$\mathcal{H}_* = \mathcal{H}_e/\mathcal{H}_s, \tag{37}$$

which can be used to gauge the relative efficiency of $\mathcal{M}_1$ over $\mathcal{M}_0$. If $\mathcal{H}_* < 1$, then the gains made by increasing knowledge about the error structure are too costly. On the other hand, if $\mathcal{H}_* > 1$, the gains are worthwhile. Since all definitions in the two models are identical with the exception of $\mathbf{A}$, these computations can be taken to mean the following: If one has to give up too much information on the signals in order to gain information about the errors, then the data are clearly not supporting that error structure. On the other hand, if the data do support the hypothesized error linkages, then the gains in information about the errors should far outweigh the losses we incur in terms of the signals.

Finally, if we have several models that encompass the same underlying model—for example, $\mathbf{A} = \mathbf{I}$ is encompassed by all models with $\mathbf{A} \neq \mathbf{I}$ other than $\mathbf{A} = \mathbf{0}$—then we can compare the composite relative efficiency measure across all models that are worthwhile (i.e., $\mathcal{H}_* > 1$) and select the one that offers the highest gains. This model can be viewed as the one that is favored by the sample as being the closest to the underlying data-generating process among all competing models and, in that sense, should be considered the "best" model.

2.5. *Discussion*

Several special considerations must be kept in mind for the count outcome models. The first is the issue of "population-at-risk." Clearly, allowing T to vary across observations is a trivial extension in the noiseless moment constraints setting. It complicates issues considerably, however, when dealing with the heteroskedastic and/or autocorrelated errors case. It is simpler to use the population-at-risk (or its natural log) explicitly as an additional predictor in the regressions. This is the approach we use in our analysis.

A second important consideration pertains to overdispersion. Typically, the Poisson assumption is a very restrictive one, as its first and second moments are equal. To allow for some flexibility, researchers rely on some variant of the traditional Poisson model that permits overdispersion. Several such variants are available, each resulting from different assumptions made about an overdispersing random variable (Cameron and Trivedi 1986). In the GCE specification described above, rather than parameterize the heteroskedasticity *indirectly* through an additional variable for which additional (often mathematically convenient) distributional assumptions must be made, we allow for heteroskedasticity *directly* by allowing an endogenous optimal reweighting of the errors.

A final consideration in count outcome models is the over-representation of zero outcomes in the sample. In such settings, it may be reasonable to model the choice between no event and some event as a different mechanism from that yielding the number of events. Extending the GCE to extract the components of these mixed processes is also part of our ongoing research and is not discussed here.

The main emphasis in this paper is on utilizing the flexibility of the GCE to deal with error-correlation across space—i.e., to treat spatial dependence as a "nuisance." Other forms of spatial structures may, of course, exist in the data. If the spatial relationships are theorized to be of a *substantive* nature, then they should be modeled as such.

There are two forms of substantive spatial processes that can be modeled. First, one may hypothesize that the signal (or expected outcome) is directly related to the observed explanatory factors in neighboring areas—i.e., where $s_n = f(\mathbf{x}'_n, \mathbf{x}'_{j \in J_n})$. Modeling substantive spatial dependence of this type is easily permitted in the current model, as explained in the preceding sections, by including $\mathbf{WX}$ (or a subset thereof) as additional variables in the design matrix constraining the probabilities of interest. Here $\mathbf{W}$ is a spatial weight matrix rather than the link matrix $\mathbf{A}$. It is typically row standardized and has $w_{nj} = 0 \ \forall n = j$ so that the nth row of $\mathbf{WX}$ (i.e., $\Sigma_j w_{nj} x_{kj} \ \forall j \in J_n$)

is, in effect, a spatially weighted average of relevant neighboring area predictors. In this paper, we explicitly estimate a set of such models that allow the spatial lag of a predictor variable to enter the hypothesized set of regressors and discuss findings.

Second, the signal may be hypothesized to depend on the observed outcomes in neighboring areas—i.e., where $s_n = f(\mathbf{x}'_n, \mathbf{x}'_{j \in J_n}, y_{j \in J_n})$. Modeling and interpreting substantive spatial effects of this kind are more difficult. From an estimation point of view, including $\mathbf{Wy}$ with the regressors constitutes a violation of the orthogonality assumption because of its endogeneity. Unlike what happens in time-series analysis, where the time lag of the dependent variable is treated as *pre-determined* and therefore uncorrelated with the current period noise, the spatial-lag term is endogenous and therefore correlated with local area errors (Anselin and Bera 1998). Therefore, even asymptotically, we should not expect $\mathbf{X'e}$ to vanish. More importantly, however, the interpretation of a significant coefficient on $\mathbf{Wy}$ in single cross-sections (such as the analysis performed in this study) is not clear (Anselin 2002). A promising specification that the GCE framework may permit is one where *signal*-autocorrelation is modeled directly rather than via a functional dependence on $\mathbf{Wy}$. This avenue of research has the potential for allowing a *simultaneous* approach to modeling substantive spatial dependence.

3. THE DATA

For this paper we analyzed data obtained from public sources about violence in the city of Chicago. These data were obtained at the lowest unit of analysis—the census tract (CT)—and were later aggregated up to the neighborhood cluster (NC) level. The neighborhood clusters are defined by the Project on Human Development in Chicago's Neighborhoods (PHDCN) as combinations of Chicago's 865 census tracts that are "geographically contiguous and socially similar" (Morenoff, Sampson, and Raudenbush 2001). The mapping of census tracts to neighborhood clusters was obtained directly from Dr. Robert Sampson of the PHDCN.

Using 1990 geographic definitions, there were 865 census tracts with an average population of approximately 3200 people. The aggregated 343 neighborhood clusters had an average population of roughly 8000 people. The disaggregated homicide types analyzed in this paper are described next, followed by a description of the independent variables used in modeling them.

3.1. *Disaggregated Homicide Counts*

Data on the dependent variable, the Disaggregated Homicide Victimization Counts over the three-year period (1989–1991), were obtained from *ICPSR 6399: Homicides in Chicago, 1965–1995 (Part 1, Victim Level File)*. That data file is a compilation of all homicides reported to the police between 1965 and 1995 (Block and Block 1998). This file contains detailed information on victim, offender, and the circumstances of each homicide as well as the offense date. Additionally, it contains a variable that indicates the "type" of homicide. This variable, SYNDROME, distinguishes between the various homicide subtypes that were analyzed in this paper. The original coding in the data contains 10 different categories, which include gang-related (01), sexual assault (02), instrumental (03), spousal attack (04), child abuse (05), other family expressive (06), other known expressive (07), stranger expressive (08), other (09), and mystery (10). We recombined these into six categories by collapsing values 04, 05, and 06 into a generic "Family" related expressive category and 02, 09, and 10 into the "Other" category. The Other category was intended to be a "catch-all" category for homicides that were not classified in any of the remaining types. Since the numbers for sexual assault homicides were very small, they were included in this category. All analysis, therefore, is performed on the six disaggregated homicide types that are classified as being gang-related (**GNG**), instrumental (**INS**), family related expressive (**FAM**), known person expressive (**KNO**), stranger expressive (**STR**), and other (**OTH**), in addition to a model estimated for all homicides combined (**ALL**).

Each victimization in this file is flagged by the location where the victim's body was found. In the public release version of the data, this information is provided only by a census tract number. Using this information, along with the recoded homicide-types, raw counts were computed at the census tract levels for a three-year time frame spanning the years 1989, 1990, and 1991. Raw counts were then aggregated up to the neighborhood cluster level. Figure 1 shows the distribution of the disaggregated homicide counts measured at the

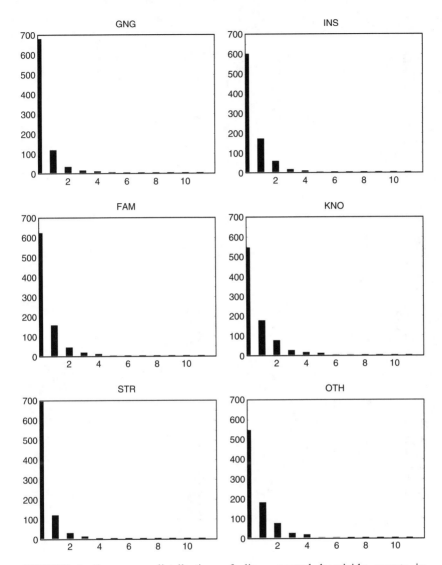

FIGURE 1. Frequency distribution of disaggregated homicide counts in Chicago's 865 census tracts (1989–1991).

census tract level, whereas Figure 2 shows the same at the neighborhood cluster level. It is clear from these figures that the distributions of the criterion measures are highly skewed and that large numbers of areal units have zero counts. In fact, the number of neighborhood

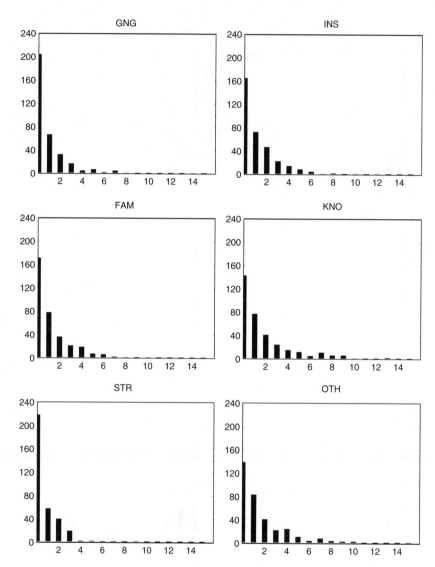

FIGURE 2. Frequency distribution of disaggregated homicide counts in Chicago's 343 neighborhood clusters (1989–1991).

clusters with no reported victims range from a low of about 40 percent (KNO) to a high of about 63 percent (STR) of the sample. Similarly, the number of census tracts with no reported homicide victims range from a low of 63 percent (KNO) to a high of 80 percent (STR) of the sample.

Next, in order to assess whether the criterion measures are randomly distributed across space, they were mapped for visual analysis. Though not a formal procedure, we also computed simple linear regression coefficients for each of these crime counts regressed on their first-order spatial lags (using the queen contiguity criterion) to get an idea of the extent and direction of spatial autocorrelation. The models were specified as $y_n = \alpha + \beta\{\mathbf{Wy}\}_n + e_n$. Table 1, where these coefficients ($\hat{\alpha}$ and $\hat{\beta}$) are displayed, along with visual inspection of the maps in Figure 3 and Figure 4, indicates that the dependent variables being analyzed are not randomly distributed across space and, in all cases, they appear to be positively autocorrelated.

3.2. *Independent Variables*

The structural, social, and economic indicators used to model these disaggregate homicide counts were obtained from the Neighborhood Change Database (NCDB) maintained by the Urban Institute in Washington, D.C. The NCDB contains social, demographic, economic, and housing data on census tracts in the United States for 1970, 1980, 1990, and 2000. Data in the NCDB are based on information gathered

TABLE 1

OLS Regression Coefficients of Disaggregated Homicide Counts (1989–1991) Regressed on Their First-order Spatial Lag (Using a Queen Contiguity Criterion) and an Intercept

	ALL	GNG	INS	FAM	KNO	STR	OTH
Unit of Analysis: Neighborhood Cluster ($N = 343$)							
Intercept	0.29	0.20*	0.21*	0.40**	0.22	0.28**	0.29*
	(0.390)	(0.114)	(0.120)	(0.123)	(0.154)	(0.082)	(0.158)
Wy (spatial lag of **y**)	0.93**	0.79**	0.81**	0.63**	0.88**	0.59**	0.80**
	(0.054)	(0.092)	(0.072)	(0.079)	(0.065)	(0.083)	(0.071)
Unit of Analysis: Census tract ($N = 865$)							
Intercept	0.53**	0.12**	0.19**	0.20**	0.21**	0.17**	0.32**
	(0.142)	(0.035)	(0.041)	(0.043)	(0.053)	(0.029)	(0.054)
Wy (spatial lag of **y**)	0.73**	0.66**	0.59**	0.53**	0.69**	0.35**	0.50**
	(0.047)	(0.058)	(0.055)	(0.063)	(0.052)	(0.067)	(0.057)

*$p < 0.1$ using conventional t-tests. **$p < 0.05$.

Unstandardized linear regression coefficients with asymptotic standard errors appear in parenthesis.

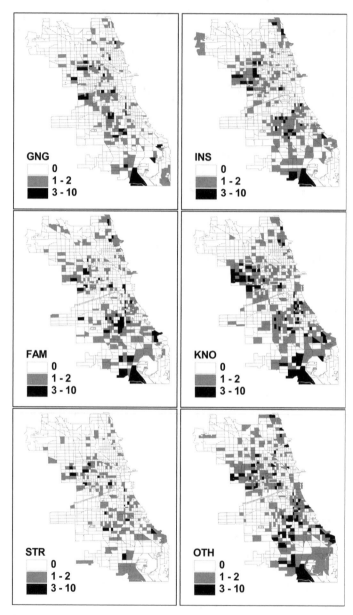

FIGURE 3. Geographic distribution of disaggregated homicide counts in Chicago's 865 census tracts (1989–1991).

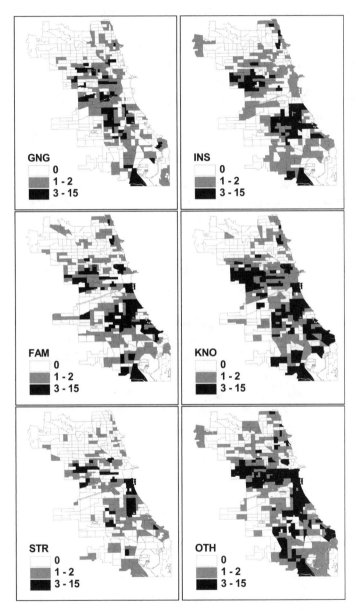

FIGURE 4. Geographic distribution of disaggregated homicide counts in Chicago's 343 neighborhood clusters (1989–1991)

by the U.S. Census Bureau in its decennial censuses. The bureau makes census tract data available to the public in both printed and machine-readable formats. The NCDB contains this public information in one database.

For this analysis, we constructed nine measures of the structural, social, and economic conditions within the areal unit being analyzed. The definition of the measures was kept constant across the two levels of areal aggregation. Data were collected at the CT level and later aggregated to the NC level of analysis. Data not available or computable at the census tract level were imputed from the relevant neighborhood cluster level. That is, the value for a given characteristic at the neighborhood level was used as the assigned value for a census tract missing that information. A description of each of these measures, along with the source of the measure and the number of census tracts missing that measure (in parentheses), is provided below.

SHRBLK   *Proportion of the neighborhood population that is black.* This variable, quantifying racial makeup of the community, was obtained directly from the NCDB (# missing = 14).

SHRHSP   *Proportion of neighborhood population that is Hispanic.* This variable, also quantifying the racial makeup of the community, was directly obtained from the NCDB (# missing = 14).

PNFH   *Proportion of neighborhood households that are nonfamily.* This variable was included to measure social disorganization and family structure and was directly obtained from the NCDB (# missing = 14).

FEMH   *Proportion of neighborhood households with children that are headed by females.* This variable was also included to measure social disorganization and family structures and was also directly obtained from NCDB (# missing = 25).

YMEN   *Young men aged 15–25 as a proportion of area's total population.* This variable was computed by dividing the count of relevant young men by the total area population. It was included to measure the prevalence in the population of persons who are typically thought of as committing violent crimes (# missing = 14).

UNEMP   *The neighborhood unemployment rate as defined by the Census Bureau.* This variable includes persons over the age of 16 who were in the civilian labor force but were unemployed. The variable was obtained directly from the NCDB and was included to assess the effects of one form of economic deprivation on violence (# missing = 17).

POVRT   *Proportion of neighborhood population below the poverty line (as defined for 1989).* This variable was also included as another measure of economic deprivation and was obtained directly from the NCDB (# missing = 14).

RESST   *Residential stability in the area.* This variable was computed as the proportion of owner-occupied housing units where the head of household has lived for at least five years (# missing = 14).

LPOP   *The natural log of the total residential population of the areal unit.* This variable was included as a control for variations in population-at-risk among the areal units (# missing = 14).

Univariate characteristics and bivariate correlations of the resulting measures reveal that the data are highly collinear (see Table 2). In order to mitigate the ill effects of collinearity, we used a data-reducing technique common in this literature. We first assessed the extent to which these data elements could be collapsed into underlying latent constructs using factor analysis on all the included variables (except LPOP). Then, having decided on a set of covariates that constitute meaningful latent constructs, we used a confirmatory factor analysis to create the latent constructs. This procedure was repeated at both the NC as well as the CT levels of analysis. Similar results were obtained at both levels. Using a retention criterion of a minimum eigenvalue of 1, we obtained three significant latent constructs. The first one indicated high (larger than 0.5) factor loadings of SHRBLK, FEMH, UNEMP, and POVRT, resulting in a measure that captures underlying resource deprivation. The second construct indicated high loadings of SHRSHP and YMEN, not yielding any clear meaning to the underlying latent construct; and the third factor indicated high loadings of PNFH and RESST, once again not yielding any clear meaning for the underlying

TABLE 2

Bivariate Correlation Coefficients and Descriptive Statistics for the Areal Macrocharacteristics Used in the Analysis

	SHRBLK (1)	SHRHSP (2)	FEMH (3)	PNFH (4)	YMEN (5)	UNEMP (6)	POVRT (7)	RESST (8)	LPOP (9)
Unit of Analysis: Neighborhood Cluster (N = 343)									
(1)	1	-0.53**	0.88**	-0.23**	0.10*	0.71**	0.55**	0.19**	-0.16**
(2)		1	-0.32**	-0.19**	0.43**	-0.16**	0.04	0.15**	-0.07
(3)			1	-0.15**	0.16**	0.84**	0.78**	0.31**	-0.23**
(4)				1	-0.29**	-0.31**	-0.13**	-0.04	0.27**
(5)					1	0.24**	0.28**	0.11*	-0.14**
(6)						1	0.88**	0.32**	-0.27**
(7)							1	0.42**	-0.23**
(8)								1	-0.15**
(9)									1
Mean	0.42	0.20	0.40	0.32	0.08	0.14	0.23	0.14	8.94
S.D	0.43	0.26	0.23	0.15	0.02	0.10	0.17	0.04	0.37
Unit of Analysis: Census Tract (N = 865)									
(1)	1.00	-0.54**	0.83**	-0.16**	-0.02	0.66**	0.56**	0.13**	-0.11**
(2)		1.00	-0.31**	-0.21**	0.22**	-0.17**	-0.03	0.07**	-0.02
(3)			1.00	-0.09**	0.03	0.74**	0.73**	0.17**	-0.26**
(4)				1.00	-0.06*	-0.21**	-0.09**	0.10**	-0.17**
(5)					1.00	0.08**	0.10**	-0.02	-0.01
(6)						1.00	0.81**	0.15**	-0.28**
(7)							1.00	0.26**	-0.34**
(8)								1.00	-0.08**
(9)									1.00
Mean	0.43	0.19	0.42	0.34	0.08	0.15	0.26	0.14	7.75
S.D	0.44	0.26	0.25	0.19	0.04	0.12	0.20	0.08	0.97

*p < 0.1. **p < 0.05.

276

latent construct. Therefore, for purposes of the regression analysis, we computed a single resource deprivation index (RESDEP) using the four covariates that loaded high on it and used the remaining covariates in their manifest forms. In all the regression models, therefore, the basic set of explanatory measures used are RESDEP, SHRHSP, PNFH, YMEN, RESST, and LPOP (in addition to an intercept term).

Despite the reduction in the dimensionality of the regressors, collinearity among the predictors still remains. Using the design matrix condition number (Belsley 1991), defined as $\kappa(\mathbf{X}'\mathbf{X}) = \eta_+/\eta_-$ where $\eta_{(+,-)}$ are the highest and lowest singular values of the data matrix $\mathbf{X}$ (with columns scaled to unit length), we assessed this collinearity to still be serious. At the NC level the data matrix has a condition number of 218.7 whereas at the CT level it is 176.3. A condition number of 1 implies a perfectly orthogonal design matrix. Condition numbers as low as 30 can indicate potentially damaging multicollinearity whereas condition numbers as high as 900, that are not uncommon in real-world design matrices, can result in degrading multicollinearity.

In the next section, we provide results of the various models analyzed using the data described above.

4. FINDINGS

This section presents the findings from applying the methods explained in Section 2 to the data described in Section 3. Baseline models are first estimated using the maximum-likelihood framework for comparison purposes. Next, using the neighborhood cluster (NC) level model for the total homicide counts (ALL) as an example, the workings of the GCE estimator are presented and discussed for various hypothesized error structures. Models for the disaggregated homicides are then presented and findings are discussed only for the best models (as gauged by $\mathcal{H}_*$). In order to assess whether and to what extent spatially lagged exogenous predictors may influence the criterion measures, models that include a spatially lagged variable are presented and discussed in light of the spatial spillover effects they imply. The chapter concludes with a summary discussion of the findings.

Before presenting and discussing the findings, a word of caution is in order.[1] All model estimates presented and discussed in this paper assume exogeneity of the regressors. This is a simplifying assumption made in order to isolate the problem of spatially correlated error structures and to highlight the workings of the proposed analytical framework. Endogeneity of regressors is very likely in this as well as other similar types of areal analysis (Dietz 2002). Extending the GCE framework to incorporate more real-world features, such as the potential endogeneity of some or all of the regressors, is left for future work (see discussion in Section 5.2.2).

4.1. *The Baseline Count Outcome Models*

Table 3 presents estimates of a basic set of models estimating the effects of these predictors on the count of the various disaggregated homicide types. The models are estimated using the traditional Poisson regression framework available in most statistical software.

There are several points worth noting here. The first is that resource deprivation (RESDEP) is a strong and persistent predictor of all the types of homicides analyzed at both the NC and CT levels. In a similar manner, the log of the total population (LPOP) is a significant predictor of the total count of homicides as well as all disaggregate homicide types at both levels of analysis. Additionally, the estimated coefficient on LPOP in most of the models is close to 1, indicating the possible appropriateness of a rate transformation. Modeling a rate-transformed count outcome as a Poisson process is the same as modeling the original count outcome with the coefficient on the log of the rate divisor set equal to 1.

The similarity across the models, however, ends there. The Poisson models show evidence of distinct homicide-type and analysis-level specific processes.

At the NC level of analysis, increases in the percentage of Hispanics in the total population are positively associated with only the total (ALL), gang-related (GNG), stranger-related (STR), and other types (OTH) of homicides. Similarly, increases in the proportion

---

[1] We thank an anonymous reviewer for pointing this out.

TABLE 3

Maximum-Likelihood Coefficient Estimates of Baseline Poisson Regressions with Disaggregated Homicides (1989–1991) Modeled on Area Macrocharacteristics

	ALL	GNG	INS	FAM	KNO	STR	OTH
Unit of Analysis: Neighborhood Cluster ($N = 343$)							
INTERCEPT	−7.79**	−9.34**	−8.69**	−10.26**	−10.48**	−8.86**	−8.68**
	(0.611)	(1.441)	(1.311)	(1.406)	(1.120)	(1.740)	(1.134)
RESDEP	0.85**	0.79**	0.80**	0.85**	0.87**	0.93**	0.86**
	(0.029)	(0.077)	(0.061)	(0.063)	(0.051)	(0.081)	(0.052)
SHRHSP	0.97**	2.53**	0.08	0.42	0.11	0.97**	0.46*
	(0.122)	(0.264)	(0.283)	(0.301)	(0.241)	(0.361)	(0.244)
PNFH	0.37**	−1.47**	0.37	0.47	0.16	0.14	1.17**
	(0.183)	(0.559)	(0.382)	(0.389)	(0.328)	(0.537)	(0.321)
YMEN	1.10	0.65	6.64**	−4.89	7.10**	−3.23	2.25
	(1.365)	(3.300)	(2.797)	(3.165)	(2.351)	(4.088)	(2.506)
RESST	−0.03	1.38	−1.46	−1.09	−0.07	0.49	0.42
	(0.578)	(1.394)	(1.277)	(1.316)	(1.055)	(1.623)	(1.057)
LPOP	0.98**	0.95**	0.91**	1.16**	1.12**	0.90**	0.91**
	(0.067)	(0.161)	(0.143)	(0.151)	(0.122)	(0.189)	(0.123)
Unit of Analysis: Census Tract ($N = 865$)							
INTERCEPT	−7.08**	−9.34**	−8.15**	−10.93**	−8.42**	−8.82**	−7.16**
	(0.310)	(0.773)	(0.658)	(0.736)	(0.559)	(0.877)	(0.547)
RESDEP	0.87**	0.82**	0.86**	0.89**	0.94**	0.97**	0.84**
	(0.029)	(0.081)	(0.062)	(0.065)	(0.052)	(0.081)	(0.051)
SHRHSP	0.99**	2.58**	0.29	0.31	0.41*	0.87**	0.42*
	(0.111)	(0.244)	(0.263)	(0.278)	(0.221)	(0.332)	(0.219)
PNFH	0.24	−1.00**	0.27	0.49	0.59**	0.17	0.60**
	(0.162)	(0.485)	(0.336)	(0.353)	(0.281)	(0.463)	(0.281)
YMEN	0.41	1.57	0.69	−1.07	1.39	−0.54	0.91
	(0.763)	(1.966)	(1.554)	(1.909)	(1.255)	(2.298)	(1.308)
RESST	0.08	0.99	−2.21**	0.32	−0.18	0.54	0.64
	(0.439)	(1.148)	(0.992)	(1.033)	(0.781)	(1.190)	(0.727)
LPOP	0.91**	0.93**	0.91**	1.20**	0.92**	0.87**	0.76**
	(0.035)	(0.087)	(0.075)	(0.082)	(0.062)	(0.098)	(0.061)

$*p < 0.1.$ $**p < 0.05.$

Unstandardized coefficients with asymptotic standard errors appear in parenthesis

of NC households that are nonfamily is positively associated with other types (OTH) of homicides but negatively associated with gang-related (GNG) homicides and not the rest. Increases in youthfulness of the underlying population, as measured by the proportion of young males in the underlying population (YMEN), are somewhat surprisingly associated only with instrumental (INS) and known expressive (KNO), but not other types of homicides. Residential stability (RESST) is not significantly associated with any of the homicide subtypes analyzed nor with the count of all homicides.

Similar findings were observed at the CT level, although there are some important distinctions. Unlike the NC level, the proportion of CT households that are nonfamily is no longer significantly associated with the total count of ALL homicides. For the instrumental homicides (INS), youthfulness of the underlying population (YMEN) is no longer significantly associated with the criterion measure, whereas increases in residential stability (RESST) are now negatively associated with instrumental homicide counts. In a similar manner, YMEN is no longer a significant determinant of known person related expressive homicides (KNO) while the proportion of CT households that are nonfamily (PNFH) and the proportion of CT population that is Hispanic (SHRHSP) are now both significantly and positively related to the criterion measure.

When compared with the total homicide counts (ALL) models at both the NC and CT levels, it is evident from these basic models that ignoring differences in homicide types can severely distort inferences. Moreover, there is evidence of the modifiable areal unit problem (MAUP)—that is, the processes that operate at the NC level may, in some instances, be *qualitatively* different from the processes that operate at the CT level.

4.2. *Structured Error Models*

In order to avoid making the strong distributional assumptions of the Poisson models, as well as to allow for potentially heteroskedastic and/ or autocorrelated errors, we next turn to the GCE framework described in Section 2. In all the GCE models estimated below, we retain the same definitions of the signal and error supports. That is, we define each signal as a sum of T binary choices with each choice defined over the support $z = (0, 1)$ with uniform prior probabilities. Also, we define the error associated with each binary choice with a support of $v = (-1, +1)$, also with uniform prior probabilities. Finally, for each sample, we define the number of binary choices being summed (T) as $3 \times \max(y)$. With these specifications, the resulting Lagrange multipliers are not directly comparable with the Poisson regression coefficients. Therefore it is more appropriate to display and discuss the marginal effects.

Under information-theoretic approaches in general, the Lagrange multipliers typically have interesting *application*-specific meaning and can sometimes be identical to sample-theoretic parameters. For example, in discrete choice models, the Lagrange multipliers are identical to the linear β weights of an underlying latent process (i.e., the logit model parameters). On the other hand, irrespective of the application, a marginal effect ($\hat{\gamma}$) is interpreted as a change in expected outcome (i.e., the $\hat{s}_n$) with respect to a unit change in the predictor (i.e., the x_{kn}).[2] In the current application, for example, the marginal effects of a one-unit increase in the percentage of nonfamily households (PNFH) can be expected to be associated with a 2.13 increase in the total number of homicides (see the appropriate value under Model I in Table 4). Since PNFH is a percentage (i.e., $PNFH_n \in (0, 1)\ \forall n$), a *one*-unit increase in PNFH implies a 100 percent rise in PNFH. Hence, the marginal effect can also be interpreted as implying that a 10 percent increase in PNFH is expected to be associated with 0.213 more homicides. In addition to caution in interpreting their meaning, since marginal effects are unit-dependent, caution needs to be taken in interpreting *quantitative* differences across various levels of aggregation. Such differences, if found, could simply be because of a scaling of the dependent variables. Comparisons of *qualitative* differences in inferences are, however, perfectly valid across levels of aggregation. Below, we restrict all cross-level analysis to the latter kind.

4.2.1. *An Example: All Homicides at the NC Level*

In order to explain the workings of the GCE estimator, we first provide detailed analysis for the regression model of ALL homicides when analyzed at the NC level (see again Table 4). Five alternate models, corresponding to five types of error structures, were estimated. Model I most closely corresponds to the baseline Poisson regression specification as $A^* = 0$. Model II allows for only heteroskedasticity. Models III, IV, and V allow for heteroskedasticity and, respectively, first-order local error-correlation, first-order local error-correlation with distance-based decay, and global error-correlation

---

[2]Under specific assumptions these marginal effects also reduce to more traditional parameters. For example, assuming $s_n = \mathbf{x}'_\mathbf{n}\boldsymbol{\beta}$ means that the kth marginal effect *is* the $\boldsymbol{\beta}_k$ of the linear model.

TABLE 4
GCE Estimates of the Lagrange Multipliers and Relevant Marginal Effects for a NC Level Model of ALL Homicides (1989–1991) Using Various Error-Structure Specifications

	Model I $A^*=0$		Model II[a] $A^*=I$		Model III[b] $A^*=I+C$		Model IV[b] $A^*=I+\exp(-D)\cdot C$		Model V[b] $A^*=\exp(-D)$	
	$\hat{\lambda}$	$\hat{\gamma}$	$\hat{\lambda}$	$\hat{\gamma}$	$\hat{\lambda}$	$\hat{\gamma}$	$\hat{\lambda}$	$\hat{\gamma}$	$\hat{\lambda}$	$\hat{\gamma}$
INTERCEPT	−13.31**	−70.21**	−12.17**	−67.27**	−11.85**	−66.95**	−12.49**	−69.13**	−12.59**	−69.66**
	(0.643)	(3.454)	(0.607)	(3.401)	(0.603)	(3.466)	(0.620)	(3.461)	(0.623)	(3.482)
RESDEP	0.95**	5.00**	0.86**	4.76**	0.84**	4.75**	0.87**	4.82**	0.89**	4.90**
	(0.031)	(0.165)	(0.029)	(0.161)	(0.029)	(0.163)	(0.029)	(0.163)	(0.030)	(0.164)
SHRHSP	1.06**	5.56**	0.90**	4.97**	0.88**	4.99**	0.92**	5.08**	0.96**	5.32**
	(0.127)	(0.658)	(0.120)	(0.655)	(0.119)	(0.665)	(0.121)	(0.662)	(0.122)	(0.665)
PNFH	0.40**	2.13**	0.31*	1.72*	0.16	0.93	0.30*	1.67*	0.34*	1.85*
	(0.192)	(1.009)	(0.180)	(0.994)	(0.179)	(1.011)	(0.181)	(1.000)	(0.183)	(1.012)
YMEN	1.05	5.54	0.46	2.55	0.08	0.43	0.43	2.37	0.60	3.30
	(1.454)	(7.663)	(1.381)	(7.632)	(1.399)	(7.903)	(1.404)	(7.772)	(1.415)	(7.826)
RESST	0.08	0.41	0.21	1.14	0.40	2.26	0.15	0.81	0.14	0.77
	(0.605)	(3.188)	(0.576)	(3.183)	(0.574)	(3.242)	(0.584)	(3.236)	(0.587)	(3.248)
LPOP	1.09**	5.72**	0.98**	5.42**	0.95**	5.39**	1.02**	5.63**	1.02**	5.66**
	(0.070)	(0.369)	(0.066)	(0.364)	(0.066)	(0.372)	(0.068)	(0.371)	(0.068)	(0.373)
Model Diagnostics										
$\mathcal{L}^D_{GCE}$	16916.0		16644.4		16595.5		16648.0		16661.2	
Pseudo R^2	66.4		68.3		68.1		68.2		67.8	
$\mathcal{H}_e$	—		1.055		1.020		0.9995		0.996	
$\mathcal{H}_s$	—		1.166		1.195		0.9996		0.978	
$\mathcal{H}_*$	—		1.105		1.172		1.0002		0.983	

Note: Unstandardized Lagrange multipliers ($\hat{\lambda}$) and associated marginal effects ($\hat{\gamma}$) with asymptotic standard errors appear in parenthesis.
[a]For computing $\mathcal{H}_*$ the encompassed model is I. [b]For computing $\mathcal{H}_*$ the encompassed model is II.
*$p<0.1$. **$p<0.05$

282

with distance-based decay. For each of these specifications, Table 4 displays the Lagrange multipliers as well as the computed marginal effects with associated asymptotic standard errors.

Visual comparison across the specifications illustrates the difference is parameter values that emerges as a result of the various forms of flexibility afforded to the basic model. The Lagrange multipliers as well as the marginal effects for models II–V are invariably smaller in absolute value than those for model I. Also, the estimated standard errors for these parameters are invariably lower for models II–V than for model I. That is, affording the model some flexibility does seem to result in more conservative but more stable parameter estimates.

Although there are no sign changes across the various specifications, the reliability of predictors sometimes changes considerably across the specifications. For example, the proportion of NC households that are nonfamily (PNFH) would seem to have a significant positive association with all homicide counts (ALL) if one did not permit error structures. On the other hand, allowing heteroskedasticity along with first-order local error-correlation (Model III) renders that predictor insignificant.

In order to select from the various specifications, we computed the composite relative information gain/loss measures for each of the models. These measures are displayed in the lower panel of Table 4. They are not applicable for model I as it is never the alternate model. Model II is assessed against the null of model I. Clearly, allowing heteroskedasticity alone is a desirable form of flexibility as $\mathcal{H}_* = 1.105 > 1$. Next models III, IV, and V are compared against model II. Here we find that models III and IV are *more* desirable than model II ($\mathcal{H}_* > 1$) but model V is less desirable ($\mathcal{H}_* < 1$). Between models III and IV, model III is clearly more desirable, as the gain in information about the noise component outweighs the loss in information about the signal by a much larger proportion. Therefore, it seems that among all the models tried here, a first-order local error-correlation structure is the closest approximation to the underlying data-generating process.

Although this is not always to be expected, in the sample analyzed above, the Pseudo R^2 measure (defined here as the proportion of observed variance in the criterion measure explained by the predictors) increases relative to model I where error structure was not permitted. This is somewhat surprising given that approaches that exactly match the observed and expected moments, such as likelihood-based methods, are designed for optimal predictive-accuracy *within* the sample being analyzed.

4.2.2. *Disaggregated Homicide Models*
We next estimated the models for each of the disaggregated homicides. Using the $\mathcal{H}_*$ criterion as a guide, we selected one of the several models as being the best. In all cases, model III appeared to be the error specification closest to the underlying data-generating process. Marginal effects implied by these models are presented in Table 5.

Rather than examine these final models in isolation, we discuss our findings only in relation to the baseline Poisson models. That is, had we ignored the possible structure in the error, how different qualitatively would our inferences have been?

Three sets of findings are worth highlighting. First, at the NC level some predictors are now significantly related to the criterion measures while under the baseline Poisson model they were not (e.g., RESST in the GNG model and YMEN in the FAM model). Alternately, while PNFH was significantly related to the total count of homicides (ALL), its no longer a significant predictor of it under the GCE specification.

Second, these qualitative differences are *not* observed at the CT level of analysis. Therefore, allowing error structure flexibility further highlights the MAUP resulting in more differences in the macroprocesses operating at the two different levels.

Finally, the fact that qualitative differences are not obtained between the baseline Poisson models and those obtained by the GCE setting at the CT level could be because the amount of error correlation at the CT level is lower than that at the NC level. One finding that lends support to this interpretation is the absolute size of the regression coefficients presented in Table 1, where it appears that the amount of spatial-correlation among the criterion measures is stronger (larger coefficients) at the NC level than at the CT level. Hence, even though correcting for error correlation may yield quantitative changes in inferences derived, qualitative findings could remain largely unaltered.

4.2.3. *Spatially Lagged Regressor Models*
In order to assess whether spatial lags of the most important predictor—resource deprivation (RESDEP)—may influence the criterion

TABLE 5
GCE Marginal-Effect Estimates of Area Macrocharacteristics on
Disaggregated Homicides (1989–1991)

	ALL	GNG	INS	FAM	KNO	STR	OTH
Unit of Analysis: Neighborhood Cluster ($N = 343$)							
INTERCEPT	−66.95**	−11.14**	−13.66**	−14.57**	−23.40**	−7.50**	−19.13**
	(3.466)	(1.418)	(1.631)	(1.620)	(2.003)	(1.246)	(1.914)
RESDEP	4.75**	0.59**	0.93**	0.96**	1.51**	0.60**	1.38**
	(0.163)	(0.067)	(0.074)	(0.073)	(0.093)	(0.056)	(0.087)
SHRHSP	4.99**	2.10**	0.06	0.50	0.12	0.58**	0.67**
	(0.665)	(0.246)	(0.334)	(0.332)	(0.404)	(0.247)	(0.392)
PNFH	0.93	−1.67**	0.01	0.17	−0.22	−0.26	1.35**
	(1.011)	(0.456)	(0.474)	(0.456)	(0.573)	(0.374)	(0.543)
YMEN	0.43	0.01	6.51**	−7.62**	10.49**	−3.92	0.82
	(7.903)	(3.352)	(3.644)	(3.803)	(4.331)	(3.036)	(4.389)
RESST	2.26	2.29**	−0.82	−0.35	0.96	1.06	1.98
	(3.242)	(1.337)	(1.575)	(1.528)	(1.847)	(1.160)	(1.787)
LPOP	5.39**	0.76**	0.97**	1.22**	1.84**	0.52**	1.36**
	(0.372)	(0.152)	(0.175)	(0.172)	(0.213)	(0.133)	(0.205)
Unit of Analysis: Census Tract ($N = 865$)							
INTERCEPT	−24.78**	−4.45**	−5.31**	−6.15**	−7.93**	−3.08**	−6.73**
	(0.702)	(0.308)	(0.320)	(0.353)	(0.403)	(0.252)	(0.361)
RESDEP	1.95**	0.27**	0.41**	0.40**	0.65**	0.26**	0.54**
	(0.065)	(0.028)	(0.029)	(0.031)	(0.037)	(0.023)	(0.033)
SHRHSP	2.12**	0.90**	0.15	0.16	0.28**	0.22**	0.27**
	(0.240)	(0.090)	(0.122)	(0.121)	(0.147)	(0.088)	(0.139)
PNFH	0.38	−0.30**	0.07	0.16	0.32**	0.01	0.32**
	(0.350)	(0.155)	(0.159)	(0.157)	(0.191)	(0.123)	(0.182)
YMEN	0.42	0.42	0.19	−0.66	0.78	−0.26	0.44
	(1.733)	(0.729)	(0.776)	(0.877)	(0.906)	(0.641)	(0.883)
RESST	0.56	0.45	−0.85**	0.28	0.05	0.21	0.51
	(0.955)	(0.401)	(0.463)	(0.455)	(0.528)	(0.318)	(0.470)
LPOP	1.99**	0.31**	0.42**	0.51**	0.62**	0.23**	0.49**
	(0.070)	(0.029)	(0.032)	(0.033)	(0.040)	(0.025)	(0.036)

$*p < 0.1.$ $**p < 0.05.$
Unstandardized marginal effects with asymptotic standard errors appear in parenthesis.

measures directly, we re-estimated the models with a spatial lag of
the resource deprivation index included as one of the predictors. In
most of the models, we find that the spatial lag term is highly significant, albeit with a smaller coefficient implying a distance decay
effect.

Table 6 displays the marginal effects of the "own" and "cross" areal unit effects of resource deprivation (RESDEP) on the various disaggregated homicide types analyzed. Once again the findings presented here are for models deemed the "best" using the $\mathcal{H}_*$ criterion described before. Of course, changing the model specification may change inferences regarding all the remaining independent variables. However, for purposes of discussion, only the marginal effects of RESDEP and its spatial lag term are displayed in Table 6.

Three important points are worth noting here. First, resource deprivation of neighboring area has a positive effect on almost all types of homicides observed in the central area. That is, increases in the resource deprivation of surrounding areas are associated with an increase in the amount of violence we can expect in central units, even if the extent of resource deprivation in the central unit remains unaltered. This also implies that an increase in the resource deprivation in one area spreads out to its neighboring areas. Therefore, changes in resource deprivation have a *spillover* effect on the amount of violence in neighboring areas.

Second, there is evidence of distance decay. That is, the effects of changes in neighboring area resource deprivation (i.e., the "cross" effects) are usually weaker than the effects of an area's resource deprivation on its level of violence (i.e., the "own" effect).

TABLE 6

GCE Marginal-Effect Estimates of RESDEP and Its Spatial Lag on
Disaggregated Homicides (1989–1991)

	ALL	GNG	INS	FAM	KNO	STR	OTH
Unit of Analysis: Neighborhood Cluster ($N = 343$)							
RESDEP	3.91**	0.50**	0.73**	0.77**	1.29**	0.52**	1.29**
	(0.222)	(0.098)	(0.104)	(0.102)	(0.125)	(0.078)	(0.118)
RESDEP_L	1.45**	0.16**	0.35**	0.32**	0.39**	0.14**	0.17
	(0.245)	(0.114)	(0.116)	(0.114)	(0.136)	(0.088)	(0.132)
Unit of Analysis: Census tract ($N = 865$)							
RESDEP	1.45**	0.16**	0.29**	0.28**	0.51**	0.25**	0.43**
	(0.098)	(0.043)	(0.046)	(0.046)	(0.054)	(0.033)	(0.051)
RESDEP_L	0.87**	0.18**	0.21**	0.20**	0.25**	0.03	0.21**
	(0.111)	(0.049)	(0.053)	(0.052)	(0.061)	(0.038)	(0.059)

$*p < 0.1.$ $**p < 0.05.$
Unstandardized marginal effects with asymptotic standard errors appear in parenthesis.

Finally, as with the other models, there is some evidence of differences in the processes linking disaggregate homicide types to resource deprivation. For instance, the spatial lag of RESDEP does not seem to be associated with local area stranger-related homicides (STR) at the CT level, but it is a significant predictor of STR at the NC level. The reverse is obtained for the models relating spatially lagged RESDEP to the other homicides (OTH).

4.3. *Summary of Findings*

The findings discussed in this section may be summarized as follows:

1. Whether or not we allow for spatial structure in the errors, we find some evidence of distinct homicide-type and analysis-level specific macroprocesses. This finding is consistent with other studies that have recently reported similar differences (Kubrin 2003). On the other hand, we also find evidence that resource deprivation is a strong, reliable, and persistent predictor of all the homicide types analyzed and at all levels of analysis. This finding is also consistent with prior research.

2. Extending traditional Poisson regression models to allow for auto-correlated structures in the errors yields two important findings. First, at the NC level, the differences in inferences regarding homicide-type specific macroprocesses becomes more pronounced. Second, this finding is not replicated at the CT level. Given that the rough measure of autocorrelation in the outcomes used in this study suggests stronger spatial autocorrelation at the NC level than at the CT level of analysis, this finding suggests that allowing spatial structure in the errors helps *clarify* the underlying macroprocesses when the flexibility is desired but does not contaminate inferences when it is unnecessary.

3. Allowing error structures almost always yields more conservative (smaller in absolute value) but more stable (smaller standard errors) marginal effects. This is consistent with the following view of information recovery: If we assume away structure in the errors, then we are assuming *more* than we know. To the extent that this assumption is not supported by the data, we are probably deriving misleading and biased inferences from the data. Allowing flexibility

in the moments simply means we let the data decide whether or not to use the flexibility. If the hypothesized error structure is present in the underlying data-generating process, the model utilizes this flexibility and yields more conservative and more stable estimates.

4. Of all the types of structures we permitted in the models, the data seem to favor the local first-order spatial error-correlation structure. This structure is most similar to a spatial moving average (SMA) process in the errors. On the other hand, a global error-correlation structure with distance-based decay would be similar to the spatial autoregressive (SAR) structure in the errors. The samples used in this analysis seem to favor the SMA process over the SAR.

5. There seems to be evidence of spillover effects of the resource deprivation measure. For convenience we used a simple SAR process with first-order spatial contiguity to model this spillover. Other processes may, of course, be very possible. Defining contiguity using distance bands, or a fixed number of neighbors, may provide better fit and more meaning in some contexts. Similarly, the spillover effects may be facilitated via socioeconomic distance rather than purely geographic distance. Such considerations may further allow interesting insights into distinct homicide-type specific macroprocesses.

6. There are several aspects of the analysis that may be sensitive to the level of aggregation used—i.e., the modifiable areal unit problem (MAUP). In comparing results across relevant NC and CT level models, it is worth noting that some variables (such as RESDEP) remain significant predictors of the criterion measure at both levels while inferences about some predictors (such as YMEN) vary substantially across levels of aggregation. The analysis presented here does not, of course, allow us to ascertain which of these levels of aggregation may be more appropriate. Rather, it merely suggests caution on relying exclusively on one level of areal aggregation for deriving inference. At the same time, the analysis does suggest more confidence in some of the predictors (than could be claimed by analysis of any one level of aggregation) as inferences about their impacts are invariant across levels of areal aggregation.

These findings are further discussed in the next section in light of their implications for modeling rare crimes that are not randomly distributed across geographic space.

5. CONCLUSIONS

In this section we discuss conclusions resulting from this research effort and enumerate some promising future avenues of research. The research effort described in the preceding sections has important substantive, methodological, and practical implications.

5.1. *Implications*

5.1.1. *Substantive Implications*
We conclude from this analysis that ignoring knowledge of the spatial positioning of sample units can yield misleading inferences. This research effort confirms that some predictors would have been erroneously deemed irrelevant and some would have been erroneously deemed significant had spatial error correlation not been allowed. In addition, unlike the linear models case, we find changes in parameter and marginal effect estimates to be quite substantial across various hypothesized error structures. This implies that, unlike linear models, where ignoring error correlation does not bias results but leads only to inefficiency, in nonlinear models for count outcomes, the parameters may in fact be substantially biased in addition to being inefficient.

On the other hand, we also find that ignoring spatial spillover effects of predictors in one location on the criterion measures in neighboring locations can not only result in models with poorer fit but can also lead researchers to underestimate or underpredict the overall (systemwide) effects of policy measures. For example, if policy measures are aimed at reducing resource deprivation in order to reduce violence, then changing resource deprivation levels in one area should have an effect on the levels of violence in neighboring areas as well. Any such policy measures must take into account anticipated benefits that accrue not only from "own" area effects but also any "cross" area effects that may exist. Therefore, the impact of citywide policy initiatives targeted at improving resource deprivation, for example, can have an aggregate benefit larger than the sum of its benefits on each areal unit individually. In this research exercise, the spillover effects analyzed were found to be positive. However, the effects would be reversed had a negative spillover effect been found. Then, the overall benefit from a citywide initiative would be dampened. Therefore, this analysis suggests careful consideration of the spillover effects of intervention and other policy initiatives when they are aimed at affecting outcomes across areal units that are spatially linked in some meaningful manner.

5.1.2. *Methodological Implications*

From a methodological point of view, the GCE approach seems to offer a variety of desirable benefits over fully parametric likelihood-based methods. Most importantly, it allows us to model heteroskedastic and autocorrelated error structures without making strong distributional assumptions. In small, finite, nonexperimental samples, it uses more flexible constraints and therefore yields more stable/reliable solutions (see the appendix for a discussion). As found in this analysis, some GCE models that allow error flexibility even offer higher in-sample predictive powers than those that do not permit error structures.

As described in this paper, modeling autocorrelated error structures within the GCE framework does *not* entail an increase in the parameter space. That is, even though the errors are allowed to be heteroskedastic and autocorrelated, these structures are allowed nonparametrically. Additionally, in the error-correlation case, the dual objective function is not defined in terms of the full $N \times N$ spatial link matrix ($\mathbf{A}$). It is defined in terms of $\tilde{\mathbf{X}} = \mathbf{A}'\mathbf{X}$. Therefore, this matrix can be computed once and for all outside a numeric optimization routine. This reduces the memory requirement and increases the efficiency of the optimization problem immensely.

5.1.3. *Practical Implications*

The methodology described in this paper is fast becoming available as part of conventional econometric software. The next release of SAS is slated to have a procedure explicitly dedicated to entropy-based model estimation (PROC ENTROPY). As yet, this procedure does not have the explicit capability to model spatially correlated error structures. Future releases should provide enhanced capabilities.

As of now, spatial and nonspatial count outcome models may be modeled using manually programmed statements (available from the author upon request). An outstanding and complicating issue is how one computes and accesses the spatial weight matrix. For this research, we computed the weight matrix using SpaceStat and then imported it into SAS. Given the GIS capabilities of SAS, however, it is conceivable that SAS will be able to perform these computations efficiently in the near future.

Finally, it is possible to perform the nonlinear numeric optimization in other software such as GAUSS. Since SpaceStat is able to read/write matrices to GAUSS format, it may be feasible to simply read the weight matrices directly into a GAUSS program that uses an optimization module within GAUSS to do the analysis.

5.2. *Future Research*

5.2.1. *More Flexibility*

The flexibility of the GCE method was used for a very narrow purpose in this paper: to allow for spatial error correlation in count outcome models. However, the GCE framework allows for a lot more flexibility than that. Future research may utilize this flexibility to, for example, gauge the effects of increasing the density of the support spaces in derived inferences. In this paper we defined $L = M = 2$. By increasing $L > 2$ or $M > 2$, we should be able to recover higher moments of each and every signal and noise term. This may yield increased clarity and precision.

In addition, future research may utilize the flexibility of the GCE to allow for a mixture of binary (yes/no) process with the count process. Such a setting would allow researchers to model the so-called zero-inflated count outcome models. In this paper this issue was largely ignored with the aim of isolating and addressing the problem of error-correlation. With a large number of units yielding no homicide victims, however, especially at the CT level of analysis, models that permit this flexibility while allowing error-correlation may yield clearer insights into the underlying data-generating processes.

Finally, when modeling true binomial counts where the maximum number of observable events are finite, known explicitly, and vary over the areal units, values of a *variable T_n* rather than a *fixed T* are available to the research. As such, the information-recovery problem should utilize this knowledge by redefining moment constraints accordingly. Future research may extend the current formulation to allow that flexibility.

5.2.2. *Endogenous and Simultaneous Processes*

In this paper we modeled the criterion measure on a set of exogenous predictors. This meant an ability to assume away the problem with endogenous regressors. In reality, of course, data are generated from more complex processes where some or several of the predictors may be endogenous. This commonly occurs, for example, in models of substantive spatial process where the outcomes in neighboring areas are theorized to influence the expected outcomes in the central areas. In addition, other neighborhood characteristics that are typically used in modeling areal data may also be endogenous (Dietz 2002). In such settings, we obtain single equation models with potentially endogenous regressors, and some form of an instrumental variable approach is required. Extending the GCE to model count outcomes with endogenous regressors in an instrumental variables framework is a promising avenue of future research.

That avenue of research can also be extended to include simultaneous equation models for count outcomes where errors may be correlated within equation (across space) and across equation (within observational units). In a similar manner, when repeated observations may be available for the same set of areal units over time, the GCE method should extend easily to provide a robust setting for assessing spatial and spatiotemporal dynamics.

5.2.3. *More Tests*

Finally, future research may evaluate the predictive accuracy of the models either in repeated samples and/or in fresh samples. Assessing the ability of an estimator to yield accurate expectations when the true underlying data-generating process is known to the researcher (such as in Monte Carlo experiments) is an ideal means of comparing competing estimators in their ability to properly recover the data-generating process. In prior applications, GME and GCE estimators have been shown to have superior properties with such simulated data, especially when the sample sizes are small (Golan, Judge, and Miller 1996).

The increased stability of the GCE estimators in all finite samples seems to also suggest that they should provide superior out-of-sample predictions. Examining the performance of models in fresh samples will provide a means of assessing whether or not the increased stability of estimated parameters translates into increased predictive powers of future events—an essential component of any modeling exercise if it is to have policy relevance.

Exploring the aforementioned extensions and performing detailed diagnostic testing are needed. We believe the findings reported here suggest that the GCE framework is well suited to incorporate the more realistic and more complex processes noted above with minimal reliance on distributional assumptions. Accordingly, it provides a more conservative but reliable analytical strategy for recovering information and, ultimately, for informing policy.

APPENDIX: SAMPLE-THEORETIC PROPERTIES OF THE GCE LAGRANGE MULTIPLIERS

As noted by several reviewers of an earlier draft, the hypothesis-testing apparatus described in Section 2.4.1 is based on *sample*-theoretic consideration. Clearly, if the information-theoretic framework is employed for recovering a set of Lagrange multiplers from *one* specific sample, then it is of obvious interest to study how these recovered Lagrange multipliers may vary across different samples—i.e., to study their sampling variability. In this appendix we provide a brief discussion of the sampling properties of the Lagrange multipliers.

To keep the discussion and derivations below as generic as possible, we write the GCE dual objective function as

$$\mathcal{L}_{GCE}^{D} = \sum_{k} \lambda_k \mu_k - f_s(\boldsymbol{\lambda}) - f_e(\boldsymbol{\lambda}) \qquad (A.1)$$

where $\mu_k = \Sigma_n x_{kn} y_n$ are the sample statistics (not functions of $\boldsymbol{\lambda}$). The traditional as well as the extended (heteroskedastic and autocorrelation consistent) GCE dual objective functions may be obtained by appropriate specification of the nonlinear functions f_s and f_e. For example, in the heteroskedastic-consistent GCE formulation of (27), $f_s(\boldsymbol{\lambda}) = \Sigma_n \ln \Omega_n$ and

$f_e(\lambda) = \ln\Gamma$. In addition, eliminating $f_e(\lambda)$ from this specification altogether yields the pure (noiseless) cross entropy dual objective function.

The optimal solutions for this unconstrained *maximization* problem is found by simultaneously solving the K first-order conditions

$$\frac{\partial \mathcal{L}^D_{GCE}}{\partial \lambda_k} = \mu_k - \frac{\partial}{\partial \lambda_k}\{f_s(\lambda) + f_e(\lambda)\} = 0 \qquad \forall k \qquad (A.2)$$

and ensuring that, at the optimal solutions, the Hessian matrix, computed as

$$\frac{\partial^2 \mathcal{L}^D_{GCE}}{\partial \hat{\lambda}_k \partial \hat{\lambda}_{k'}} = -\frac{\partial^2}{\partial \lambda_k \partial \lambda_{k'}}\{f_s(\hat{\lambda}) + f_e(\hat{\lambda})\} \qquad \forall k,k', \qquad (A.3)$$

is negative definite. Given the logarithmic forms of the functions f_s and f_e, the dual objective function is *strictly* concave thereby ensuring a unique global maximum.

We can study variations in the *optimal* Lagrange multipliers that can be expected due to fluctuations in the sample statistics μ_k (from one sample to another) by taking the total derivative of the K first-order conditions (A.2) with respect to each $\{\mu_k\}$ and $\{\hat{\lambda}_k\}$. In matrix notation, this may be written as the following system of K differential equations

$$d\boldsymbol{\mu} - \frac{\partial^2}{\partial \hat{\boldsymbol{\lambda}} \partial \hat{\boldsymbol{\lambda}}'}\{f_s(\hat{\boldsymbol{\lambda}}) + f_e(\hat{\boldsymbol{\lambda}})\}d\hat{\boldsymbol{\lambda}} = \mathbf{0}. \qquad (A.4)$$

Using the definition of the Hessian from (A.3) and rearranging terms, we obtain the desired relationship between variations in the optimal Lagrange multipliers and variations in the sample statistics as

$$\frac{d\hat{\boldsymbol{\lambda}}}{d\boldsymbol{\mu}'} = \left\{-\frac{\partial^2 \mathcal{L}^D_{GCE}}{\partial \hat{\boldsymbol{\lambda}} \partial \hat{\boldsymbol{\lambda}}'}\right\}^{-1} \qquad (A.5)$$

This relationship implies that if we can make certain assumptions about how the sample statistics (μ_k) vary across slightly different samples then we can make claims about the implied distribution of the Lagrange mulipliers across these samples. For the former, we can rely on the central limit theorem according to which, irrespective of the population distribution of a random variable, computed sample statistics (such as sums or means) of this random variable taken across several samples of a given size, will be normally distributed even if these samples (that these statistics are based on) are as small as 30 to 40 units. Here the μ_k are one such sample statistic that can therefore be assumed to have a normal distribution *across* repeated samples of sizes as low as 30 to 40 units. Consequently, we may assume that the optimal Lagrange multipliers are normally distributed as well. The value about which these Lagrange multipliers are normally distributed is, of course, a function of the size of the sample as well as the definition of the problem. There is *no* implied population Lagrange multiplier about which the sample specific values are distributed.

This point is important to stress. Within sample-theoretic settings, the distribution of a parameter's sample estimate is considered about a fixed but unknown population value (sometimes referred to as the "true" value). In small samples, however, this population value remains fixed but the variability of the sampling distribution about it increases, thereby rendering its estimate from any one sample less reliable (more unstable). Under the GME/GCE setting, with small/ finite samples, the Lagrange multipliers shrink toward 0 (i.e., they are more conservative) without compromising their stability (i.e., they are relatively more stable). In effect, the Lagrange multipliers adjust, thereby "buying" them some stability.[3] Of course, the *relative* gains of having more conservative but more stable estimates for any specific formulation can only be assessed in simulated (controlled) repeated sampling experiments. We leave the task of assessing the empirical small-sample gains of the *extended* GCE formulation for future work. Interested readers are, nevertheless, referred to Golan, Judge, and Perloff (1996) as well as the Golan, Judge, and Miller (1996) monograph throughout which the *empirical risk*, in the sense of mean squared error loss, of various GME/GCE estimators are compared to their sample-theoretic counterparts. There the superior small-sample

---

[3]Perhaps a more intuitive way of putting this is that by formulating generalized (more flexible) constraints, the GME/GCE framework allows us to recover *weaker* signals in any given sample that are more *stable* across repeated samples.

performance of the *traditional* GME/GCE formulation is demonstrated under a variety of settings and sample sizes.

Even if the superior small-sample performance of the traditional GCE estimator can be *conjectured* to hold for the extended formulation, the extended formulation was introduced in this paper to accomodate heteroskedastic and autocorrelated error structures. Hence, a related and important question to address is whether this extended GCE formulation provides the "correct" or "appropriate" metric for the covariance matrix to converge toward *asymptotically*.[4]

The desirable large-sample properties of the traditional GME/GCE formulations are based on their asymptotic equivalence to the pure (noiseless) ME/CE problems. The extended GCE formulation, however, *does not* reduce to a noiseless CE formulation. Note that all the GCE formulations differ from the noiseless CE formulation only with regard to the term $f_e(\lambda)$ in (A.1). In order to study the asymptotic properties of various GCE formulations, therefore, we may consider what happens to this last term asymptotically.

First, consider this term for the traditional GCE formulation. As given in (18), this last term is

$$f_e(\lambda) = \sum_n \ln \Psi_n = \sum_n \ln \left\{ \sum_m w_m^0 \exp\left(\frac{v_m}{N} x_n'\lambda\right) \right\},$$

so that as $N \to \infty$, since $\mathbf{v}$ is symmetric about 0 and bounded (by construction), the term inside the exponent shrinks pointwise to 0 $\forall m$, n. Hence, $\lim_{N \to \infty} \sum_n \ln \Psi_n = \sum_n \ln \left(\sum_m w_m^0 \cdot 1 \right) = \sum_n \ln (1) = 0$ where the last step simply invokes the adding-up property of the proper prior probabilities (by construction). Therefore, asymptotically, the traditional GCE dual objective function reduces to the pure (noiseless) CE dual objective of (13).

Under the heteroskedastic consistent formulation of the GCE problem of (27), however, this term is

$$f_e(\lambda) = \ln \Gamma = \ln \sum_{n,m} q_{mn}^0 \exp(v_m x_n'\lambda) = \ln \frac{1}{N} \sum_n \left\{ \sum_m \frac{1}{M} \exp(v_m x_n'\lambda) \right\},$$

$$\text{(A.6)}$$

---

[4]We thank an anonymous reviewer for raising this important point.

where, based on discussion following (23), $q_{mn}^0 = \pi_n^0 w_m^0$, $\pi_n^0 = \frac{1}{N}$, and $w_{mn}^0 = \frac{1}{M} \forall m, n$. Now, as $N \to \infty$ the term inside the exponent will $\neq 0$ $\forall n, m$. Therefore, simply increasing the sample size will not make the term inside the exponent disappear. Since $\exp(v_m \mathbf{x}_n' \boldsymbol{\lambda}) > 0 \ \forall n, m$ and since $\mathbf{v}$ is symmetric about 0, then, writing $\varphi_n = \sum_m \frac{1}{M} \exp(v_m \mathbf{x}_n' \boldsymbol{\lambda})$, we have $\varphi_n > 1 \ \forall n$. Therefore, we obtain $\lim_{N \to \infty} \ln \Gamma = \ln\left(\frac{1}{N}\sum_n \varphi_n\right) > 0$. Now, if we assume that the independent variables ($\mathbf{x}_n$) are bounded, then, given that $\mathbf{v}$ is bounded by construction, we find that this last term converges asymptotically to a strictly positive but *finite* (bounded) value. The heteroskedastic-consistent formulation of the GCE therefore converges to a *different optimization problem* than the noiseless CE one. In a similar manner, we may study the asymptotic behavior of the last term in the autocorrelated error case.

That the extended GCE formulation results in a "different" asymptotic problem than the noiseless CE is, however, insufficient to establish whether it results in an "appropriate" problem. To investigate the appropriateness of the asymptotic behavior of the extended GCE formulation, we hence need to understand its implication for the asymptotic covariance matrix of the optimal Lagrange multipliers. To study this, note that a typical element of the heteroskedastic-consistent GCE Hessian matrix may be derived as

$$\frac{\partial^2 \mathcal{L}_{GCE}^D}{\partial \hat{\lambda}_k \partial \hat{\lambda}_{k'}} = -\sum_n x_{kn} \left\{ \mathbf{z}^{2'} \hat{\mathbf{p}}_n - (\mathbf{z}'\hat{\mathbf{p}}_n)^2 \right\} x_{k'n} - \sum_n x_{kn} \left\{ \mathbf{v}^{2'} \hat{\mathbf{w}}_n - (\mathbf{v}'\hat{\mathbf{w}}_n)^2 \right\} \hat{\pi}_n x_{k'n}$$

$$- \left\{ \sum_n (x_{kn}\hat{e}_n)\hat{\pi}_n (x_{k'n}\hat{e}_n) - \sum_n (x_{kn}\hat{e}_n\hat{\pi}_n) \sum_n (x_{k'n}\hat{e}_n\hat{\pi}_n) \right\}$$

$$= -\sum_n x_{kn}\left(\hat{\sigma}_n^2(s)\right)x_{k'n} - \sum_n x_{kn}\left(\hat{\sigma}_n^2(e)\right)\hat{\pi}_n x_{k'n} - \hat{\boldsymbol{\Xi}} \qquad \text{(A.7)}$$

where $\hat{\sigma}_n^2(s)$ and $\hat{\sigma}_n^2(e)$ are the second central moments of the recovered signal and noise terms implied by the probabilities $\hat{\mathbf{p}}_n$ and $\hat{\mathbf{w}}_n$.[5] Based on these derivations, the asymptotic covariance matrix of the heteroskedastic-consistent GCE estimator of $\boldsymbol{\lambda}$ may be written, in matrix notation, as

[5]Detailed derivations are available from the author upon request.

$$\Sigma^{\text{het}}_{\lambda(GCE)} = \left\{ \mathbf{X}'\hat{\Lambda}_s\mathbf{X} + \mathbf{X}'\left(\hat{\Pi}\hat{\Lambda}_e\right)\mathbf{X} + \hat{\Xi} \right\}^{-1} = \left\{ \mathbf{X}'\left(\hat{\Lambda}_s + \hat{\Pi}\hat{\Lambda}_e\right)\mathbf{X} + \hat{\Xi} \right\}^{-1}$$

(A.8)

where,

$$\hat{\Pi} = \begin{pmatrix} \hat{\pi}_1 & & & \\ & \hat{\pi}_2 & & \\ & & \ddots & \\ & & & \hat{\pi}_N \end{pmatrix} \quad \text{and}$$

$$\hat{\Lambda}_* = \begin{pmatrix} \hat{\sigma}_1^2(*) & & & \\ & \hat{\sigma}_2^2(*) & & \\ & & \ddots & \\ & & & \hat{\sigma}_N^2(*) \end{pmatrix} \quad \forall * = s, e. \quad (A.9)$$

In a similar manner, we may derive the asymptotic covariance matrix of the Lagrange multipliers under the autocorrelated-error setting as

$$\Sigma^{\text{het/auto}}_{\lambda(GCE)} = \left\{ \mathbf{X}'\hat{\Lambda}_s\mathbf{X} + \tilde{\mathbf{X}}'\left(\hat{\Pi}\hat{\Lambda}_e\right)\tilde{\mathbf{X}} + \hat{\tilde{\Xi}} \right\}^{-1} = \left\{ \mathbf{X}'\left(\hat{\Lambda}_s + \mathbf{A}\hat{\Pi}\hat{\Lambda}_e\mathbf{A}'\right)\mathbf{X} + \hat{\tilde{\Xi}} \right\}^{-1}$$

(A.10)

where $\tilde{\mathbf{X}} = \mathbf{A}'\mathbf{X}$ and $\mathbf{A}$ is the row-standardized hypothesized spatial link matrix defined in Section 2.2.2. Since the $f_e(\lambda)$ term does not drop out of the objective function, even asymptotically, we have $\lim_{N\to\infty}\hat{\Lambda}_e \neq \mathbf{0}$. This suggests why the asymptotic covariance of the optimal Lagrange multipliers recovered from the extended GCE setting are *deviations* from the traditional CE-based covariance matrix, which is defined as $\Sigma_{\lambda(CE)} = \left\{ \mathbf{X}'\hat{\Lambda}_s\mathbf{X} \right\}^{-1}$. Moreover, the deviations are based on the appropriate quantities—the error weights $(\hat{\Pi})$ in the heteroskedastic-consistent case and, additionally, the link matrix $(\mathbf{A})$ in the autocorrelation-consistent case.

REFERENCES

Anselin, Luc. 1988. *Spatial Econometrics: Methods and Models*. Dordrecht, Netherlands: Kulwer Academic Publishers.

Anselin, Luc. 2002. "Under the Hood: Issues in the Specification and Interpretation of Spatial Regression Models." *Agricultural Economics*. 27(3):247–67.

Anselin, Luc, and Anil K. Bera. 1998. "Spatial Dependence in Linear Regression Models with an Introduction to Spatial Econometrics." Pp. 237–89 in *Handbook of Applied Economic Statistics*, edited by Amman Ullah and David A. Giles. New York: Marcel Dekker.

Anselin, Luc, Jacqueline Cohen, David Cook, Wilper Gorr, and George Tita. 2000. "Spatial Analysis of Crime." Pp. 213–262 in *Criminal Justice 2000, Volume 4: Measurement and Analysis of Crime and Justice*, edited by David Duffee. Washington, DC: National Institute of Justice (NCJ 182411).

Avakame, Edem F. 1998. "How Different is Violence in the Home? An Examination of Some Correlates of Stranger and Intimate Homicide." *Criminology*. 36(3):601–32.

Bailey, Trevor C., and Anthony C. Gartell. 1995. *Interactive Spatial Data Analysis*. Essex, England: Addison Wesley Longman Ltd.

Balkwell, James W. 1990. "Ethnic Inequality and the Rate of Homicide." *Social Forces*. 69:53–70.

Baller, Robert D., Luc Anselin, Steven F. Messner, Glenn Deane, and Darnell F. Hawkins. 2001. "Structural Covariates of U.S. County Homicide Rates: Incorporating Spatial Effects." *Criminology*. 39(3):561–90.

Belsley, David A. 1991. *Conditioning Diagnostics: Collinearity and Weak Data in Regressions*. New York: J Wiley.

Besag, Julian. 1974. "Spatial Interaction and the Statistical Analysis of Lattice Systems." *Journal of the Royal Statistical Society, Series B (Methodology)*. 36(2):192–236.

Block, Carolyn Rebecca, and Richard L. Block. 1998. *Homicides in Chicago: 1965–1995, Part I (Victim-Level Data), Codebook*. Ann Arbor, MI: Inter-University Consortium for Political and Social Research.

Bolduc, Denis, Bernard Fortin, and Stephen Gordon. 1997. "Multinomial Probit Estimation of Spatially Interdependent Choices: An Empirical Comparison of Two Techniques." *International Regional Science Review*. 20(1–2):77–101.

Braithwaite, John, and Valerie Braithwaite. 1980. "The Effect of Income Inequality and Social Democracy on Homicide." *British Journal of Criminology*. 20:45–53.

Cameron, Colin A., and Pravin K. Trivedi. 1986. "Econometric Models Based on Count Data: Comparisons and Applications of Estimators and Tests." *Journal of Applied Econometrics*. 1:29–54.

Case, Anne. 1992. "Neighborhood Influence and Technological Change." *Regional Science and Urban Economics*. 22:491–508.

Clayton, David, and John Kaldor. 1987. "Empirical Bayes Estimates of Age-Standardized Relative Risk for Use in Disease Mapping." *Biometrics*. 43:671–781.

Cressie, Noel, and Ngai H. Chan. 1989. "Spatial Modeling of Regional Variables." *Journal of the American Statistical Association*. 84(406)393–401.

Cressie, Noel, and Timothy R. C. Read. 1989. "Spatial Data Analysis of Regional Counts." *Biometrical Journal*. 31(6):699–719.

Cubbin, Catherine, Linda Williams Pickle, and Lois Fingerhut. 2000. "Social Context and Geographic Patterns of Homicide Among U.S. Black and White Males." *American Journal of Public Health*. 90(4):579–587.

Dietz, Robert D. 2002. "The Estimation of Neighborhood Effect in the Social Sciences: An Interdisciplinary Approach." *Social Science Research*. 31:539–575.

Felson, Richard B., and Steven F. Messner. 1998. "Disentangling the Effects of Gender and Intimacy on Victim Precipitation in Homicide." *Criminology*. 36(2):405–23.

Golan, Amos. 2002. "Information and Entropy Econometrics—Editor's View." *Journal of Econometrics*. 107(1–2):1–15.

Golan, Amos, George Judge, and Douglas Miller. 1996. *Maximum Entropy Econometrics: Robust Estimation with Limited Data*. Chichester, England: J Wiley.

Golan, Amos, George Judge, and Jeffrey M. Perloff. 1996. "A Maximum Entropy Approach to Recovering Information from Multinomial Response Data." *Journal of the American Statistical Association*. 91(434):841–53.

Greene, William A. 2000. *Econometric Analysis* 4th ed. Upper Saddle River, NJ: Prentice-Hall.

Heagerty, Patrick J., and Subhash R. Lele. 1998. "A Composite Likelihood Approach to Binary Spatial Data." *Journal of the American Statistical Association*. 93(443):1099–111.

Imbens, Guido W., Richard H. Spady, and Phillip Johnson. 1998. "Information-Theoretic Approaches to Inference in Moment Condition Models." *Econometrica*. 66(2):333–357.

Jaynes, Edwin T. 1957a. "Information Theory and Statistical Mechanics." *Physics Review*. 106:620–30.

Jaynes, Edwin T. 1957b. "Information Theory and Statistical Mechanics II." *Physics Review*. 108:171–90.

Jaynes, Edwin T. 1979. "Where Do We Stand on Maximum Entropy?" Pp. 15–118 in *The Maximum Entropy Formalism*, edited by Raphael D. Levin and Myron Tribus. Cambridge, MA: MIT Press.

Judge, George G., R. Carter Hill, William E. Griffiths, Helmut Lütkepohl, and Tsoung-Chao Lee. 1988. *Introduction to the Theory and Practice of Econometrics*, 2d ed. New York: J Wiley.

Kaiser, Mark S., and Noel Cressie. 1997. "Modeling Poisson Variables with Positive Spatial Dependence." *Statistics and Probability Letters*. 35:423–32.

Kennedy, Leslie W., Robert A. Silverman, and David R. Forde. 1991. "Homicide in Urban Canada: Testing the Impact of Income Inequality and Social Disorganization." *Canadian Journal of Sociology*. 16:397–410.

Kitamura, Yuichi. 1997. "Empirical Likelihood Methods with Weakly Dependent Processes." *Annals of Statistics*. 25(5):2084–102.

Kitamura, Yuichi, and Michael Stutzer. 1997. "An Information-Theoretic Alternative to Generalized Method of Moments Estimation." *Econometrica*. 65(4):861–75.

Kubrin, Charis E. 2003. "Structural Covariates of Homicide Rates: Does Type of Homicide Matter?" *Journal of Research in Crime and Delinquency*. 40(2):139–70.

Kullback, J. 1959. *Information Theory and Statistics*. New York: J Wiley.

Land, Kenneth C., Patricia L. McCall, and Lawerence E. Cohen. 1990. "Structural Covariates of Homicides Rates: Are There Any Invariances Across Time and Social Space?" *American Journal of Sociology*. 95(4):922–63.

LeSage, James P. 1999. *Spatial Econometrics*. http://www.rri.wvu.edu/WebBook/ LeSage/spatial/spatial.html. Accessed May 15, 2003.

Levine R. D. 1980. "An Information Theoretic Approach to Inversion Problems." *Journal of Physics A*. 13:91–108.

McMillen, Daniel P. 1992. "Probit with Spatial Autocorrelation." *Journal of Regional Science*. 32(3):335–48.

Messner, Steven F., and Luc Anselin. 2004. "Spatial Analysis of Homicides with Areal Data." Pp. 127–44 in *Spatially Integrated Social Sciences*, edited by Michael F. Goodchild and Donald G. Janelle. New York: Oxford University Press.

Messner, Steven F., Luc Anselin, Robert D. Baller, Darnell Hawkins, Glenn Deane, and S. Tolnay. 1999. "The Spatial Patterning of County Homicide Rates: An Application of Exploratory Spatial Data Analysis." *Journal of Quantitative Criminology*. 15(4):423–50.

Mittelhammer, Ron C., George G. Judge, and Douglas J. Miller. 2000. *Econometric Foundations*. Cambridge, England: Cambridge University Press.

Morenoff, Jeffrey D., Robert J. Sampson, and Stephen W. Raudenbush. 2001. "Neighborhood Inequality, Collective Efficacy, and the Spatial Dynamics of Urban Violence." *Criminology*. 39(3):517–59.

Osgood, Wayne D. 2000. "Poisson-Based Regression Analysis of Aggregate Crime Rates." *Journal of Quantitative Criminology*. 16(1):21–43.

Parker, Karen F., and Patricia L. McCall. 1999. "Structural Conditions and Racial Homicide Patterns: A Look at the Multiple Disadvantages in Urban Areas." *Criminology*. 37(3):447–477.

Pinske, Joris, and Margaret E. Slade. 1998. "Contracting in Space: An Application of Spatial Statistics to Discrete-Choice Models." *Journal of Econometrics*. 85:125–54.

Reiss, A., and Jeffrey Roth. 1994. *Understanding and Preventing Violence*. Washington, DC: National Academies Press.

Rosenfeld, Richard, Timothy M. Bray, and Arlen Egley. 1999. "Facilitating Violence: A Comparison of Gang-Motivated, Gang-Affiliated, and Non-Gang Youth Homicides." *Journal of Quantitative Criminology*. 15:495–516.

Shannon, Claude. 1948. "A Mathematical Theory of Communication." *Bell System Technical Journal*. 27:379–423.

Smith, William R., Sharon Glave Frazee, and Elizabeth L. Davison. 2000. "Furthering the Integration of Routine Activity and Social Disorganization Theories: Small Units of Analysis and the Study of Street Robbery as a Diffusion Process." *Criminology*. 38:489–523.

Soofi, Ehsan S. 1994. "Capturing the Intangible Concept of Information." *Journal of the American Statistical Association*. 89:1243–54.

Waller, Lance A., Bradley P. Carlin, Hong Xia, and Elan E. Gelfand. 1997. "Hierarchical Spatio-Temporal Mapping of Disease Rates." *Journal of the American Statistical Association*. 92(438):607–17.

Williams, Kirk R., and Robert L. Flewelling. 1988. "The Social Production of Criminal Homicide: A Comparative Study of Disaggregated Rates in American Cities." *American Sociological Review*. 53(3):421–31.

𝕩 5 𝕩

IMPROVED REGRESSION ESTIMATION OF A MULTIVARIATE RELATIONSHIP WITH POPULATION DATA ON THE BIVARIATE RELATIONSHIP

Mark S. Handcock*
Michael S. Rendall†
Jacob E. Cheadle‡

Regression coefficients specify the partial effect of a regressor on the dependent variable. Sometimes the bivariate or limited multivariate relationship of that regressor variable with the dependent variable is known from population-level data. We show here that such population-level data can be used to reduce variance and bias about estimates of those regression coefficients from sample survey data. The method of constrained MLE is used to achieve these improvements. Its statistical properties are first described. The method constrains the weighted sum of all the covariate-specific associations (partial effects) of the

This work was funded by grants from the National Institute of Child Health and Human Development to the first two authors (R01-HD043472-01), to the Penn State University Population Research Institute (Core Grant R24 HD41025 and for Interdiciplinary Training in Demography 5T32 HD07514), and to the University of Washington Center for Studies in Demography and Ecology (Core Grant R24 HD41025). We thank Leslie Benson for programming assistance and Sanjay Chaudhuri for useful comments.

*University of Washington, Seattle
†RAND and Pennsylvania State University
‡Pennsylvania State University

*regressors on the dependent variable to equal the overall associa-
tion of one or more regressors, where the latter is known exactly
from the population data. We refer to those regressors whose
bivariate or limited multivariate relationships with the dependent
variable are constrained by population data as being "directly
constrained." Our study investigates the improvements in the
estimation of directly constrained variables as well as the
improvements in the estimation of other regressor variables
that may be correlated with the directly constrained variables,
and thus "indirectly constrained" by the population data. The
example application is to the marital fertility of black versus
white women. The difference between white and black women's
rates of marital fertility, available from population-level data,
gives the overall association of race with fertility. We show that
the constrained MLE technique both provides a far more powerful statistical test of the partial effect of being black and purges
the test of a bias that would otherwise distort the estimated
magnitude of this effect. We find only trivial reductions, however, in the standard errors of the parameters for indirectly
constrained regressors.*

1. INTRODUCTION

A typical situation in the social sciences is that data are available in aggregate levels of a societal unit but have too little detail. These data are therefore considered useful only at a level of preliminary description or for cross-societal comparison. The best known and most general of societal data collections in the United States is the decennial census of households and individuals, offering both published aggregate tabulations and the opportunity for researchers to estimate bivariate and limited multivariate associations from microdata samples that are large enough to approximate population data. A glance at national or subnational statistical yearbooks, however, reveals many other population collections or registers of events of potential interest to sociologists. Individuals, businesses, and nonprofit institutions register their coming into being, their ceasing to exist, and certain changes to their legal identity. Annual income is recorded in corporate and individual tax returns. Entry to, and exit from, governmental support programs (low-income benefit programs, unemployment insurance, old-age and disability insurance, etc.) and punishment or supervision programs (prisons, probation, restraining orders, child-support orders) at the national, state, and local levels are typically registered and compiled. Limited amounts of information about the individuals experiencing the events are typically also collected.

Standard regression modeling techniques are not appropriately used with these population-level data, as there are too few variables to estimate behavioral models. Putting this into a statistical framework, sociologists employing regression methods are typically interested in studying the association between a dependent variable and an explanatory variable of interest (a "target variable"). The estimates of this association are of more interest after controlling for confounding associations of variables related to both the outcome variable and the explanatory variable of interest ("control variables"). Not infrequently, data at the population level are available for the outcome variable and the target variable but not for an adequate set of control variables. In this case, only a "misspecified" model may be estimated with these population data. The sociologist then turns to survey data to specify the model more fully. Typically she or he then abandons the information on the overall associations between the outcome and target variable provided by the population data.

That social scientists are forced to choose *either* population data *or* sample data, however, need not be assumed. The advantages and disadvantages of sample versus population data collections point strongly to their being complementary to each other. The advantages of population data are that they are without sampling error and may be much less subject to biases due to nonresponse. These advantages mirror the main disadvantages of survey samples: sampling error and bias due to nonresponse. The main advantage of sample surveys is that a large amount of information is collected about individuals, often with special thought in the selection of variables toward those that may have causal associations. These are the variables from which a behavioral model may be specified. The challenge then is to develop and apply statistical methods that combine population data's more precise and less biased estimates of the overall associations between the outcome and target variables with survey data's breakdown of these overall associations into multivariate associations between outcome, target, and control variables. The main purpose of the present study is to describe and illustrate a statistical method that combines the respective advantages of survey and population data. The method is constrained maximum likelihood estimation (MLE). Population-level data provide the constraints, in the form of information about the overall association between an outcome variable y and a target explanatory variable x. Estimates of the multivariate associations between outcome variable y, target variable x, and control variables z using survey data are then constrained to equal the overall associations.

1.1. Statistical Theory of Constrained Maximum Likelihood Estimation and Other Methods for Combining Population and Survey Data in Regression Analysis

The traditional statistical method for combining survey and aggre-gated population data is poststratification (Kish 1965; Lohr 1999). Broadly defined, poststratification refers to methods for adjusting bias and reducing variance in survey results by reweighting observa-tions after selection (Smith 1991). Until recently, the statistical litera-ture on the statistical properties of poststratified estimates has been relatively sparse (Holt and Smith 1979), but it has been applied also to the modeling of survey data through the use of constraining informa-tion from population data (Deming and Stephan 1942; Ireland and Kullback 1968). More recently, Qin and Lawless (1994) develop methods for combining information from multiple sources when the information about the parameters of interest can be expressed in terms of unbiased estimating equations. They establish some theore-tical properties of contingency tables with population data for mar-ginal probabilities. Their equations are applied in conjunction with the empirical likelihood for the sampled information to estimate the parameters. This approach is closely allied to the econometric approaches we discuss below.

The lack of development of the post-stratification approach to modeling has been in part due to the fact that it has been largely motivated by, and is usually applied in, design-based inference. However, the ubiquitous nature of nonresponse and attrition has led many researchers to consider instead model-based inference. In design (i.e., randomization) based inference, the population values are regarded as fixed numbers and inference is based on the probability sampling scheme for the survey. If nonresponse exists, design-based inference is inappropriate except under very strict assumptions about the nature of the nonresponse. In the alternative, model-based perspective, nonresponse and attrition are regarded as further sample selection, and the ultimate sampling scheme must be inferred from a selection model and the observed data. In this case, poststratification can be used to make the nonresponse ignorable for inference in the sense of Little and Rubin (1987). From this perspective the combination of survey and population data should be model-based (Little 1991, 1993, 1995). Little and Wu (1991) compare the design-based and model-based approaches when the sampled population differs from the population data due to nonresponse or coverage errors.

Little (1993) develops a Bayesian model-based approach to combine information from sample surveys and population data (see also Elliott and Little 2001). The approach assumes that the population distribution of a categorical variable in a simple random sampled sample survey is determined from the population information. His approach is to poststratify on the variable using a Gaussian model for the response given the poststratification variables. This approach is also useful when the survey is subject to simple forms of nonresponse and coverage errors. Further, the model is easily extended to the case where a joint distribution of multiple variables is available from the population data. Application to multiple data sets, some with fewer covariates, is also possible. This is analogous to population-level data with fewer variables combined with survey data with more variables. This may be restated as a partially missing regressors problem (Little 1992). Including observations with some missing regressors nevertheless increases the efficiency of the estimation of parameters for the regressors that are present. In this way, missing data observations are treated as a second type of sample that must be combined with the sample of complete data observations. This framework can be extended to cover situations in which samples are combined from different studies with overlapping, but not completely identical, sets of regressors. Gelman and Little (1998) and Gelman and Carlin (2001) develop further methods of adjustment that are based on modeling population structure. Bethlehem (2002) shows how the Dutch POLS social survey can be adjusted for unit nonresponse by including population level data.

A closely related literature is that on ecological regression (Goodman 1953; Firebaugh 1978). Originally the focus was on the potential biases of using population- or aggregate-level information alone to infer individual-level processes. However, recent developments in ecological inference emphasize the use of individual-level information to address these concerns (Wakefield and Salway 2001).

There is a well-developed literature on the econometric theory for combining population-level and sample-survey data. This work dates back to at least Manski and Lerman (1977). The approach is closely related conceptually to what econometricians refer to as choice-based, or endogenously stratified, random sampling. In (bio)statistics this is often studied under the title of case-control or retrospective sampling schemes (Prentice and Pyke 1979; Breslow and Day 1980). Of most direct importance is the work by Imbens and Lancaster (1994, 1996) and Hellerstein and Imbens (1999). This is a very active research area in econometrics that has direct relevance to other social science fields. Imbens and colleagues (Imbens and Lancaster 1994; Hellerstein and Imbens 1999) explore the benefits of combining population with survey data, using economic data in a generalized method of moments (GMM) regression framework. Imbens and Lancaster (1994) consider the estimation of parameters in the regression model under moment restrictions on the survey data contributed by population data, and report large gains in efficiency by incorporating marginal moments from census data with sample-survey joint distributions. Hellerstein and Imbens (1999) give an example of the bias-reduction possibilities of including aggregate data in the context of estimating wages from survey data. In that case, the survey data suffer from possibly nonrandom attrition. They also show how this may be addressed by means of a reweighting scheme under an implicit assumption that the values are missing at random. This approach can be seen as an extension of poststratification using a special case of the empirical-likelihood estimator (Qin and Lawless 1994; Imbens, Johnson, and Spady 1998). While the approach does not require parametric assumptions about the error distributions, it does not benefit from this information either. This reduces small-sample statistical efficiency and excludes Bayesian extensions relaxing the assumption that the constraint values are exact. In addition, the approach does not adjust for nonresponse that is not missing at random. Likelihood-based methods and maximum likelihood estimators in particular are more frequently found in sociological and much other social-scientific modeling work, due to their good statistical properties and because likelihood-based methods provide a general conceptual and inferential framework.

There is also a tradition of combining population and sample data in macro-level demographic analyses, using techniques that include "model" life tables and indirect standardization (Smith 1992). More recently, Handcock, Huovilainen, and Rendall (2000) demonstrated the potential feasibility of a constrained maximum likelihood estimator (MLE) to combine sample survey data with birth registration data in the estimation of a multivariate model of fertility. Large gains in efficiency were achieved through the intercept term of their logistic regression equation. The variance about the intercept parameter was halved when the general fertility rate constraint was introduced. Since the covariate-specific birth probabilities are always functions of the intercept parameters, the reduction in variance in the constrained model was similarly large (around 50 percent) for both covariate-specific birth probabilities. Handcock et al. did not, however, use any population-level information on fertility rates by model covariates, and so gains were confined to the intercept parameter and functions of it. The present paper extends the Handcock et al. results to consider possible gains in efficiency and unbiasedness additionally for the *coefficient* parameters of regression equations. As with that earlier paper, we treat the case of exact population data for the constraints. In Section 2, we describe the statistical theory of variance and bias reduction for the constrained maximum likelihood estimator, with particular application to logistic regression. In Section 3, we describe how this estimator may be used in a sociological application that combines panel survey data with population data on black and white marital fertility in a test of the minority-group hypothesis of fertility. In Section 4, we present the results. Section 5 concludes with a discussion.

2. STATISTICAL THEORY

We outline here the statistical principles of variance and bias reduction when combining survey and population data in a likelihood framework. The exposition is oriented toward the type of estimators and assumptions about the nature of the survey and population data of our subsequent empirical application. We describe the theory of constrained MLE for survey data that are subject to varying degrees and types of nonresponse and attrition when exact population-level data are available to constrain the regression estimates. Further, we describe implementation with constraints on the weighted sum of conditional probabilities when the weights may be known from either population or survey data or both, and when the unconditional probabilities are known from population-level data. The conditional probability function described is the logit, although the method of constrained MLE generalizes to other functional forms. The basic principles also apply to nonlikelihood-based regression methods such as least squares and method of moment estimators. We make reference to these generalities in the course of the exposition.

2.1. *Representative Survey Data Combined with Exact Population Values*

In this section, we consider what improvements could be achieved by combining survey data that are representative of our target population with accurate population-level data. To say that the survey data are "representative" corresponds in the terminology of missing data to "ignorable" nonresponse (Rubin 1976), encompassing as special cases standard survey designs where data are "nonmissing," "missing completely at random," "missing at random," or subject to "covariate only missingness." We say that the population data are "accurate" to mean that they are without substantial nonsampling error such as undercounting or misclassification. Because they are collected for all members of a target demographic population, we assume that they are statistically precise (that is, not subject to sampling error). In this section we show how the population values may be used to reduce sampling variance about survey estimates. We give a formula (equation 8 below) for the reduction in variances about the regression parameters, which demonstrates that the standard errors of the estimates when using the population information will always be lower than when this information is ignored. This formula applies to the reduction in standard errors on both the intercept and coefficient parameters in the regression.

We start by writing the joint distribution of a response Y and covariates X as

$$P(Y = y,\ X = x\ |\ \theta_0) = P(Y = y\ |\ X = x, \theta_0)(X = x), \qquad (1)$$

where θ_0 is the unknown parameter vector of interest describing the relationship between Y and X. These may, for example, be the regression parameters in a logistic or probit regression of Y on X or, less frequently in contemporary sociological research, discriminant analysis (e.g., Efron 1975; Ruiz-Velasco 1991). Suppose the universe consists of women within a given range of childbearing ages, and that the response variable Y has two levels: 0 denotes no birth, and 1 denotes a birth, during the year $(t - 1, t]$. Suppose further that the only covariate in this model is a dichotomous "premarital children" variable X for whether there are any children from before this marriage in the family unit at time $t - 1$. The binomial logistic regression model for the birth probability $P(Y = 1|X = x, \theta_0)$ is given by

$$\text{logit}[P(Y = 1|X = x, \theta_0)] = \beta_0 + \beta_1 x. \qquad (2)$$

Here the parameter is $\theta_0 = (\beta_0, \beta_1)$. Denote the survey data by $D = (y_i, x_i)$, $i = 1,\ldots,$ n. If this is all the information we have, under standard regularity conditions, the value of θ that maximizes the likelihood

$$L(\theta; y, x) = \prod_{i=1}^{n} P(Y = y_i, X = x_i\ |\ \theta)$$

$$= \prod_{i=1}^{n} P(Y = y_i\ |\ X = x_i, \theta)P(X = x_i) \qquad (3)$$

is an asymptotically efficient estimator of θ_0. Under these conditions, the estimator is also asymptotically unbiased and Gaussian with asymptotic variance V_s, where V_s is the inverse of $E_{\theta_0}[\partial \log[L(\theta; y|x)]/\partial\theta_{ij}]$, the Fisher information matrix for θ (Rice 1995). Note that as the sampled distribution of the covariates does not depend on θ_0 the same estimator is produced by maximizing the constrained likelihood

$$L(\theta; y|x) = \prod_{i=1}^{n} P(Y = y_i|X = x_i, \theta). \qquad (4)$$

Intuitively this means that information about the population distribution of the covariates does not affect the estimator. Thus population information about a function of X alone would not improve the estimation of θ_0.

Now suppose that we supplement the survey data by population information about some function of the response and covariate variables, which we denote by $g(y,x)$. The function may be bivariate, or multivariate if information about multiple characteristics is available. As the information tells us something about how Y and X relate to each other, we might expect that it will also help us infer the value of θ_0. We assume that the information can be expressed as a mean of a multidimensional function over the population

$$C(\theta_0) = E_{\theta_0}[g(Y, X)], \qquad (5)$$

where the value of $C(\theta_0)$ is known from the population data to be ϕ, for example. Most information can be expressed in this form by a judicious choice of $g(y,x)$. Returning to the example, consider the above model for birth probabilities in terms of presence of premarital children. Population data supply the annual probability of childbearing among all married couples in that wife's age group, ϕ. Survey data are used to estimate the proportion of couples with and without premarital children, $\rho = P(X = 1)$ and $1 - \rho = P(X = 0)$. By choosing

$$g(y, x) = \begin{cases} 1 & y = 1 \\ 0 & y \neq 1 \end{cases},$$

and using the above expressions for the covariate-specific birth probabilities, the constraint (5) is

$$P(Y = 1 | X = 0, \theta_0)(1 - \rho) + P(Y = 1 | X = 1, \theta_0)\rho = \phi \qquad (6)$$

In general, a constraint for covariates x and outcome variable y is of the form

$$C(\theta) = E_\theta[g(Y, X)] = \int_x \int_y g(y, x) P(Y = y | X = x, \theta)(X = x)dy\,dx \qquad (7)$$

If the marginal distribution of the covariate X, $P(X = x)$, is known then this constraint is a known function of θ. Hence (5) constrains this function of θ to equal its known population value ϕ. If we maximize the above likelihood subject to this constraint using the procedure described in Handcock et al. (2000), the estimator is still asymptotically efficient, unbiased, and Gaussian. However, while the asymptotic variance in the unconstrained version is given by the Fisher information matrix V_s, in the constrained version the asymptotic variance is

$$V_S - V_S H^T [H V_S H^T]^{-1} H V_S, \tag{8}$$

where $H = [\partial C_i(\theta)/\partial \theta_j]$ is the gradient matrix of $C(\theta)$ with respect to θ. As the second term in this expression is positive definite, the inclusion of the population information always leads to an improvement in the estimation of θ_0. In particular, the standard error of the estimator in the version using the population information (the constrained model) will always be less than the one that ignores it (the unconstrained model). A further result of (8) is that the asymptotic ratio of the variances of the constrained to unconstrained parameters is independent of the survey sample size. Thus, the *percentage* reduction in the standard errors of the regression parameters will be approximately the same for all sample sizes.

It is also important to note that both V_s and H in (8) can be estimated from the survey data using the unconstrained model. The efficiency gain from including population information can then be estimated before running a constrained model, and so before obtaining the population data. Alternative choices for $g(y,x)$ can then be compared in terms of their statistical efficiency and ease of collection of the population information. Note that the increase in efficiency from including population data will be reduced if the population distribution of the covariates is not known. Typically in demographic applications, the population data will provide information about the univariate or bivariate distributions of at least some of the covariates, but survey data will be needed to provide information about the multivariate dimensions of the covariate vector.

The effect of including the population data is presented graphically in Figure 1. This is a stylized representation of the relative

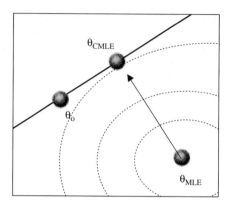

FIGURE 1. The relationship between estimates when representative sample data
alone are used (MLE) and when they are augmented by exact
population information (CMLE).

positions in a two-dimensional parameter space of the various models.
The target population model is represented by θ_0. The dashed curves
are the contours of the unconstrained likelihood (3) with the maximum
likelihood estimator using only the sample survey represented by θ_{MLE}.
The models satisfying the constraints (5) on the parameters imposed by
the population data are represented by the thick line. Note that θ_0 is
always on this line if the population data are from the target population. The constrained MLE θ_{CMLE} is the value on this line that maximizes the likelihood subject to the constraints. The variance formulas
given above show that θ_{CMLE} is, on average, closer to θ_0 than is θ_{MLE}.
The exact size of the improvement depends on constraints, but it is
calculable from (8) for given $g(y,x)$, independently of the actual value
of the constraint ϕ. Because the survey data are representative, though,
the expected values of both the constrained and unconstrained parameters are equal to the population parameter θ_0. The gains realized
through the introduction of the population data will be in variance
reduction only, as the unconstrained estimator is already unbiased with
respect to the target population.

It is worthwhile to be explicit about the situation where the
survey suffers from nonresponse but is still assumed to be representative. The simplest case is where the values of D that are missing are a
simple random sample from the complete sample. This is known as
the *missing completely at random* condition (Little and Rubin 1987).

Denote the observed part of D by D_{obs}, and the missing part by D_{mis} so that $D = (D_{obs}, D_{mis})$. As the mechanism that determines which values are missing is independent of the response, covariates and θ_0, the likelihood for the data is just the product (3) taken over the observed cases. In addition, the constrained MLE is still asymptotically unbiased, efficient, and Gaussian. The asymptotic efficiency for the observed data relative to the complete data is just the proportion of the complete data that is missing. Hence the inclusion of the population data has the same *rate* of increase in efficiency that it has in the complete data case.

This assumption can be weakened to allow values to be missing differentially by covariates but independent of the response and of the vector of parameters θ_0 relating the response variable to the regressors. We call this *covariate only nonresponse* (Rubin 1977). In our example, this would mean that childless women could have a different response rate to women who had at least one child at time $t - 1$, as long as the rate was the same for all women in each category regardless of their birth status during the year. That is, the reason for nonresponse is then perfectly related to the measured covariates. As the constrained likelihood is expressed in terms of the conditional distributions $P(Y = y_i \mid X = x_i, \theta)$, and these are unchanged, the likelihood for the data is again just the product (3) taken over the observed cases. Thus even though the observed sample distributions of the covariates are biased, the inclusion of the population information is unaffected and the constrained MLE is asymptotically unbiased, efficient, and Gaussian. The asymptotic efficiency for the observed data relative to the complete data is again just the proportion of the complete data cases that is missing.

Suppose now that the nonresponse also depends on the response Y. Suppose that the probability that an observation is missing may depend on D_{obs} but not on the missing part D_{mis}. This is known as *missing at random*, in the sense of Rubin (1976). This is less restrictive than covariate only nonresponse, which is in turn less restrictive than missing completely at random. Missing at random allows the probability that a datum is missing to depend on the response and covariate of the datum itself, but only indirectly through the quantities that are observed. Let us assume that the parameters of the nonresponse mechanism are distinct from the parameters of interest θ_0. If both the missing at random and the distinctness conditions hold, then the missing-data mechanism is said to be *ignorable* (Little and Rubin 1987). This is an important concept, because we can still model an ignorable nonresponse mechanism as a function of what we have observed and obtain efficient inference for θ_0. Finally, note that this assumption, like all those made about missing data, cannot be verified from the observed data alone; support must come from expertise or information external to the data. For example, we might know from other studies that women's marital fertility by premarital fertility does not differ by whether they respond to surveys, even if, say, women with no premarital children are less likely to respond.

If there is nonresponse, the observed information includes not only the observed values of the response and covariates but also a variable R indicating whether the case was observed or not. Hence the likelihood for the observed data is the joint likelihood for D_{obs} and R. However, if the missing data mechanism is ignorable, the joint likelihood is

$$L(\theta; y_{obs}, x_{obs}, R) = P(R \mid Y = y_{obs}, X = x_{obs}) P(Y = y_{obs} \mid X = x_{obs}, \theta)$$
$$= P(R \mid Y = y_{obs}, X = x_{obs}) L(\theta; y_{obs} \mid x_{obs}). \qquad (9)$$

The first term is independent of θ so the likelihood is proportional to the constrained likelihood for the observed values of the response and covariates. Hence the MLE is just the constrained MLE under $L(\theta; y_{obs} \mid x_{obs})$, independent of the missing data mechanism. That is, under our approach we can achieve fully efficient inference without modeling the missing data mechanism explicitly for likelihood-based inference about θ_o. The constrained MLE under $L(\theta; y_{obs} \mid x_{obs})$ is asymptotically unbiased, efficient, and Gaussian. The asymptotical efficiency for the observed data relative to the complete data is just the proportion of the complete data that is missing. Hence again the inclusion of the population data has the same *rate* of increase in efficiency as it has in the complete data case.

2.2. *Nonrepresentative Survey Data Combined with Exact Population Values*

In this section, we consider what improvements could be achieved using accurate population-level data to supplement "nonrepresentative" survey data, meaning survey data that are less than perfectly representative of the population on at least one dimension related to the estimation problem. In our regression case, this refers to representativeness of the conditional expectations of the dependent variable Y on regressors X. In missing data terminology, the effective survey sampling mechanism then incorporates nonresponse that is no longer ignorable. The statistical properties of estimators that combine nonrepresentative survey data with exact population values, however, apply more broadly than to the case of "nonignorable" survey nonresponse. They can be extended also to respondent misreporting (Schafer 1997) and to survey sampling designs that do not exactly match the target population.

The main result of using constraints from the target population in combination with the above kinds of survey data is that the more population information we introduce, in the form of constraints about the relationship between Y and X, the closer we will get to unbiased regression estimates of target population relationships.[1] We describe this below in terms of the synthetic population that is formed by the combination of elements from both the representative and nonrepresentative effective sampling frames respectively from the population-level and survey data. The inclusion of population constraints moves this synthetic population toward the target population. The more constraints used, the closer is the synthetic population to the target population, and the greater the reductions in bias about parameters estimated from this synthetic population.

Following Little and Wu (1991) and Hellerstein and Imbens (1999), we refer formally to the survey data's distribution as the *sampled population*, with parameter θ_{sample}. We distinguish this from

---

[1] A reviewer correctly points out that this does not necessarily hold in the case where population information *on the distribution of the regressor X* alone is used to estimate the unconditional expectation of Y, where the sample and population distribution of X differ due to informative (nonignorable) nonresponse (that is, nonresponse depends on Y in addition to X). In this case population-level information on the joint distribution of Y and X is required. The population-level information we consider for constrained MLE, however, is information about the relationship between Y and X—that is, information on the association between Y and some subset of the regression vector X. We consider the use of population data in the estimation of the distribution of regressor X when we also have information on the association between Y and X in the bottom two paragraphs of Section 2.3 below.

the *target population*, with parameter θ_o. The MLE will approach θ_{sample}. If the survey is representative, $\theta_{sample} = \theta_0$; otherwise the difference between them represents the bias of the sample survey. The inclusion of population information will, in general, reduce this bias. Suppose we use the constrained MLE to estimate θ_0. Consider the synthetic population that satisfies the constraints (5) defined by the population data and that is closest to θ_{sample} in terms of likelihood (see Figure 2). This population is in a sense a combination of the sampled population and the target population. We denote the parameter for this synthetic population by $\theta_{combined}$. The constrained MLE θ_{CMLE} will approach $\theta_{combined}$, as the sample size increases, rather than the true value θ_0. Thus the difference between $\theta_{combined}$ and θ_0 is a measure of the bias that remains after introducing population constraints. In this sense it is the *bias of the combined survey and population information*. In general $\theta_{combined}$ will be closer to the true value θ_o than θ_{sample}, so the inclusion of the population data improves the estimates. The development of the properties of the constrained MLE in Section 2.1 still applies, with θ_o now replaced by $\theta_{combined}$. In particular, the variance formulas given above now apply for θ_{CMLE}, which is, on average, closer to θ_o than is θ_{MLE}. Hellerstein and Imbens (1999) derive these results in the special case of linear regression.

Computational limitations for the maximization problem may be encountered when many population constraints are simultaneously applied. To circumvent this problem, the poststratification

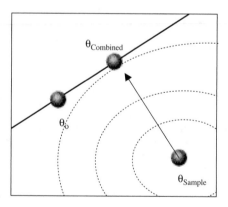

FIGURE 2. The relationship between the estimated parameters of the unconstrained ("sample") and constrained ("combined") and the population parameter when the sample survey is not representative.

reweighting approach of Hellerstein and Imbens can be used. Those authors demonstrate the equivalence between the constrained estimation and the reweighting approaches in the linear regression context. They show that the empirical likelihood MLE can be expressed as a weighted linear regression estimator, where the weights are a by-product of calculating the MLE and can be interpreted as poststratification weights. This approach has a major advantage: Once the weights are calculated, the weighted data set can be used within standard statistical packages, and interpreted accordingly. Both the constrained methods and the reweighting methods lead to identical estimators. The choice of method can then be made on the basis of ease of programming and statistical computational efficiency.

Misreporting of respondents can be statistically treated in a similar way to nonignorable nonresponse. It requires the modeling of the misreporting mechanism just as the nonresponse is modeled. Even parameters of the misreporting (i.e., the misreporting probability) can be included as parameters. A good example is Heitjan and Rubin's (1989) treatment of respondents' rounding of answers (e.g., age and income); Heitjan (1990) also reviews these methods.

2.3. *Application to Logistic Regression*

Let Y be a binary response variable modeled via a logistic regression on covariates $X = \{X_1, X_2, \ldots, X_q\}$:

$$\text{logit}[P(Y = 1 | X_1 = x_1, X_2 = x_2 \ldots, X_q = x_q, \theta_0)] = \sum_{k=1}^{q} \theta_{0k} x_k. \quad (10)$$

The responses are assumed to be conditionally independent given the covariates. We next introduce constraints on the total effects of each variable. Let ϕ_{ij} be the proportion of positive responses $(Y = 1)$ in the population with $X_i = j$. The corresponding constraint functions $C_{ij}(\theta)$ are each of the form

$$\phi_{ij} = C_{ij}(\theta) = E_\theta[g_{ij}(Y, X)]$$
$$= \sum_{x:x_i=j} P(Y = 1 | X = x, \theta)\pi(X = x | X_i = j), \quad (11)$$

where

$$g_{ij}(y, x) = \begin{cases} 1 & \text{when } y = 1 \text{ and } x_i = j \\ 0 & \text{otherwise} \end{cases}$$

The constraint function (11) is expressed as the sum of two product terms (on the right-hand side of the constraint function). The first term is the probability of a positive response conditional on the value of the regressor vector x. The second term is the proportion of the population with a specific set of values on the regressor variables given that $X_i = j$.

Consider now the case in which there is a constraint function defined for each possible value j that variable X_i may take. For example, X_1 may be a race variable that takes the value of $X_1 = 0$ for whites and $X_1 = 1$ for blacks. Given the individual is white or black, there will in general be different distributions on other regressor variables—for example, on the distribution of socioeconomic status. Hence $\pi(X = x \mid X_1 = 0) \neq \pi(X = x \mid X_1 = 1)$, where vector X includes both race and socioeconomic status.

Continuing this example, let response variable Y indicate whether a birth occurs in the year. Then $\{\phi_{11}, \phi_{10}\}$ represents the bivariate association of race with fertility in the population of whites and blacks. For example, ϕ_{11}/ϕ_{10} expresses the ratio of black to white fertility. The two constraint functions $C(\theta_{11})$ and $C(\theta_{10})$ then together constrain the marginal effects in the behavioral model that includes socioeconomic status to preserve this overall ratio of black to white fertility that is known from the population data. When a set of constraints of this type is applied, such that for a given regression variable X_i (in the example, race), its bivariate association with Y is completely specified for the population, we say that the regression variable X_i has been *directly constrained*. For other variables in the equation (e.g., socioeconomic status), we say they are *indirectly constrained*, since each constraint potentially influences every parameter value via the interrelationships between the covariates, assuming nonzero covariances—i.e., $cov(X_i, X_j) \neq 0$. Hence a direct constraint on one variable indirectly influences the values of the other parameters and their standard errors. While these indirect effects may be expected to be larger if the covariates are closely related (for example, if a variable is an interaction between a directly constrained variable and another variable), Imbens and Lancaster (1994) found in a Monte Carlo simulation that only for regressor variables that are extremely highly correlated will population information limited to one of the variables' relationship with the dependent variable have any variance reduction on the parameter estimate for the other. We similarly find that only the coefficient parameters of the "directly-constrained" variables are significantly influenced by the population data in our empirical application reported in the results section below.

In general, the population proportions $\pi(X = x \mid X_i = j)$ may be estimated from survey or population data, or a combination of the two. Estimating them from the survey data is useful to ensure conformity of the variable definitions between the first and second terms on the right-hand side of the constraint equation (11)—that is, between the definitions of X measured in the regression sample observations (y,x) and X measured in the data (sample or population) used to estimate the distribution of X, $\pi(X = x \mid X_i = j)$. "Nonconformity" of definitions may be restated as the case that the sample is "population-representative" with respect to the distribution of X but that there is no population data source for which there is a set of identically measured variables on all dimensions of vector X. Estimation of the distribution of X from the regression sample data introduces a source of variability in the constraint function. It is possible to modify equation (8) to include a component due to this uncertainty. The constrained estimator is still used, but with the constraint functions conditional on the distribution of the regressors estimated from survey data. Let $g(x;\theta) = E_{Y \mid X=x;\theta}[g(Y, x)]$ be the conditional expectation of $g(Y, X)$ given $X = x$. The variation of $g(X;\theta)$ determines the variation in the constraints. The variance of the constrained estimator is given by Imbens and Lancaster (1994) as

$$V_{CU} = [V_S^{-1} + H^{\mathrm{T}}\Delta_g^{-1}H]^{-1} = V_S - V_S H^{\mathrm{T}}[HV_S H^{\mathrm{T}} + \Delta_g]^{-1}HV_S,$$

where Δ_g is the covariance matrix of $g(X; \theta_0)$. Compared to equation (8), it can be seen that Δ_g represents the cost of not knowing $\pi(X = x \mid X_i = j)$ and this inflates the variance of the estimator. When Δ_g is close to zero—that is, the constraint right-hand side varies little from sample to sample—the two formulas are very close. The effect of using sample data to estimate population proportions

$\pi(X = x \mid X_i = j)$, however, is to unambiguously reduce the effect-iveness of constrained estimation. By just how much will vary from application to application.

A second case of difference between the sample and population distributions of regressors X is when the investigator estimates the distribution of X from regression sample data that are not "popula-tion-representative" with respect to the distribution of X. This case belongs to the class of *covariate-only non-response* discussed in Section 2.1. Again, using the sample data in place of the population data in the right-hand side of the constraint function will unambiguously reduce the effectiveness *with respect to the variance reduction* of using population data to constrain the estimation. However, as dis-cussed in Section 2.1, even though the observed sample distributions are biased, the constrained MLE of the regression parameters is asymptotically unbiased.

3. A CONSTRAINED MLE TEST OF THE 'MINORITY-GROUP STATUS' HYPOTHESIS OF FERTILITY

The example introduced above in the context of the theoretical prop-erties of constrained ML estimators can now be elaborated and estimated. Specifically, we consider a test of the "minority-group-status" hypothesis of couple fertility. We demonstrate the constrained maximum likelihood method by testing this hypothesis on the marital fertility of black and white couples in which the wife is aged between 30 and 34 years old. According to the 'minority-group status' hypoth-esis, fertility will be lower for a minority group of otherwise equal economic status (Goldscheider and Uhlenberg 1967). In previous tests of the hypothesis applied to minority black versus majority white women (Johnson 1988; Boyd 1994), the strength of empirical support for the hypothesis has varied, and the hypothesis has undergone refinements (Johnson 1979) that have sought to limit its applicability to women with higher socioeconomic statuses. Our test of the minor-ity group status hypothesis does not attempt to contribute substan-tively to this literature, but instead is presented to show concisely how to apply the constrained MLE method to test hypotheses of theore-tical interest in sociology. Thus our test of the hypothesis uses the simplest "strong form" of the hypothesis in which women of all socioeconomic statuses are expected to be similarly affected, and uses a sample confined to married women in the 30- to 34-year-old age group. While limiting the age range in this way will mix childbearing quantity with timing effects, we include regressors (in particular, for marital duration) that control for timing associations.

The minority-group status hypothesis of fertility differentials was originally proposed when fertility within marriage predominated among both majority and minority groups. Thus it is appropriate for us to apply the hypothesis to marital fertility. It is important, however, to take into account the potentially confounding effect of fertility before the marriage began. This may be nonmarital fertility, either with a woman's current husband or with a previous partner. It may also be fertility within a previous marriage. In either case, we expect and find that this depresses fertility in the current marriage. Because, as we show, premarital fertility is substantially more common among black married women than among white married women, it is important to include a control for any premarital children in addition to other sociodemographic and economic variables.

We obtain the bivariate associations between race and fertility from the population data: the race- and year-specific marital fertility rates for 30- to 34-year-old women from 1984 to 1993. The population data are estimates of annual marital fertility rates by five-year age group and race of the woman published by the National Center for Health Statistics (NCHS 1999). The NCHS makes these estimates by using as their numerator all marital births in a given year between 1984 and 1993 to married mothers of that racial group,[2] and by using as their denominator the Census Bureau's midyear population estimates by sex, age, and marital status. We assume that the marital age-, period-, and race-specific fertility rates have zero sampling variance, and that the age, race, and period definitions are those of the target population for our analyses. That is, we assume that the NCHS data represent the true population values exactly.

In general, when jointly using survey and population data, there will seldom be an exact match between the population and survey universes and variable definitions. In the present study, we

---

[2]In general, these are 100 percent samples, but some states provide 50 percent samples for the national compilation by NCHS, who then weight them to the population total.

specify the population about which we wish to make inferences on the basis of the population data, and we use the survey data to best approximate that. This allows us to explore empirically the statistical properties of the case for which we have described above in terms of statistical theory. This is the case in which the population values are known exactly and the sample may or may not have been drawn (or have subsequently evolved) in a way that can be said to exactly represent that target population.

The survey data we use are from the Panel Study of Income Dynamics (PSID, Hill 1992). These data have the advantages of coming from a very long-running panel survey with covariates for socioeconomic and demographic variables for each year. For the present study, it is especially advantageous to have economic status measured directly each year with an income variable. We make estimates for the years 1984 to 1993. The latter year is the most recent year for which "final release" files, including generated variables such as the family income-to-poverty ratio, were available from the Survey Research Center when we coded our survey data. The PSID sample uses an unequal probability sample design. We account for this by conducting our estimation with the PSID's individual sample weights. Thus we account for both initial sample design effects and some of the biases introduced by attrition. The PSID's sampled population may, however, have drifted away from target population universe over time, through differential attrition (Fitzgerald, Gottschalk, and Moffitt 1998), and through its not capturing the processes of population change through immigration. We interpret such drift in terms of *bias* with respect to the target population.

The universe consists of years of exposure to marital fertility in the period 1984 to 1993 among white and black married couples in which the wife is aged 30 to 34 years old. The survey data were collected at annual intervals late in the year, with age recorded in completed years at last birthday. Using these data to best approximate our calendar-year universe, we select our sample to consist of all survey year-pairs $(t - 1, t]$ in which the wife was aged from 29 to 34 in year $t - 1$, and hence aged 30 to 35 in year t. The part-year exposure while still aged 29 is then balanced by part-year exposure at age 35. The matching of survey period to calendar year is done at year t of the $(t - 1, t]$ survey period, since the survey data are collected late in each year, and thus the majority of exposure in each $(t - 1, t]$ year occurs during calendar year t. Married couples each contribute up to six couple-years of exposure in the 1984 to 1993 period. This results in a sample of 8,266 person-years. We ignore variance-estimation complications due to the repeated observation of individuals in the panel. Because we use the same data for both the constrained and unconstrained estimates, introducing this further complication should not change our main results.[3]

The variables from the PSID that are used in the regression are as follows. The dependent variable Y has two levels: 0 denotes no birth and 1 denotes a birth to the couple, during the year $(t - 1, t]$. Using the PSID's panel data only, we code a birth when a child aged less than 2 has entered the family unit since the previous year. This assumes that the parents and child live together at the survey interview immediately following the birth, and that infant mortality between birth and survey is zero. Improvements to the accuracy of coding of births could presumably be achieved through supplementing the panel data with the PSID's fertility histories. For the present study's methodological objectives, though, the panel data are sufficient.

Next, we consider the explanatory variables. A fully specified model of the determinants of the marital birth event would include a variety of demographic, economic, and sociological variables

---

[3]While corrected standard errors could in theory be computed for both the unconstrained and constrained cases, in practice, the considerable additional computational burden imposed by constrained estimation makes such a procedure feasible only for the unconstrained case. A computationally feasible approach would be to use the unconstrained estimator to calculate the design effect (ratio of the variance of the actual sample to the variance under the assumption of a simple random sample), and to apply this ratio to the constrained variances. This would also adjust for other attributes of the sample that inflate the standard error. The PSID's guidance on these design effects are that the *standard errors* should be inflated by a factor of 1.5 for whites and 2.25 for blacks (Morgan et al. 1974, appendix B), due to both higher degrees of clustering and the dual-sample frame that includes more blacks than whites in the low-income subsample. When we conducted our own bootstrap estimates of the design effects for transitions between family statuses (including through childbearing) for white and black women, we found somewhat smaller magnitudes of design effects: 1.18 for white women and 2.01 for black women. These lower magnitudes, especially for whites, were despite our having included multiple observations of the same individual in the PSID sample, suggesting that the effects of the overall sample design are likely to be more important than the effects of repeated observation.

influencing the probability of a birth in the year. The demographic variables might include the single-year ages of both the wife and the husband; length of the marriage; and number of, and years since, previous births within this marriage, for this couple (allowing for children born to the couple before they married), and outside this couple. The economic variables might include the husband's and the wife's current and opportunity wages (the latter affected by education and years of working experience), and the couple's net worth. Sociological variables, such as religious affiliation and behavior, and attitudes toward marriage and family, might also be included. Our intention in this example is to include a reduced set of these variables that is sufficient to illustrate the statistical issues and advantages when using constrained MLE as opposed to the usual, unconstrained technique.

As proxies for a full set of *demographic* variables, we include single-year durations of marriage up to 10 years and over, and whether the age of any child in the current family unit is greater than the duration of the marriage (a "premarital children" variable). As a proxy for a full set of *economic* variables, we include dummies for the family's tercile income-to-poverty ratio. This defines lower-, middle-, and upper-income married couples of this age group. The cut points are at 3.15 and 5.16 times the PSID's approximation of the official poverty ratio. Since the poverty ratio is determined by size of family, this also proxies partially for that demographic variable. As a proxy for *sociological* variables that have changed over time, including attitudes to marriage and the family, we include single-year period dummies for 1984 to 1993. These period dummies will, of course, proxy also for changes in other unobserved variables, including contemporary labor-market conditions.

Finally, *race* of the couple is coded from the "race of the Family Unit Head" variable in the PSID. A more complete model would allow for the race of the husband and wife to differ, but again, our simplification is adequate for illustrative purposes. Race is also interacted fully with each of the year dummies and with the dummy for whether there are any premarital children. The choice of these particular interactions is more for the purposes of illustration than for substantive or model-fitting reasons. The year dummies are interacted with race because the population data allow us to do so very precisely. The 'premarital children' variable allows us to explore the effect of interacting a variable for which the population data do not provide direct information, with a variable (race) that is directly constrained. We explore the effect of constraints on the black dummy and its interactions with premarital children and period, under different model specifications and sample sizes. A major focus of our study is the improvements of estimation and inference with respect to the directly constrained coefficients for race and race-by-year interactions, as it is these that allow us to test the minority-group hypothesis of fertility.

Formally, the covariates in this model are represented by the vector x, measured at time $t - 1$. The binomial logit model for the birth probability $P(Y = 1 | X = x, \theta_o)$ is given by equation (10). In the unconstrained case, we use the survey data alone to estimate the value of θ_0 that maximizes the unconstrained log-likelihood.

We next introduce constraint functions. Let ϕ_{tr} be the NCHS fertility rate for black and white couples ($r = 0, 1$, respectively) in year $t = 1984, \ldots 1993$. These fertility rates are used to constrain the black and white couples' annual probabilities of a marital birth. The 20 constraint functions $C_{tr}(\theta)$ are each of the form seen in equation (11) above:

$$\phi_{tr} = C_{tr}(\theta) = \sum_{x:year=t,\ race=r} P(Y = y \mid X = x, \theta) \times$$
$$P(X = x \mid year = t, race = r) \tag{12}$$

Thus the constraint functions are of the form in which the value of the outcome variable is known exactly for race and period subpopulations of the overall population of 30- to 34-year-old married women. The bivariate association of race with fertility is then implicitly constrained for all 30- to 34-year-old married women in any given year. The first term on the right-hand side of the constraint function is the probability of a birth in year t conditional on the value of the regressor vector x. The second term is the proportion of the population of that race in year t with a specific set of values for the regressor variables. Here, it is the proportion of the population with a specific number of years marital duration, presence or absence of premarital children, and family income-to-poverty tercile (that is, values on the regressors that are not directly constrained). We estimate those proportions from the survey data. In a simple specification of the model from our example problem, variance reduction in the estimation of our parameter of interest (the coefficient on the black dummy) was little changed when variability about the regressor distribution *was* accounted for—down from a 98.4 percent reduction over the unconstrained estimate's variance to a 97.0 percent reduction. Variance reduction in the intercept parameter, however, was more substantially affected—down from a 94.9 percent reduction to only a 73.2 percent reduction. For simplicity, the results presented below do not account for this source of variability in the estimates of variance reduction.

The maximum likelihood estimator under constraints is the solution of

$$\max_{\theta} \left[L(\theta; y|x) \right] \quad \text{subject to} \quad C_{tr}(\theta) = \phi_{tr} \quad t = 1, \dots 10, r = 0, 1$$

The estimator is asymptotically efficient, unbiased, and Gaussian with covariance matrix approximated by (8). To evaluate the gains obtained by imposing additional constraints from the population data, we estimate both the unconstrained and constrained versions of our model, and compare the parameters and their standard errors.

We implement our constrained ML estimator using the PROC NLP procedure of the SAS/OR package (SAS Institute 1997). This procedure allows for a wide range of objective functions and for a large number of either linear or nonlinear constraints. In the present logistic regression case, the constraints are nonlinear due to the non-linearity in the logistic cumulative density function. The NLP procedure also calculates the covariance matrix and standard errors, using the standard asymptotic approximation of the inverse of the Fisher information matrix. The NLP procedure is relatively simple to implement, and converges within a reasonable time (under two hours CPU time) for the specification presented here. In more complex specifications with larger survey samples, however, more flexible and efficient programming implementations may be required.[4]

---

[4]The main programming disadvantage of the NLP procedure is that it does not allow for the specification of the constraint function in matrix form. Thus it becomes unwieldy when the number of possible regressor-vector values to sum over becomes large. Code for example implementations including for the present study are available at **http://www.stat.washington.edu/~handcock/ combining**.

4. RESULTS

Comparisons between the population and survey estimates of the annual marital fertility for white and black married women aged 30 to 34 are shown in Figures 3 and 4 for the years 1984 to 1993.[5] Here, as throughout the analyses, the survey estimates are weighted. Here alone, however, the confidence intervals account for deviations of the sample from a simple random sampling design. We do so by applying inflation factors of 1.18 and 2.01 respectively to the standard errors of white and black women, as calculated separately in a bootstrap estimation of standard errors in the PSID.

The degree of fluctuation due to sampling error is high for both races. This is seen both in the confidence intervals that are plotted with the point estimates and in comparison with the population rates. The population rates show clear upward trends and very little fluctuation from year to year, for both whites and blacks. The upward trends are not clearly visible in the highly fluctuating survey rates. Several

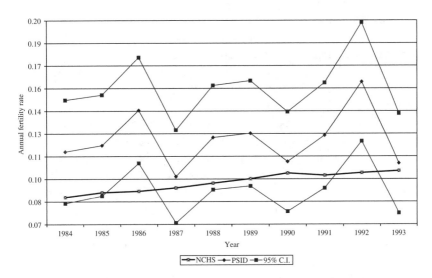

FIGURE 3. Survey (PSID) versus population (NCHS) marital fertility rates of 30- to 34-year-old white women.

[5]Strictly, the annual probability of a birth is estimated in the PSID, but this is equivalent to a fertility rate due to the negligible mortality at the child-bearing ages.

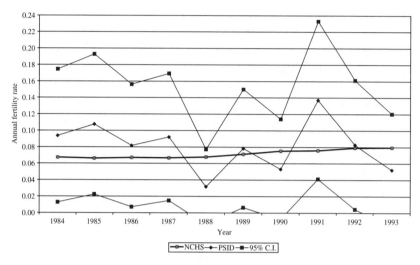

FIGURE 4. Survey (PSID) versus population (NCHS) marital fertility rates of
30- to 34-year-old black women.

features stand out when comparing the white and black rates. First,
the black fertility rates in the survey fluctuate more than the white
fertility rates. This is as expected given the smaller sample sizes of
married black women—approximately 250 person-years of exposure
per year, compared to married white women's approximately 600
person-years of exposure per year.

Second, the black survey rates fluctuate both above and below
the population rates, while the white survey rates appear to be systematically higher than the population rates, even if the difference is
statistically significant in only two years (1986 and 1992). This finding
is important for the statistical testing of the minority-group hypothesis, as it could induce a finding of lower marital fertility among black
women that is due to bias in the sample if population data were not
used to correct this bias. We conduct a formal test for such a bias in
the regression estimates below.

Third, in both the population and survey rates, the marital
fertility of blacks is substantially lower than that of whites. This is
seen clearly in the population rates, in which the black rates are
consistently lower by about 20 percent. The black rates increase
from an annual rate of .0675 in 1984 to .0796 in 1993, while white
rates increase from .0830 to .1004 in the same period. These differences

are the population estimates of the bivariate association of race and fertility. While this direction of differences is consistent with the minority-group hypothesis (at least in its "strong version"), before drawing a conclusion it is necessary to control for socioeconomic covariates that may depress black marital fertility rates relative to those of whites of the same age group.

For the minority-group status hypothesis to be supported, we should find that black women's fertility is substantially lower *after* controlling for sociodemographic and economic variables. To do so, we allow the survey data to contribute information on premarital children, on duration of the current marriage, and on the economic condition of the family. After including these demographic and socio-economic control variables, the coefficient for the race variable together with dummies for the interaction of race by year provide a test of the minority-group hypothesis.

The distributions of blacks and whites on the covariates, and the proportions giving birth by covariate and race, are shown in Table 1. Black women are likely to have been married fewer years (29.1 percent fewer than 5 years, compared to 23.0 percent of white couples). They are much more likely to have a child present from before the marriage (19.7 percent, compared to only 7.5 percent of white couples). They are also much more likely to be in the lower income-to-poverty tercile (50.3 percent, compared to 31.1 percent of white couples), and much less likely to be in the upper income tercile (16.7 percent, compared to 35.3 percent of white couples).

Two of these racial covariate distributions would point to black couples having lower birth probabilities than white couples, and one points in the reverse direction. Having a premarital child and being in lower income categories are associated with substantially lower probabilities of giving birth: 0.035 with a premarital child compared to 0.116 without a premarital child; and 0.074 in the lower income category compared to 0.152 in the higher income category. Birth probabilities are higher, however, at shorter marital durations (the third and fourth years being the peaks), with the exception of the first year of the marriage. The lower marital fertility rates of 30- to 34-year-old married black women that are seen in the population data, therefore, may be due to socioeconomic covariate differences by race, not to a "minority-group" effect. Hence, as proposed by the minority-group hypothesis, it is necessary to control for these

TABLE 1

Blacks' and Whites' Covariate Distributions and Bivariate Relationships of These Covariates to Marital Fertility

	Proportion		
	Whites	Blacks	Birth Probability
Marital Duration			
1 year	0.034	0.043	0.013
2 years	0.040	0.056	0.112
3 years	0.045	0.057	0.191
4 years	0.052	0.066	0.191
5 years	0.059	0.069	0.177
6 years	0.063	0.064	0.163
7 years	0.062	0.068	0.167
8 years	0.070	0.071	0.144
9 years	0.075	0.076	0.127
10+ years	0.500	0.430	0.068
Premarital Child			
None	0.926	0.806	0.116
One or more	0.074	0.194	0.035
Family Income-to-Poverty Ratio			
Lowest third	0.311	0.503	0.074
Middle third	0.336	0.330	0.100
Top third	0.353	0.167	0.152
Sample N (person-year pairs $t - 1,t$)	5,813	2,453	

Source: PSID 1984 to 1993.

covariates to assess whether there is a depressing effect of minority status on fertility.

We estimate the model with socioeconomic covariates under two regression specifications, alternately including and excluding the income variables (see Table 2). In both models, we control for marriage duration and presence of a premarital child when estimating the year-by-year effects of being black on having a birth. For each specification, we estimate the models alternately in their unconstrained and constrained versions. Comparing the specifications alternately with and without the income-to-poverty variables, a test of increase in the log-likelihood reveals that in both the unconstrained and constrained versions, inclusion of the income-to-poverty variables improves the fit ($p < .001$). The values of the log-likelihood for each equation are

TABLE 2
Unconstrained and Constrained Regression Estimates

(a) Without Income Variable

	Unconstrained		Constrained		
	Parameter	Standard Error	Parameter	Standard Error (s.e.)	Percent Reduced (s.e.)
Intercept	−1.328**	0.169	−1.564**	0.115	31.8
Premarital child	−1.449**	0.228	−1.441**	0.227	0.1
Year 1985	0.078	0.170	**0.027****	**0.008**	95.2
Year 1986	0.297	0.164	**0.056****	**0.012**	92.4
Year 1987	−0.119	0.178	**0.077****	**0.010**	94.5
Year 1988	0.115	0.170	**0.041****	**0.008**	95.2
Year 1989	0.028	0.168	**0.082****	**0.009**	94.6
Year 1990	−0.178	0.175	**0.114****	**0.010**	94.1
Year 1991	0.023	0.169	**0.040****	**0.013**	92.2
Year 1992	0.243	0.165	**0.053****	**0.013**	92.2
Year 1993	−0.098	0.172	**0.102****	**0.011**	93.4
Marriage duration 1 year	−2.864**	0.541	−2.854**	0.540	0.0
2 years	−0.622**	0.212	−0.618**	0.212	0.4
3 years	0.011	0.181	0.010	0.180	0.6
5 years	−0.106	0.171	−0.105	0.170	0.6
6 years	−0.220	0.172	−0.218	0.171	0.6
7 years	−0.195	0.171	−0.193	0.170	0.6
8 years	−0.345*	0.171	−0.341*	0.170	0.5
9 years	−0.541*	0.173	−0.536**	0.172	0.5
10 or more years	−1.277**	0.138	−1.267**	0.137	0.5
Black	0.086	0.458	**−0.017****	**0.050**	89.0
Black*pre-marital child	−0.023	0.617	−0.011**	0.614	0.4
Black*year 1985	−0.029	0.639	**−0.090****	**0.027**	95.8
Black*year 1986	−0.935	0.697	**−0.225****	**0.025**	96.4
Black*year 1987	0.109	0.618	**−0.338****	**0.027**	95.6
Black*year 1988	−1.242	0.774	**−0.338****	**0.029**	96.2
Black*year 1989	−0.645	0.636	**−0.414****	**0.033**	94.8
Black*year 1990	−0.687	0.692	**−0.291****	**0.025**	96.3
Black*year 1991	0.108	0.595	**−0.089****	**0.019**	96.7
Black*year 1992	−1.106	0.734	**−0.050****	**0.022**	97.1
Black*year 1993	−1.035	0.739	**−0.242****	**0.023**	96.9
2nd tercile income-to-poverty	—	—	—	—	
3rd tercile income-to-poverty	—	—	—	—	
−2 log-likelihood	2673.3		2703.6		

(continued)

TABLE 2
Continued

| | (b) With Income Variable | | | | |
| | Unconstrained | | Constrained | | |
	Parameter	Standard Error	Parameter	Standard Error (s.e.)	Percent Reduced (s.e.)
Intercept	−1.628**	0.185	−1.930**	0.138	25.4
Premarital child	−1.319**	0.229	−1.310**	0.229	0.2
Year 1985	0.081	0.170	**0.099****	**0.010**	94.3
Year 1986	0.291	0.164	**0.120****	**0.009**	94.4
Year 1987	−0.133	0.178	**0.132****	**0.007**	96.3
Year 1988	0.095	0.171	**0.091****	**0.009**	94.6
Year 1989	0.022	0.169	**0.145****	**0.008**	95.3
Year 1990	−0.195	0.176	**0.168****	**0.008**	95.5
Year 1991	0.019	0.169	**0.106****	**0.012**	93.0
Year 1992	0.229	0.166	**0.106****	**0.012**	92.9
Year 1993	−0.105	0.172	**0.165****	**0.008**	95.1
Marriage duration 1 year	−2.833**	0.541	−2.820**	0.540	0.1
2 years	−0.611**	0.213	−0.606**	0.212	0.5
3 years	0.019	0.181	0.018	0.180	0.6
5 years	−0.104	0.172	−0.101	0.171	0.6
6 years	−0.222	0.172	−0.221	0.171	0.6
7 years	−0.190	0.172	−0.199	0.170	0.7
8 years	−0.316*	0.172	−0.312	0.171	0.5
9 years	−0.503**	0.173	−0.496**	0.172	0.5
10 or more years	−1.173**	0.140	−1.164**	0.139	0.5
Black	0.175	0.458	**0.141****	**0.054**	88.2
Black*premarital child	−0.051	0.617	**−0.047****	0.615	0.4
Black*year 1985	−0.056	0.639	**−0.186****	**0.030**	95.3
Black*year 1986	−0.968	0.698	**−0.327****	**0.027**	96.1
Black*year 1987	0.107	0.619	**−0.411****	**0.027**	95.6
Black*year 1988	−1.221	0.774	**−0.385****	**0.029**	96.3
Black*year 1989	−0.635	0.636	**−0.474****	**0.033**	94.9
Black*year 1990	−0.721	0.692	**−0.393****	**0.028**	96.0
Black*year 1991	0.089	0.596	**−0.129****	**0.022**	96.3
Black*year 1992	−1.091	0.734	**−0.102****	**0.023**	96.9
Black*year 1993	−1.003	0.738	**−0.281****	**0.025**	96.5
2nd tercile income-to-poverty	0.222*	0.099	0.219*	0.099	0.4
3rd tercile income-to-poverty	0.439**	0.096	0.434**	0.095	0.4
−2 log-likelihood	2662.4		2693.7		

Note: Directly constrained coefficients are shown in bold; statistically significant coefficients are indicated by *p < .05 and **p < .01.

given in Table 2. As the standard errors for these parameters are trivially reduced by introducing constraints, it follows that the test for improving the model fit is almost identical when comparing the two specifications in the constrained models and in the unconstrained models.

Our main focus is on the differences between the unconstrained and constrained estimates. As described in the theory section, the parameters can be divided into those that are directly constrained and those that are not. The former category consists of the year variables, the black variable, and the black-by-year interactions. For each year, there are black and white constraints. The difference between them measures the bivariate association of race with fertility in that particular year. For each year there is a survey variable whose regression coefficient measures the *marginal effect* of being black in that particular year. Thus these variables fit our definition from the theory section of having "directly-constrained parameters." The category of indirectly constrained parameters consists of those for the premarital child, marital duration, and income-to-poverty variables, plus the variable for the interaction of black and premarital child.

We consider first efficiency gains from constraining the survey estimates. Consistent with the statistical theory presented above, the standard errors on all parameters are lower in the constrained equation than in the corresponding unconstrained equation. For the variables that are directly constrained, the reductions in standard errors are extremely large. For the year dummies, the reductions are by factors of more than 15, while for the black-by-year interactions, the reductions are by factors of up to 30. The reductions in standard errors about the black variable are by factors of about 9. Accordingly, the magnitudes of the coefficients for the year dummies and black-by-year interactions vary much less in the constrained model than in the unconstrained model.

The reductions in standard errors are of trivial magnitudes, however, for all indirectly constrained variables, in all cases by less than 1 percent. Noteworthy here is that even for the interaction variable between black and premarital child, the standard error is reduced by less than 1 percent. This negligible reduction is in spite of the strong correlation between being black (a directly constrained variable) and having a premarital child (seen above). This example points to the likelihood that any reductions in the standard errors of other than directly constrained variables in sociological research will be very modest.[6]

The intercept parameter is a special category that is subject to a direct constraint: the fertility rate of the reference white group in the reference year 1984. However, the intercept parameter measures more than just an implicit marginal effect of being white in 1984, measuring also the implicit marginal effects of being in the reference categories of the variables that are not directly constrained. The standard error reduction is by "only" one-third about the intercept variable. The statistical interpretation here is that the intercept is related both to the directly constrained variable (black versus white) and the unconstrained variables (marital duration and premarital child and, in the second specification, also income level). The more indirectly constrained parameters there are in the model, the less will the intercept term be determined by the value of the constraint on the reference year 1984 for reference race "white."

Comparing the specifications alternately with and without the income-to-poverty variables is instructive here. The reduction in the standard error about the intercept term is proportionately smaller when the income-to-poverty variables are additionally included (by 25.4 percent, versus by 31.8 percent in the model without the income-to-poverty variables). There are not, however, any substantial differences in the directly constrained parameters with the additional indirectly constrained parameters included. This is an important result because the present study has used a simpler specification of the socioeconomic and demographic variables than would typically be used. The finding of almost equally large reductions in the standard errors when further indirectly constrained regressors are added indicates that directly constraining a regressor of interest can also be expected to yield very large efficiency gains in a fully specified regression model.

We now proceed to evaluate the effects of these reductions in standard errors on our statistical evaluation of the minority-group hypothesis. We do so for the specification that includes the income-to-poverty variables. Because we have interaction dummies for nine

---

[6]We further confirmed this finding in results not reported here in which we experimented with simulated data that we created to have very high correlations between directly constrained and other variables.

years as well as a black dummy, there are ten statistical tests of the minority-group hypothesis that may be performed in each equation. A measure of the black minority-status effect for 1984 is the coefficient of the black dummy. For each of the years 1985–1993, we can use the sum of the black dummy and the black-by-year interaction dummy. Each minority-status effect can be evaluated using a t-test whose test statistic is constructed by dividing the black-effect estimate by its standard error.[7] We then construct confidence intervals around the estimate for each year. These are shown in Figure 5.

The unconstrained model estimates of the year-by-year black minority-status effect have large confidence intervals around them, such that in no year is the estimate significantly different from zero. While point estimates are relatively evenly spread between being above and below zero (six above and four below), those below zero are further from zero, suggesting a possible effect that the statistical test may not be powerful enough to detect. This suggestion is supported by the results for the constrained model. Seven out of ten years have a point estimate below zero, and six of these are statistically significantly different from zero. Only one of the years (1984) has a point estimate that is above zero and statistically significant.

We next assess whether and by how much we have reduced bias by constraining the estimates. As discussed in Section 2.2, the survey data are unbiased if $\theta_{sample} = \theta_0$. We can test the overall hypothesis of equality between these two parameter vectors using a Wald test statistic:

$$(\theta_{MLE} - \theta_{CMLE})^T (V_S - V_C)^{-1} (\theta_{MLE} - \theta_{CMLE}).$$

This is asymptotically Chi-squared with degrees of freedom equal to the number of constraints.

As these models are nested, this difference is asymptotically chi-squared with degrees of freedom equal to the number of constraints. For the model including the poverty variables the test

---

[7]For the years 1984–1993, the test statistics are the sum of the two estimated coefficients (the black dummy and the black *year interaction) and so the standard errors can be calculated from a quadratic form in the appropriate variance-covariance matrix. This is V_s in the unconstrained case and V_c in the constrained case.

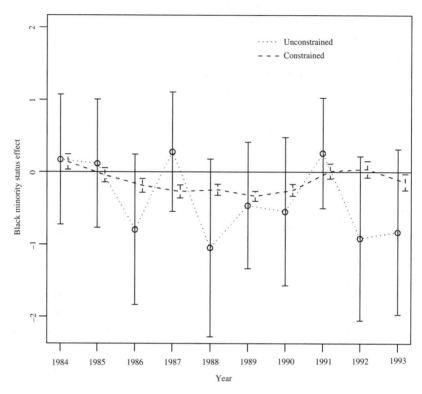

FIGURE 5. Estimates of the black minority-status effect.
Note: Effect is estimated by the sum of the "black" parameter estimate and the 'black-by-year' parameter estimate for that year.

statistic is 69.86. The *p*-value based on the chi-squared with 20 degrees of freedom is <0.001. Hence we can reject the null hypothesis of no bias against the alternative of bias in at least one parameter. The result is unsurprising given the comparisons between the sample and population fertility rates shown above for whites in particular (see again Figure 3). In particular, it seemed that one reason that black marital fertility in the PSID might be lower than white fertility is that white fertility might have been upwardly biased.

We calculate the bias in terms of the log-odds of having a birth calculated from the constrained model estimates minus the log-odds of having a birth calculated from the constrained model estimates. This calculation of the log-odds is just the right-hand side of equation (10). We calculate this bias for the reference category on the other regressors—that is, no premarital child, marital duration four years, and bottom tercile income-to-poverty ratio. We do this separately for whites and blacks (see Figures 6 and 7). The log-odds are seen to be upwardly biased in five of the ten years for whites, but in none for blacks.

Returning to the results of Figure 5, we saw that there appeared to be a tendency for a downward black minority-status effect on fertility in the unconstrained model, but one for which the year-by-year statistical tests were not powerful enough to detect. One way of increasing the power of the test is to consider an average of each of the annual effects. This permits an overall test of the minority-group status hypothesis for the 1984–1993 period. We calculated the

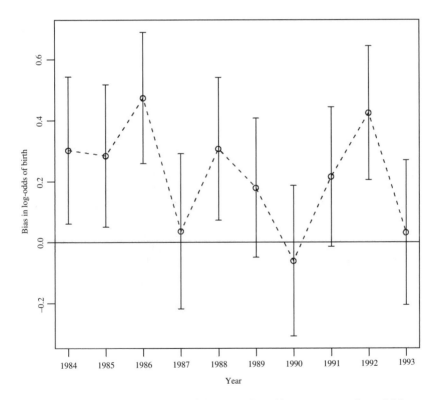

FIGURE 6. Estimates of the bias of the PSID for white no pre-marriage children, married four years, and lowest income-to-poverty tercile.
Note: Bias is estimated by the unconstrained log-odds minus the constrained log-odds.

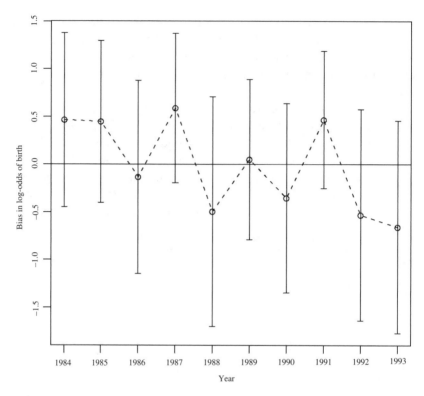

FIGURE 7. Estimates of the bias of the PSID for black no pre-marriage children, married four years, and lowest income-to-poverty tercile.

Note: Bias is estimated by the unconstrained log-odds minus the constrained log-odds.

average "black" effect in the constrained and unconstrained models as the mean of the annual differences in the log odds, and calculated the standard error about this mean.[8] The mean effects are then $-.375$ (0.165 standard error, p = .02), or 0.687 odds-ratio for the unconstrained model, and $-.128$ (.0445 standard error, p = .004), or 0.880 odds-ratio for the constrained model. This compares to mean odds ratios for the mean black-to-white race-specific fertility rates as presented in Figures 3 and 4 of 0.641 for the PSID sample data and 0.755 for the NCHS population data. Thus adding the covariates moderates

---

[8]The average "black" effect is a linear combination of the coefficients, and its variance is then the corresponding quadratic form in the variance-covariance matrix; see also footnote 7.

the black-white difference from 0.641 to 0.687 in the unconstrained (sample) version, and from 0.755 to 0.880 in the constrained (population) version (Table 3). These are very good summary measures of the effect of constraining the survey estimates of the marginal race effect to known population values of the overall race and fertility association. The unconstrained model indicates that black marital fertility in this age group is as much as one-third lower than white marital fertility (in terms of odds of having a birth in the next year), after controlling for socioeconomic variables and variables for marital and fertility history. This difference is statistically significant at the .05 level but not at the .01 level. Thus although the magnitude of the effect is apparently very high, the statistical test is only just powerful enough to detect it. The constrained model indicates that the effect of black minority status is much smaller— 12 percent lower odds than for whites of having a birth in the next year. The test for the minority effect, however, is a very powerful one. The standard error about the average effect is only one-quarter that of the unconstrained model, and thus the relatively small difference between black and white marital fertility is significant at the .004 level.

Finally, we conduct a test of whether the mean black effect (that is, the black log-odds minus the white log-odds) estimated with the unconstrained model is biased. The standard error of the difference in the mean black effect between the unconstrained and constrained models (0.247) is 0.159, or a p-value of .060. Taking the constrained model's average "black" effect as unbiased, we can say

TABLE 3

Mean 1984–1993 Odds Ratios of Black-to-White Fertility in the Sample and Population Data at the Predicted Values from the Unconstrained and Constrained Regression Estimates

	Ratio of Black Odds of Birth to White Odds of Birth
Bivariate Relationships	ratio
PSID (sample)	0.641
NCHS (population)	0.755
Partial (Regression-Predicted) Relationships	
Unconstrained regression	0.687
Constrained regression	0.880

that the apparent upward bias in the unconstrained model's black effect, estimated by comparing the mean effect between the constrained and unconstrained models, is close to being statistically significant at the .05 level.

5. SUMMARY AND DISCUSSION

We first described the statistical properties of the general constrained ML estimator. We then illustrated its application with a particular type of constraint function in which the weighted sum of all the covariate-specific associations (partial effects) of the regressors on the dependent variable is constrained to equal the population association of one or more of the regressors. We refer to those regressors whose bivariate or limited multivariate relationships with the dependent variable are constrained by population data as being "directly constrained." Our study estimated the improvements in the estimation of directly constrained variables and also improvements in the estimation of other regressor variables that may be correlated with the directly constrained variables, and thus indirectly constrained by the population data.

We showed with an empirical example that partial effects from survey data may be reestimated with a large reduction in variance by specifying population constraints on their overall association with the dependent variable. The example application consisted of a test of the "minority-group" hypothesis of fertility for the marital fertility of black and white couples in which the wife is aged between 30 and 34 years old. According to the minority-group hypothesis, fertility will be lower for a minority group of otherwise equal economic status.

The population data were age-, year-, and race-specific marital fertility rates calculated from birth-registration data combined with census-based estimates of the married population by age and race. The survey data were from the Panel Study of Income Dynamics (PSID). These survey data contribute additional information on premarital children, on duration of the current marriage, and on the economic condition of the family.

The standard error about the coefficients was shown to be substantially, even drastically, reduced under constrained MLE as compared to under unconstrained MLE. The indirectly constrained coefficients, however, were changed negligibly in both point estimate and standard error about the point estimate. We also used the comparison between constrained and unconstrained MLE to test for bias in the survey data, and found evidence of upward bias for white couples but not for black couples. Thus we have shown that the constrained MLE technique both provides a far more *powerful* statistical test of the minority-group hypothesis and purges the test of a bias that would otherwise favor a finding in support of the minority-group hypothesis.

Substantively strong but statistically weak support for the minority-group hypothesis is found in the estimates from the unconstrained version of our model. The conclusion from the constrained version is that a statistically significant but substantively small minority-group effect is indicated. The difference in these two conclusions from the point of view of the sociologist is potentially very large. As we noted above, earlier tests of the hypothesis for black versus white fertility have yielded mixed findings. These studies are not directly comparable to the present study, due among other things to the restriction of the present study to married women in their early 30s. Nevertheless, the results of the present study suggest that one factor contributing to the mixed findings in previous studies may be weaknesses in the empirical tests—either due to bias in the data of one or the other of the black or white groups (as we found here for whites); or due to the large sampling error that arises in testing in relatively small subpopulations. It is indicative here that researchers frequently turn to large sample data sets such as Census PUMS when analyzing racial and ethnic differences (e.g., Bean and Swicegood 1985), trading off sampling error for the problem of having fewer socioeconomic variables available to specify a behavioral model. In the present study, we direct sociologists to an alternative approach that allows for the use of a smaller survey data set and thus a more fully specified behavioral model, but using known population relationships to greatly increase the statistical power of the regression estimates.

As a caveat here to the finding of a small minority-group status effect, the relatively simple set of socioeconomic variables regressors used here, and the lack of attention to hypothesized interactions between socioeconomic status and a minority-group status effect in more refined statements of the hypothesis, may have resulted in marital fertility equations that are misspecified. If the specification were improved by the inclusion of more regressor variables—for example, to specify such socioeconomic by minority-group status interactions, or to include more demographic or economic variable detail—the black minority-group status effect might be reduced still further. In that case, we would be able to conclude against the operation of a substantial minority-group status effect using a much more powerful test than one that used survey data only. The comparisons we made between the models before and after adding more socioeconomic regressors (the income-to-poverty ratio dummies) indicate that little reduction in statistical power would result from adding more regressors to the model.

Finally, we note that the statistical structure assumed for the population and survey data here will not always be realistic. In particular, we assumed that the population constraints were known exactly, in terms of both the associations of race and year with fertility (the marital fertility rates provided by NCHS) and the distributions of regressor variables (estimated from sample, not population, data). Future research on, and development and implementation of methods to account for, these sources of uncertainty in the constraint functions and values are recommended.

REFERENCES

Bean, F. D., and G. Swicegood. 1985. *Mexican American Fertility Patterns.* Austin: University of Texas Press.

Bethlehem, J. G. 2002. "Weighting Nonresponse Adjustments Based on Auxiliary Information." Pp. 289–302 in *Survey Nonresponse*, edited by R. M. Groves, D. A. Dillman, J. L. Eltinge, and R. J. A. Little. New York: Wiley.

Boyd, R. L. 1994. "Educational Mobility and the Fertility of Black and White Women: A Research Note." *Population Research and Policy Review* 13(3):275–81.

Breslow, N. E., and N. E. Day. 1980. *Statistical Methods in Cancer Research.* Vol. 1, *The Analysis of Case-Control Studies.* Lyon, France: IARC.

Deming, W. E., and F. F. Stephan. 1942. "On the Least Squares Adjustment of a Sampled Frequency Table When the Expected Marginal Tables Are Known." *Annals of Mathematical Statistics* 11:427–24.

Efron, B. 1975. "The Efficiency of Logistic Regression Compared to Normal Discriminant Analysis." *Journal of the American Statistical Association* 70(352):892–98.

Elliott, M. R., and R. J. A. Little. 2001. "A Bayesian Approach to Combining Information from a Census, a Coverage Measurement Survey and Demographic Analysis." *Journal of the American Statistical Association* 95(450):351–62.

Firebaugh, G. 1978. "A Rule for Inferring Individual Level Relationships from Aggregate Data." *American Sociological Review* 43:557–72.

Fitzgerald, J., P. Gottschalk, and R. Moffitt. 1998. "An Analysis of Sample Attrition in the Michigan Panel Study of Income Dynamics." *Journal of Human Resources* 33:251–99.

Gelman, A., and J. B. Carlin. 2001. "Poststratification and Weighting Adjustments." Pp. 289–302 in *Survey Nonresponse*, edited by R. M. Groves, D. A. Dillman, J. L. Eltinge, and R. J. A. Little. New York: Wiley.

Gelman, A., and T. C. Little. 1998. "Improving Upon Probability Weighting for Household Size." *Public Opinion Quarterly* 62:398–404.

Goldscheider, C., and P. R. Uhlenberg. 1967. "Minority Group Status and Fertility." *American Journal of Sociology* 74:361–72.

Goodman, L. A. 1953. "Ecological Regressions and the Behavior of Individuals." *American Sociological Review* 18:663–64.

Handcock, M. S., S. M. Huovilainen, and M. S. Rendall. 2000. "Combining Registration-System and Survey Data to Estimate Birth Probabilities." *Demography* 37(2):187–92.

Heitjan, D. F. 1990. "Inference from Grouped Continuous Data; A Review" (with discussion). *Statistical Science* 4:164–83.

Heitjan, D. F., and D. B. Rubin. 1989. "Inference from Coarse Data via Multiple Imputation. *Journal of the American Statistical Association* 85(423):304–14.

Hellerstein, J., and G. W. Imbens. 1999. "Imposing Moment Restrictions from Auxiliary Data by Weighting." *Review of Economics and Statistics* 81(1):1–14.

Hill, M. S. 1992. *The Panel Study of Income Dynamics: A User's Guide*. Newbury Park, CA: Sage.

Holt, D., and T. F. M. Smith. 1979. "Post-Stratification." *Journal of the Royal Statistical Society, Series A*, 142:33–46.

Imbens, G. W., Johnson, P., and Spady, R. H. 1998. "Information Theoretic Approaches to Inference in Moment Condition Models." *Econometrica* 66:333–59.

Imbens, G. W., and T. Lancaster. 1994. "Combining Micro and Macro Data in Microeconometric Models." *Review of Economic Studies* 61:655–80.

———. 1996. "Efficient Estimation and Stratified Sampling." *Journal of Econometrics* 74(2): 289–318.

Ireland, C. T., and S. Kullback. 1968. "Contingency Tables with Given Marginals." *Biometrika* 55:179–88.

Johnson, N. E. 1979. "Minority-Group Status and the Fertility of Black Americans, 1970: A New Look." *American Journal of Sociology* 84(6):1386–1400.

———. 1988. "The Pace of Births Over the Life Course: Implications for the Minority-group Status Hypothesis." *Social Science Quarterly* 69(1):95–107.

Kish, L. 1965. *Survey Sampling*. New York: Wiley.

Little, R. J. A. 1991. "Inference with Sample Weights." *Journal of Official Statistics* 7:405–24.

———. 1992. "Regression with Missing X's: A Review." *Journal of the American Statistical Association* 87(420):1227–37.

————. 1993. "Post-stratification: A Modeler's Perspective." *Journal of the American Statistical Association* 88(423):1001–12.

Little, R. J. A., and D. B. Rubin. 1987. *Statistical Analysis of Missing Data*. New York: Wiley.

Little, R. J. A., and N. Schenker. 1995. "Missing Data". Pp. 39–76 in *Handbook for Statistical Modeling for the Social Sciences*, edited by G. Arminger, C. C. Clogg, and M. E. Sobel. New York: Chapman Hall.

Little, R. J. A., and M. M. Wu. 1991. "Models for Contingency Tables with Known Margins When Target and Sampled Populations Differ." *Journal of the American Statistical Association* 86(413):87–95.

Lohr, S. L. 1999. *Sampling: Design and Analysis*. Pacific Grove, CA: Brooks-Cole.

Manski, C. F., and S. R. Lerman. 1977. "Estimation of Choice Probabilities from Choice Based Samples." *Econometrica* 45(8): 1977–88.

Morgan, J. N., K. Dickinson, J. Dickinson, J. Benus, and G. Duncan. 1974. *Five Thousand American Families: Patterns of Economic Progress*. Vol. 1, *An Analysis of the First Five Years of the Panel Study of Income Dynamics*. Ann Arbor: Survey Research Center, University of Michigan.

National Center for Health Statistics. 1999. *Vital Statistics of the United States 1993*. Volume 1, *Natality*. Hyattsville, MD: National Center for Health Statistics.

Prentice, R. L., and R. Pyke. 1979. "Logistic Disease Incidence Models and Case-control Studies". *Biometrika* 66:403–11.

Qin, J., and J. Lawless. 1994. "Empirical Likelihood and General Estimating Equations." *Annals of Statistics* 22(1):300–25.

Rice, J. A. 1995. *Mathematical Statistics and Data Analysis*. Pacific Grove: Wadsworth.

Rubin, D. B. 1976. "Inference and Missing Data." *Biometrika* 63:581–92.

————. 1977. "Formalizing Subjective Notions About the Effect on Non-respondents in Sample Surveys." *Journal of the American Statistical Association* 72(405):538–43.

Ruiz-Velasco, S. 1991. "Asymptotic Efficiency of Logistic Regression Relative to Linear Discriminant Analysis." *Biometrika* 78(2):235–43.

SAS Institute. 1997. *SAS/OR Technical Report: The NLP Procedure*. Cary, NC: SAS Institute.

Schafer, J. L. 1997. *Analysis of Incomplete Multivariate Data*. London: Chapman and Hall.

Schoen, R., and R. M. Weinick. 1993. "The Slowing Metabolism of Marriage: Figures from 1988 Marital Status Life Tables." *Demography* 30(4):737–46.

Smith, D. P. 1992. *Formal Demography*. New York: Plenum.

Smith, T. F. M. 1991. "Post-stratification." *Statistician* 40:315–23.

Wakefield, J., and R. Salway. 2001. "A Statistical Framework for Ecological and Aggregate Studies." *Journal of the Royal Statistical Society, Series A*, 164:119–7.

ERRATA

The following are corrections for volumes 32 and 34, *Sociological Methodology*.

In Reardon and Firebaugh (2002), equations (27) and (28) and the surrounding text (pp. 54–55) should read:

> An index S meets the grouping decomposability criterion if we can write
>
> $$S = f(S_N) + \sum_{n=1}^{N} g(S_n),\qquad(27)$$
>
> where S_N is the segregation calculated among the N supergroups, S_n is the segregation among the groups making up supergroup n, and f and g are strictly increasing functions on the interval $[0,1]$ with $f(0) = g(0) = 0$.
>
> ... Reardon, Yun, and Eitle (2000) show that H can be written as
>
> $$H = \frac{E_N}{E} H_N + \sum_{n=1}^{N} \frac{t_n E_n}{TE} H_n,\qquad(28)$$

where E_N and H_N are the entropy and segregation calculated among the N supergroups, T and E are the size and entropy of the population as a whole, and t_n, E_n, and H_n are the size, entropy, and segregation within supergroup n, respectively.

Likewise, in Reardon and O'Sullivan (2004), equations (20) and (21) and the surrounding text (pp. 149–150) should read:

Following Reardon and Firebaugh (2002), a spatial segregation index $\widetilde{S}$ meets the grouping decomposability criterion if we can write

$$\widetilde{S} = f(\widetilde{S}_N) + \sum_{n=1}^{N} g(\widetilde{S}_n), \qquad (20)$$

where $\widetilde{S}_N$ is the segregation calculated among the N supergroups, $\widetilde{S}_n$ is the segregation among the groups making up supergroup n, and f and g are strictly increasing functions on the interval $[0,1]$ with $f(0) = g(0) = 0$. ... the decomposition of $\widetilde{H}$ into between- and within-supergroup components has the same form as the aspatial H:

$$\widetilde{H} = \frac{E_N}{E} \widetilde{H}_N + \sum_{n=1}^{N} \frac{t_n E_n}{TE} \widetilde{H}_n. \qquad (21)$$

REFERENCES

Reardon, S. F., and G. Firebaugh. 2002. "Measures of Multigroup Segregation." Pp. 33–67 in *Sociological Methodology*, Vol. 32, edited by Ross M. Stolzenberg. Boston, MA: Blackwell Publishing.

Reardon, S. F., and D. O'Sullivan. 2004. "Measures of Spatial Segregation." Pp. 121–62 in *Sociological Methodology*, Vol. 34, edited by Ross M. Stolzenberg. Boston, MA: Blackwell Publishing.

Reardon, S. F., J. T. Yun, and T. M. Eitle. 2000. "The Changing Structure of School Segregation: Measurement and Evidence of Multi-racial Metropolitan Area School Segregation, 1989–1995." *Demography* 37(3): 351–64.